Contestations in Contemporary Southeast Asia

This Palgrave Macmillan book series publishes research that displays strong interdisciplinary concerns to examine links between political conflict and broader socio-economic development and change. While the emphasis is on contemporary Southeast Asia, works included within the Series demonstrate an appreciation of how historical contexts help to shape present-day contested issues in political, economic, social and cultural spheres. The Series will be of interest to authors undertaking single country studies, multi-country comparisons in Southeast Asia or tackling political and socio-economic contestations that pertain to the region as a whole. Rather uniquely, the series welcomes works that seek to illuminate prominent issues in contemporary Southeast Asia by comparing experiences in the region to those in other parts of the world as well. Volumes in the series engage closely with the relevant academic literature on specific debates, and include a comparative dimension within even single country studies such that the work contributes insights to a broader literature. Researchers based in Southeast Asian focused institutions are encouraged to submit their work for consideration.

More information about this series at
http://www.palgrave.com/gp/series/16279

Maznah Mohamad

The Divine Bureaucracy and Disenchantment of Social Life

A Study of Bureaucratic Islam in Malaysia

palgrave
macmillan

Maznah Mohamad
Department of Malay Studies and Department of
Southeast Asian Studies, Faculty of Arts and Social Sciences
National University of Singapore
Singapore, Singapore

ISSN 2661-8354 ISSN 2661-8362 (electronic)
Contestations in Contemporary Southeast Asia
ISBN 978-981-15-2092-1 ISBN 978-981-15-2093-8 (eBook)
https://doi.org/10.1007/978-981-15-2093-8

This Palgrave Macmillan imprint is published by the registered company Springer Nature Singapore Pte Ltd.
The registered company address is: 152 Beach Road, #21-01/04 Gateway East, Singapore 189721, Singapore

Preface and Acknowledgements

Most observers of Islam try to construct the religion as an edifice of distinctive and exclusive essences. Lately, I have been more preoccupied with unmasking it, to strip it down to something less obvious, to peel off its every layer to uncover a wisp of the unseen or forgotten. To do so means fully understanding the seen and what is apparent. For the last few years, my research has been about trying to find similarities rather than differences between religious systems and other social formations. Could Islam through its material manifestations be just another expression of modern secularism, constitutionalism, patriarchy and even rationalism?

As I recall, in the four-decade-long academic work and research in which I have been involved, the focal point of the Malay village has always been the *madrassah* (community prayer centre), as Malay villagers would call it. In the first village in which I worked, this was a two-storey wooden house in a centralised location of the *kampong* (village) donated by one of the wealthier families. It served as a social rather than a worship area or religious learning centre. The upstairs area was used for communal prayers performed only by men. The downstairs was where all the 'life' was. Women and children dominated this space. In the day, the ground floor was used as a kindergarten for the village children. During special occasions or thanksgiving feasts, the cooking would be done within the compounds of the *madrassah*. The downstairs section was a place for storytelling and bawdy banter, a sort of 'chill-out' place to break away from the drudgery of backbreaking work in the fields. Religious life was interwoven within these social interludes. *Dakwah* (Islamic propagation) was unheard of. It was not religion but the development dream that drove many young villagers in their pursuits. Newly married couples eagerly waited for their time to be resettled at a new land scheme somewhere else, where there was commercial cultivation of oil palm. This was their ticket to social mobility, not a passport to heaven.

I then moved on to study the handloom weavers in the east coast *negeri* (States) of Terengganu, Kelantan and Pahang. What was the nature of their religious sensibility? Islam was hardly 'hegemonic', although it was here, there and everywhere. Weavers would mechanically weave template-motifs set up by the master weavers. Did they know that the motifs were symbolically Islamic in nature? Did they know that Terengganu, Kelantan and Pahang also happened to be within the trade routes plied by Muslim merchants between India and China? Did they know that the market for their ornate textiles was the scattered Malay nobility who had set up court in port cities throughout the archipelago, invoking divine rule through the aura of Islam? The weavers were oblivious to these facts. Yet, Islam and their identity as artisans coexisted without much fuss.

In the early 1980s, Islam was globalised, meaning the consciousness of local Muslims was suddenly enmeshed and united (inorganically, I would say) into a common Muslim history. The 1979 Iranian Revolution sparked a movement among Muslims (from Pakistan to Malaysia), to also execute their own violent or velvet revolution as the case may be, to Islamise state and society. This took the route of constitutionalism and legalism, which seemed to be the most preferred mode since it was believed that Islam would only be legitimised as a social system—and ironically as a past civilisation—through the image of the modern nation-state. It is thus untrue that religious legal-bureaucratic elites shunned secularisation as a process of modernisation (through functional differentiation and temporalisation). This was deemed necessary.

Here is where the construction of a new 'Muslimness' began to take concrete shape, by reinventing the past and inventing a new presence. Before the rise of codified rules and laws, the pressure to Islamise was mainly effected through a form of social panopticonism, such as voluntary veiling and altered life-styling (to the trope of the Police's, *every breath you take, every move you make, every bond you break, every step you take, I'll be watching you…can't you see you belong to me?*). This worked, but it may not have been good enough, at least to the bureaucrats. Hence the rise of law, a much more effective 'revolution' in the real sense than social movements. The bureaucracy has been part of governance, with a legal status, invested with salaries, empowered to dictate what is the 'right' Islam, yet in all these, never having needed to be accountable to voters nor taxpayers.

Religion dominates the everyday lives of Malays today, not as culture but as law, order, regulation, method and official creed. Religiosity is achieved by the extensive tentacles of the legal bureaucracy, reaching out into every aspect of Muslim life, from schooling to sex. In one of my most recent fieldwork forays, I met up with Administrative Director of an Islamic religious department in a northern *negeri* (State) in Peninsular Malaysia. So modern was the set-up of this office and its personnel that it was hard to differentiate it from the office of the Department of Immigration next door. The director herself was not a graduate in Islamic Studies but in Business Administration. She prided herself in being a 'professional civil servant' who could be transferred to any government department, be it defence, finance or welfare. It has come to a stage where Islam needs to be managed, not just preached.

What then to make of all this? It would seem that religious life is being interwoven within the interstices of secular sensibility, rather than replacing the secular state. True to my hunch, unmasking and peeling off the layers of organised Islam revealed something that is not easily seen or even what it imagines itself to be. Are the whisperers of enchanted social life losing their affective everyday appeal by metamorphosing into power-wielding purveyors of disenchantment? This is the basic question of this book.

Answering a simple question requires an extensive answer and, without the collective effort and help of so many individuals and institutions, this task would have been extremely arduous and possibly unfulfilled.

I would like to record my acknowledgement to the National University of Singapore (NUS) for providing the grants that went into researching this book. Most notably, I received the NUS Start-Up Grant for the study on "State, Syariah in a Post-Secular World" and the research grant from the Centre for Family and Population Research on "Protecting and Perfecting the Muslim Family". I would like to thank Norhayati Kaprawi, Noraisah Yusop and Nurul Fadiah Johari who assisted me in conducting the research. To the many inquisitive and probing students who took my module on "Religion, Society and Politics in Southeast Asia" offered over so many semesters, I owe them gratitude for sharpening many of the ideas that went into this book. I have been fortunate to have supportive colleagues and heads of departments at NUS who believed in my work and provided academic vision and inspiration in the writing of this book. I am heartened by the camaraderie and guidance given by colleagues—Noor Aisha Abdul Rahman and Suriani Suratman from the Malay Studies Department and Goh Beng Lan and Itty Abraham from the Southeast Asian Studies Department.

During the period of my writing, I was affiliated with the Gender Studies Programme of the University of Malaya. I am thankful for the valuable support extended by Rusaslina Idrus, Shanthi Thambiah, Alicia Izharuddin and Lai Suat Yan, which allowed me to be in the convivial company of Gender Studies scholars in Malaysia.

I was fortunate to have shared company and conversations with scholars whose erudition could be seen throughout the pages of this book. They include Sharifah Zaleha Syed Hassan, Wazir Jahan Karim, Norani Othman, Clive Kessler, Moshe Yegar, Donald Horowitz, Michael Peletz, Ahmad Fauzi Abdul Hamid, Mohamed Nawab Mohamed Osman, Patricia Sloane-White, Kikue Hamayotsu and Dominik Muller. I especially owe much to the illustrious Judith Nagata, who became both friend and family.

Without the passionate social activism and engaged intellectualism of Cecilia Ng, Zarizana Aziz, Siti Hawa Ali, Rashidah Shuib, Zainah Anwar, Marina Mahathir, Norhayati Kaprawi, Suri Kempe, Rozana Isa, Mohamed Imran Mohamed Taib, Vivienne Wee, Halijah Mohamed, Zubee Ali, Nurul Fadiah Johari, Filzah Sumartono, Siti Hazirah Mohamad and all friends in the Wali group, this study would be absolutely meaningless. This book imbibes the presence of their spirit (*semangat*).

To my editor-extraordinaire, tan beng hui, who was not only meticulous, fastidious and precise with punctuations, letter-casing and choice of words, but a virtuoso in improving ideas, concepts and arguments throughout the book, I offer my heartfelt thanks. She generously lent much of her own scholarly expertise on gender and Islam in Malaysia into the pages of the book.

My family has been the bedrock of my life and work. To Adil and Nabilah, I am grateful for the use of their ideal, efficient apartment for my self-incarceration to finish up the book and nothing else. To Asha, I thank her for the many moments of joy in the company of her delightfully unconditional assertive self. Ashman was born in August after the intense period of the book writing and was a delight when he came. I am thankful to Rosa, who provided much long-distance empathy and kindred spirit throughout my writing process. We were in a similar race to the finishing line, if on different roads, and completed what we started on the same week. To Jayam, with all my love, thank you for the many long hours and months of compassionate internment, care and concern over the quality of the book and more.

Singapore
October 2019

Maznah Mohamad

Contents

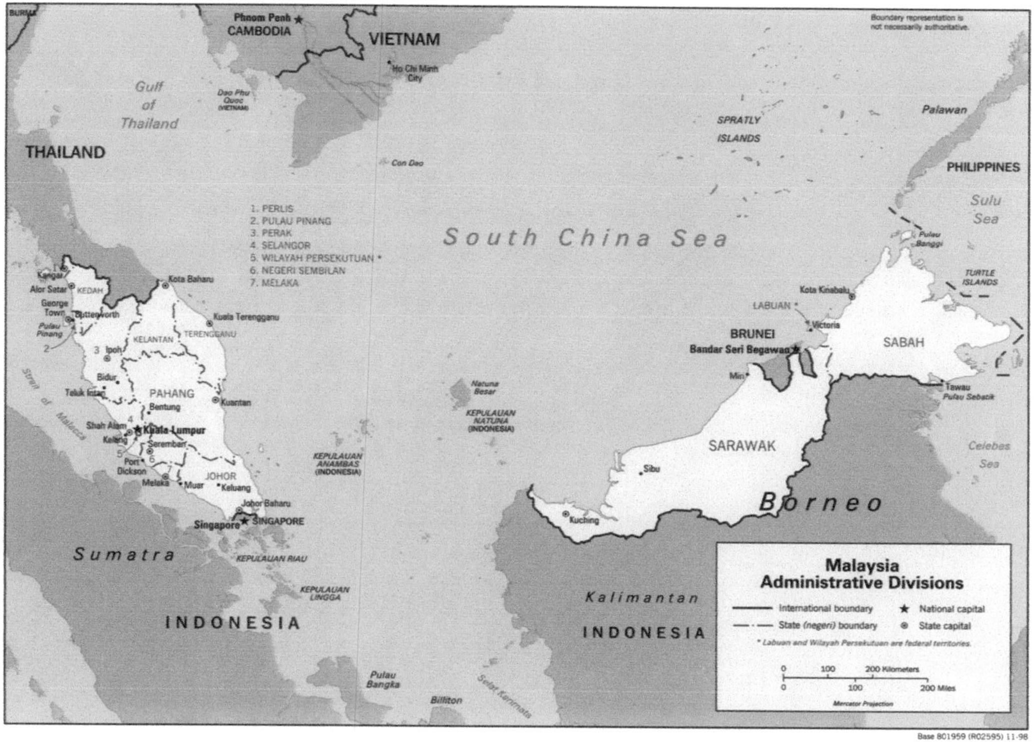

Map of Malaysia: Administrative Divisions. (Source: ASEAN UP, https://aseanup.com/wp-content/uploads/2018/05/malaysia-administrative-divisions-1998.jpg)

A Note on Abbreviations and Acronyms, Non-English Words or Terms, Malay Names and Terminology

Abbreviations and Acronyms
Abbreviations are capitalised when not pronounceable, for example, JKSM, GLC and NGO. Along with acronyms, abbreviations that are pronounceable are capitalised at the first letter, while the rest are in lowercase, as in Jakim, Umno and Pas.

Non-English Words or Terms
All non-English words or terms are italicised. Those that have been translated and transliterated from other languages are spelt out according to the source materials. As such there will be a variation in spellings of the same term, for instance, *kathi*, *qadi* or *kadi*. Likewise, the word '*syariah*' is spelt according to source materials as well as time and place. In this study, it is used as an adjective rather than a noun or proper noun—hence spelt in lowercase—since the term connotes laws or rules that are derived from Islamic sources, as much as it represents the qualities of being Islamic or the requirements for Islamic compliance and conformity.

Malay Names
Malay names are patronymic and do not come with family surnames. Hence, works of Malay writers based in Malaysia are cited by their first names.

Terminology—Negeri (State) and State
The nation-state of Malaysia comprises 14 decentralised administrative units, which will be referred to as the 13 States or *negeri* (in Malay) and

three Federal Territories or Wilayah Persekutuan (in Malay). The 13 States or *negeri* are Perlis, Kedah, Pulau Pinang, Perak, Selangor, Negeri Sembilan, Melaka, Johor, Pahang, Terengganu, Kelantan, Sabah and Sarawak. The Federal Territories have three non-contiguous geographical entities, namely Kuala Lumpur, Putrajaya and Labuan. Throughout the text, the term *negeri* refers to the 13 States within the federated system under which Malaysia is governed. This is distinguished from the conceptual notion of the 'state' to mean a central government or national authority.

Acronyms and Abbreviations

Abim	Angkatan Belia Islam Malaysia (Malaysian Islamic Youth Movement)
AG's Chambers	Attorney General's Chambers
Amle	Administration of Muslim Law Enactment
ASB	Amanah Saham Bumiputera
ASN	Amanah Saham Nasional
ASNB	Amanah Saham Nasional Berhad
ASWJ	Ahli Sunnah Wal Jamaah (followers of Sunni Islam)
Baheis	Bahagian Hal Ehwal Islam (Division of Islamic Affairs)
Baka PDRM	Bahagian Agama dan Kaunseling Polis Diraja Malaysia (Division of Religion and Counselling Royal Malaysian Police)
BBA	bai' bi thaman ajil
BMMB	Bank Muamalat Malaysia Berhad
BN	Barisan Nasional (National Front)
BNM	Bank Negara Malaysia (Central Bank of Malaysia)
BSK	Bahagian Sokongan Keluarga (Family Support Division)
CEO	Chief Executive Officer
DAP	Democratic Action Party
Felda	Federal Land Development Authority
FMS	Federated Malay States
FT	Federal Territories/Federal Territory
GLC	Government-Linked Corporation
GSI	International Global Standard
HDC	Halal Industry Development Corporation
IAIS	International Institute of Advanced Islamic Studies

IFI	Islamic Financial Institutions
Ikim	Institut Kefahaman Islam Malaysia (Institute of Islamic Understanding)
Iksim	Institut Kajian Strategik Islam Malaysia (Institute of Islamic Strategic Research Malaysia)
Inceif	International Centre for Education in Islamic Finance
Indah	Institut Dakwah dan Latihan Islam (Islamic Dakwah and Training Institute)
Intan	Institut Tadbiran Awam Negara (National Institute of Public Administration)
IRF	Islamic Renaissance Front
ISA	Internal Security Act
Isma	Ikatan Muslimin Malaysia (Alliance of Malaysian Muslims)
Isra	International Syariah Research Academy
Jais	Jabatan Agama Islam Selangor (Selangor religious department)
Jakim	Jabatan Kemajuan Islam Malaysia (Department of Islamic Advancement Malaysia)
JAM	Jemaah Al-Quran Malaysia
Jawhar	Jabatan Wakaf, Zakat dan Haji (Department of Wakaf, Zakat and Hajj)
Jawi	Jabatan Agama Islam Wilayah Persekutuan (Federal Territories religious department)
JCorp	Johor Corporation
JIL	Jaringan Islam Liberal
JKSM	Jabatan Kehakiman Syariah Malaysia (Syariah Judicial Department Malaysia)
JMC	BMMB and PWS Joint Management Committee
JMM	Jaringan Melayu Malaysia (Malaysian Network of Malays)
JPBK	Jawatankuasa Penyelarasan Baitulmal Kebangsaan (National Committee for the Coordination of Baitulmal)
JPSM	Jabatan Pendakwaraya Syariah Malaysia (Syariah Prosecution Department Malaysia)
Kagat	Kor Agama Angkatan Tentera (Religious Corp of the Malaysian Army)
KMM	Kumpulan al-Maunah Malaysia
LGBT	lesbian, gay, bisexual, transgender
LTH	Lembaga Tabung Haji (Pilgrims Fund Board)
Maik	Majlis Agama Islam Kedah (Kedah State Islamic Religious Council)
Main	Majlis Agama Islam Negeri (State Islamic Religious Councils, SIRCs)

Maipp	Majlis Agama Islam Pulau Pinang (Penang State Islamic Religious Council)
Maiwp	Majlis Agama Islam Wilayah Persekutuan (Federal Territories State Islamic Religious Council)
MD	Managing Director
Mida	Malaysian Industrial Development Authority
MISB	Muamalat Invest Sdn Bhd
Miti	Ministry of international Trade and Industry
MKI	Majlis Kebangsaan bagi Hal Ehwal Agama Islam (National Council for Islamic Religious Affairs)
MoF	Ministry of Finance
MSWP	Mahkahmah Syariah Wilayah Persekutuan (Federal Territories Syariah Court)
Mui	Majlis Ulama Indonesia
MWDC	Malaysian Wakaf Development Corporation
NEP	New Economic Policy
NGO	Non-Governmental Organisation
OIC	Organisation of Islamic Countries
Pas	Parti Islam Se-Malaysia (Pan-Malaysian Islamic Party)
pbh	peace be upon him
Perkim	Pertubuhan Kebajikan Islam Malaysia (Malaysian Muslim Welfare Association)
PH	Pakatan Harapan (Alliance of Hope)
PKR	Parti Keadilan Rakyat (People's Justice Party)
PM	Prime Minister
PNB	Permodalan Nasional Berhad
PPIM	Persatuan Pengguna Islam Malaysia (Muslim Consumer Association of Malaysia)
PPZ	Pusat Pungutan Zakat (Zakat Collection Centre)
PPZ-Maiwp	Pusat Pungutan Zakat – Majlis Agama Islam Wilayah Persekutuan (Zakat Collection Centre – Federal Territories State Islamic Religious Council)
PSRM	Parti Sosialis Rakyat Malaysia (People's Socialist Party of Malaysia)
PUM	Persatuan Ulama Malaysia (Ulama Association of Malaysia)
PWNB	Perbadanan Wakaf Nasional Berhad (National Wakaf Corporation Bhd)
PWS	Perbadanan Wakaf Selangor (Selangor Wakaf Corporation)
SAC	Syariah Advisory Council
SCM	Securities Commission of Malaysia
SIRC	State (*negeri*) Islamic Religious Council
Sis	Sisters in Islam

SPPIM	Sistem Pengurusan Perkahwinan Islam Malaysia (Malaysian Islamic Marriage Management System)
Uda	Urban Development Authority
Umno	United Malays National Organisation
UMS	Unfederated Malay States
USM	University of Science Malaysia
Yadim	Yayasan Dakwah Islamiah (Islamic Missionary Foundation)
Yapeim	Yayasan Pembangunan Ekonomi Islam Malaysia (Islamic Economic Development Foundation of Malaysia)
YWM	Yayasan Wakaf Malaysia (Wakaf Foundation of Malaysia)

List of Diagram and Charts

List of Tables

CHAPTER 1

Bureaucratisation and Disenchantment

Introduction

This study seeks to understand why and how Islamisation in a multireligious society such as Malaysia[1] has flourished successfully to the point of distressing multicultural cohesion, though without the outbreak of open, violent and prolonged conflicts. How can one understand why and how this has been so? While there have been bursts of ethnic contestations, no recurring and large-scale religious violence has erupted in the country,[2] as compared to other Muslim-majority nations such as Indonesia and Turkey (Chernov-Hwang 2009). Nevertheless, surface incidents of inter-religious as well as intra-Islamic disputes and controversies have become a constant feature of everyday life. The early answer to the question posed is that there is a seeming paradox—despite the presence of a strong and overpowering Islamism, this overhang is also tempered by the mediation of tensions that remain below the surface.

These trends have produced a stable disquiet of multireligious conflict and coexistence. This study postulates that the reasons for this condition lie in understanding Islam as a process ensconced within the ambit of a bureaucracy, which is rules based and a rational system that brooks no disputation and disharmony of its subjects. Religion is entrusted to a bureaucracy that intends to be in the service of the Divine and does so through the means of a typically modern and rational organisation. This bureaucracy systematically and methodically subjects all manner of

M. Mohamad, *The Divine Bureaucracy and Disenchantment of Social Life*, Contestations in Contemporary Southeast Asia,
https://doi.org/10.1007/978-981-15-2093-8_1

religious expressions to some determinate and secular standards as benchmarks for Islamic society. This bureaucracy, the Divine Bureaucracy, functions within and straddles the dual spheres of secularism and otherworldliness. It forms the subject of exploration and analysis of this book.

Some key concepts are useful and necessary to position this study as a new way of looking at the power of religion, while locating its significance within the wider study of religion and state. I find the concepts bureaucratisation, rationalisation and disenchantment; notions of bureaucratic power, secularism and modernity; and the oscillating nature of enchantment and disenchantment in religious expression particularly forceful for the purpose of this study. It does not merely detail the interrelationship between state and religion, but rather how and why, in certain instances, they fuse. Going beyond relationships of actors within the two domains of state and religion, the study uncovers their new amalgamated realm of state religion, and the religious state, through its Divine Bureaucracy.

The utility of Max Weber's 'bureaucratisation', 'rationalisation' and 'disenchantment' became clear when I was struck by the distinctive quality of Islamic development programmes undertaken by the Malaysian state during the early 2000s. That these activities were visible and palpable in everyday lives would sometimes be associated, mistakenly for the most part, with the rise of what was previously studied as religious fundamentalism (Marty and Appleby 1991; Mohaddessin 1993). However, this line of inquiry did not seem adequate or accurate for the deeper understanding of particular national variants of the Islamisation project. In one of my earliest articles on this phenomenon, I posited that the *syariah*-aspiring[3] bureaucracy—rather than political agents or pious subjects—was behind the ascendance of Islam in Malaysia (Maznah 2010, 506). The identification of the bureaucracy as having extraordinary powers was due to its oversight over *syariah* laws and public institutions, and its imbibement of a 'routinised charisma' within the Weberian notion of a legal rational bureaucracy. This article focuses on developing arguments about the secularisation of *syariah*, as there was much denouncement then of 'secularism' being an ideology that was the antithesis of Islam.[4]

As it turned out, there was much to be further investigated and learned about the workings of this *syariah*-aspiring bureaucracy, as well other concerns beyond secularism. This book can thus be considered the extension and hopefully a betterment of two of my previous works on this topic (Maznah 2010, 2013). Here, it is not only about deepening the knowledge on the workings of the *syariah* bureaucracy as drivers of change but, more crucially, it is about highlighting the ascendance of a particular form of Islamisation—'bureaucratic Islam'—led by a distinctive bureaucracy, which I have named the Divine Bureaucracy.

This study interrogates the complexity of religious life in the modern nation-state of Malaysia. Here, a bureaucracy on Islamic matters is being developed to control, regulate and organise religious life through a secularisation or, more precisely, a disenchantment process. In doing so, this bureaucracy also whittles away the enchantment of a religious life leading to more worldly concerns through the routes of politics or economics. More directly, this bureaucracy enforces the proscription of what it routinely labels the 'deviant' departures from an Islam that is authorised by state officials. While the dominant perception is of religious piety or political Islam on the rise, another reading of this phenomenon is of a bureaucratic Islam in ascendance through its creation of a disenchanted religiosity. Family, identity and money, the main empirical focus of this study, are but some of the many social realms that this bureaucracy subjugates and shapes through its laws, its methods and its rationality, thus explaining the overwhelming role of religion in everyday, this-worldly affairs.

The legal narratives of correctness, compliance, injunctions and sanctions are expected to lead Muslims to a perfect religious life. This Divine Bureaucracy does not necessarily lend itself to a peaceful mediation of inter-religious and even intra-religious conflict. However, it does provide its own impact to societal transformation by intensifying discourse, dissent and negotiations in the public sphere over its actions. Although divisive and contentious, these processes can be put on hold to prevent open skirmishes on the streets.[5] In this manner, the Divine Bureaucracy perpetuates itself as a distinct power base—just like most bureaucracies with intrinsic qualities—thus enabling it to be the symbol as well as the basis of modernity.

Bureaucratisation and the Rationalisation of Religion

Making sense of Islam and how it is used as a source of governance, if not domination, in Malaysia today would require stepping back to re-evaluate the meaning of religion in its broadest context. Is religion a form of superstition? At first impression, it may be considered a form of irrational belief system, aspiring towards an other-worldly fulfilment, but in the course of history this changed. What Weber observed in his *The Religions of Asia*, first published in 1917, was that Asian religions (including Confucianism, Hinduism, Buddhism, Judaism and Islam) were unlike Christianity of the West in the Middle Ages and largely lacked having a "single dominant church" (Weber 1978a, 192). He suggested that these religions placed more emphasis on life after death, showed indifference towards earthly concerns and largely saw the world as an "enchanted garden", providing little basis for the development of a "rational, inner-worldly ethics of action", such as that achieved by Protestantism in the West (Weber 1978a, 198–199). Mystical Asian religions' aim of "emptying of worldly relationships and concerns" was praiseworthy from the point of view of the practitioners since it allowed them to reach a "positive state of unutterable blessedness", akin to *Nirvana* (Weber 1978a, 201). Nevertheless, the outer-worldly aspirations held by the literati, sages and mystics caused a division of society between them, on the one hand, and the uneducated masses, on the other. The latter needed prophets to lead them on an ethical mission which could only be imposed through a rational narrative on their this-worldly everyday lives. This then was precisely what characterised the transformation of all world religions, including Hinduism, Buddhism and Islam, from a 'non-rational' past dominated by mystics, sages, sorcerers and saints to the present time when faith is outlined by an authority structure legitimised by rationalisation.

Weber provides a tool for understanding the reification of religion in its absorption of a legal and administrative structure, and through its process of bureaucratisation. Essentially, 'bureaucracy' and its method of 'bureaucratisation' is another form of domination, based on knowledge and rules (Swedberg and Agevall 2016, 20–21), or a technical superiority over all other forms of organisations through the execution of functions based on "calculable rules" (Weber 1978b, 351).

The ideal types of legitimate authority have been divided into at least three types: traditional, charismatic and legal rational. Traditional authority is based on the sanctity of beliefs and traditions, charismatic authority on exceptional and personal appeal of leaders, while legal rational authority is based on rules by which office holders are put into positions of power (Allen 2004, 100). As Weber puts it in his *Economy and Society*, first published in 1922, the bureaucracy bases its domination and legitimacy on a "rationally consociated conduct", patriarchalism on "social conduct bound in relationships of traditional authority" and charismatic domination "upon a concrete individual which is based neither upon rational rules nor upon tradition" (Weber 1966, 336–337).

These conditions for domination are only ideal types, with Weber admitting that this is not necessarily a pure categorisation, but could be combined, mixed, adapted or modified throughout historical periods. Accordingly, hierocracy, or rule by those associated with religion, can be "permanently institutionalised" through the means of continuous domination, "be it bureaucratic, patrimonial or feudal" (Weber 1978c, 250). In short, religion can prosper under all three forms of domination structure, be it bureaucratic, patriarchalism or charismatic, a condition which could best characterise the modern Divine Bureaucracy of this study.

In *Economy and Society*, Weber's rational bureaucracy is differentiated from the power of charismatic authority:

> In contrast with all forms of bureaucratic administrative system, the charismatic structure recognizes no forms or orderly procedures for appointment or dismissal, no 'career', no 'advancement', no 'salary'; there is no organized training either for the bearer of charisma or his aides, no arrangements for supervision or appeal, no allocation of local areas of control or exclusive spheres of competence, and finally no standing instructions comparable to bureaucratic governing bodies independent of persons and of their purely personal charisma. (Weber 1978b, 227)

The root word of bureaucracy is the literal term bureau or drawers, or the bureau as in a branch of government. This form of governance is to be distinguished from the rule by monarchs (monarchy) or aristocrats (aristocracy)—hence the nomenclature, bureaucracy. In its earliest origin, the bureaucracy was beholden directly to an ascriptive authority, usually hereditary monarchs. With the advent of popular government democratically elected by the people, the role of bureaucrats took on a different form, in that while bureaucrats are answerable to elected representatives, they are also in the service of new clients—the people or the public. Weber refers to the power position of the bureaucrats as "overtowering" so much so that the "political master" can find himself in the position of the "dilettante who stands opposite the expert, facing the trained official who stands within the management of administration" (Weber 1991a, 232). In its modern incarnation, the bureaucracy thus sits between the governing class and the governed masses, potentially wielding power in a distinctive realm, "which could readily control or outmanoeuvre" those sitting above and below them (Beetham 1987, 60).

Other Weberian categorisations include the "patrimonial bureaucracy", an in-between form of domination sharing the rationality of modern legal elements, yet partly suffering from the "arbitrariness of traditional domination" (Lai 2015, 50). Studies on the bureaucracy have also focused on problems and paradoxes of bureaucratisation. The modern bureaucracy can expand in uncontrollable ways to the extent of encroaching upon wide spheres of social life while using its own power for self-aggrandisement through the proliferation of more bureaucratisation (Eisenstadt 1958, 103). As bureaucracies develop into complex organisations through structures of routinisation, rationalisation and formalisation of skills and functions, they are also inclined towards the self-perpetuation, self-maintenance and self-preservation of these structures (Tchalian 2013, 2–4). Where control is concerned, bureaucracies are capable of being the "instrument of power that take on lives of their own" permeated with a Foucauldian capacity to "form models of social life that compete with, erode, and exclude other models for human activity" (Heyman 2004, 489–490).

A modern bureaucracy is dependent on the exercise of calculable rules and laws. But what forms of laws and legal systems are considered germane to the functioning of a bureaucracy according to Weber? Here again the typology of laws suggested by Weber in *Economy and Society* is often difficult to understand, particularly when applied to contemporary situations. Weber's use of the term *kadijustiz* or '*kadi*-justice' is used to describe how laws are used in Islamic societies, but his categorisation of it does not necessarily fit with the present practice of *syariah* law application and administration. He makes a distinction between 'charismatic', '*kadi*' and 'empirical' forms of justice. Charismatic justice is based on non-rational revelations in the form of "oracles, prophecy or trials by ordeals", while *kadi*-justice is based on "informal decisions" and also on "ethical" or "value-judgements". Empirical justice is recognised as formal decisions that are not based on rational concepts but on "analogies" or "precedents". All have a combination of a "thoroughgoing traditionalism" on the one hand and "arbitrary will and favour of the lord" on the other (Weber 1978c, 352).

Nevertheless, by no means does he preclude the coexistence of the various systems in any form of legal practice. The point is that all three do not lead to a bureaucratic form of domination with a rational-formal basis to its laws. Weber's typology of laws also includes concepts of the irrational-substantive, which are not guided by general rules but are reactions on an individual case basis, as well as the rational-substantive, which means law as guided by general rules and principles of specific ideologies (Rheinstein 1966, l). Hence, *syariah* laws today can encompass and criss-cross many of the ideal types conceived by Weber. For example, they can be both rational, in that they are guided by general rules of lawmaking that see passage through a parliamentary procedure and also have a substantive component that contains principles of ethics, morality and religion beyond that of the law itself. Rheinstein (1966) describes Weber's *kadijustiz* as "a term of art to describe the administration of justice which is oriented not at fixed rules of a formally rational law but at the ethical, religious, political, or otherwise expediential postulates of a substantively rational law" (213 fn 48). The significance of this observation is that *syariah* law may contain the basis of rationalism even if it is still short of rational scientific principles required of a Weberian bureaucracy.

Some six decades ago, Eisenstadt (1958, 103) proposed some intriguing possibilities of inquiry on the relations between the bureaucracy with its acquisition of power through legitimate means and the usurpation of power through unintended goals, as well as due to its own internal expansion. The absorption of religious aura subject to the Weberian "calculable rules" of bureaucratic domination is one of the unintended consequences of an enlarged bureaucratic structure. As these have not been rigorously interrogated in relation to emergent and contemporary variants of the bureaucracy, this study intends to pursue these questions in its analysis of the expansion of Islam through a Divine Bureaucracy.

Secular, Secularism, Secularisation

Besides bureaucratisation, religion and its meaning in social life are frequently approached through debates around the notions of modernisation, disenchantment and secularism; the most cited works are Casanova (2009), Taylor (2007) and Asad (2003). Secularism (often the synonym for de-religionisation) and religion (sometimes the synonym for de-secularisation) are posed by some scholars as being mutually exclusive and oppositional, but this binary and dichotomous divide in social paradigms has been critiqued, revised and reworked (see, for example, Dressler and Mandair 2011; Cinar et al. 2012). One of the most lucid ways of explaining the noun 'secularism' is to distinguish its variants or cognates: "secular" as a central modern epistemic category, "secularization" as an analytical conceptualisation of modern world-historical processes, and "secularism" as a worldview (Casanova 2009, 1049).

Casanova (2009) further distinguishes secularism as a "modern statecraft", from secularism as an "ideology", hence attributing a plurality of meanings to the concept. Certain presumed "dyadic pairs" of synonymy as in "sacred" versus "profane", "transcendent" versus "immanent" or "religious" versus "secular" are no longer relevant given that secular phenomena like "nation, citizenship, and human rights" are in themselves sacralised (1061–1064). In a state where the bounds of politics and religion cloud one another, it is difficult, if not pointless, to ascertain if a social phenomenon is religious or secular. In Egypt, for example, its Constitution denotes Islamic law as the main source of the country's legislation, although the legal system in which the law originates is European law, hence giving the state its paradoxical quality (Agrama 2012, 2–6). Asad views the meaning of modern religion as shaped by the worldview of "secularism", and vice versa:

> "[R]eligion" is a modem concept not because it is reified but because it has been linked to its Siamese twin "secularism." Religion has been part of the restructuration of practical times and spaces, a rearticulation of practical knowledges and powers, of subjective behaviors, sensibilities, needs, and expectations in modernity. But that applies equally to secularism, whose function has been to try to guide that rearticulation and to define "religions" in the plural as a species of (non-rational) belief. (Asad 2001b, 221)

The dyadic and binarial presupposition is largely invoked as political and ideological rhetoric, as a means of simplifying or metaphorically drawing battle lines between what is desirable and what is undesirable in the aspirations for reforms around religion (Salama and Friedman 2012).

Enchantment, Disenchantment

Weber's conceptualisation of disenchantment emerged from the rationalisation of Western civilisation and the role of Judaism and Protestant literalism in their prohibition of idolatry (Yelle 2012, 7). Secularism brought by Western colonialism differentiated religious beliefs between one that was based on a canonical source against that of idolatry, and relegated traditional religion as inferior and pre-modern.

To render all the above points in greater clarity requires dissecting the usefulness of the concept of 'disenchantment' as used by Weber in his *Science as a Vocation*, first delivered as a lecture in 1918 (Weber 1991b, 129–156). The conception of secularism is less useful in understanding the dynamics of religion than disenchantment. Disenchantment can be defined as a condition where the world and its mysteries are no longer explained by magic but is demystified by science, rationalism and secularism (Swedberg and Agevall 2016, 86–87). When religion is rationalised,

> There are no mysterious incalculable forces that come into play, but rather that one can, in principle, master all things by calculation. This means that the world is 'disenchanted'. One need no longer have recourse to magical means in order to master or implore the spirits, as did the savage, for whom such mysterious powers existed. Technical means and calculations perform the service. (Weber 1991b, 139)

The interconnectedness of debates and discourse around modernisation, secularism and disenchantment shows them to be essential epistemic categories in the understanding of religion in modern times (Asprem 2016; Grosby 2013; Saler 2006). Seeing religion as hovering around or actually occupying the spaces of secularism and disenchantment dispels the notion or ideology of religion as being antithetical to secularism or that religion is a social system impermeable to change and transformation.

How can the idea of disenchantment be affixed to the outcome of a modern religious bureaucracy? Weber's notion of disenchantment refers to the ability to "control by means of calculation" and to be free from the rule of "mysterious, unpredictable forces" (Grosby 2013, 302). The waning of enchantment comes with the advent of scientific method, reason and rationality, since beliefs in spirits and the supernatural would be demystified with new ways of discovering the world. A more simplistic secularisation thesis consigns religion to the periphery of social life, with a dichotomy represented between the "porous, premodern self" inclined towards "enchantment", and the "buffered" and "disenchanted" modern self more impervious to the influence of religion (Lyons 2014, 873–874).

Nevertheless, many scholars have dismissed the suggestion that Weber's intention was to portray disenchantment as the desirable aspect of modernisation. Weber himself did not see religion phasing out with the advent of scientific rationalism associated with modernity. Far from it, "religious belief, as the quintessential bearer of meaning of life, is inexpungeable"

(Grosby 2013, 304). Weber did not see disenchantment as a higher form of sensibility able to free people from illusions and irrational beliefs, but was aware that the costs to all this would be a deepening bureaucracy in the exercise of rationalising scientific and economic advancement (Main 2017, 1101–1102). A disenchanted world is bound to be controlled by a meddling state and its enlarged bureaucracy, usurping individual freedom and liberal democracy (Grosby 2013, 308–309).

Hence, far from discounting the value of enchantment as a human need, Weber's views of this were said to be more intricate than just putting science, reason and rationality on a pedestal at the expense of magic. Weber also foresaw a disenchanted world that would lead to the waning of public life as people recede to their private spaces to fulfil their transcendent beliefs. Accordingly, such unfavourable consequences of disenchantment can be attributed to the inadequacy of science in filling "the vacuum left by the diminishment of religion" and its incapability of answering questions related to ethics and morals (Chua 2010, 2). It is perhaps possible to correct Chua's assumption here that religion not only would be diminished by disenchantment but, more broadly, can also be reconfigured through disenchantment. The disenchantment process results in a paradoxical process of rationalising religion to the extent of augmenting, rather than diminishing, religion itself.

As to the scripturalist turn in Islam, the primary source of wisdom, learning and reference for action and behaviour is the Quran, and even this is adapted to fit within a "scientific idiom", by fashioning its magical aspects as rational (Eneborg 2014, 420). This particular exercise of instrumentalising the Quran for a variety of purposes may be seen as the "modernizing of magic" rather than the purification of the religion (Eneborg 2014, 428). Can modernity flourish alongside elements of enchantment? Very much so. An antinomial approach as opposed to the binarial view allows envisioning "a specifically modern enchantment [which] might be defined as one that enchants and disenchants simultaneously: one that delights but does not delude" (Saler 2006, 702).

Geoffrey Benjamin's work on the religious transformation of the Temiars, an indigenous group of people, the Orang Asli, who live in the upland settlements of Kelantan, Perak and northern Pahang in Peninsular Malaysia, has been illuminating in the application of the bureaucratic rationalisation thesis as to how religion today is largely about its "repackaging", to become "*teachable*", with "*written* sources as the guarantors of religious truth" (2014, 301).

To date, studies on the disenchantment of religion have been predominantly applied to Christianity and non-Eastern religions (e.g. Yelle 2012; George 2017; Zisook 2017). The dependability of scripturalism became the foundation of religion and, with European colonialism, the codification of tradition. Henceforth, the written text was privileged to justify political projects (Yelle 2012, 9). Stated differently, even from a Weberian perspective, religion can be rationalised in modernity, particularly when there is a trend of revivalism and intensification. These "patterns of rationalization and secularization" can also include an Islamic resurgence induced by modern "nationalist expressions against Western secularization" (Lee and Ackerman 1997, 5–6).

By conceptualising, identifying and deconstructing the notion of a Divine Bureaucracy and its relationship to the enchantment and disenchantment of religion, this study hopes to elucidate the character of religion that can be subjected to various transformative motivations, among small or big cultural groups, in the West or otherwise. Enchantment and disenchantment as well as modernity and religion can coexist at the same time. This explains why it is possible to see the full flourishing of a religious bureaucracy with its absorption of secularism's sensibility and modern rationality while wielding its patrimonial powers and sacred authority through the simulacrum of enchantment. Modern religion is fixated on purifying, codifying and organising a system of belief to the point of disenchanting religious life, yet it is this very quality that exalts religion as an 'enchanted' process organised by a distinct structure. As religious authority is imbibed into a modern bureaucracy, this bureaucratisation takes on a more secularised character, progressively disenchanting and demystifying religious meanings by turning them into calculable, reducible, uniform and operable set of actions and rules that can be applied to all—consented, coerced or legalised subjects of the faith.

Bureaucratising Islam

Weber had an impression of the dichotomy between European Puritan asceticism and Asian religions with their mystical traditions. Within this he placed Islam as a test of his thesis on asceticism and rational economic activities (Turner 1974, 230). Did Islam have elements of rationality that would make it tenable as a basis for the development of capitalism? Nevertheless, given his limited observations of the capacity of Islam to accommodate modernisation and vice versa, Weber's main concern was deducing if capitalism could be developed under an Islam bogged down by values and systems of patrimonialism and its other enemies—"fatalism, passivity, mysticism" (Turner 1974, 240). There was certainly a profusion of mystical and magical practices prevalent within the Islam he had observed.

By the time Islamic reformism advanced in the twentieth century, a modern religious bureaucracy had been put in place, and some of the disjuncture between *syariah*, the law, and its judicial procedures as observed by Weber had begun to be addressed. These observations were limited to circumstances of the pre-modern Arab and Ottoman variety and did not anticipate that modern *syariah* could evolve as a full-blown system of formal, rational laws, with little room for arbitrariness and inflexibility. Whether in Iran, Egypt or Saudi Arabia, *syariah* came to be legitimised through its inception into the country's constitution as codified statutes (Schacht 1959; Coulson 1964). Here is when Islamic values, beliefs and goals were subjected to a rationalised system, accompanied by the professionalisation of its legal agents, and supported by a bureaucratic administration which could only pursue Islamic reform through secularisation (Asad 2001a).

One of the first studies on the bureaucracy within an Islamic setting assesses the modernising role and the failure of the bureaucracy in the history of the Ottoman Empire (Weiker 1968). Another is a study of corruption within the sixteenth-century Ottoman bureaucracy (Fodor 1995). Both of these studies focus on the internal elements of the bureaucracy, with Ottomanism rather than Islam as the core narrative. It was only in the 2000s that the phenomenon of Islamic religiosity was first explored through the lens of bureaucratisation. Antoun's study on the Jordanian religious bureaucracy makes the case where the state co-opts religion by increasing the number of religious specialists and differentiating government religious structures within the system (2006, 374). A more recent work on the Moroccan Islamic bureaucracy also situates the significance of bureaucratisation as a centralising and co-optation strategy to combat terrorism within "the infrastructure of the state" (Wainscott 2017, 14).

In studying religion and modernisation in Malaysia, Lee and Ackerman (1997) incisively discuss the distinct role of bureaucratisation in shaping Malay ethnicity, starting from the inclusion of Malay elites into the colonial civil service to their privileging through affirmative action policies of the New Economic Policy (NEP)[6] to the centralisation of Islamic administration (33–39). Mention or discussion of the bureaucracy has also been included as part of a larger study on state-religion relations in the context of the advent of political Islam (Liow 2009, 44–72). However, despite the important observations made, the bureaucracy was still a peripheral category in their overall examination of the major religions in Malaysia.

My earlier study attempted to outline some of the features of the emergent "legal-bureaucratic Islam" in Malaysia, although the focus was on its secularising tendencies (Maznah 2010). There have also been two other works with the term 'bureaucratisation' attached to their examination of Islam in Malaysia, although they adopt a state-religion political relations approach. These studies contain rich details of how regulatory and administrative structures have been established, resulting in both the successful and contentious management of Islam by the state (Mohd Azizuddin 2015; Liow 2009).

In the studies above, the bureaucracy was largely regarded as a structural means to fulfilling the ends of the state rather than an end in and of itself, or as the very embodiment of the religion. Conceptually, none engage extensively with bureaucratisation as a paradigm to interrogate the growing complexity of Islam's ascendency by means of a formal, rational organisation and a religiously enabled absolute bureaucratic authority, as this book attempts.

From Sacred Authority to Ulama *to Divine Bureaucracy*

Who holds the central authoritative leadership in Islam? Traditionally, this position has been associated with the *ulama* (Islamic scholars) but exactly who the *ulama* are is not easily defined. The *hadith* or word of the Prophet (pbh) considers *ulama* as "heirs to the prophets" or "people that bind and unbind" (Kramer and Schmidtke 2006, 11). Commonly, they are referred to as "traditionally educated scholars" (Eickelman and Piscatori 2004, xvii). Norshahril (2018) has a more elaborate description where Muslims distinguish them from other elites in their society "by virtue of their education". Furthermore, *ulama* are trained in Islamic disciplines or revealed knowledge, which can include "law, exegesis, theology, and traditions of the Prophet" (Norshahril 2018, 23). Saeed (2004) distinguishes two groups of *ulama*: official ones who are absorbed by the state bureaucracy and non-official ones who are independent of the state (2004, 14). *Ulama* are also "representatives of the Islamic religious and scholarly tradition" (Zaman 2012, 2) and "gatekeepers of Islamic learning" (Hatina 2009, 3). In Islam, *hadith* and *sunna* (ways of the Prophet), words derived from the foundational texts of the Quran, are sacred, eternal and inviolable; hence, the *ulama* as authoritative interpreters of these texts are rendered as key and vital (Kramer and Schmidtke 2006, 3). There is certainly the idea of a "sacred authority" in Islam, one whose legitimacy is determined by a set of ideological, locational and functional factors (Eickelman and Piscatori 2004, 57–59). Although these studies have identified the salient role and presence of *ulama* in Muslim social and political life, the designation remains ambiguous as those who hold the title are placed in many locations and sites of authority, from the informal to the formal.

Sharifah Zaleha's 1985 study on the shifting features of Islam in the Malay World opens up new and pioneering observations about the region's changing authority figures:

> For doctrinal justification, the new form of Islam turns to the teachings of orthodox rather than mystical Islam about the need to acknowledge the supremacy of the Divine Law. This shift in the religious focus of Malaysian Islam implies that beliefs need to be systematized, Islamic rituals and non-ritual activities standardized, and religious authority centralized and placed in the hands of the **ulama-bureaucrats** [my emphasis in bold]. (159)

Zaleha shows that the transformation of Islam pivots upon key agents, shifting from "saints" to "teacher-scholars" and finally to "religious bureaucrats". This identification of a new form of Islam emerging at the beginning of the twentieth century as bureaucratic, systematised, standardised, centralised and led by "*ulama*-bureaucrats" is a theme that this study will be advancing. In Muslim-majority nations, particularly in Malaysia, the *ulama*, or members of Islam's 'sacred authority', are now largely located within an official structure, holding much of state power (Norshahril 2018). The use of the term 'Divine Bureaucracy' will hopefully capture these new dynamics in this study of authority in religion.

Weber's concept of routinised charisma or charisma attached to an office rather than to a personality or leadership could be applied to the Islamic bureaucracy as well. A traditional authority of religion elevated into a salaried and professional class, the *ulama* is Malaysia's version of this charismatic bureaucracy, where it is routinised to take on the form of modern officialdom. A formerly existing *ulama* tradition of affective and "*guru*-disciple"[7] legitimacy is promoted through its graduation into a bureaucracy (Nagata 1982, 56). Even if this bureaucracy may not fully resemble the neutral, legal, rational ideal type of Weber's evolutionary organisation, it nevertheless adapts and attempts to be congruent with other existing structures of rationalised administration. A charismatic bureaucracy containing both elements of modernity and divinity promises more authority and distinctiveness. Had it been just one without the other, it would not have gained such importance.

Bureaucratisation, Judicialisation, Corporatisation

Over the years, there has been much more directed scholarship in using 'bureaucracy' as an epistemic category for charting newer dynamics of religion in state and society. Recent studies on this subject can be found in the special issue volumes of two journals: the *Journal of Law and Religion* (2018, Vol. 33, No. 2) with the theme "The Bureaucratization of Religion in Southeast Asia" and the *Journal of Current Southeast Asian Affairs* (2018, Vol. 37, No. 1) on "The Bureaucratisation of Islam in Southeast Asia: Transdisciplinary perspectives". These groundbreaking studies on state-religion relations use the prism of bureaucratisation to understand the transformation of society through religion. As the articles attest, the ramifications of the bureaucratic overlay on religious transformations have been considerable, though understudied (Kunkler 2018; Larsson 2018; Muller 2018; Hamayotsu 2018; Fenwick 2018; Nisa 2018). The authors assert that bureaucratic forms have "profound consequences for social and cultural transformation, alongside changes of the very social, political and doctrinal meanings(s) of Islam" (Muller and Steiner 2018, 12). Change through bureaucratisation has been affected in quieter ways than by social forces such as radical movements and political parties, hitherto the focus of most studies on Islam in past decades. However, the bureaucracies of religion have evolved from erstwhile "servants" of larger ideological state projects to becoming "major producers of religious authority, and as such have entirely transformed national landscapes of religious life" (Kunkler 2018, 196). The use of bureaucratic institutions and codes for the administration of Islam has produced a "special brand of Islam" (Steiner 2018, 28).

Through calculated rationality and systematisation of purpose, bureaucratisation achieves at least two outcomes, the objectification of religion and its functionalisation (Kunkler 2018, 194). Objectification systematically classifies and categorises (Eickelman 1992, 647), while functionalisation translates knowledge and discursive contents into pragmatic and serviceable ends (Starrett 1998, 9–10). According to Muller (2018), the language of bureaucracy lends power to transform Muslim society through the imposition of "categorical schemes" allowing for the "translation" of Islam into codes, procedures and symbols (214). Beyond considering the bureaucratisation of Islam as a strategy for political control and neutralising opposition, such a study allows for interrogating related, though no less imperative, questions involving the "production of social meanings", its "discursive contexts" and "social changes" at the micro level (215).

Hamayotsu (2018) focuses on the expansion of the Islamic court and its deeper integration into the state justice system as a form of bureaucratisation to fulfil external goals of political alliances rather than a professed goal of Islamising society. Beyond religion, a tight bureaucratic structure fulfils the needs and interests of political and religious elites to sustain dominant rule on the basis of communal identity (249–250). Bureaucratising Islam or expanding its governmentality inevitably leads to an Islamisation of the state, with the position of the majority religion strengthened. It would be in the self-interest of those within the bureaucracy were it to be expanded, hence validating the self-preservation of the bureaucracy thesis (268). The external implication of this is the deterioration of freedom and plurality in society. In Malaysia, contentious cases of apostasy, conversion, marriage, divorce, custody of children and inheritance involving Muslim-non-Muslim litigants are some of the indications of this trend (270).

Besides bureaucratisation, judicialisation has also been identified as a site in the regulation of religion (Peletz 2015; Kunkler 2018; Dressel 2012; Moustafa 2018). Judicialisation has been referred to as the rapid and increasing reliance on courts and judicial systems to address societal problems, from moral questions to public policy and political contentions (Dressel 2012, 1). It involves the resolution of religious conflict through the judicial process whereas bureaucratisation entails a specialised agency to delineate what is 'right' or 'wrong' in religious practices. Bureaucratisation in some ways precludes the need for judicial intervention (Sezkin and Kunkler 2014, 449–451). Judicialisation endeavours to defuse conflicts, while bureaucratisation attempts to lock the conflicts within, resulting in various instances of judicialisation intensifying identity politics and ethno-religious divides (Sezkin and Kunkler 2014, 451). Like bureaucratisation, however, judicialisation has a similar latitude to affect social change outside of the courts, with its ability to spur public debate, constitute political coalitions and incite the participation of non-specialists, eventually leading to the "production of new religious knowledge" (Moustafa 2018, 705–706).

A related institutional form to both bureaucratisation and judicialisation is corporatisation. The rise of Islamic corporate governmentality, combining elements of divinity with work styles, methods, assessment procedures and target goals of the modern corporation, can be seen as a heightening of bureaucratised Islam (Peletz 2015). Deeper than just work styles, corporatisation sets in as an inevitable organisational model when financial resources are marshalled and valorised by capitalist logic for the benefit, and in the name, of Islam (Sloane-White 2017). The chapters that follow utilise the notions of bureaucratisation, judicialisation and corporatisation as interrelated conceptual tools in comprehending the power of the Divine Bureaucracy.

Why Divine Bureaucracy, Why Disenchantment of Social Life?

Reconfiguring Weber's line of arguments, I make a case in this study that a specific bureaucracy, the Divine Bureaucracy, can paradoxically surface through a form of rationalisation and the eschewing of all incalculable forces as in magic and enchantment, while at the same time reinforcing itself through its strong "possession of sacred values" (Weber 1991c, 352). Yet another paradox is the disenchantment of social life through this Divine Bureaucracy. While rationalisation strips religious life of its mystical elements through guided rules, sanctions and doctrines, the authority of the bureaucracy can only be exercised rationally through a form of authoritarian, perhaps irrational domination, whereby the ruler influences the conduct of the ruled, as if the content of the command is also "the maxim of their conduct for its very own sake. Looked upon from the other end, this situation will be called *obedience*" (Weber 1966, 328).

However, not to simplify the idea of "obedience", Weber qualified this as something that can be the outcome of varied factors—from "empathy or through inspiration or through persuasion by rational argument or through some combination of these", even "by the ruled's own conviction of its propriety, or by his [*sic*] sense of duty, or by fear, or by dull custom, or by a desire to obtain some benefit for himself [*sic*]" (ibid.). The shifting between the rational and irrational motivation on the part of the administered suggests a form of 'divination' in the quality of bureaucracy that is at work.

This study will show how the functioning of a bureaucracy for Islamic development in Malaysia resembles a quintessential secular arrangement. The Divine Bureaucracy is tasked with codifying an often unstructured piety and its aura of fluid enchantment into a disenchanted performative religiosity achieved through the application of literal, unambiguous and categorical rules upon everyday conduct. The features of officials in this bureaucracy are one of shifts and transferals—at one level, implementing legal and formal technicalities on their juridical subjects as rational, efficient civil servants, and, on another, exuding the celestial air of being God's representatives who cannot be reproached. This assumed interchangeable role privileged upon the Divine Bureaucracy is the source and basis of its power.

Following Benjamin (2014), the book-based "emissary prophet" approach is more applicable to Malaysia's Divine Bureaucracy as opposed to that of the "exemplary prophet", which is associated with the idea of charismatic leadership and those whose beliefs are multistranded. The former "leads rapidly to the characterising of certain religious practices as *correct* and others as *incorrect*—a distinction fundamental to the schoolmasterly authority that underpins the position of the clergy in many religious traditions" (337–338). Benjamin's division amounts to formal rationality, domination, emissary prophecy and disenchantment on one side and substantive rationality, autonomy, exemplary prophecy and re-enchantment on the other side (338).

The "potentialities of secularism", as suggested by Agrama (2012, 6), might include the religious bureaucracy, where instead of producing agents or representatives of the non-secular, this bureaucracy—even as it propounds worldviews inimical to secular values—has instrumentally found its flourishing within the sphere of secularism. Such a possibility has been both initiated and spurred by an objectified Muslim consciousness in the modern era to critically question what it means to be a believer and why certain actions are taken to reaffirm such faith. Objectification of a once mystical, even fluid, belief system requires that this be re-understood as a precisely outlined "self-contained system" that can be distinguishable from other competing belief systems (Eickelman and Piscatori 2004, 38). It is about an Islam reimagined through the use of *syariah* idioms, "the flexibility and interpretability of its constructs, and the open structure of its texts which eventually serves a select form of political and cultural affirmation" (Messick 1993, 3).

There is also the reinvention of being pious through the construction of new lifestyles which incorporate social distancing and community enclaving (Nasir, Turner and Pereira 2010). For all such tendencies to cohere necessitates some form of authority, that is, a religious bureaucracy able to systematise and functionalise religion, altering religious discourse and shifting control to other central authorities or groups not necessarily associated with traditional forms and structures (Starrett 1998, 6). I argue here that the objectification of Islam or of a heightened Muslim consciousness would inevitably have to find its foothold within a systematic and routinised system of secular governance. All of this would be manifested through codified laws, debates and discourses based on textualised sources, differentiation of administrative and judicial functions and rationalisation of resources for utilitarian and economic goals.

When contextualised against the backdrop of the rising interdependency between religion and the state for mutual legitimacy and survival, this lends credence to the emergent demand for not just a new but a zealous bureaucracy. The bureaucracy over religious matters in Malaysia was initially limited, fulfilling the goals of pacifying and neutralising a potentially antagonistic Islamic civil society (Liow 2009; Mohd Azizuddin 2015; Hayamotsu 2018). But as has been observed of most bureaucracies (Heyman 2004, 489), it was subsequently able to evolve into an "instrument of power" with a life of its own. With power, the Malaysian religious bureaucracy could set in motion a train of disenchantment over a wide spectrum of social life, relying on the discourse and idioms of both *syariah* and scientific rationality.

When a modern bureaucracy (typified as a legal rational system) confronts religious traditions (with elements of non-rational presuppositions), it may be inevitable that a new religious imagination would have to be invented. The creation of "discrete, rule-following 'bureaus' or offices" is the logic of bureaucracy (Han 2015, 80). Religion will thus be organised as "an object of continual management and intervention", while religious life and sensibility will be made to fit dominant presumptions and conditions of governance of the time (Agrama 2012, 18).

The disenchantment of social life in this study refers to the phenomenon of a legal rational instrument, the Divine Bureaucracy, delivering a 'categorically objectified' Islam. What is inaccurately perceived as a steep rise in religiosity among Muslims or of a sense of creeping Islamisation is, in actual fact, the proliferation of a disenchanted Islam constructed by an omniscient state officialdom. The establishment of this Divine Bureaucracy is derived from the dividends of political pacification, neutralisation and co-optation of revivalist, extremist or radical Islam of the past decades (Kamarulnizam 1999; Hamayotsu 2005; Ahmad Fauzi 2007). In Malaysia's project of majoritarian ethnic and religious dominance, the notion of Ketuanan Melayu[8] has also provided another source of sustenance for the enlargement of the Divine Bureaucracy (Maznah 2010; Hamayotsu 2018) through its "hegemonic narrative of supremacy and exclusion" (Liow 2016, 135).

In this book, I expand upon previous studies on Islamic bureaucratisation by identifying the bureaucratic apparatus not just as the means to address state-religion tensions or the facilitation of ethnic-elite rule preservation, but to regard the Divine Bureaucracy as a distinctive power base generating new meanings in the construction and re-delineation of Islamic subjectivity, as well as new ways of confronting diversity, plurality and democracy in society. In previous conceptualisation and studies, sites of bureaucratic, Islamic power are seen to lie within the modes of classification (Muller 2018), objectification (Eickelman 1992) and functionalisation (Starrett 1998). My own conceptualisation of the power of Islamic bureaucratisation includes all of the above, as well as its micro-capacity to standardise, ring-fence, finalise and cleanse social life, while making the process explicit, definite, precise, doctrinally justifiable and rules based in its intent, method and ends to achieve the higher purpose of a religious, even enchanted, life. There are paradoxes and ironies in all of these for while the bureaucracy's tool is rational and secular, its authority is founded on a sense of divinity, and though the 'higher purpose' of religion preaches to a form of enchantment, the worldly pathway is one of disenchantment.

Dissension against this categorical objectification of religion and religious subjects may find expression in the longing for a return to the enchantment of spiritual life, which would embody penchants for decentralisation, diffusion, the blurring of boundaries, capacious spatial manoeuvres, equivocality as value in negotiations and, above all, more tolerance and inclusivity of the Other. The magical qualities of religion, disavowed by a de-magicalised bureaucracy (Weber's *Entzauberung*), with its sense of mystery and the unknowable, are still holding sway among many, as this study will show. Hence, it is also a mistaken assumption to accept that a disenchanted religiosity has broadly and deeply swept through society. Recurrent intra-Muslim contestation over what is to be construed as the 'better', 'preferred', 'perfect' or 'most enchanting' Islam persists, which ironically has also cut out the work for statist Divine Bureaucracy for a long time to come as it persistently seeks out methods, edicts, rules and lawmaking to cleanse the space for only one version of Islam.

What is in This Book

Together with its introductory and concluding chapters, this book comprises eight chapters. Following this Introduction, Chap. 2 traces the origin of Islam's bureaucratisation in contemporary Malaysia to the foundation and intentions of British colonial rule. Governing on the basis of formalised laws led to the engraining of a proto-bureaucracy within the purview of indigenous and customary realms of power. What the colonial lawmakers variously termed *Hukum Syarak*, and *Mohammedan* or *adat* (customs) laws, were codified and systematised to administer affairs within the delineated sphere of Islamic religion and Malay custom. In the first decade after decolonisation, the administration of Islamic law and affairs maintained a secularising framework, and power was limited to the confines of traditional authority—the ruling and religious elites of decentralised *negeri* (State, subnational units of governance within the federated system). Two decades after national independence in 1957, a Muslim public sphere—often associated with the *dakwah* of Islamic resurgent movements—was considerably enlarged, enabling contestations over Islam by agents outside the circle of traditional authority. Such challenges were considered risky to the Malay-led national leadership under the ruling party the United Malays National Organisation (Umno), as it feared the fragmentation of the Malay vote bloc due to such Muslim contestations. The Islamist mobilisation thus forced the state to redress Muslim grievances and competition through policies of accommodation, neutralisation and co-optation. This included the ironic adoption of the very goals propounded by the mobilisers who themselves had initially been impeded by the state. Such a structural reconstitution of Islam could only be effected through a bureaucratic pathway, the outcome of which was an augmented bureaucracy over Islamic matters and subjects, with unparalleled expanded domains.

Chapter 3 details the contemporary features of this augmented bureaucracy over Islam, extending to become the Divine Bureaucracy. It identifies this entity's three distinctive levels of power acting in tandem or autonomously from one another: *negeri*, federal and corporate Islamic bureaucracies. The first is the decentralised, *negeri*-based traditional

Islamic bureaucracy first established under British colonialism, which has continued in strength through the present time. The federal Islamic bureaucracy refers to the second domain, which is the central or federalised bureaucracy over Islam, which took shape during the third decade of postcolonial governance. The corporate Islamic bureaucracy, the third domain, is engendered by the growth of an Islamic banking and financial sector. This chapter explains and argues why and how the Divine Bureaucracy and its association with the promotion and advancement of Islam made it exceptional, superseding powers of other national institutions of authority.

The bureaucratisation of religion through the strengthening of the Divine Bureaucracy added new challenges to being and becoming 'Muslim'. This will be expounded in Chap. 4. The goal of homogenisation is imperative as it concurs with the Divine Bureaucracy's function to standardise, uniformise and centralise. This chapter, along with Chap. 5, explains how the bureaucracy confronts and deals with the plurality of identities, whether based on gender, sexuality, ethnicity or competing Islamic religiosity within its midst. As the ubiquity of the Divine Bureaucracy increases, various groups of Muslims have found themselves designated as incorrect, improper, impure and in contravention of formalised *syariah*'s rules and regulations. The Divine Bureaucracy acts as a force of salvation and deliverance, with religious expression and identity codified and defined in accordance with acceptable official interpretations. Two processes of Islamic and Muslim homogenisation have gone hand in hand in this exercise. One was the standardisation of faith in that only an officially designated Islam would be legitimately accepted and supported by state. The other was the ring-fencing of constituents to outlaw the Muslim subject from exiting the *syariah* juridical bound.

While Chap. 4 examines and analyses cases of why and how the standardisation of faith has been enforced upon both individuals and collectives, Chap. 5 explores the notion of ring-fencing as intrinsic to the Divine Bureaucracy's project to homogenise the expressions of Islam and the Muslim subject's identity. The case studies expounded in this chapter will show that both *syariah* and civil laws delineate the boundaries of group identity by playing a gatekeeping function, defining who should be outlawed as Muslim 'deviants' and who should be rehabilitated back into the fold of group legitimacy. One of the most palpable, if not infallible, gatekeeping devices for ring-fencing is the legal prohibition against Muslims opting out of Islam as apostates. Yet ring-fencing goes beyond outlawing apostasy; religious deviancy, forbidden marriages and sexual waywardness are part of a broad syndrome to be contained as well. To ring-fence subjects within these conditions of decreed wrongfulness requires that Muslim subjects suspend their civic identity and civil rights, a role that has devolved upon the Divine Bureaucracy.

Chapter 6 investigates several premises that underscore the quest for the perfection of the Islamic family, as directed and envisioned by the Divine Bureaucracy. The reformulation of *syariah* family law to embody a new Malay-Muslim masculinity and femininity is a foremost priority of the Divine Bureaucracy. The second policy goal is to enforce a mandatory marriage education programme for Muslim couples planning to marry. While moral panic over marital breakdown and rising rates of Muslim divorce may have provided the early impetus for this extensive nationwide undertaking, it has been more successful in providing a first-entry level exposure on the makings of a better and more authentic Islamic family. A third priority is the regulation of Muslim marriage and family units by laying emphasis on the supremacy of Islam as a constitutional entitlement, along with the elevation of Muslim masculinity as a right in society. This inclination is demonstrated through the judicialisation of Muslim-non-Muslim marital legal contestations, the role of the Divine Bureaucracy, and the *syariah* and civil judiciary in determining these outcomes. In all of these matters, the Divine Bureaucracy acts as the key agent in making and unmaking family.

A corporate Islamic bureaucracy laying the foundations and driving the growth of an Islamic-oriented finance and banking sector is the subject of Chap. 7. Constituting the third of the Divine Bureaucracy's three arms, the chapter shows how the corporate bureaucracy linked to Islam is distinct, autonomous and distanced from the other two bureaucracies of *negeri* and federal Islam. The sector of Islamic finance capitalism provides an interesting case study as a representation of Islamic moneymaking, the quintessence of an economic model driven by faith. The social agents driving and sustaining the industry are not bureaucrats entrenched within formal *syariah* institutions but nevertheless function within an organisational bureaucracy leveraged upon an economy based on Islam. Similar to the other two levels of the Divine Bureaucracy, corporate Islamic bureaucracy also rides on the exceptionalism of Islamic national supremacy.

The growth of Islamic capitalism is driven by an autonomous class of non-theological agents. While dependent on religious discourses and textual prescriptions for legitimising the purposes of Islamic finance, these actors have the power to overlook the encumbrances of religion whenever it is necessary to promote the goals of capital accumulation over Islamic orthodoxy. The corporate Islamic bureaucracy comprises technocrats who function within a transnational network of state agents, investors, bankers, economists and scholars in Islamic commercial law. The Syariah Advisory Council of Malaysia's Central Bank (Bank Negara Malaysia) and the Securities Commission of Malaysia (SCM) play a key role in these movements. Institutions and agencies entrusted to generate an Islamic economic sphere serve to systematise, construct, appraise, certify and accredit what is allowable in *syariah*-compliant financial transactions. The ethical justification for the 'purification' of money ultimately also serves the end material goal of wealth accumulation in accordance with a capitalistic logic, and hence is potentially contentious.

The concluding chapter (Chap. 8) restates the main analytical framework of this study, as a newer way of understanding the wide and deep mobilisation of religious symbols and material resources in the transformation of state and society. The expanding visibility and palpability of Islamic piety has strong links to the proliferation, enlargement and accretion of institutions of religious governance, almost wholly funded by the state. This immense sense of the reorganisation and disenchantment of social life is driven not only by spiritual devotion or cultural ideology but also by the instrumentalist goals of power and control. This final chapter also reviews some of the nascent reform overtures and policies with regard to Islamic matters, of Malaysia's newly elected Pakatan Harapan (Coalition of Hope) government that ousted the 61-year-old government of the Barisan Nasional (National Front) in 2018. Although too early to give conclusive insights on this, it can be seen that the Divine Bureaucracy was too formidable an edifice to chisel at, its power going beyond any elected authority. It may be incorrect to conclude that the power of the Divine Bureaucracy is unappealing or repressive, since disenchantment in its orderliness may be the draw to many of its adherents.

Conclusion

This introductory chapter has critically reviewed concepts and theories relevant for an inquiry on the bureaucracy, religious authority and social life. It has explored the concepts of bureaucratic power, secularism, modernity, rationality and the oscillating nature of enchantment and disenchantment in religious expressions. It has also made a case for developing a new typology of bureaucracy, namely the Divine Bureaucracy, to fill the gaps in understanding how contemporary state Islamisation evolves and functions. It demonstrated how the theoretical explications and insights presented point to the germaneness of the epistemic categories around bureaucracy and bureaucratisation as another way of understanding the transformation of social and religious life in society. The Divine Bureaucracy studied in this book typically has all the features of the Weberian legal rational organisation, and, in line with the modernisation thesis, it performs the function of ordering religious society through a systematic and rules-based process of rationalising its subjects and objects of governance.

The specific functions of this bureaucratisation include the mode of a multiple-layered and extensive explication and categorisation of rules and guidelines on worship, conduct, consumption, contracts, exchange and all aspects of cultural, social, political and economic life outlined, and justified along select scriptural and textual sources. The latter is yielded as sacred and divine, providing the bureaucracy its greatest source of power, while the systematisation exercise manifests the intense objectification of Islam "as an abstract system of ideas that can be distinguished from other such systems" (Eickelman and Piscatori 2004, 38). The outcome of disenchantment is not only in its Weberian connotation, of an extensive rationalisation and de-personalisation process, but also in its literal, popular and everyday signification of leading to a state of discontentment and disillusionment among opponents.

This is particularly felt by politically despondent civil rights advocates, challenging the violations of human rights by the Divine Bureaucracy; or by Muslim subalterns who, by returning to a religious enchantment of mysticism, idolatry and magic, would be persecuted and prosecuted for transgressing the norms, rules and laws under the charge of this bureaucracy. Hence, while the Divine Bureaucracy thrives within a space of secularisation, it does not endear itself to the secular subject and vice versa. This bureaucracy identifies the secular subject—the emancipated woman, the liberal Muslim, the multicultural inclusivist, as well as the wrongful 'un-secular' subject (the supernatural-worshipping 'deviant')—amongst its most discernible 'enemies'. The significations of modernity, secularism and religion occupying a space which is neither here nor there, or 'either/or', but rather, within an antinomial site, increases the complexity of governance and decreases the possibilities for the resolution of societal conflicts.

The Divine Bureaucracy provides one trajectory in understanding the role of religion in a post-secular and postmodern world where the exercise of domination, through religion, can emanate from a range of organisational sources. The seemingly neutral and non-aligned bureaucratic system is one of these. Bureaucratisation, secularism, enchantment and disenchantment are useful epistemic concepts as they help to clarify debates about whether what is in fact occurring in many Muslim-majority societies today should be understood as a movement of aggressive Islamisation, or a process of perilous de-secularisation, or the secularisation of religious life. In Malaysia, at least, it is more apt to recognise that it is the disenchantment of social life, the demystification of faith and the objectification of religiosity that constitute the most pervasive trends. These sum up the purposes and the consequences of religious bureaucratisation. It is this bureaucratisation that constitutes state Islamisation. But more than just a variant, bureaucratic Islam is *the* definitive Islam in modern life.

Notes

1. This study of Islam is situated in Malaysia, a multicultural, mid-sized and middle-income country which has seen a turnover in its ruling government for the first time in 2018, after some 60 years. In its governance and political, cultural and economic practices, Islam is a strong feature because of its Muslim-majority population.
2. On 13 May 1969, riots broke out on the streets of Kuala Lumpur. This was by far the most significant violent episode in Malaysia's post-independence history. Most accounts of the incidence document it as an ethnic clash involving Malays and Chinese, rather than a conflict based on religion. See, for example, Malaysia (1969), Comber (1983) and Kua (2013).
3. The term, which is taken to mean 'Islamic law', can be spelt differently in different national contexts as '*sharia*', '*shariah*' or '*syariah*'. When not citing the term from other sources, the spelling adopted in this book is '*syariah*' and treated as an adjective rather than noun, hence in small rather than in capital letters.
4. At the popular level of discourse, but presented as an academic study, see, for example, Haslinda (1999).
5. In a comparative study of Islamist mobilisation in Turkey, Indonesia and Malaysia, the latter had the lowest incidence of political violence, largely because the state had made the cost of employing violence "too high" (Chernov-Hwang 2009, 111). Inter-religious infractions too have been

relatively minimal with the spectre of May 1969, the most prominent interracial riots in Malaysian history, used as a fearful disincentive.

6. The NEP was an affirmative action policy to reduce the socio-economic disparity between the indigenous population (the majority being Malays) and others (primarily Chinese). It was implemented in 1970 and regarded as a policy response to the ethnic riots of May 1969 (Jomo 2005).
7. This refers to a tradition of learning which places great reverence and authority on teachers who pass on knowledge to their pupils, with this line of discipleship credited to its originator.
8. The political narrative of Ketuanan Melayu is used to denote the supremacy or entitled deservedness of the Malays in controlling politics in the country.

References

Agrama, Hussein Ali (2012) *Questioning Secularism Islam, Sovereignty, and the Rule of Law in Modern Egypt*, Chicago: Chicago University Press.

Ahmad Fauzi, Abdul Hamid (2007) "Patterns of State Interaction with Islamic Movement in Malaysia during the Formative Years of Islamic Resurgence", *Southeast Asian Studies*, Vol. 44, No. 4, 444–465.

Allen, Kieran (2004) *Max Weber: A critical introduction*, London, Ann Arbor, MI: Pluto Press.

Antoun, Richard T (2006) "Fundamentalism, Bureaucratization, and the State's Co-optation of Religion: A Jordanian case study", *International Journal of Middle East Studies*, Vol. 38, No. 3, 369–393.

Asad, Talal (2001a) *Thinking About Secularism and Law in Egypt*, Leiden: International Institute for the Study of Islam in the Modern World (ISIM).

——— (2001b) "Reading a Modern Classic: WC Smith's 'The Meaning and End to Religion'", *History of Religions*, Vol. 40, No. 3, 205–222.

——— (2003) *Formations of the Secular: Christianity, Islam, modernity*, Stanford, CA: Stanford University Press.

Asprem, Agil (2016) *The Problem of Disenchantment: Scientific naturalism and esoteric discourse 1900–1939*, Leiden, Boston: Brill.

Beetham, David (1987) *Bureaucracy*, Milton Keynes: Open University Press.

Benjamin, Geoffrey (2014) *Temiar Religion 1964–2012: Enchantment, disenchantment and re-enchantment in Malaysia's uplands*, Singapore: National University of Singapore Press.

Casanova, Jose (2009) "The Secular and Secularisms", *Social Research: An international quarterly*, Vol. 76, No. 4, 1049–1066.

Chernov-Hwang, Julie (2009) *Peaceful Islamist Mobilization in the Muslim World: What went right*, New York: Palgrave Macmillan.

Chua, Eu Jin (2010) "Disenchantment", in Mark Bevir (ed), *Encyclopedia of Political Theory*, Thousand Oaks: Sage Publications, 1–2.

Cinar, Alev, Srirupa Roy and Maha Yahya (eds) (2012) *Visualizing Secularism and Religion: Egypt, Lebanon, Turkey, India.* Ann Arbor: University of Michigan Press.

Comber, Leon (1983) *13 May 1969: A historical survey of Sino-Malay relations*, Kuala Lumpur: Heinemann.

Coulson, NJ (1964) *A History of Islamic Law*, Edinburgh: Edinburgh University Press.

Dressel, Bjorn (2012) "The Judicialization of Politics in Asia: Towards a framework of analysis", in Bjorn Dressel (ed), *The Judicialization of Politics in Asia*, New York: Routledge.

Dressler, Markus and Arvind-Pal S Mandair (eds) (2011) *Secularism and Religion-Making*, Oxford, New York: Oxford University Press.

Eickelman, Dale F (1992) "Mass Higher Education and the Religious Imagination in Contemporary Arab Societies", *American Ethnologist*, Imagining Identities: Nation, culture, and the past, Vol. 19, No. 4, November, 643–655.

Eickelman, Dale F and James Piscatori (2004) *Muslim Politics*, Princeton: Princeton University Press.

Eisenstadt, SN (1958) "Bureaucracy and Bureaucratization", *Current Sociology*, Vol. 7, No. 2, 99–124.

Eneborg, Yusuf Muslim (2014) "The Quest for 'Disenchantment' and the Modernization of Magic", *Islam and Christian-Muslim Relations*, Vol. 25, No. 4, 419–432.

Fenwick, Stewart (2018) "Eat, Pray, Regulate: The Indonesian Ulama Council and the management of Islamic affairs", *Journal of Law and Religion*, Vol. 33, No. 2, 271–290.

Fodor, Pal (1995) "How to Forge Documents? (A case of corruption within the Ottoman bureaucracy around 1590)", *Acta Orientalia Academiae Scientiarum Hung. Tomus*, Vol. XLVIII, No. 3, 383–389.

George, Jibu Matthew (2017) *The Ontology of Gods: An account of enchantment, disenchantment and re-enchantment*, Palgrave Macmillan.

Grosby, Steven (2013) "Max Weber, Religion, and the Disenchantment of the World", *Culture and Society*, Vol. 50, Issue 3, June, 301–310.

Hamayotsu, Kikue (2005) "Demobilizing Islam: Institutionalized religion and the politics of co-optation in Malaysia", PhD thesis, Australian National University.

——— (2018) "The Political Origins of Islamic Courts in Divided Societies: The case of Malaysia", *Journal of Law and Religion*, Vol. 33, No. 2, 248–270.

Han, Sam (2015) "Disenchantment Revisited: Formations of the 'secular' and 'religious' in the technological discourse of modernity", *Social Compass*, Vol. 62, No. 1, 76–88.

Haslinda, binti Hasan (1999) "Sekularisme: Sejarah kelahiran dan kesannya terhadap peradaban Islam dengan penumpuan terhadap serangan pemikiran", MA thesis, University of Malaya.
Hatina, Meir (2009) "Introduction", in Meir Hatina (ed), *Guardians of Faith in Modern Times: 'Ulama' in the Middle East*, Leiden: Brill, 1–17.
Heyman, Josiah McC (2004) "The Anthropology of Power-Wielding Bureaucracies", *Human Organization*, Vol. 63, No. 4, 487–500.
Jomo, KS (2005) "Malaysia's New Economic Policy and National Unity", in Yusuf Bangura and Rodolfo Stavenhagen (eds), *Racism and Public Policy*, UNRISD and Palgrave Macmillan, 182–214.
Kamarulnizam, Abdullah (1999) "National Security and Malay Unity: The issue of radical religious element in Malaysia", *Contemporary Southeast Asia*, Vol. 21, No. 2; 261–282.
Kramer, Gudrun and Sabine Schmidtke (2006) "Introduction—Religious Authority and Religious Authorities in Muslim Societies: A critical overview" in Gudrun Kramer and Sabine Schmidtke (eds), *Speaking for Islam: Religious authorities in Muslim Societies*, Leiden: Brill, 1–14.
Kua Kia Soong (2013) *May 13 Fact and Fiction: Malaysian challenges*, Petaling Jaya: Suaram.
Kunkler, Mirjam (2018) "The Bureaucratization of Religion in Southeast Asia: Expanding or restricting religious freedom?", *Journal of Law and Religion*, Vol. 33, No. 2, 192–196.
Lai, Junnan (2015) "'Patrimonial Bureaucracy' and Chinese Law: Max Weber's legacy and its limits", *Modern China*, Vol. 41, No. 1, 40–58.
Larsson, Tomas (2018) "Buddhist Bureaucracy and Religious Freedom in Thailand", *Journal of Law and Religion*, Vol. 33, No. 2, 197–211.
Lee, Raymond LM and Susan E Ackerman (1997) *Sacred Tensions: Modernity and religious transformations in Malaysia*, Columbia, SC: University of South Carolina Press.
Liow, Joseph Chinyong (2009) *Piety and Politics: Islamism in contemporary Malaysia*, Oxford: Oxford University Press.
——— (2016) *Religion and Nationalism in Southeast Asia*, Cambridge: Cambridge University Press.
Lyons, Sara (2014) "The Disenchantment/Re-Enchantment Of The World: Aesthetics, secularization, and the Gods of Greece from Friedrich Schiller to Walter Pater", *The Modern Language Review*, Vol. 109, No. 4, October, 873–895.
Main, Roderick (2017) "Panentheism and the Undoing of Disenchantment", *Zygon*, Vol. 52, No. 4, 1098–1122.
Malaysia (1969) *The May 13 Tragedy: A report*, Kuala Lumpur: National Operations Council.

Marty, Martin E and R Scott Appleby (eds) (1991) *Fundamentalisms Observed*, A study conducted by the American Academy of Arts and Sciences, Chicago: University of Chicago Press.

Maznah, Mohamad (2010) "The Ascendance of Bureaucratic Islam and the Secularization of the Sharia in Malaysia", *Pacific Affairs*, Vol. 83, No. 3, 505–524.

——— (2013) "Legal-Bureaucratic Islam in Malaysia: Homogenizing and ring-fencing the Muslim subject" in Hui Yew Foong (ed) *Encountering Islam: The politics of religious identities in Southeast Asia*, Singapore: ISEAS, 103–132.

Messick, Brinkley (1993) *The Calligraphic State: Textual domination and history in a Muslim society*, Berkeley: University of California Press.

Mohaddessin, Mohammad (1993) *Islamic Fundamentalism: The new global threat,* Washington, DC: Steven Locks Press.

Mohd Azizuddin, Mohd Sani (2015) "Islamization Policy and Islamic Bureaucracy in Malaysia", *Trends in Southeast Asia*, No. 5, Singapore: ISEAS Publishing, pp. 1–29

Moustafa, Tamir (2018) "The Judicialization of Religion", *Law and Society Review*, Vol. 52, No. 3, 685–708.

Muller, Dominik M (2018) "Bureaucratic Islam Compared: Classificatory power and state-ified religious meaning-making in Brunei and Singapore", *Journal of Law and Religion*, Vol. 33, No. 2, 212–247.

Muller, Dominik M and Kerstin Steiner (2018) "The Bureaucratisation of Islam in Southeast Asia: Transdisciplinary perspectives", *Journal of Current Southeast Asian Affairs*, Vol. 37, No.1, 3–26.

Nagata, Judith (1982) "Islamic Revival and the Problem of Legitimacy Among rural religious elites in Malaysia", *Man,* New Series, Vol. 17, No. 1, March, 42–57.

Nasir, Kamaludeen Mohamed, Bryan S Turner and Alexius A Pereira (2010) *Muslims in Singapore: Piety, politics and policies*, London: Routledge.

Nisa, Eva F. (2018) "The Bureaucratization of Muslim Marriage in Indonesia", *Journal of Law and Religion*, Vol. 33, No. 2, 191–309.

Norshahril, Saat (2018) *The State, Ulama and Islam in Malaysia and Indonesia*, Singapore: ISEAS Publishing.

Peletz, Michael G (2015) "A Tale of Two Courts: Judicial transformation and the rise of a corporate Islamic governmentality in Malaysia", *American Ethnologist*, Vol. 42, No. 1, 144–160.

Rheinstein, Max (1966) (ed) *Max Weber on Law in Economy and Society,* (with an introduction and annotation), 2nd ed, Cambridge: Harvard University Press.

Saeed, Abdullah (2004) "The Official Ulema and Religious Legitimacy of the Modern Nation State" in Shahram Akbarzadeh and Abdullah Saeed (eds), *Islam and Political Legitimacy*, London: Routledge, 14–28.

Salama, Mohammad and Rachel Friedman (2012) "Locating the Secular in Sayyid Qutb", *The Arab Studies Journal*, Vol. 20, No. 1, 104–131.
Saler, Michael (2006) "Modernity and Enchantment: A historiographic review", *The American Historical Review*, Vol. 111, No. 3, 692–716.
Schacht, Joseph (1959) "Islamic Law in Contemporary States", *The American Journal of Comparative Law*, Vol. 8, No. 2, 133–147.
Sezkin, Yuksel and Mirjam Kunkler (2014) "Regulation of 'Religion' and the 'Religious': The politics of judicialization and bureaucratization in India and Indonesia", *Comparative Studies in Society and History*, Vol. 56, No. 2, 448–478.
Sharifah Zaleha, Syed Hassan (1985) "From Saints to Bureaucrats: A study of the development of Islam in the State of Kedah, Malaysia", PhD thesis submitted to Cornell University
Sloane-White, Patricia (2017) *Corporate Islam: Sharia and the modern workplace*, Cambridge: Cambridge University Press.
Starrett, Gregory (1998) *Putting Islam to Work: Education, politics, and religious transformation in Egypt*, Berkeley: University of California Press.
Steiner, Kerstin (2018) "Branding Islam: Islam, law, and bureaucracies in Southeast Asia", *Journal of Current Southeast Asian Affairs*, Vol. 37, No.1, 27–56.
Swedberg, Richard and Ola Agevall (2016) *The Max Weber Dictionary: Key words and central concepts* (Second Edition), Stanford: Stanford University Press.
Taylor, Charles (2007) *A Secular Age*, Cambridge: Harvard University Press.
Tchalian, Hovig (2013) "Bureaucracy" in Vicki Smith (ed), *Sociology of Work: An encyclopedia*, Thousand Oaks: Sage Publications, 1–9.
Turner, Bryan S (1974) "Islam, Capitalism and the Weber Theses", *The British Journal of Sociology*, Vol. 25, No. 2; 230–243.
Wainscott, Ann Marie (2017) *Bureaucratizing Islam: Morocco and the war on terror*, Cambridge: Cambridge University Press.
Weber, Max (1966) "Domination", in Max Rheinstein (ed), *Max Weber on Law in Economy and Society*, Cambridge: Harvard University Press, 322–337.
——— (1978a) "The Religions of Asia" (first pub. 1917), in WG Runciman (ed) and E Matthews (trans), *Max Weber: Selections in translations*, Cambridge: Cambridge University Press, 192–205.
——— (1978b) "The Development of Bureaucracy and its elation to Law" (first pub.1922), in WG Runciman (ed) and E Matthews (trans), *Max Weber: Selections in translations*, Cambridge: Cambridge University Press, 341–354.
——— (1978c) "The Nature of Charismatic Domination" (first pub. 1922), in WG Runciman (ed) and E Matthews (trans), *Max Weber: Selections in translations*, Cambridge: Cambridge University Press, 226–250.
Weber (1991a) "Bureaucracy", in HH Gerth and C Wright Mills (trans and eds), *From Max Weber: Essays in sociology*, London: Routledge, 196–252.

——— (1991b) "Science as a Vocation", in HH Gerth and C Wright Mills (trans and eds), *From Max Weber: Essays in sociology*, London: Routledge, 129–156

——— (1991c) "Religious Rejection of the World and Their Directions", in HH Gerth and C Wright Mills (trans and eds), *From Max Weber: Essays in sociology*, London: Routledge, 323–359.

Weiker, Walter F (1968) "The Ottoman Bureaucracy: Modernization and reform", *Administrative Science Quarterly*, Vol. 13, No. 3, 451–470.

Yelle, Robert (2012) *The Language of Disenchantment: Protestant literalism and colonial discourse in British India*, New York: Oxford University Press.

Zaman, Muhammad Qasim (2012) *Modern Islamic Thought in a Radical Age: Religious authority and internal criticism*, Cambridge: Cambridge University Press.

Zisook, Jonathan J (2017) "Disenchantment of the Word: Weber, Judaism, and Maimonides", *Journal of Classical Sociology*, Vol. 17, Issue 3, 173–190.

CHAPTER 2

Origins of the Divine Bureaucracy

Introduction

The beginnings of the bureaucratisation of Islam in Malaysia can be traced to the period of British colonial administration. The rule of law introduced during this time was an entry point for engraining a proto-bureaucracy within the purview of religious, traditional and customary practices. A distinctive bureaucracy then surfaced out of the need to systematise the management of a precolonial and colonial legal order, which included formalising, supervising and adjudicating what the British recognised to be an assortment of Malay, tribal, *adat* (customs),[1] Mohammedan or Muslim laws (Taylor 1937; Buss-Tjen 1958; Hooker 1976). In the early years before national independence in 1957, these plural sets of laws and their administration maintained the secular framework instituted by the British. Any contentions over this or competition for legitimacy was limited within the confines of the indigenous or British ruling circle, with *adat* versus Islamic worldviews the most dominant source of conflict (de Josselin de Jong 1960; Hooker 1971; Maznah 2016a, b).

As the sphere of public concern grew larger and more actors outside the circle of ruling and religious elites came to be involved, this gave rise to newer forms of contentions, with *adat* concerns receding into the margins of Malay social life. More articulations and resistance were directed towards official control over Islam. This was what placed it even more firmly within the ambit of the state, which resulted in the scope of

M. Mohamad, *The Divine Bureaucracy and Disenchantment of Social Life*, Contestations in Contemporary Southeast Asia,
https://doi.org/10.1007/978-981-15-2093-8_2

bureaucratised Islam widening in an unparalleled way. The motivation to structurally reconstitute Islam through a bureaucratic pathway came from having to neutralise challenges from other non-state, Muslim actors.

This chapter discusses these developments in two parts. The first addresses the colonial construction and usage of the law to institute early bureaucratic structures around Islam. The introduction of the rule of law—which some deem a 'rule by law'—served to legitimise British governance, at the same time that it facilitated the pacification of native ruling elites, the containment of chaos and the maintenance of peace, alongside systematic and increased revenue collection to ensure stability of the colonial presence. It was within the rubric of laws exclusively applied to Malays that the earliest legal rational bureaucrats emerged. The civil service introduced by the British had a distinctive character: "it was, and continues to be dominated by Malays". Moreover, colonial rule was meant to be executed "through indigenous authorities", with *adat* and Islam to be the essential foundation of Malay civil service officers' training (Khasnor 1984, 1–7, 169–183).

Hence, the seeds of bureaucratised Islam were planted very early since colonial times. In instances which had depicted a power play in the transformation of Islam from a private, unregulated, ritualistic, syncretic religion to an authoritative system of rules and regulation, these were mainly the outcome of an intra-elite contestation, between and among Malay rulers and British administrators (Maznah 2016b, 26–30). An early eruption of Malay division on the basis of Islam between the Kaum Tua (Old Guards) and Kaum Muda (Young Turks) factions did not culminate in a religious revolution, with the latter summarily suppressed by the former's colonial-aligned bureaucratic alliance between Malay rulers and traditional religious elites (Roff 1967, 56–90).

The second part of the chapter deals with the period of a maturing decolonisation, from the 1970s onwards, during which the institutional justification for this bureaucracy was questioned and challenged by the emergence of state and religious civil society contestation. The sphere of a politicised Muslim community had become enlarged. However, the episodes of dissension were not always about reforming or 'purifying' Islam but also represented a sense of movement towards its re-enchantment through a resurgent *dakwah*[2] led by young people, including charismatic leaders outside the traditionalist and official *ulama* (Islamic scholar) circles. As these developments constituted a threat to statist Islam, the imperative of fully enclosing Islam within the bureaucratic realm became a serious consideration. There were reactions and counter-reactions from the state to challenges mounted by fervent Islamist mobilisation, which were ultimately redressed and countervailed through policies of accommodation, neutralisation and co-optation. The outcome of this was an augmented bureaucracy over Islamic matters and subjects, widening and expanding itself in various domains of social life.

Colonial Construction of a Divine Proto-Bureaucracy

In the Malay World, the disenchantment/enchantment of religion began and ended not in the present century but some time ago, from the nineteenth century. The displacement of the 'monistic' idea of a single element God-king by a 'theocentric' Islam with the separation of humans and God was followed by a period of European colonialism. The sequence usually began with a formal agreement between the British and the local ruler to 'apportion' the power of administering the various *negeri* (States, subnational units of governance) under the respective rulers, followed by the progressive and inevitable introduction of the rationalisation process. Through this, old patrimonial power was replaced with British 'rational' patrimonialism "conducted through the organs of [the] colonial bureaucracy" (Lee and Ackerman 1997, 31–32). Islamic traditions were mixed with indigenous customary practices of *adat* and elements of magical and mystical beliefs and rituals (Gullick 1965, 138–143; Sharifah Zaleha 1985, 29–77). There were diverse and plural features of governance at the local level in the various *negeri*. Traditional Malay rulers, later conferred with the royal titles of sultan or raja, were made absolute heads of each *negeri* aided by an embryonic bureaucracy that was patrimonial rather than legal rational. Today, the generic term for Malaysian monarchs is 'sultan'.

Under the Malay sultanate in the nineteenth century, there was no predominant religious authority, although in Kelantan, the *mufti* (jurisconsult) was prominent as representing the highest authority of the *syariah* court system. There, the Mahkamah Adat (Customary Court) and Mahkamah Negeri (Territorial Court) existed on the same level as the *syariah* court, indicating the divisibility of religious matters from other civil matters (Abdullah Alwi 1996, 9). In other Malay States, the equivalent of the Mufti's Office (Pejabat Mufti) was the Orang Kaya Imam Tuan (community religious leader) in Perak, a *negeri*-level *kadi* (judge or registrar of an Islamic court) in control of mosques in Negri Sembilan, and a *kathi* (kadi) in Kedah, but most *imam* (head of prayer) and *kadi* were village-level personages responsible for managing the mosques and providing religious education to children (Yegar 1979, 92). The *imam* in 1870s Perak was among the "principled men" of the village: the *penghulu* (headman), the *bilal* (caller to prayer), the *khatib* (*quranic* reciter/orator) and even the *pawang* (healer) (Gullick 1965, 36–37). The *penghulu* in most Malay *negeri*, the *to' kweng* (community heads) in Kelantan and the *lembaga* (clan chiefs) in Negri Sembilan were key village leaders who did not carry out religious functions (Gullick 1965, 30–31; Hooker 1969, 155–157; Abdullah Alwi 1996, 6–7). The distinctive 'Islamic' personages, the *imam* and *kathi*, were paid from proceeds of *zakat* (religious tithe/tax) collection rather than from state revenues (Abdullah Alwi 1996, 6). There was clearly a division of authority among these men and between religious and secular responsibilities.

Territorial administration was designated by *mukim* (subdistrict) in which the *imam*, *bilal* and *surau* (community prayer hall) staff were answerable to the sultan. The functions and delineations of the *syariah* court were less clear and largely confined to personal matters of a religious nature, for example, punishing Muslims for not fasting during Ramadan, failing to attend Friday prayers, being involved in *khalwat* (close proximity) or defaulting on *zakat* payments. These courts were also responsible for issuing payments to the *surau* and *raja* (ruler), solemnising marriage contracts and validating divorces, and registering marriages. The designated functions of the *imam* could overlap "as a religious teacher, a prosecutor, a land officer, a registrar of marriages and divorces, an advocate, a policeman, and a judge in the *syariah* court, in his own *mukim*" (Abdullah Alwi 1996, 18).

In Kelantan, a judicial system was already in place by the eighteenth century, where the designations of *mufti*, *hakim* (judge) and *kadi* had become part of the administrative ensemble of the ruler. The laws of a *negeri* were derived from both Islamic and Malay customary canons, with the former substantively drawn from Arabic treatises translated into Malay such as the *Bughyat al Mustarshidin* and *Mu'in al-Hukkam* (Abdullah Alwi 1996, 3).[3] In Negri Sembilan, traditional justice was exacted in a more complicated and democratic way through several levels of authority. Disputes would first be resolved within one's own *suku* (clan) and also at the *perut* (sub-clan) levels, with the *ibu buapak* (lesser chief) as mediator. They could also be brought to judgement before the *undang* (chiefs) within the *luak* (district). The disputants would consult the *lembaga* before a final decision was reached through a process of unanimity (*kebulatan*) (Gullick 1981, 7–12).

It is interesting that out of the three positions of *mufti*, *kadi* and *imam*, the *kadis* had the least religious significance as, under Malay sultans, they were to mainly assist the *mufti*. Besides the *mufti*, the *imam* also had a more direct religious role, such as conducting Friday prayers, collecting *zakat*, mediating family disputes, solemnising marriages and generally enforcing what was then known as *Hukum Syarak* (*syariah* law) at the village level. Perhaps because of the 'clerical', or even 'secular', nature of *kadi* duties, the British formalised this role more than that of other Islamic functionaries, with the first *kadi* nominated in 1880 in the British protectorate of Perak (Gullick 1965, 139). It was also one of the first administrative positions created by the British in the Straits Settlements and the Federated Malay States (FMS) to deal with matters falling under the rubric of Islam.

In the Straits Settlements and the Federated Malay States,[4] one of the first administrative positions the British created to deal with Islamic affairs was that of the *kadi*. As early as 1875, Arab subjects in the Straits Settlements had petitioned the colonial authority to codify and standardise laws for Muslim marriage, as they found it disconcerting that local *kadi* were not exercising rules on marriage in a uniform way to guide court litigations (Nurfadzilah 2015, 501–506). As Arabs were merchant travellers, they would have married local women and had families in different places; therefore, a more standardised system would benefit them when it came to rulings affecting the status of family and marriage (Nurfadzilah 2015, 497–500). However, even when the position of *kadi* was first legislated under colonial rule, there was confusion about its actual function. This was initially understood as 'celebrating' or performing the marriage ceremony. It was only later in subsequent legislation that this role was specified as an official who presided over such a ceremony—a contractual agreement to be precise—which could only be solemnised by the *wali* (lawful guardian giving away the bride to marriage) and two male witnesses. Hence, the *kadi*'s role was merely as an official of the ceremony and to whose office such union had to be registered.

The act of registering marital unions and dissolutions was an important aspect of early colonial governance as this helped establish the status of family members in property disputes, besides serving as a useful modality to obtain a population database. *Kadi* were appointed for each district (*daerah*) and numerous *naib kadi* (deputy *kadi*) were placed in the *mukim*. Despite the small role assigned to this office, the *kadi* was still recognised as the foremost religious official in the Malay *negeri* then (Sharifah Zaleha 1985, 129). Kelantan, one of five Malay *negeri* under the Unfederated Malay States (UMS), gave much greater prominence to the role of the *mufti* rather than the *kadi* as was the case in the FMS or the Straits Settlements. Hence, in Kelantan, it was the *mufti*'s position which was bureaucratised first within the Islamic administrative system of the country (Abdullah Alwi 1996, 35–41).

Formal Court System and Secular Statutes

The colonial government introduced an organised courts structure while coding and systematising a plethora of laws, customs and norms into legislation that could be extended universally to whomever the statutes applied. The establishment of new ways of governing involved a balancing act of accommodating concerns of the local ruling elites while imposing an external system of crafting the state through the rule of law. British administrators rationalised, if not revamped, the seeming arbitrariness of local judicial traditions by delimiting the jurisdictions of their courts, specifying differentiated roles for the *mufti*, *kadi* and *imam*, and legislating English (or secular) procedural regulations in court proceedings involving Islamic matters. The goal was to centralise Islamic authority within each *negeri*, and then to 'pigeon-hole' Islamic law and its administration to the domain of a lower court so as not to interfere or overlap with other legal and governmental reforms introduced for other areas of public life. It was this process of modernisation which eventually reconstituted and embedded the legality of Islam in its relation to 'Malayness'. Before this "there was no organized class of *ulama*, and Islam was not a State religion in the formal sense of the term", and that while the "Malay sultanates were undoubtedly considered Muslim States; the legal identity of Malay and Muslim was defined later" (Yegar 1979, 92).

The first complete courts system in the Malay *negeri* was established in 1890 in Perak (Yegar 1979, 152). As recorded in the Perak Government Gazette of 1890, the court structure comprised seven tiers: the Residency Court, Senior Magistrate's Court, Courts of the Magistrates of the first class, Courts of the Magistrates of the second class, Courts of the Magistrates of the third class, Courts of Kathis and Assistant Kathis, and Courts of Penghulus. This hierarchy reflected the jurisdictional powers of each court and the maximum penalty, in terms of imprisonment and fines, that could be imposed. While the colonial government appointed all the other court officials, those in the Courts of Kathis and Assistant Kathis, and Courts of Penghulus, received their *kuasa* (authority) from the sultan. Their termination was also determined by the ruler. The Courts of Kathis were specific and had their powers limited to "all matters concerning Mahomedan religion, marriage and divorce, and in all matters regulated by Hukum Sharah as [was] defined in his kuasa, under the hand and seal of His Highness the Sultan, and countersigned by the British Resident, in each case". Furthermore, a *kadi* could only impose a fine not exceeding ten dollars, and an assistant *kadi* was limited to a maximum fine of five dollars. Likewise, the Courts of Penghulus would only hear suits "brought by Malays and other Asiatics, where the debt, damage, demand, or matter in dispute [did] not exceed twenty-five dollars" (Perak Government Gazette 1890). Only in Kedah and Perlis was the nomenclature "*Shari'a*" given to the name of courts with Islamic jurisdictions (Yegar 1979, 162–163). Unlike all the other *negeri*, both did not have the Courts of Penghulus. This diversity of systems under the various Malay sultanates was one of the more pronounced aspects of how Islam was administered under British colonialism.

After the courts system was put in place, all disputes had to be adjudicated in the formal court setting, which was almost always presided by British judges. In cases involving Muslims and Islamic or *adat* law, these judges, lacking in local viewpoints, turned to the Muslim elite as assessors or advisers. This was how this group of 'local assessors' came to be co-opted into the colonial court system. As assessors, their job was to aid the court which, "on the conclusion of such case, require[d] the assessor or each of the assessors to state his opinion orally, [as well as] record his opinion". Nevertheless, the court was also not bound to accept the assessors' views in its judgements (Perak Government Gazette 1890). In 1917, Perak appointed 76, and Pahang 28, Malay assessors under the provision of 'The Muhammadan Laws Enactment[5] 1904', for both *negeri*. Their occupations, among others, were listed in Perak as Penghulu, Padi Inspector, Guru Agama, Koran teacher and Planter; and in Pahang, as Member of State Council, Government Officer, Naib Kathi, and Landowner (FMS Government Gazette 1920a). Sometime in the 1930s, a member of the public complained about their lack of knowledge and urged the government to start a "religious college to turn our men with a thorough knowledge of the Mohammedan religion to guide the 2,500,000

Mohammedan Malays of this country into broad-minded Mohammedans" (The Straits Times 1935, 7).

By the 1930s, the British had developed uniform religious organisations to deal with matters of Islam. These took the form of several governing and legislative structures at different times of their rule, for example, the Council of Chiefs and Ulama in Perak; the *Shaikh al-Islam* (head of Islam) in Kedah, Perlis and Terengganu; and the Majlis Ugama Islam dan Isti'adat Melayu (Majlis, Council of Islamic Religion and Malay Custom) of Kelantan (Yegar 1979, 93). The last structure, the Majlis, became the template for subsequent emplacement of Islamic bureaucratisation for the other *negeri*. Kelantan was the first to establish its Majlis in 1915, followed by Kedah in 1948, and then in other Malay *negeri* by 1959. The Kelantan Majlis had "its own constitution which declare[d] it to be the principal authority in each state on all matters concerning Islamic religion and Islamic Malay custom" (Abdullah Alwi 1996, 70). When this Majlis was established, a new law was also enacted to specify the powers of its members—from supervising *surau* and mosques, to issuing *fatwa* (legal opinion), to managing the *baitulmal* (Islamic treasury) and its trusteeship of *wakaf* (endowments), to centralising the collection of *zakat*, *fitrah* (dues) and other charitable collections (Abdullah Alwi 1996, 71–73).

The Codification of Traditions

As expected, an early goal of the colonial administration was to legitimise its actions by promulgating new laws and reformulating and codifying old traditions and norms. A reconstituted governance structure wrested from the old ways of local autocracy and anarchy to becoming one based on a written Constitution and a legislative body, the State Council—the latter with a membership appointed from among local ruling elites and headed by the sultan and the highest British official within the *negeri*. All enactments were deliberated and passed through this Council, hence institutionalising a government by the rule of law, more accurately, 'rule by law', as it was not a government installed through the popular will of the people. In turn, the bureaucracy through which these laws were actualised was the crucial, if not, primary, pillar of successful colonial governance.

Colonial missions were involved not only in a great deal of lawmaking but also in the demarcation of autonomous spheres to enable a system of differentiated authority. Ensuring the separate spheres of governance between British administrators (as modernisers) and the local rulers (as legitimators of the colonial presence and linkage to traditions) was one of the more strategic moves in the ultimate control of the colony. Through major agreements, such as the Raffles Memorandum to the Sultan of Johore in 1823 and the Pangkor Treaty of 1874, local rulers were given autonomy, but only to rule over the sphere of Malay customs and Islamic affairs.[6] Under colonial indirect rule, which incorporated the Residential system (for the FMS of Perak, Selangor, Pahang and Negeri Sembilan) and Advisory system (for the UMS of Kelantan, Terengganu, Kedah, Perlis and Johor), the British entered into treaties with respective Malay rulers to ensure that general administration and collection of revenues would be under their control. In return, English laws were applied to all except when it was considered to be the turf of *adat* or Islam. The introduction of a formal, written Constitution was adopted by two *negeri*: Johor drafted by an English law firm in Singapore and Terengganu by British advisers. These Constitutions protected the sovereignty and power of the sultans with two conditions: first, successors to their respective thrones were to be the legitimate descendants of the male line, Malay and Muslim; and, second, that Islam was to be declared the "national" religion for Johor and the "State" religion for Terengganu (Yegar 1979, 76–85).

British public opinion in the late nineteenth century was wary of interfering with any local laws, especially Islamic laws, as expressed by a letter to a newspaper at the time:

> I feel satisfied that whatever may be the decision of a Magistrate, the Chief Justice will decline to recognise any act likely to infringe on the law, in such case made and provided, by another religion. If once we begin to allow our legislative codes to interfere with the religious rites and regulations of our subjects, except where humanity demands it, then look out for squalls—we shall have deserved it. (*Singapore Free Press and Mercantile Advertiser* 1891, 3)

In all of the Malay *negeri*, the significance of the application of Islamic law was recognised, and the solution to accommodating this was to confine its implementation to a specific court, the Kathi Courts or the Shari'a Courts (in the case of Kedah and Perlis).

The first laws on Muslim divorce did not specify *syariah* conditions for validity and only sought to make marriages and divorces official through a process of registration. In Perak, divorces were conferred through a decree (Perak Government Gazette 1889), and similarly for marriages in Johor, a copy of the registration was provided so that these documents, "certified under the signature and seal" of the *kathi*, would constitute "prima facie evidence in all Courts of the State" (Johore Government Gazette 1914). In Johor, from 1914 onwards, another layer of bureaucracy was created with the appointment of the 'Registrar of Muhammadan Marriages and Divorces', different from the role of the *kadi*. It was compulsory to register a marriage, divorce or revocation of divorce; failure to do so would result in offenders fined up to 50 dollars. The legal certification for marriage and divorce comprised a copy of the entry by the *kadi* into the record book, duly signed by the parties concerned, and confirmed with the seal of the *kadi*'s office. Each district *kadi* then forwarded all the entries in his record book to the Registrar. The copies of these entries were also made under oath. All the *kadi*, *naib kadi* and Registrars were to be paid a fee for every registration made, for issuing certified copies of records and for court summonses. Three *kadi* and 38 *naib kadi* for each of the subdistricts in the *negeri*—where all but one carried the honorific 'Haji' or 'Syed' or 'Lebai' before their names—were appointed by the sultan of Johor (Johore Government Gazette 1914). Through this restructuring and reform, religious personages who once occupied informal roles had then been elevated to hold formalised administrative positions.

The terms of Muslim marriage were spelt out more elaborately in a 1920 Pahang statute. This emphasised the role of the *wali* as the person to "celebrate" or solemnise the ceremony, and that, subsequently, "he shall, with two witnesses, report the proceedings to the person authorised to register marriages within the period of three days and pay the prescribed fees" (FMS Government Gazette 1920b). Under the enactment too, the registration of marriage and divorce was systematised with a formal certificate, and fees were collected for each registration, whether marriage or divorce. A typical marriage and divorce certificate included the names of the parties involved as well as their fathers and the *penghulu*; in the case of Negeri Sembilan, the registration enactment required that the "tribe" and "*lembaga*" of each party, the names of the "*wali*" and witnesses, and the amount of "*mas kahwin*" (dowry) paid be recorded (Negeri Sembilan Government Gazette 1900).

As a means to collect and systematise knowledge about the governed population, the implementation of rules for the registration of Muslim marriage and divorce was done by the *kadi* or Registrar. This was the first involvement of grassroots or local-level authority in the gradual bureaucratisation of religious affairs. Throughout this, there was no determinate set of 'Islamic' laws that could decide conclusively on many family matters, from inheritance to sexual and marital wrongs or rights. Hence, early litigation depended on the varying opinions and services of special Muslim advisers to the courts.[7]

Decentralised Islamic Authority and Administration

A few other elements about the administration of Islam in the colonial period are notable. First, the process was elite-centric and involved intra-elite contestation; second, the institutionalisation was within a limited domain of legislative and public policy involvement; and third, the nature of Islamic administration was only standardised within individual *negeri*, most notably only among those within the FMS. Wider colonial penetration into the peninsular territories was made possible through the exchange of spheres of control between Malay rulers and British administrators After the Federation of Malaya was formed in 1948, laws pertaining to Islam and its administration continued to remain within the powers of the Malay sultans and the State Councils. This post-Second World War phase strengthened a bureaucratised Islam with a Malay *qua* Islamic identity. The symbolism of the Malay *raja* (ruler) as the highest authority over Islam, and of the *rakyat* (subjects) under this rule, was integral to the construction of the modern Malaysian Malay identity.[8] Here, communal religiosity was reinvented or reconstituted by the secularising process of statute-making and institution-building around Islam. At this point, the once *adat*-centric, magic-believing and privately pious community became more disenchanted of its erstwhile religious identity.[9] Before even the onset of a nationalist movement for decolonisation, there was already an "authoritarian form of religious administration" with a religious bureaucracy strengthened on the basis of "doctrinal and administrative authority in the hands of a hierarchy of officials" under the strong patronage of the nine traditional rulers or sultans (Roff 1967, 72).

Territorial Identities in Laws and Courts System

The rise of judicialisation related to matters of Islam and for Muslims within the court system had two effects. First, Islam became a matter of the state; second, religious concerns became more differentiated within the hierarchy of civil administration. In the early twentieth-century Kelantan, for example, there were many issues which led to a rethinking of how Islam could be administered while locating the power to do so within certain sections of the local ruling and religious elites. A study by Abdullah Alwi (1996) is instructive in detailing the various separation of powers between sultan and religious authority. For instance, the power of the Mufti's Office as Appeal Court Judge in the Muslim court system, and as jurisconsult in the issuance of *fatwa*, was considerably greater than in all the other Malay *negeri* to the point of threatening the authority of the sultan. Dissatisfaction among the aristocratic and religious elites towards colonial reforms was reinforced with the introduction of a policy that displaced local leaders with British-appointed District Officers. This gave the former cause to lead peasants aggrieved by new systems of taxation and land registration (Cheah 2006). Such resistance was put down but it later guided the British to be more sensitive to local demands.

In 1915, three influential *ulama* who had been educated in Mecca and Egypt, and with the support of the sultan of Kelantan, proposed and founded the idea of a religious council, the Majlis, that would serve the political as well as economic interests of a burgeoning class of reformist religious leaders. Politically, as head of the Majlis, the sultan would unequivocally assume the headship of Islam without having to contend with other authoritative rivals. On the economic front, the Majlis was empowered to systematise the collection of *zakat* and other religious taxes in the *negeri*. Proceeds from these taxes were apportioned with two-fifths going to the local *imam* in charge of a district and the remaining to the sultan and the Majlis. Two-thirds of the remaining three-fifths share went to the former (Abdullah Alwi 1996, 79–81).

The formation of the Majlis was legalised through a statute, as were the rules that defined the powers and roles of its members.[10] By legitimising and enforcing its powers, the Majlis proposed at least 12 new laws to the State Council within a year of its formation. These ranged from *zakat* collection procedures to the supervision of mosques to compulsory attendance at Friday prayers and to the eviction of prostitutes and pimps from town. The Majlis in effect was a parallel institution to the State Council. Only in 1966 were its legislative powers removed through a new enactment—the Council of Religion and Malay Custom Enactment, No. 2 of 1966 (Kelantan)—which redefined its roles.

Nevertheless, by influencing other *negeri* to establish similar bodies, the Kelantan Majlis played a major role in furthering Islamic governance and bureaucratisation. If the colonial State Councils were the highest governing bodies during the British administration, it appeared that religious elites sought to replicate this structure to thrust themselves to be on par with the government of the day. The Majlis was not established in other Malay *negeri* during British rule, as most matters involving the Islamic religion were brought up in the State Council rather to a separate governing structure. Later, the formation of the Majlis became an important postcolonial edifice for the centralisation of state Islam, and eventually every *negeri* had its own Majlis Agama Islam Negeri or State Islamic Religious Council (SIRC), the highest authority on Islam and Malay customs. This was made possible through the passing of statutes from 1951 in Perak to as late as 2004 in Sabah.

The main features of these SIRCs in their early years of existence included the following:

1. Existing as a corporation or statutory body
2. Aiding and advising the ruler of each *negeri* on all matters concerning Islam and Malay custom
3. Managing the *baitulmal*, collect *zakat* and *fitrah*
4. Administering estates, and owning and disposing of property
5. Acting as trustees of mosques and *wakaf* in specific *negeri*
6. Making and establishing *fatwa*
7. Constituting Courts of Kathis
8. Appointing *mufti* and *kadi* (Ahmad Ibrahim 1965, 147–175)

Every *negeri* also had a well-placed *syariah* courts system while still exhibiting variation and distinctiveness among them (Malaya 1944, 111–117). In the FMS, there were five levels in the court hierarchy, the highest being the Supreme Court, and at the lowest rungs were the Courts of Kathis and Assistant Kathis, and Courts of Penghulu. There was wider variation in the UMS, with the exception of Johor which had the same system as in the FMS. Kedah had only four tiers, with the 'Sharaiah' Courts below the Magistrates Courts. Perlis also had a four-tiered court system, but this comprised the Court of the Raja, Senior Court, Junior Court and, finally, the 'Sheriah' Court. The system in Kelantan and Terengganu had six levels; in the former, the last three tiers were the courts for Muslims and small offences—Court of the Chief Kathi, Court of District Kathis and Court of Penggawas (heads of parishes)—while in the latter, the Courts of Kathis and Courts of Penghulus occupied the fifth and sixth rungs. All these meant that the differentiation of functions even within the Islamic governance hierarchy was starting to become extensive and wide-ranging. More accurately, it was an Islamic judicial system modelled after the English court system.

Postcolonial Malaysia: Augmenting the Administration of Islam

By the time of Malaya's independence, traditional rulers had been transformed into constitutional monarchs, and hence had no power to legislate or impact policy in any substantial way. The Islamic courts and religious councils as within the purview of local ruling elites during British rule had demarcated the spheres of control between what may have seemed to be between 'religious' and 'secular' spaces. Within these sites of bureaucratisation, Islam provided the cause for the consolidation of a Malay-Muslim sovereignty and its effects thereafter. The period after national independence brought newer and a wider variety of agents and contenders into the picture.

During the postwar colonial years, from 1945 to the early 1950s, nationalist and perhaps ambivalently pro-royalist movement gained new momentum, with a more pronounced Malay-ethnic agenda (Ariffin 1993). By this time, the Malay sultans were losing power to the new ruling elites, who were not tied to the royalty and came from within the ranks of the professional class. The new elites were modernist in perspective and though they held Islam to be an important basis of Malay identity, the place of religion was still at the level of personal law rather than extended to overall matters in Muslim life. British-instituted *syariah* courts still had little clout as they occupied a lower rung within the hierarchy of the courts system, while Islamic administration continued to be devolved within the respective *negeri*. The various enactments for Muslims also remained within the purview of *negeri* rulers rather than the federal government.

Since Islam was under the ambit of individual *negeri*, each enacted its own laws to govern Muslims within their boundaries; hence, some laws differed from one *negeri* to another. An early period of statutory rationalisation mainly involved the passage of one comprehensive set of laws for Muslims to consolidate or repeal the various separate enactments that existed during colonial times. The first "single omnibus statute" was adopted in Selangor in 1952 (Horowitz 1994, 258). The legislation was called the Administration of Muslim Law Enactment of Selangor (1952) and it integrated the previously separate enactments as in the Muhammadan

Law and Malay Custom (Determination) Enactment 1930, the Muhammadan Marriage and Divorce Registration Enactment 1931, the Muhammadan (Offences) Enactment 1938 and the Council of Religion and Malay Customs Enactment 1949 into one major statute for Muslims. Given that all laws for Muslims were still governed under the separate *negeri* governments, there was little power for the federal authority to intervene in Islamic matters.

During this phase, the characteristics of Islamic laws continued to be one of diversity and plurality. Matters of marriage, divorce, custody and maintenance were inserted under a few sections within the general law meant for Muslims. For example, the Administration of Muslim Family Law (Penang) Enactment 1959 had only 25 sections on marriage and divorce out of a total of 172 sections. In this early stage, each *negeri* also had its own set of Islamic family laws whose contents often differed from each other, while their *syariah* courts were administered independently of federal intervention.

As noted earlier too, the court which dealt with Muslim marriages was the Kathi Court, which had the status of a lower court. Lawyers were not usually appointed to represent the plaintiff and the defendant, and most of the judgements were made by the *kadi*. The laws were probably less developed and therefore more flexible in terms of interpretation and enforcement. The *kadi* was at liberty to express his views judiciously without being bound by precedence, dogma and text. In Malaysia, Islamisation was largely expanded through lawmaking, due to the early incorporation of religious rules through bureaucratisation—"the Islamization of law proceeded more methodically" and that "in the span of a decade, dozens of new statutes and judicial decisions [had] clarified, expanded, and reformulated the law applicable to Muslims" (Horowitz 1994, 236). In this period, *syariah* was constructed within the ambit of English statute law, and the features of laws for Muslims were plural in scope and jurisdiction as well as hybridised in almost all aspects (Yegar 1979, 119). What was meant by 'Islamic law' was a combination of laws informed by custom as well as by modern ideas of progress. The politics of naming the title of laws also indicated the changing nature of Islamisation that occurred, as in from 'Muhammadan' to 'Muslim' to 'Islamic' to '*syariah*' laws, denoting a change from the subject or object of the law (Muslims) to the quintessence of the law (Islamic) (Moustafa 2018, 39).[11]

Gradually, and even ironically, the Federal Constitution of an independent Malaysia itself became the new 'sacred' text for debates on all sides of the divides, when it came to the status of Islam. The constitutional provision, Schedule 9, List II, Paragraph 1, confers powers on State Legislative Assemblies to enact laws on Islamic matters, hence providing for the separation of powers between Federal and State (*negeri*) legislatures. Another legal interpretation also says that, in actuality, power over Islam is shared between the central and *negeri* governments. The interpretation of Article 3(1), which stipulates that Islam is the religion of the Federation, allows for the promotion of Islamic education, the establishment of Islamic institutions and a national budget for Islamic causes (Faruqi 2016, 58–59, 62–63). It was around these purposive legal ambiguities that a bureaucratic Islam around administration, enforcement and narrational authority would also be constructed, especially on the constitutional basis that Islam was not only to be protected but promoted by the state.

Islam and Malay Populist Support

Importantly, the new national landscape involved a representative government chosen by popular will. If there was to be any negotiation and bargaining over Islam, it had to extend beyond a small circle of elites. Early prime ministers, Tunku Abdul Rahman and his successor Abdul Razak Hussein, continued to engage with Islamic religious elites whose influence at the rural level remained strong and intact, largely because the identity of 'Malayness' could not be de-coupled from its Islamic core. Besides, the almost absolute authority over Islam still resided with the Malay rulers even as they became constitutional monarchs through a relatively peaceful process of bargaining, negotiations and power transfers (Abdul Rahman 1984; Harper 1998; Cheah 2002). For the most part though, during these early years following independence, the development of Islam remained confined to the private sphere of affective time-honoured ritualistic communion of praying, fasting, the offering of tithes and pilgrimage.

Tunku Abdul Rahman founded the Pertubuhan Kebajikan Islam Malaysia (Perkim, Malaysian Muslim Welfare Association) in 1960 and was its president from 1971 to 1989. Perkim was a Muslim converts association but in line with Tunku's secular outlook, which sought to keep some distance from the more dominant Islamic organisations. In 1971, after he stepped down as Prime Minister in the aftermath of the 1969 riots,[12] Tunku took up the position of Secretary-General of the Islamic Secretariat of the Organisation of Islamic Countries (OIC) and cultivated good relations with the government of Saudi Arabia (Singapore Herald

1971). In 1980, Perkim received a donation of RM25 million from the Saudi government (Straits Times 1980), and, the following year, Tunku was involved in talks with the Saudis to establish Bank Islam (Berita Harian 1981). Abdul Razak had provided federal financial support to the Majlis of Kelantan in 1967 (Abdullah Alwi 1996, 119), and he formalised the establishment of the Yayasan Dakwah Islamiah (Yadim, Islamic Missionary Foundation) in 1974.

As seen above, the development of Islam under colonialism and the early post-independence years had been methodically circumscribed, although a substantial infrastructure around civil administration, courts, schools and taxation system was also set in place. As will be seen in Chap. 3, consolidating populist support meant having more of these institutions, rather than less, as unfolding events would later dictate. The ruling Malay party Umno (United Malays National Organisation), which the prime ministers of the country headed, had to serve both Malay and Islamic interests as the primary path to securing and sustaining power.

Postcolonial Enlargement of the Muslim Public Sphere

By the early 1970s, new ways of expressing Islam appeared outside the expectations of the national ruling elites. The enlargement of the 'public sphere', a concept developed by Jurgen Habermas (1991), appears to characterise a movement of an emerging Malay middle class claiming a public space which hitherto had been dominated by state authorities.[13] The *dakwah* movement among students and youths, and the growth of a variety of religious and 'resurgent' (Chandra 1987) or 'revivalist' (Hussein 1988) movements among the Malay middle class, presented a different set of challenges. Existing institutions and laws on Islamic matters seemed inadequate in their encounters with these new forms of faith-based activism. The New Economic Policy (NEP) affirmative action plan favouring *bumiputera* (sons of the soil, *lit.*), defined as Malays and other indigenous citizens, introduced after the watershed May 1969 'racial riots', could seemingly address Malay discontent (Faaland, Parkinson and Saniman 1990). During this period, however, vociferous demands were made for Malay dominance through calls such as adopting Malay as the national language, converting national schools into Malay-medium education, opening up higher education for more Malay enrolment, and restructuring the economy to generate greater wealth for the Malays and reduce inter-ethnic inequality. The Islamic resurgence represented a Malay-Muslim phenomenon that was outside the parameters of the NEP.

In their early years, the formation of *dakwah* movements created a stir and unsettled Umno's sense of dominance over the Malays. This Islamic revivalism can be understood as a form of re-enchantment given that the 'technicalisation' and rationalisation of Islam through rules, procedures, laws, systems and the continuity of regulation had been going on uninterruptedly since the beginning of the twentieth century. Previously under colonialism, bureaucratisation was the route to accommodate the sovereignty of Malay rulers while containing Islam within a restricted public sphere. Islam, in a sense, was stripped of its divine essence and turned into a 'state religion' that did not offer anything more than the bare services of adjudicating the business of marriage and divorce, maintaining mosques and *surau*, supervising schools, collecting taxes, punishing offenders, providing religious instructions, and coordinating pilgrimage funds and travels. Religiosity had transmuted into an ordinary form of everyday rituals, much as it had contributed to an effectively satisfying sense of well-being. Nevertheless, some sections of the Muslim society felt alienated from the essence of the religion's spiritual and magical core. The implementation of the NEP addressed most of the 'secular' demands of Malay nationalists, but it left untouched the religious ethos, disposition, conduct and spirit of Malay social life, leaving room for the burgeoning of Islamic civil society and the birth of new Islamic causes, though of a different nature to those negotiated between the British administrators, sultans and the *ulama*.

A new upsurge of public expressions around the late 1960s was unlike the Malay divides of before, from the early 1900s to the 1940s, which had stemmed from a diversity of educational orientation: between Islamic or pan-Islamic schooling networks, a socialist-oriented group originating from a Malay language-based schooling and literary movement, and English-educated Malay aristocratic and administrative elites (Roff 1967, 91–247). The new postcolonial Malay movements had 'Islam' as their unequivocal calling. When waves of the Islamic movement burst forth in the post-1969 period, many read this as the eruption of the old Malay schism between rural Malays of "humble origins and inspired by Middle-Eastern Islamic modernism" and Malays of the "well-born, English-educated, highly anglicized" administrative and aristocratic class (Kessler 1980, 6). Others saw it as a new cleavage developing between "devout

Muslims who [had] found and understood the totality of Islam as a way of life" and the "secular Westernized Malays whose priorities [lay] with modernization and development" (Zainah 1987, 90). While such perspectives may be valid, they did not fully explain the fact that scores of Malays were on both sides of the divide, whether English educated or Middle Eastern trained. Moreover, many of such Malays chose to veer towards messianic movements, such as the Darul Arqam (also known as Al-Arqam), or to embrace Islam as a holistic system but doing so through a *modus operandi* indistinguishable from the route of conventional modernisation.

This is not to say that such divergent tendencies among Malays did not exist during colonial times, notably between the Kaum Tua and Kaum Muda. Malay nationalism itself was carved along many different roads and aspired goals (Roff 1967). An Islam that was saint-oriented had also been part of the fabric of Malay society but was overtaken by the dominance of teacher-scholars and, later, religious bureaucrats (Sharifah Zaleha 1985, 10). In the *dakwah* movements of the 1970s, it seemed as if the past elements of religious expressions had never disappeared, but had been revived and reinvented for the present. These postcolonial Islamic resurgent movements have been well studied (Nagata 1984; Chandra 1987; Zainah 1987; Hussein 1988; Mohamad Abu Bakar 1991). While rich and insightful, these accounts saw such movements as forms of 'dissenting' Islam with their particular dynamics analysed in the framework of state-society contentions.

Missing from this rich corpus of work was an understanding of these movements from the perspective of the disenchantment/enchantment thesis. While these movements no doubt emerged as challengers to official or state Islam then, their attraction also lay in the affective appeal of transformative experiences. Could the reason for their appeal also have been the rediscovery of the enchantment of religion or of an unfulfilled re-enchantment? Many of these movements had a political agenda or the intention of reforming the mainstream system, and they were not necessarily anti-modernist. Appendix 1 'Timeline on the formation of religion-related social movements and incidences of political conflict and violence in Malaysia' lists episodes involving the formation of movements, and incidences of political conflicts and violence, perpetrated by either the civil society or the agents of the state. It demonstrates a recurrent feature and concern of the state in 'managing Islam', from as early as 1968 to the present period of the study.

Ways of Re-Enchantment

There were a variety of organised groups in the early 1970s with different ways and goals of re-Islamising society. Besides Darul Arqam, another significant player was Angkatan Belia Islam Malaysia (Abim, Malaysian Islamic Youth Movement). For most observers, both movements occupied the same terrain of Islamic renewal. In fact, they had widely divergent characteristics, as symbolised by their respective charismatic leaders, Ashaari Muhammad, on the one hand, and Anwar Ibrahim, on the other. Darul Arqam focused on building an informal autonomous sphere of worshippers and followers, while Abim acted as a legal, non-confrontational pressure group vis-à-vis the state. Their existence, nonetheless, drew a uniform reaction from the state.

Although a political pressure group, Abim also had amongst its followers, those who experienced an affective enchantment of discovery, passion and a sense of purpose with an Islam that was distinguishable from the sterile variety passed on and regulated by the traditional bureaucracy. Two of its founding members, Razali Nawawi and Mohd Dahlan Arshad, were conscientised in Egypt and England, respectively. Both started out as students in Egypt and were influenced by the anti-Nasserite Islamic movement, the *Ikhwan al-Muslimin* (Muslim Brotherhood), founded by Hassan al-Banna. Recalling this period, Mohd Dahlan attributes the roots of his awareness to the discovery of a renewed Islam inspired by this movement.[14] While still in Malaysia, his connections to the radical beliefs of this group caused him to be harassed by the Malaysian government. He was forced to relocate to London, where he joined the Islamic Centre, a movement of diasporic Muslims based in the United Kingdom. Through his association with this group, he began to be disaffected with the lifestyle of other Malay overseas students. He wrote disapprovingly of some of their more popular activities: "In England there was a Malay Union of United Kingdom, an organization established in 1930 by Tunku Abdul Rahman. The main annual activity was *Hari Raya Dancing*" (Mohd Dahlan 1996, 20).

For some, contacts with a transnational brethren of faithfuls were akin to an epiphany that would leave deep and lasting impressions about the 'universality' of the Islamic faith, such as that experienced by Anuar Tahir, one of the early members of Abim:

> I heard the cry "Narai Takbir" and other resounding calls in foreign words which I remember to this day such as "Biplop! Biplop! Biplop!"...which

> means revolution, "Zindabad! Zindabad! Zindabad!"...or live! and then the slogans shouted in high spirits "la syarqiya wal la gharbiyya! Islamiah ... Islamiyah" in Arabic...and then interspersed with Urdu, Benggali and English, "neither East or West, Islam is The Best". (Anuar 1996, 52; translated from Malay)

Pakistani scholar and activist, Abul A'la Maududi, was one of the greatest heroes of this Islamic revolutionary spirit. Whenever his name was mentioned in Anuar's own speeches, there were thunderous cheers and approval.

> A few anecdotes about the resilience and courage of Maududi would greatly enliven the spirit of the camp's participants. My speech was halted several times to allow for the audience to shout their Takbir and other fiery slogans. Until this day that experience has remained a sweet memory which I will never forget. (Anuar 1996, 52–53, translated from Malay)

Unlike the young leaders of Abim, those in Darul Arqam were not influenced by Islamic reformists from outside the Malay World. The mystical inspiration of its leader, Ashaari Muhammad, was a nineteenth-century Javanese saint, Syeikh Suhaimi. Born in 1843 in Wonosobo, Central Java, the Syeikh had his religious education in the *pondok* (traditional religious) schools of Java and is said to have travelled to Mecca, Syria, Iraq, Jerusalem and Egypt to further his study of Islam. It is also believed that he received the message to start his *tariqah* (Sufi sect) upon receiving the *amanat* (mandate) to enter the *ka'abah* (sacred structure at the centre of mosque complex in Mecca) after midnight to commune with the spirit of the Prophet. Thereafter, he was ordained to begin his order, *Aurad Muhammadiyah*, and his following increased after his disciples reported experiencing significant benefits. Due to suppression by Dutch authorities, he moved to Singapore and started his congregation there, before branching out to the Malay Peninsula, particularly in Johor, Melaka, Negeri Sembilan and Selangor (Simatupang 1988; Ahmad Fauzi 2013, 70–74; Md Taha, n.d.).

Writing in the Darul Arqam journal, *Al Munir*, Ashaari proclaimed that Syeikh Suhaimi did not die but would return as the Imam Mahdi; thus, his followers had to prepare for this eventuality to be on the right side when it happened (Ashaari 1988a; Idrus 1988). The Imam Mahdi was the messiah incarnated as the "divinely guided person" who will lead a revolution, end tyranny and restore peace and justice in this world before the Day of Judgement or *kiamat* (doomsday) (Sachedina 2012, 738). Ashaari himself penned a poem, '*Imamul Mahdi*', on how it would not be too long before the messiah would "defend what is right and fight all that is evil, and at that moment the righteous will win and the immoral [will be] defeated".[15]

Darul Arqam had a particular appeal among the Malay middle class, from about the 1970s onwards, and attracted a following with its novel and radically new ways of being Muslim. This was a movement that was messianic, mystical and eschatological in character and had no overt intention to pressure the government to reform, much less displace it. During the British rule, this variant of Islamic practices and adherents was ignored by the colonial administration given that these followers were far from the circle of local elites the British recognised, and as such were excluded from negotiations over jurisdictional authority. However, in a modern setting, the presence of a group like Darul Arqam with its "sufi-conditioned Islamization" was perceived as a great threat to the rationalised Islam that the state bureaucracy promoted (Ahmad Fauzi 2013, 68). In Darul Arqam, the use of the Quran as the "most intimately negotiated, vernacularly creative, and magically effective venue of religious action" (O'Connor 2001) was revived in an aura of enchantment:

> As a *tariqah*, the Aurad Muhammadiah consists of the recitation, individually after each daily prayer and preferably in congregation on Thursday nights, of seven verses in the correct order, preceded by reading the first chapter of the Qur'an. These verses, four and three of which are to be read ten and fifty times respectively, are together a collection of Qur'anic verses the twin attestation of faith to Allah and the Prophet Muhammad. (Ahmad Fauzi 2013, 72)

In many ways then, these two movements—Darul Arqam and Abim—were as different as night and day, although what they had in common was the opportunity to be re-enchanted with a new way of expressing faith. The former found its origins in a home-grown or Malay World Sufistic tradition with its devotional core in the mystical powers of the *zikir* (incantations) and a belief in the coming of Imam Mahdi, while also holding a deeply misogynistic worldview on gender relations.[16] It was funded primarily by its own small business operations and donations from members (Hussein 1988, 234–241; Ahmad Fauzi 1999). Abim was a reformist, this-worldly, politically oriented, with state-capture as an agenda, and at the same time drawing its inspiration from Muslim reformist scholars from Pakistan and Egypt, namely Abul A'la Maudoodi and Syed Qutb. It also had strong links with the Saudi-based World Assembly of Muslim Youths (Wamy) and other Arab countries; at one point, it received Saudi funds and would have received much more if not for restrictions by the government (Hussein 1988, 251–252).

Regardless of intentions, both movements had the same effect of enlarging the Muslim political community. With Islam's rich reservoir of scriptural sources, idiom-rich knowledge base as well as tradition of enchantment from which the multifarious projection of human needs could be expressed and fulfilled, the 'reformist', 'dissenting', 'revivalist' or 'deviationist' groups came to be aligned along this wide spectrum of the faith's callings. The examples of Darul Arqam and Abim provide a broad narrative of the growth of new actors in civil society, which were either pressure groups or competed with the Umno-led government for Malay loyalty and unity, even if this was an imagined aspiration rather than a probable reality. At a time when Umno was riding on a wave of near-absolute consensual support from Malays,[17] especially with the uncompromising implementation of affirmative action programmes through the NEP, any possibility of this 'unity' cracking rang alarm bells.

Besides the more visible revivalist movements, which also affected state responses to the unexpected rise of a motley variety of Islamic expressions, there were other notable parallel developments. In the 1974 general election, Parti Islam Se-Malaysia (Pas, Islamic Party of Malaysia) entered into a coalition partnership with Umno and won state power in Kelantan. By 1977, this partnership had broken down due to disagreements over *negeri* versus federal rights, leading to street demonstrations and the declaration of an emergency rule in Kelantan by the Umno-led federal government (Saravanamuttu 2016, 122–123). This was an indication that Malay unity, which Umno had purportedly sought through its overture of an alliance with an Islamic party, was not a sufficient condition for eliciting a persuasive Malay 'consensus'.

Other means of 'expressing Islam', seen by the state as a sign of both Malay disunity and challenges against traditional Islam, were a series of violent incidents perpetrated by hitherto unknown advocates of a dissenting Islam. In February 1978, four Muslim men ran amok and destroyed idols at a Hindu temple in Kerling, Selangor, before being killed by caretakers of the temple. In 1980, 6 attackers dressed in white and armed with swords slashed 23 people at a police station in Batu Pahat, Johor. The six were shot to death. In 1985, one of the most dramatic incidences to shake the state was the killing of 18 people and 4 policemen in the village of Memali in Kedah. According to the White Paper released by the government, the police had gone to the village to arrest Ibrahim Mahmood (also known as Ibrahim Libya) under the Internal Security Act (ISA) for allegedly plotting to violently overthrow the government in the name of Islam. When the police surrounded his house, hundreds of his followers holed themselves up with him. Ibrahim was said to have convinced them through various speeches before this that they were leading a *jihad* (call to holy war) against a *kafir* (infidel) government and that they would die as martyrs (*mati syahid*) in any ensuing fight. After 4 policemen were killed in the raid, a shootout resulted in the deaths of 18 people, including Ibrahim Libya himself (Malaysia 1986).

There were hints of the mystical and supernatural in how this charismatic movement created an appeal among its followers. In believing that they would be immune to bullets, Ibrahim Libya's 'soldiers' were told to wear talismans, with the following instructions:

> To paste band-aid on the palm of the hand while supplicating and reciting the *Fatihah* ten times; followed by supplication on the Prophet for ten times, with both palms up as in the state of *doa* rub the face up to the hair and down over the whole body ending up at the navel; Then to paste the band-aid stuck with tiny sticks on the navel while reciting "*Nawaitul Jiha Fi Sabillillah*"... a whole tub of water had also been casted a spell (*jampi*) for drinking. According to Ustaz Ibrahim the talisman and the water will prevent any danger, [and] they will be invincible. (Malaysia 1986, 16–17)[18]

Another less-known incident was the attack at a police station in Sandakan in 1988, where eight men armed with machetes and dressed in white and red robes were shot to death (The Straits Times 1988). The 1970s and 1980s were thus a moment of 'debate' and 'comparisons', of making a choice as to how one should define one's own subjectivity as being Malay *and* Muslim. There was Islam as lived routinely, and there were 'Islams' as presented by myriad groupings and charismatic leaderships, all legitimately propounding their causes under the safe umbrella of the faith. The weapons of the dominant were resources, patronage and instruments of legal coercion, while the weapon of the 'weak' dissidents was the appeal of a re-enchanted Islam.

Accommodation and Solution in State and Muslim Society Engagement

> [T]he Malaysian Islamic Youth Movement concentrate [*sic*] on working with youths, Darul Arqam on the general public, Pusat Ugama (Religious Centre) in the Prime Minister's Department on civil servants including police and army personnel while the Dakwah Foundation of Malaysia tries to coordinate the activities of the various Dakwah groups. (Ismail 1978, 10–11)

In 1978, the above rendition was how one journalist described the burgeoning influence and targets of the various *dakwah* and Islamising activities in the country. Unlike the colonial period, which only saw the involvement of elites in shaping the meaning of Islam in public and private life, postcolonial possibilities for the masses to participate in and influence the Islamic sphere were not only endless but also an undertaking that could be done safely and defiantly under the umbrella of a 'Malay-Islamic' government. Its control of the newly declared sphere of Islamic morality required no rules or legislation to be passed, as Muslims could be policed in a self-directed way. A young man described the growing strength of the *dakwah* movement in universities in 1978 as follows: "[P]reviously we went to clubs instead of praying. Now you see less of this in Malaysia. Also, there are fewer women wearing mini-skirts" (Borsuk 1978, 14).

However, as early as 1982, it appeared that the revivalist movements were on the wane as the government had managed to pacify, neutralise, accommodate and respond to their demands and proposals for more Islamisation in society (Hussein 1988, 643–648). In actuality, Islamisation was not on the decline. It was only that those who promoted this outside of the ambit of the state were not welcomed, but those who were with the state could find new opportunities for Islam's flourishing. Umno battled Pas not only on the electoral front, and won, but, in courting potentially influential leaders into its fold, it was also more successful than Pas. Umno prevailed too on what was to be the meanings of correct and authentic Islam as the bureaucracy was firmly under its control.

The vanquished included the non-state Islamic movements discussed above. Abim was inducted into the mainstream with the co-optation of Anwar Ibrahim into Umno in 1982. Darul Arqam was banned in 1994 by both national and *negeri fatwa* committees on charges of being a deviant stream of Islam, while it was banned by the Home Ministry as a security threat to the country. In the case of Abim, political parties Umno and Pas fought over winning its leader Anwar Ibrahim to their side. Pas first eyed him as its potential leader, given that the party was in a disarray after its separation from the Umno-led ruling coalition in 1977. It needed new leadership legitimation after this conflict and the fervour of the Iranian Revolution also motivated Pas to inject a fresh Islamism within the party. Anwar was sought by Umno where calls for more Islamisation in public life were getting louder in the party, and there was growing pressure to reform from within by presenting a more Islamic image to balance its ethnic Malay identity. Anwar had a strong bargaining position and whoever could deliver the promise of an Islamisation agenda would trump. He eventually chose Umno for a variety of reasons, including family ties to the party, his own background of secular schooling and early association as a student leader with Mahathir Mohamad. Mahathir was then the Umno leader and critic of Tunku Abdul Rahman, Malaysia's first Prime Minister. Last but not least, Umno was *the* ruling party which controlled the government of the day (Hussein 1988, 595–600).

When the dust of some of these episodic contestations had settled, Umno, under the premiership of Mahathir from 1982 onwards, seemed set on having the upper hand in determining the Islamic agenda or at least checked it from falling into the hands of its rivals. After initial moves to establish and consolidate many more Islamic bodies under the federal government, as well as having Anwar Ibrahim as the eminent symbol and promoter of the government slogan and policy of *Penerapan Nilai-Nilai Islam dalam Pentadbiran* (The Integration of Islamic Values in Administration), the expansion of religious administration, upgrading of the status of *syariah* courts and the corporatisation of Islamic wealth followed closely.

As a political party, Umno had intended that the Islamisation or 'out-Islamisation' exercise, particularly in relation to its electoral rival, Pas, would continue giving it legitimacy among the Malay-Muslim constituency (Liow 2004). The institutionalisation of Islam within the legal-bureaucratic sphere—exclusive only to the Muslim citizenry, and purportedly not touching the affairs of non-Muslims—seemed a logical and natural route. The expansion and intensification of institutional Islam inevitably led to the strengthening of bureaucratic Islam, and the creation of a powerful 'religiocracy' of sorts, especially among the *ulama* class (Norshahril 2018). While Umno may have patronised this class, state Islamisation also became a successful symbol of the party's legitimacy. As such, it was difficult to suppress the growing influence of this bureaucratic authority, even if some of its stances went against Umno's—or rather, Mahathir's—image of Islamic moderation and secular developmentalism.

How was post-independence 'Islamisation' different from that 'created' by the British, which seemingly drew neat legal boundaries around the limited scope of Islam's jurisdictions in public life, and empowered only those with *kuasa* from the sultan to play any legitimate role in this domain? The answers to this question are helpful in uncovering the burgeoning features of a distinct state apparatus dedicated solely to addressing the religious rumblings of those perceived as falling on the other side of the divide of the Malay ruling elite. Conflicts and tensions between the Umno-ruled government and the opposition party Pas, the youth-led pressure group, Abim, the Sufistic Darul Arqam and a host of other atypical devotional groups found their resolution in various ways. Without doubt, the state had the upper hand in determining the outcome given the range of methods, or combination of them, that it had at its disposal—for example, coercion, demonisation, persuasion, cooperation, accommodation and, finally, Islamisation (Hussein 1988, 39).

Clearly, however, it would be more complicated in the postcolonial setting. While Malay monarchs were legally still the highest authority on Islam in their respective *negeri*, they had to contend with popularly elected Malay leaders, a relatively unshackled public sphere (particularly when it came to expressing Islam), and an established, though latent, bureaucracy already built around Islam. Although the jurisdiction of Islam in public life and the authority around its governance could still be circumscribed and legally demarcated, it had become increasingly difficult to prevent the boundaries of both from enlarging. Technically, the model of Islamic governance from colonial to postcolonial times has remained the same, that is, it is an administrative authority, validated by statute and having the credentials to institute laws applicable only to Muslims. What changed in the postcolonial situation were the special characteristics of the Islamic bureaucracy, its dramatic growth and its control over Muslims.

The face of Islamisation in postcolonial Malaysia was thus in the form of a gradual, but extensive, proliferation of Islamic institutional bodies, a process which was not entirely top-down nor fully state-driven. Islamic development was fuelled by the mixed motivations of the state, which included the pacification of dissenters and accommodation of their demands on the one hand and institute a policy of Malay-preferentialism as a symbolic and substantive marker of its post-1969 governance on the other hand. In this new phase, it seemed that all the stakeholders of Islam had fortuitously aligned as a powerful constellation of forces at the right political moment. Malay and Islamic political parties had every opportunity to promote a viable agenda of reinforcing their Malay-Islamic credentials for electoral gain, while dissenting Islamic movements found that many of their demands and agitation for more Islamisation could readily be converted into policy.

To pre-empt any potential eruption of Islamic radicalism, the government had to capitalise on the new political environment to accommodate the heterodoxy of Islam. Religious bureaucrats, previously marginal agents of Islamic transformation, now found themselves elevated as lynchpins in the progressive bureaucratisation of the faith. Nevertheless, it would be erroneous to assume that the heralding of a Divine Bureaucracy put an end to challenges against the state.

Conclusion

This chapter has argued that the manifestations of religious revivalism were merely symptomatic of the greater accessibility of an emergent aspiring middle class to the public sphere, which allowed Islam to be expressed within a larger continuum of discourse and practice. The Islamic bureaucracy that was in place through colonial times, however, was not attuned to addressing some of the newer demands of the growing Muslim middle class, and the increasingly visible Muslim civil society whose greater exposure to global influences rendered them more questioning of authority. Viewing these as either a threat or a boost to political popularity and legitimacy, the ruling elite used their political parties to adopt a strategy of absorbing rather than suppressing these emergent representations of Islam. Such a strategy could only succeed through the route of more bureaucratisation, more popularly referred to as the 'out-Islamisation' of Pas (Liow 2009, 13; Norshahril 2018, 122–126), enabling opposition Islam to be neutralised, co-opted or effectively institutionalised within a participatory state (Chernov-Hwang 2009, 111–138).

Whatever could be disenchanted through the fashioning of religion as orderly, procedure-based and legal rational sets of expressions were translated into national organisational goals. If the permeation of Islamic values in society was an objective, this was sought through a systematic process rather than being left to the caprices of civil society and other inexplicable forces. As will be shown in the following chapter, the legal rational bureaucracy does not have to depend on charismatic leadership to propagate Islam but on methodical and planned modes of operation sanctioned by legality. From family to identity to money, the reformulated, expanded and empowered bureaucracy can be seen to emplace systems and rules to achieve whatever stated objectives and sanctions determined from the start.

In colonial times, the bureaucracy was used to specify, yet delimit Islam; in the postcolonial period, the religious bureaucracy became a vessel for the appropriation and reconstitution of Islam through new modes of governance. The centralisation of authority, the standardisation of religious expression, the corporatisation of Islamic wealth and the enclosing of Muslims as a homogeneous constituency, all became the defining traits of the Divine Bureaucracy, which will be explicated in the subsequent chapters.

Notes

1. The Malay word *adat* means customs or traditions. The word used in the legal sense is also a noun, as there are bodies of traditional laws referred to by colonial scholars as Adat Temenggong or Adat Pepateh.
2. In Arabic, the word *dakwah* or *da'wah* literally means the call or invitation. Although it is also meant to denote the act of proselytisation and conversion of non-Muslims into Islam, it has been largely used in the Malay-Indonesian world to mean the reinforcement and expansion of Islamic faith and practice among Muslims themselves (Meuleman 2011, 236). In Malaysia, it is about the 'return' to Islam and adoption of Islam as a complete way of life (Ungku Maimunah 1989, 288).
3. This book has been popularly reprinted in Malay. See, for example, the blog, "*Karya* Ulama: *Beberapa catatan untuk diri dan berkongsi bersama*", http://abusyahmin.blogspot.com, accessed: 21 January 2019. This blog has an extensive compilation and explanation of many Arabic texts used by *ulama* (religious scholars) in the Malay World.
4. British Malaya consisted of three administrative governance units: the Straits Settlements (Penang, Melaka and Singapore, territorial entities without traditional Malay rulers), the Federated Malay States (Perak, Selangor, Negeri Sembilan and Pahang) and the Unfederated Malay States (Kelantan, Terengganu, Kedah, Perlis and Johor). One of the key differences between British rule in the Federated and Unfederated Malay States was that the former had a more active presence of the British Resident in the governance of these States (*negeri*), as opposed to the British Adviser in the latter.
5. Following from this colonial nomenclature, statutory provisions passed by State Legislative Assemblies (subnational Parliaments) in postcolonial Malaysia are known as 'Enactments' while Federal laws are termed 'Acts'.

6. Contents of these treaties noted that Islam and Malay customs were to be the only purview of the Malay rulers (Braddell 1931). In the Memorandum between Raffles and the Sultan of Johore, in 1823, it is stated:

   > In all cases regarding the ceremonies of religion, and marriages, and the rules of inheritance, the laws and customs of the Malays will be respected, where they shall not be contrary to reason, justice or humanity. In all other cases the laws of the British authority will be enforced with due consideration to the usages and habits of the people.

   In the Pangkor Treaty of 1874, the following was noted:

   > That the Sultan [shall] receive and provide a suitable residence for a British Officer to be called a Resident, who shall be accredited to this Court, and whose advice must be asked and acted upon on all questions other than those touching Malay Religion and Custom.

7. See details and commentaries of such cases in Taylor (1937, 15–69).
8. Malaya was the name used to refer to territorial entities under British colonial administration, which included the *negeri* of the Malay Peninsula as well as the Straits Settlements of Penang, Malacca and Singapore. The term 'Malaysia' was only adopted after the formation of the post-independence federation in 1963. Singapore, Sabah and Sarawak became part of the Federation of Malaysia. In 1965, Singapore left this federation.
9. In precolonial Malay society, faith and practice were syncretic in nature; neither Islam nor magic was a "state religion", as noted by Gullick (1965, 141).
10. The Administration Enactment, No. 4 of 196, and The Rules for Members of the Council of the Islamic Religion and Malay Custom, Kelantan, Enactment No. 14 of 1916 (Abdullah Alwi 1996, xxxv).
11. For example, the Muhammadan Marriage and Divorce Enactment 1911, Administration of Muslim Law Enactment 1952, Islamic Family Law Act 1984 and Syariah Criminal Offences Enactment 2001.
12. See endnote 2 in Chap. 1.
13. Habermas was referring to the European society of the early twentieth century, "The bourgeois public sphere may be conceived above all as the sphere of private people [coming] together as a public; they soon claimed the public sphere regulated from above against the public authorities themselves" (quoted in Bernstein 2012, 767).
14. "[I]n the Sixties, I continued my studies at the University of Iskandariah, also in Egypt… During that time, most of the local radio stations used to play (propaganda) songs in praise of the leadership of Jamal Abdul Nasir. Majority of the Malaysian students who returned from Egypt were influenced by Nasir's Arab socialism. Only a few remained loyal to Islam. It was here where I met some brothers from *Ikhwan al-Muslimin* (Muslim

Brotherhood) such as Sa'id Ramadhan (son-in-law of Imam Hasan al-Banna), al-Tilmisani, Zainul Abidin, Dr. Shara Basi and a few others whose name I could not remember" (Mohd Dahlan 1996, 20).

15. The original reads, "*Kita Yakin Mujaddid itu/Adalah Imamul Mahdi/ Pembela yang benar/Pembenteras yang salah/Di waktu itu yang benar pasti menang/Yang salah pasti kalah*" (Ashaari 1988b).
16. The group had a special magazine on women and for women, *Almukminah: Penyuluh peranan wanita Islam sebenar.* In one issue titled "Syurga – Tempat orang yang sanggup berkorban", Ashaari Muhammad answers hypothetical questions coming from a woman unhappy with her polygamous husband. It goes, "The question is, Ustaz, since getting married, my husband has not given me enough attention. His love and inclination towards his new wife is overwhelming till I feel disgraced and useless altogether". To which Ustaz Ashaari replies, "A good Muslim wife must be willing to sacrifice herself and her own rights to her husband. She is able to smile to her husband as much as it is bitter". The question and answer format goes on for two pages, with no fault attributed to the husband (Khadijah 1988, 8–9).
17. The other contending Malay-Muslim party is the Pan-Malaysian Islamic Party or Pas. Although Pas is a visible and forceful competitor to Umno, its base is predominantly in the Malay-majority state of Kelantan. In terms of electoral seats it commands, this is also of no match to that of Umno's. See Saravanamuttu (2016, 280–285)
18. In Malay: "*Meletakkan plaster di tapak tangan sambal menadahnya dan membaca Fatihah sebanyak sepuluh kali; Diikuti dengan ucapan selawat ke atas Nabi sebanyak sepuluh kali; Kedua-dua tapak tangan, seperti dalam keadaan berdoa, di mana disapukan dari muka ke atas rambut dan turun menyaluti seluruh badan dan berakhir di tengah pusat; Seterusnya plaster berlidi pun ditampal di pusat serentak dengan melafazkan "Nawaitul Jiha Fi Sabillillah"..."Sebuah kolah air juga telah dijampi untuk diminum. Menurut Ustaz Ibrahim tangkal dan air jampi itu akan mengelakkan dari bahaya, jadi kebal*" (Malaysia 1986, 16–17).

References

Abdul Rahman, Tunku Putra Al-Haj (1984) *Malaysia: The road to independence*, Petaling Jaya: Pelanduk Publications.

Abdullah Alwi, Haji Hassan (1996) *The Administration of Islamic law in Kelantan*, Kuala Lumpur: Dewan Bahasa dan Pustaka.

Ahmad Fauzi, Abdul Hamid (1999) "New trends of Islamic resurgence in contemporary Malaysia: Sufi-revivalism, messianism, and economic activism", *Studia Islamika: Indonesian Journal for Islamic Studies*, Vol. 6, No. 3, 1–74.

——— (2013) "The Aurad Muhammadiah Congregation: Modern transnational Sufism in Southeast Asia", in Hui Yew-Foong (ed), *Encountering Islam: The politics of religious identities in Southeast Asia*, Singapore: ISEAS Publishing.

Ahmad Ibrahim (1965) *Islamic Law in Malaya*, Singapore: Malaysian Sociological Research Institute Ltd.

Anuar Tahir (1996) "Menjalin Hubungan Antara Bangsa: Sebuah catatan pengalaman" in *Angkatan Belia Islam Malaysia, 1971–1996*, Selangor: Angkatan Belia Islam Malaysia, pp. 50–55.

Ariffin, Omar (1993) *Bangsa Melayu: Malay concepts of democracy and community*, New York: Oxford University Press.

Ashaari, Muhammad (1988a) "Asy Syeikh Muhammad bin Abdullah As Suhaimi masih hidup", *Al Munir: Penunjuk jalan taqwa*, No. 8, August, 18–19.

——— (1988b) "Imamul Mahdi", *Al Munir: Penunjuk jalan taqwa*, No. 9, September, 7.

Berita Harian (1981) "Bank Islam Malaysia", 5 May, 1.

Bernstein, Richard J (2012) "The Normative Core of the Public Sphere", *Political Theory*, Vol. 40, No. 6, 767–778.

Borsuk, Richard (1978) "Green and White in the Village of the Faithful: Inside Malaysia's 'dakwah' movement", *The Straits Times*, 10 October, 14.

Braddell, Roland (1931) *The Law of the Straits Settlements: A commentary*, Second Edition, Singapore: Kelly and Walsh, Limited.

Buss-Tjen, PP (1958) "Malay Law", *The American Journal of Comparative Law*, Vol. 7, No. 2, Spring.

Chandra, Muzaffar (1987) *Islamic Resurgence in Malaysia*, Petaling Jaya: Fajar Bakti Sdn. Bhd.

Cheah, Boon Kheng (2002) *Malaysia: The making of a nation*, Singapore: Institute of Southeast Asian Studies.

——— (2006) *To' Janggut: Legends, histories, and perceptions of the 1915 rebellion in Kelantan*, Singapore: Singapore University Press.

Chernov-Hwang, Julie (2009) *Peaceful Islamist Mobilization in the Muslim World: What went right*, New York: Palgrave Macmillan.

de Josselin de Jong, P (1960) Islam Versus Adat In Negri Sembilan (Malaya), *Bijdragen Tot De Taal-, Land- En Volkenkunde,* Vol. 116, No. 1, 158–203.

Faaland, Just, JR Parkinson and Rais Saniman (1990) *Growth and Ethnic Inequality in Malaysia's Economic Policy*, London: St. Martin's Press.

Faruqi, Shad Saleem (2016) "Shariah Laws, Civil Laws and the Federal Constitution", in G25 Malaysia, *Breaking the Silence: Voices of moderation, Islam in a constitutional democracy*, Singapore: Marshall Cavendish, 55–75.

FMS Government Gazette (1920a), "The Muhammadan Laws Enactment, 1904", *CO 574/25.*

——— (1920b) "Federated Malay States, State of Pahang (1920) Enactment No. 1 of 1920, An Enactment to provide for the Registration of Marriages and Divorces of Muhammadans, Pahang 1920", *CO 574/25.*

Gullick, JM (1965) *Indigenous Political Systems of Western Malaya*, New York; The Athlone Press.

——— (1981) "Law and Adat Perpateh: A Problem from Jelebu", *Journal of the Malaysian Branch of the Royal Asiatic Society*, Vol. 54, No. 1, 7–20.

Habermas, Jurgen (1991) *The Structural Transformation of the Public Sphere: An inquiry into a category of bourgeois society*, translated by Thomas Burger with the assistance of Frederick Lawrence, Cambridge, Mass: MIT Press.

Harper, TN (1998) *The End of Empire and the Making of Malaya*, New York: Cambridge University Press.

Hooker, MB (1969) "The Relationship between Adat and State Constitutions of Negri Sembilan", *Journal of the Malaysian Branch of the Royal Asiatic Society*, Vol. 42, No. 2, 155–172.

——— (1971) "Law, Religion, and Bureaucracy in a Malay State: A study in conflicting power centers", *The American Journal of Comparative Law*, Vol. 19, No. 2, 264–286.

——— (1976) *Adat Laws in Modern Malaya: Land tenure, traditional government and religion,* Kuala Lumpur: Oxford University Press.

Horowitz, Donald L (1994) "The Qur'an and the Common Law: Islamic law reform and the theory of legal change", *The American Journal of Comparative Law*, Vol. 42, No. 2, 233–293.

Hussein, S Ahmad (1988) "Islam and Politics in Malaysia, 1969–1982: The dynamics of competing traditions", PhD thesis submitted to Yale University.

Idrus, Jamhari (1988) "Pembentukkan Zaman Ummah Kedua: Siapa di belakang Imamul Mahdi?", *Al Munir: Penunjuk Jalan Taqwa*, No. 9, September, 6–7.

Ismail, Kassim (1978) "Dakwah Dilemma", *New Nation*, 24 October, 10–11.

Johore Government Gazette (1914), 'Enactment No. 15 of 1914: An Enactment to provide for the registration of Marriages and Divorce of Muhammadans', CO 653/1.

Kessler, Clive (1980) "Malaysia: Islamic revivalism and political disaffection in a divided society", *Southeast Asia Chronicle*, Vol. 75, 3–11.

Khadijah, Aam (1988) "*Syurga – Tempat orang yang sanggup berkorban*", *Almukminah: Penyuluh Wanita Islam Sebenar*, May, 8–9.

Khasnor, Johan (1984) *The Emergence of the Modern Malay Administrative Elite*, New York: Oxford University Press.

Lee, Raymond LM and Susan E Ackerman (1997) *Sacred Tensions: Modernity and religious transformations in Malaysia*, Columbia, SC: University of South Carolina Press.

Liow, Joseph Chinyong (2004) "Political Islam in Malaysia: Problematising discourse and practice in the UMNO-PAS 'Islamisation race'", *Commonwealth & Comparative Politics*, Vol. 42, No.2, 184–205.

——— (2009) *Piety and Politics: Islamism in contemporary Malaysia*, Oxford: Oxford University Press.

Malaya (1944) *Malayan Basic Handbook: Malaya and its civil administration prior to Japanese Occupation*, Malaya: The War Office.

Malaysia (1986) *Kertas Perintah 21, Tahun 1986: Peristiwa Memali* (White Paper No 21, 1986: Memali Incident), Kuala Lumpur: Ministry of Home Affairs.

Maznah, Mohamad (2016a) "The Customary Tenure Enactment and Matrilineal Land Rights in Negeri Sembilan", *Journal of the Malaysian Branch Royal Asiatic Society* (JMBRAS), Vol. 89, Part 1, June, 15–33.

——— (2016b) "Policing and Protecting Women: Some aspects of Malay-Islamic law-making under British colonialism", *Kajian Malaysia,* Vol. 34, No. 1, 2016, 59–78.

Md Taha, Suhaimi (n.d.) "Jawapan Bagi Tuduhan Terhadap Sejarah Hidup Syeikh Muhammad As-Suhami dan Aurad Muhammadiah", https://auradmuhammadiah.wordpress.com/manaqib-sheikh-suhaimi-2/, accessed 31 January 2019.

Meuleman, Johan (2011) "Dakwah, Competition for Authority and Development", *Bijdragen tot de Taal-, Land- en Volkenkunde*, Vol. 167, No. 2–3, 236–269.

Mohamad, Abu Bakar (1991) "External influences on contemporary Islamic resurgence in Malaysia", *Contemporary Southeast Asia*, Vol. 13, No. 2, 220–228.

Mohd Dahlan, Arshad (1996) "Langkah Awalku" in ABIM, *Angkatan Belia Islam Malaysia, 1971–1996*, Selangor: Angkatan Belia Islam Malaysia.

Moustafa, Tamir (2018) *Constituting Religion: Islam, liberal rights, and the Malaysian state*, Cambridge: Cambridge University Press.

Nagata, Judith (1984) *The Reflowering of Malaysian Islam: Modern religious radicals and their roots*, Vancouver: University of British Columbia Press.

Negeri Sembilan Government Gazette (1900) Federated Malay States, Negeri of Negri Sembilan 'An Enactment to Provide for the Registration of Marriages and Divorces of Muhammadans', CO 463/2.

Norshahril, Saat (2018) *The State, Ulama and Islam in Malaysia and Indonesia*, Singapore: ISEAS Publishing.

Nurfazilah, Yahaya (2015) "Craving Bureaucracy: Marriage, Islamic law, and the Arab Petitioners in the Straits Settlements", *The Muslim World*, Vol. 105, 496–515.

O'Connor, Kathleen Malone (2001) "Popular and Talismanic Uses of the Qurʾān", in Jane Dammen McAuliffe (ed), *Encyclopaedia of the Qurʾān,* Georgetown University, Washington DC: Brill Reference Online.

Perak Government Gazette (1889), 'Order of Council No. 12 of 1889, Mohamedan Divorce', CO467/1.

——— (1890), 'Order in Council No. 11 of 1890: Constitution and powers of criminal and civil courts', CO467/1.

Roff, William R (1967) *The Origins of Malay Nationalism*, Kuala Lumpur: University of Malaya Press.

Sachedina, Abdulaziz (2012) "Mahdi", in Mark Juergensmeyer and Wade Clark Roof (eds), *Encyclopedia of Global Religion*, Thousand Oaks: Sage Publications, 738.

Saravanamuttu, Johan (2016) *Power Sharing in a Divided Nation: Mediated communalism and new politics in six decades of Malaysia's elections.* Singapore: ISEAS Publishing.

Sharifah Zaleha, Syed Hassan (1985) "From Saints to Bureaucrats: A study of the development of Islam in the State of Kedah, Malaysia", PhD thesis submitted to Cornell University.

Simatupang AH (1988) "Siapa Syeikh Muhammad As Suhaimi?", *Al Munir: Penunjuk Jalan Taqwa,* No. 8, August, 16–17, 24–25.

Singapore Free Press and Mercantile Advertiser (1891) "Mohammedan Law in the Straits", 16 September.

Singapore Herald (1971) "Tunku for Jeddah", 8 January, 13.

Taylor, EN (1937) "Malay Family Law", *Journal of the Malayan Branch of the Royal Asiatic Society*, Vol. 15, No. 1, viii-ix, 1–78.

The Straits Times (1935) "Naib Kathis: Need for a Malayan college", 10 May, 7.

——— (1980) "Saudi Gift", 24 March, 15.

——— (1988) "Sabah Police Shoot Dead Eight Men Armed with Parangs", 24 May, 1.

Ungku Maimunah, Mohd Tahir (1989) "The notion of 'Dakwah' and Its Perceptions in Malaysia's Islamic Literature of the 1970s and 80s", *Journal of Southeast Asian Studies*, Vol. 20, No. 2, 288–297.

Yegar, Moshe (1979) *Islam and Islamic Institutions in British Malaya: Policies and implementation*, Jerusalem: The Magnes Press.

Zainah, Anwar (1987) *Islamic Revivalism in Malaysia: Dakwah among the students*, Petaling Jaya, Selangor: Pelanduk Publications.

CHAPTER 3

Features of the Divine Bureaucracy

Introduction

By 1981, when Mahathir Mohamad came to power as the country's fourth Prime Minister, the seeds for the growth of the Divine Bureaucracy had already been planted. Greater centralisation of Islamic authority, more acute standardisation of religious expressions, sizeable corporatisation of Islamic monetary resources, and more extensive enclosing of Muslim subjects within *syariah* legalism were some of the features that gradually shaped this distinctive bureaucracy. Its powers and legitimacy are drawn from formal statutes, organisational systematisation, rational management of human and capital resources, and a differentiation of functions. All are typical of the Weberian rational legal bureaucracy but for one additional and crucial dimension. This dimension—sacrosanctity and inviolability derived from revelatory and founding texts of the Quran, the prophetic traditions of *hadith* (words of the Prophet) and *sunna* (ways of the Prophet), and ancient and contemporary *fiqh* (Islamic jurisprudence) texts—imprints the exceptional authority of the Divine Bureaucracy.

This chapter will detail the contemporary features of this bureaucracy, its manifold purposes and functions, and its extending scope that has gone beyond mere civil administration into the legislative and courts system, educational administration, and Islamic realms of corporatisation. From the 1980s, the Divine Bureaucracy grew into a multilevelled, multidifferentiated and multitentacled titan. There was a simultaneous and prolonged

M. Mohamad, *The Divine Bureaucracy and Disenchantment of Social Life*, Contestations in Contemporary Southeast Asia,
https://doi.org/10.1007/978-981-15-2093-8_3

proliferation and multiplication of institutions, as well as the doubling and overlapping of functions entrusted to the countless 'bureaus' and 'sections' created within each entity of administrative governance. Unlike the previous period of colonialism and early postcolonialism, today this bureaucracy has a palpable disenchanting impact on everyday lives, not just of Muslims within its jurisdiction but also of non-Muslims outside its fold.[1]

The Divine Bureaucracy as a monolithic bureaucracy has at least three arms, domains or components that have taken on lives of their own. Stemming from the three important nexus of power that act in tandem or separately from one another, the first, termed here as the *negeri* (State, subnational unit of governance) Islamic bureaucracy, grew out of its original decentralised, traditional, religious administrative units formed in each Malay territorial enclave during British rule. The second domain of bureaucratic control is that of the central or federal Islamic bureaucracy which had a more extensive authority over Islamic matters from the 1980s onwards due to the greater concentration of powers in the hands of national leaders. The third domain is occupied by a corporate Islamic bureaucracy, growing out of the development of Islamic banking and finance, and the commercialisation of *zakat* (religious tithe/tax collection), *wakaf* (religious endowment) and the *halal* industry. Together, these constitute the Divine Bureaucracy of this study, exerting authority over some of the most critical spheres of governance—civil administration, courts and corporations. The promotion and advancement of Islam have also been facilitated by the exercise of their legal and financial exceptionalism over other national institutions.

The Divine Bureaucracy and Its Components

From the 1980s onwards when national development through 'Islamisation' became a major thrust of the Mahathir-Anwar administration (Mauzy and Milne 1983; Anwar 1992; Nasr 2001; Abbott and Gregorios-Pippas 2010; Schotmann 2011), *syariah* lawmaking, court proceduralisation and corporatisation of Islamic resource management all experienced major transformation. This was primarily through the processes of centralisation, accretion, expansion, elevation, corporatisation and privatisation. 'Centralisation' is understood here as the "concentration of administrative power in a central government, authority"; 'accretion', "an increase by gradual external addition, in size or extent"; 'expansion', "anything spread out"; 'elevation', rising to "loftiness; grandeur or dignity"; 'corporatisation', "to develop into big business; bring under the control of a corporation"; and privatisation, the "transfer from public or government control or ownership to private enterprise".[2] This was how bureaucratised Islam became considerably enlarged in contemporary times to span various levels of federal and *negeri* governance, including the quasi-public sectors of money, banking and finance. Table 3.1 illustrates the differences among the Divine Bureaucracy's three domains by highlighting their location, locus of authority, and agencies and institutions under their governance.

Negeri Islamic Bureaucracy

The *negeri*-based or State-based Islamic bureaucracy was the earliest formed ensemble of institutions to oversee the affairs of Muslims and Islam in the country. The first legal authority on Islam introduced in this regard was the Majlis Agama Islam Negeri (Main, State Islamic Religious Councils—SIRCs), headed either by the respective Malay sultans or State Governors. As noted in Chap. 2, in 1915, Kelantan pioneered the creation of this structure with its Majlis Ugama dan Isti'adat Melayu, and, by 1963, this institution had been replicated and established by statutes in the other within the peninsula (Ahmad 1965, 147–169). This process was completed in 2004 when Sabah, the last *negeri* to do so, established its own SIRC.

In the aftermath of postwar developments and impending decolonisation from the end of the Second World War onwards, the subnational Islamic bureaucracy underwent reconstitution. When the British failed to form the Malayan Union in 1946 due to Malay protests, they negotiated for another entity in its place, the Federation of Malaya.[3] Cognisant of Malay demands for more rights, they strengthened the SIRCs with new laws that formalised these as a "corporate body with power to hold and dispose of property and to enter into contracts and administer estates", including being granted more powers to regulate the practice and teachings of Islam. This was a major shift from the colonial period when the SIRCs were placed under the purview of the State Councils (Ahmad Ibrahim 1965, 147–175; Abdullah Alwi 1996, 70).

By the 2000s, the SIRCs lost their old basis of authority when all existing laws governing this institution were repealed and replaced with new statutes. Though retaining their status as the main subnational authority

Table 3.1 The Divine Bureaucracy

Domain	*States*	*Federal*		*Corporate*
Location and locus of authority	Perlis, Kedah, Perak, Selangor, Negeri Sembilan, Melaka, Johor, Pahang, Terengganu, Kelantan, Sabah, Sarawak and Federal Territories	Directly under the Jabatan Perdana Menteri (Prime Minister's Department, hereon, the PM's Department)[a]	Under various federal ministries and agencies[b]	Governed by federal laws, not related or answerable to federal or *negeri* Islamic bureaucracies
Agencies and institutions	Majlis Agama Islam Negeri (SIRC, State (*negeri*) Islamic Religious Council)[c]	Jabatan Kemajuan Islam Malaysia (Jakim, Islamic Development Department of Malaysia)[d]	Ministry of Education—Islamic Education Division	Syariah Advisory Council (SAC) of Bank Negara Malaysia (BNM)
	Mufti's Office	Jabatan Kehakiman Syariah Malaysia (JKSM, Syariah Judicial Department of Malaysia)	Kor Agama Angkatan Tentera (Kagat, Religious Corp of the Malaysian Army)	Syariah Advisory Council (SAC) of Securities Commission Malaysia (SCM)
	Syariah court	Yayasan Dakwah Islamiah Malaysia (Yadim, Malaysian Islamic Dakwah Foundation)	Bahagian Agama dan Kaunseling Polis Diraja Malaysia (Baka PDRM, Division of Religion and Counselling Royal Malaysian Police)	Islamic banks—Syariah Advisory Committees
	Negeri (State) Islamic religious department	Lembaga Tabung Haji (LTH, Pilgrims' Funds Board)[e]	Attorney General's Chambers—Syariah and Harmonisation of Law Division	Lembaga Tabung Haji
		Jabatan Wakaf, Zakat dan Haji (Jawhar, Department of Wakaf, Zakat and Hajj)	Ministry of Home Affairs—Quranic Regulatory Section and Hadith Regulatory Section	Halal Industry Development Corporation (HDC)

Agencies and institutions	Institut Kefahaman Islam Malaysia (Ikim, Institute of Islamic Understanding Malaysia) Yayasan Pembangunan Eknomi Islam Malaysia (Yapeim, Islamic Economic Development Foundation of Malaysia) Yayasan Wakaf Malaysia (Wakaf Foundation of Malaysia) Al-Hijrah Media Corporation Federal Territory Mufti's Office[f] Jabatan Agama Islam Wilayah Persekutuan (Jawi, Federal Territory religious department)[f] Majlis Agama Islam Wilayah Persekutuan (Maiwp, Federal Territory SIRC)[f] Yayasan Taqwa Wilayah Persekutuan (Federal Territory Taqwa Foundation) World Zakat Organisation

[a]This listing is taken from Jakim (n.d.)
[b]This list is not exhaustive
[c]Some SIRCs have their own privatised or semi-privatised corporations for *zakat* collection and distribution, and *wakaf* development and management
[d]Jakim also has a Halal Certification Department which takes on a corporatised model
[e]Lembaga Tabung Haji is placed under the authority of the PM's Department, although it also has the characteristics of a corporate bureaucracy
[f]These organisations are under the PM's Department but are parallel and equivalent in functions to *negeri*-based institutions

on Islam, the SIRCs were no longer the "highest" (*tertinggi sekali*) body for "*Hukum Syarak*" (*syariah* law) consultation and also lost their advisory role over "Malay customs".[4] Instead, the domain of *syariah* lawmaking was to reside with *negeri* legislators when it came to passing 'Islamic' enactments, and the Mufti's Office for the issuance of *fatwa* (legal opinion). The new laws continued to recognise the sultans and agong (king) as the apex authority whose advice must be sought on all matters regarding Islam within their respective jurisdictions. However, they also elevated the *mufti* (jurisconsult) to become the chief authority "in respect of all matters of *Hukum Syarak* in every *negeri*".[5] Malay customs also were no longer tied with Islam after the provision that the SIRCs should also observe *adat* (customary) laws was removed in the new enactments. This reflected the perceived irrelevance and heterodox nature of Malay customary laws and norms, which were downplayed in the assertion of a new, resurgent and 'authentic' Islam.

Federal Islamic Bureaucracy

The next layer of the Divine Bureaucracy encompasses institutions at the federal level involved in centralising the development of Islam. Appendix 2 provides a timeline and details of their formation, those that were created under the Prime Minister's Department (PM's Department), and other related agencies. As previously noted, Islam is constitutionally governed by each individual *negeri*. Many national-level Islamic bodies that exist today are thus not products of or governed by specific statutes. Yet they have considerable clout and authority by virtue of their resources and the executive powers they derive from being part of the federal government.

The foremost institution in this regard is the Jabatan Kemajuan Islam Malaysia (Jakim, Islamic Advancement Department of Malaysia), formed for the development and management of Islam throughout the country. It began in 1974 when a Unit Agama (Religious Unit) was upgraded to the Bahagian Ugama (Religious Section) under the PM's Department. In 1984, this section was renamed and further upgraded to become the Bahagian Hal Ehwal Islam (Baheis, Division of Islamic Affairs). In 1997, Baheis became Jakim, a full-fledged department complete with its own special cabinet minister serving as the de facto Minister of Islamic Affairs. Subsequently, other 'Islamic' institutions were established under the PM's Department, the more notable ones being the Jabatan Kehakiman Syariah Malaysia (JKSM,

Syariah Judicial Department of Malaysia) in 1998, and Jabatan Wakaf, Zakat dan Haji (Jawhar, Wakaf, Zakat and Hajj Department) in 2004.

In addition, the PM's Department oversees the religious bureaucracy of the Federal Territories—comprising Kuala Lumpur, Labuan and Putrajaya—namely its SIRC, the Majlis Agama Islam Wilayah Persekutuan (Maiwp), the Mufti's Office and the Jabatan Agama Islam Wilayah Persekutuan (Jawi, Federal Territories Religious Department). Even though these operate on federal funds, they mirror the set-ups of the other *negeri*.

Corporate Islamic Bureaucracy

The domain of the corporate Islamic bureaucracy—identified in this study as the third domain of the Divine Bureaucracy—has developed around the growth of an Islamic finance and banking industry, and the corporatisation of various 'monetisable' activities under the *negeri* Islamic bureaucracy. It may have little in common with the spheres led by the administrators, *ulama* (Islamic scholar), *mufti* and *syariah* judges, who pervade and are the pillars of the federal and *negeri* Islamic bureaucracies, also referred to here as the traditional Islamic bureaucracy. Nor is it necessarily recognised as an arm of state-led Islamisation. Even so, excluding this layer from the analysis of the Divine Bureaucracy would be missing out on the large and interlocking picture of national and global Islamisation, as well as the role of money and business in religious development. While it may not be subjected to national *syariah* laws, the corporate Islamic bureaucracy has an extensive global interconnectedness and inclusivity in terms of agents, leaders and clients that distinguishes it from traditional institutions of religious regulation and control.

The two main institutions under this bureaucracy are the Syariah Advisory Council of the Securities Commission of Malaysia (SCM), formed in 1996, and the Syariah Advisory Council of the Bank Negara Malaysia (BNM, Central Bank of Malaysia) formed in 1997. Between them, the BNM's Syariah Advisory Council is more important and authoritative, where *syariah* rulings pertaining to the Islamic banking and financial sector are concerned. Increasingly, the gap between the domain of corporate Islamic bureaucracy and traditional Islamic bureaucracies has narrowed. The requisite for legitimation of the former must also derive from foundational *syariah* scriptural and textual sources, which are the knowledge and epistemological bastion of the traditional Islamic bureaucracy. Over time, mutual interests have also arisen between the traditional and corporate bureaucracies to collaborate in the development of 'Islamic' wealth and resources.[6]

Centralising the Civil Administration of Islamic Development

The centralisation of civil administration over Islam in Malaysia should not be perceived solely as a political response to neutralise challenges from Islamic civil society. Certainly, even before countering demands from revivalist Islamic groups, the government had already established the Majlis Kebangsaan Bagi Hal Ehwal Agama Islam (MKI, National Council for Islamic Religious Affairs) in 1969.[7] The creation of the Federal Territory of Kuala Lumpur in 1974, followed by Labuan in 1984 and Putrajaya in 2001, resulted in a new entity called the Federal Territories (FT) under the governance of the national government. While this has instituted the same Islamic administration structures found in the other *negeri*, the creation of Maiwp within the belly of federal governance has allowed the national leadership—through new religious elites—to mould this body in its own image of modernisation and professionalisation.

For instance, the Committee for Islamic Law under Maiwp and endorsed by the MKI was one of the first to propose that Islamic laws be standardised. Its draft of the Islamic Family Law, recommended as a standalone statute, was presented as a national model to be emulated by all *negeri*. This subsequently resulted in them promulgating the proposed law (Abdul Monir 2016, 76–77). The 1984 FT Islamic Family Law contained many progressive provisions for the protection of women's rights. This changed in the 2000s when almost every *negeri* either made extensive amendments to its legislation or repealed the existing ones altogether to reflect the ideological and ideational shifts among the emergent *syariah* elite.[8]

Other significant developments at the federal level included the progressive establishment, then upgrading and finally expansion of institutional bodies related to Islamic matters. The creation of the Perbadanan Wang Simpanan Bakal-Bakal Haji (Pilgrims' Savings and Deposits Bank) in 1962 and the Masjid Negara (National Mosque) that was built in the capital Kuala Lumpur in 1965 were both symbolic yet fundamental to the intervention of the central government into the lives of Muslims. The

Council of Rulers,[9] comprising all heads of *negeri* in the country, can also be seen as holding the national mandate over Islam as it is the body to endorse any nationally created institutions on Islamic matters such as the MKI.

The 1970s saw no less than a dozen federal initiatives pertaining to Islam. As mentioned earlier, a timeline of the formation of various key agencies in the PM's Department and related agencies is found in Appendix 2. Among the more prominent ones were the formation of a dedicated institute for *dakwah* training, Institut Dakwah dan Latihan Islam (Indah, Islamic Dakwah and Training Institute), and the Yayasan Dakwah Islamiah Malaysia (Yadim, Malaysian Islamic Dakwah Foundation); the establishment of Yayasan Pembangunan Ekonomi Islam Malaysia (Yapeim, Islamic Economic Development Foundation); and the upgrading of the Unit Agama (Religious Unit) to the Bahagian Ugama (Religion Section) in the PM's Department. It was no coincidence that the flurry of measures towards institutionalising Islam coincided with the first burst of Islamic revivalist activities at home, and the start of the impactful Iranian Revolution with its founding of the Islamic Republic of Iran.

Jakim's establishment in 1997 came 15 years after Anwar Ibrahim joined Umno from Abim, and 12 years after Mahathir's *Penerapan Nilai-Nilai Islam dalam Pentadbiran* (Integration of Islamic Values in Administration) policy in 1985. Some of the phrases contained in this policy—which incidentally is still found on the website of the Prime Minister's Office after Mahathir's return to power in 2018[10]—include Islamic values as an important factor in engendering a respectable society. What Mahathir originally construed as Islamic values were also universal values of "honesty, integrity, responsibility, industry, sincerity, well-mannerism, of society over self, of willingness to sacrifice, devoid of greed, visionary, with morals, virtuous conduct and all else", as noted in this website.

Perhaps due to the 'universality' or 'non-distinctiveness' of these so-called Islamic values, the uptake on this policy was not immediate. Ahmad Sarji Abdul Hamid, former Chief Secretary under the earlier Mahathir administration and a prolific writer on the civil service, was one of the few who commented on this policy at the time. Under a section on 'leadership values' in a 1994 report, he wrote that exemplary leadership was not just the preserve of 'Western management gurus' but was already included in *quranic* verses and prophetic traditions. He also maintained that the government's approach to quality and productive work was congruent with

Islamic values. The same report included an excerpt of a 1994 speech he made, which drew parallels between universal work ethics and values to 'Islamic management values' (Ahmad Sarji 1995, 290–293, 295).

The growth and differentiation of administrative departments, personnel and functions, and the progressive ballooning of its budget were reflective of the vast expansion in the Divine Bureaucracy. There are currently 14 agencies for 'Islamic Development' under the PM's Department alone.[11] Within 12 of these there are at least 90 departments. Diagram 3.1 maps the organisational structure of Jakim, the biggest federal Islamic body today. It has four main sections (Director's Divisions, Policy, Operations, Finance) with 25 divisions under them. However, even the Research Division (under the Policy Section) has three subdivisions with six sections and 18 units under it.[12] The graphic representation of these multitiered and multi-led departments and bureaus conveys a seemingly endless differentiation of functions that are identified in modern, managerial and technical nomenclature. There are also numerous overlapping functions. For instance, the programme for '*dakwah*' is replicated in many divisions, as are the units for *quranic* and *hadith* studies. Two divisions with core functions that overlap are Jawhar and the Yayasan Waqaf Malaysia, where both are in the business of *wakaf* (trusts/endowments) development. It is also unclear what Yapeim does to promote the development of Islamic economics since the Lembaga Tabung Haji (Pilgrims Fund Board) is also in the business of investment. Furthermore, it is questionable why a dedicated television station, Al-Hijrah Media, is necessary, since the two existing government channels could have given programmes on Islam as much air time as required. Yadim, which was formed in the 1970s under the Trustees (Incorporation) Act 1952, appears redundant now since *dakwah* activities are being executed by many other Islamic institutions, including *negeri* religious departments and schools. Even Jakim has its own Dakwah Unit.

Jakim as the Face of Central and Dominant Islam

Whether by popular imagination or scholarly account, Jakim has been considered the most important and powerful bureaucratic organ of Malaysian Islam. It is the face of the statist Islam, and actions or statements coming from its representatives have been headline-grabbing. More than just newsworthy, however, Jakim has its proverbial 'finger in every pie' of social life. In its earlier years, its role was largely to coordinate *sya-*

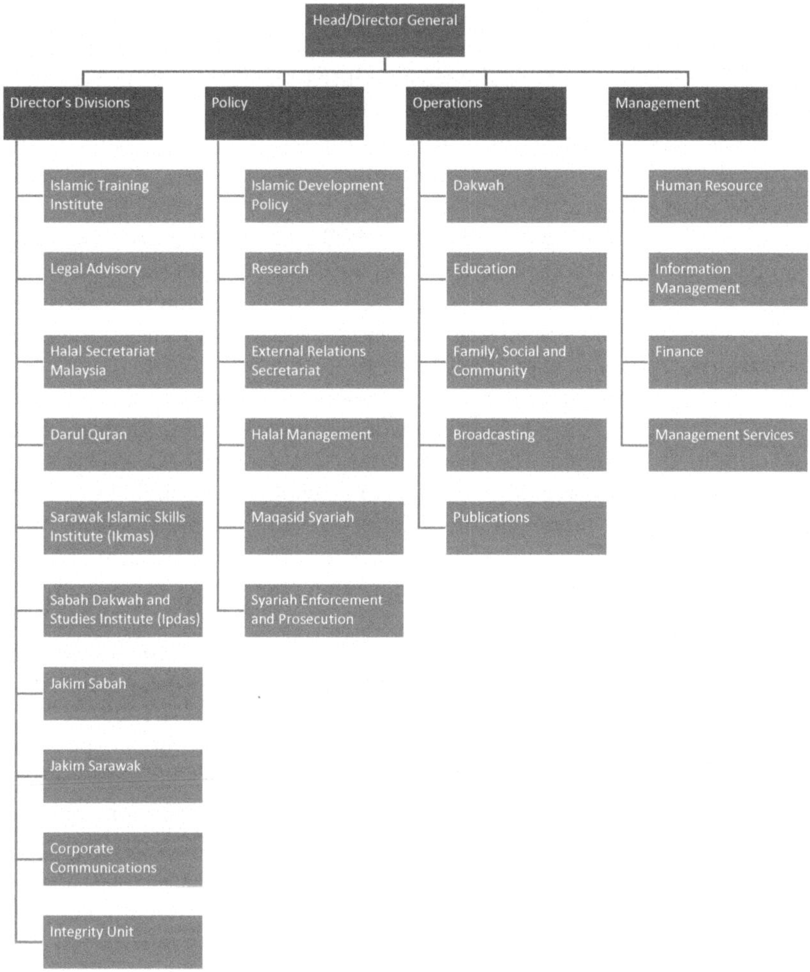

Diagram 3.1 Organisational chart of Jakim (as of April 2019). (Source: "Carta organisasi Jabatan Kemajuan Islam Malaysia (Jakim)", http://www.islam.gov.my/images/images/CARTA_Jakim_DISEMBER_2018-2.jpg, accessed 24 April 2019)

riah legislative reforms as well as to push for the elevation and standardisation of *syariah* law to have uniformity of application and enforcement across all *negeri*. In 1988, Jakim was appointed Secretariat of the Technical Committee on Syariah and Civil Laws, which sought to upgrade the status of *syariah* laws and courts in relation to the civil judiciary (Radzi 1998; Harun 1999). This 'Technical' committee was singularly an important pivot for the overall *syariahtisation* of laws in the country, as will be discussed in the sections below. Since the 2000s, Jakim's authority began to be greatly enlarged, and its presence in social life ubiquitous. There was hardly any area that was not impacted by its presence or interventions.

For instance, when the then spiritual leader of Pas was accused of calling God a gangster, he was made answerable to Jakim (Reme 2002). Its officials also saw fit to publicly reprimand the organiser of a 'I want to touch a dog' event held to get Muslims to appreciate dogs rather than view them as taboo and not to be touched, for upsetting Muslim sensitivities (Malaysiakini 2014a). It has instructed Muslims not to celebrate Valentine's Day (Looi 2011), supported a *fatwa* ban on yoga for Muslims (Hamidah 2008), and prohibited women from dressing like men to "prevent lesbianism" (Aniza 2008). In 2010, Jakim succeeded in getting a court order to stop all religions except Islam from using the word 'Allah' (Jayasankaran 2010). It monitors websites (New Straits Times 2007) and has backed the seizure and banning of books, one of the most controversial being a Malay translation of *Allah, Liberty and Love* by a Canadian author (Rahmah 2012).

In the sphere of sexual morality, Jakim has called in movie stars and directors for purported nudity in their films (The Straits Times 2002). It has issued guidelines on the dos and don'ts of concerts, carnivals and entertainment events (Hamidah 2005). In 2015, it condemned a group of young Muslim women for appearing in a widely circulated video clip of them being embraced by members of a Korean K-pop band at a concert. It also threatened to take action against the concert organisers for not consulting Jakim's entertainment guidelines (Malaysiakini 2015a). In 2018, when some segments of the public chastised a female Malay gymnast who won two gold medals at a prime regional sporting event for her allegedly revealing and body hugging outfits, Jakim asserted its authority by drawing up a dress code for all Muslim women athletes. It has previously defied a directive of the Ministry of Housing and Local Government to wait for guidelines on what constituted 'indecent acts' in public spaces, and ordered its officers to detain unmarried couples caught being publicly intimate (Hamidah 2006). There was a time too when it saw it fit to support raids conducted on those suspected of committing *khalwat* (close proximity) and snooping on people's private lives (Farrah Naz 2006; Syed Nazri 2006).

Elsewhere, Jakim was the first to centralise *halal* certification, with no other body allowed to do so (New Straits Times 2003a). It authorised raids on food outlets suspected of selling fake *halal* food (New Straits Times 2005a), and even indelible ink for use at the general election first needed its certification as *halal* (Hariz 2011; Lee 2012). Jakim has run training programmes for non-Muslim employers of foreign Muslim domestic workers (Farrah Naz and Cheema 2013), sat on a committee regarding the introduction of *quranic* studies in primary schools (New Straits Times 2004b) and selected students from religious schools to receive scholarships from corporations to study medicine in the Middle East (New Straits Times 2010). In the formulation of a national sex education curriculum, Jakim was one of the parties consulted as well (Nurris 2005). Prior to one Islamic conference on HIV/AIDS, some participants wanted this body to vet presentations with references to condoms, transsexualism and sexual orientation, fearing that these were anti-Islam (Farrah and June 2003). Even PM Abdullah Ahmad Badawi once told women's groups that organised a campaign to encourage monogamy to defer their views to this body (Firdaus 2003; Mahadeva 2003).

In aspects of policing, Jakim enforcement officers were allowed to apply for firearms licence after a *negeri* religious department enforcement officer was killed, allegedly in the course of a crackdown operation on a deviant religious sect (New Straits Times 2013). After its proposal to form a '*syariah* police unit' was criticised, the police agreed to loan their officers to assist in Jakim's enforcement of Islamic laws (New Straits Times 2014). Some have recognised its role in combating terrorism, especially the Islamic State threat, as crucial (New Straits Times 2015; Aina and Fairuz 2015).

From late 2014 onwards, however, prominent and high-profile Muslims, including one royal, began to express open and direct criticisms of Jakim. In December 2014, a group of former top Muslim civil service officers, judges, ambassadors and public scholars, who subsequently called themselves G25, wrote an open letter to PM Najib Abdul Razak. The letter noted how "disturbed and deeply dismayed" they were over the application of Islamic laws in the country, especially the way "religious bodies seem[ed] to be asserting authority beyond their jurisdiction", and called for Islamic law to be implemented with the highest standards of justice (Malaysiakini 2014b). Soon afterwards, a member of the group, Tawfik Ismail, son of former Deputy PM Ismail Abdul Rahman, gave an interview and called for Jakim's abolishment on grounds that it was not provided for in the Constitution (Anisah 2015a). Among other criticisms against Jakim was its huge budget which needed to be accounted for (The Edge Markets 2015). Tawfik was subsequently investigated under the charge for sedition (Malaysiakini 2015b). The G25 group then undertook to conduct an audit of Jakim (Malaysiakini 2015c). A month later, the Sultan of Johor also questioned why Jakim needed an allocation of RM1 billion for its operations (Malaysian Insider 2015). To what extent are these criticisms of Jakim justified? The following section examines some of the publicly aired points of contention around Jakim, particularly its budget and how public funds have been spent in the institution's mission for Islamic Development.

Islamic Affairs Budget

The federal budget for Islamic Development is itemised under the PM's Department. This includes the budget for Jakim, Maiwp, Jawi and the FT Mufti's Office (Table 3.2). However, there are also other items such as mosque building, *syariah* court construction or *wakaf* development that are not categorised under Islamic Development of the budget under the PM's Department (Table 3.3). In this study, all items that are related to Islamic expenditure will be counted as expenditure for 'Islamic Affairs'. This means that items categorised as Islamic Development are part of the total budget for Islamic Affairs. Jakim receives the lion's share of the federal budget for Islamic Affairs as seen in Table 3.4. For the ten-year period between 2009 and 2019, its average allocation of the total overall budget for Islamic Affairs was around two-thirds, that is, 66 per cent.

Chart 3.1 shows the total amount allocated for all items under Islamic Affairs. This amount increased yearly from 2009 (RM750 million) and

Table 3.2 Federal budget allocation for Islamic Development (RM) (2018 and 2019)

Year	*2018*	*2019*
Jakim	871,615,400	882,801,000
Maiwp	21,000,000	23,554,600
Jawi	119,001,300	118,553,400
FT Mufti's Office	6,721,400	6,864,500
Total	**1,018,338,100**	**1,031,773,500**

Source: Ministry of Finance (2018, 2019)

Table 3.3 Federal budget for Islamic Affairs (RM) (2019)

Islamic **Development**	**2019**
Jakim	882,801,000
Maiwp	23,554,600
Jawi	118,553,400
FT Mufti's Office	6,864,500
Total (A)	**1,031,773,500**
Other Islamic-related funds	**2019**
Islamic complex/*tahfiz*/Orang Asli Community Centre	9000,000
Mosque building	41,230,000
Halal industry development	800,000
Syariah court construction	22,000,000
Wakaf asset development	16,500,000
JKSM	68,485,000
Jabatan Pendakwaraya Syariah Malaysia (Syariah Prosecution Department)	4,148,300
Mahkamah Syariah Wilayah Persekutuan (FT Syariah Court)	22,383,500
Total (B)	**184,546,800**
Total for Islamic Affairs (A+B)	**1,216,320,300**

Source: Ministry of Finance (2019)

Table 3.4 Jakim's share of the federal Islamic Affairs budget

Year	*Jakim's budget (RM)*	*Islamic Affairs (RM)*	*Jakim's share of Islamic Affairs budget (%)*
2009	500,173,300	751,742,520	66.5
2010	353,387,300[a]	732,026,700	48.3
2011	505,131,900	928,625,630	54.4
2012	630,815,900	932,839,400	67.6
2013	685,592,200	1,009,044,200	67.9
2014	695,445,000	1,026,792,800	67.7
2015	721,700,900	1,002,857,700	72.0
2016	776,802,500	1,211,037,200	64.1
2017	744,947,800	1,069,315,800	69.7
2018	871,615,400	1,249,297,100	69.8
2019	882,801,000	1,216,320,300	72.6
All years	7,368,413,200	11,129,899,350	66.2

Source: Ministry of Finance (2009, 2010, 2011, 2012, 2013, 2014, 2015, 2016, 2017, 2018 and 2019)

[a]Jakim's budget for the year 2010 is exceptionally low. The only explanation for this is that a disproportionately high allocation of RM157 million was given to the development of *wakaf* lands and RM66 million for *syariah* courts construction during the same year. These two items received much lower allocations for the other years

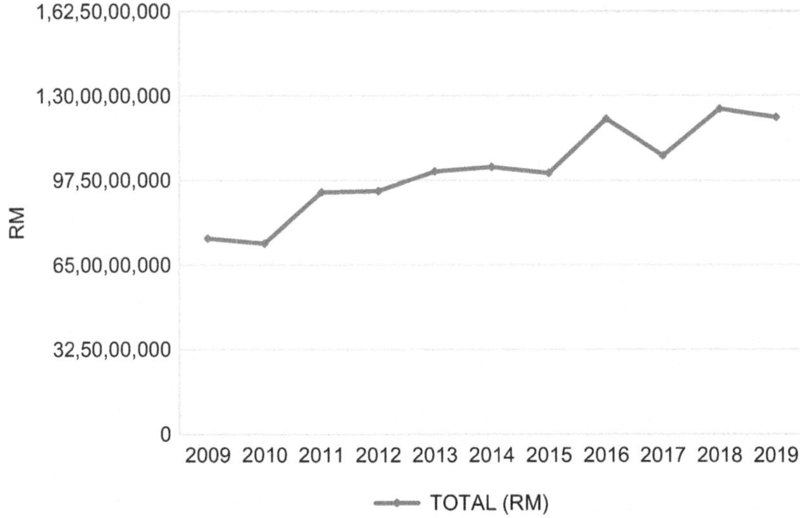

Chart 3.1 Federal allocation for Islamic Affairs (2009–2019). (Source: Ministry of Finance, 2009, 2010, 2011, 2012, 2013, 2014, 2015, 2016, 2017, 2018 and 2019)

peaked in 2018 (RM1.25 billion) before dropping slightly in 2019 (RM1.21 billion) after the newly installed Pakatan Harapan (PH) government assumed power in May 2018.

To put the federal budget for Islamic Development in perspective, Chart 3.2 demonstrates how this allocation is much larger than several important ministries, such as Foreign Affairs and Primary Industries. Chart 3.3 shows that budgets of most public universities are also smaller than that for national Islamic Development.[13] Charts 3.2 and 3.3 allow a comparison between the national budgets allocated by the two different ruling governments; under Barisan Nasional (BN) in 2018 and the newly elected PH administration in 2019. As can be seen, very little changed by way of pattern and prioritisation of Islamic Affairs funding distribution.

How and what Islamic Development funds were spent on elicited much dissatisfaction among certain sections of the Muslim public and non-Muslims whose taxes contributed to the national treasury. In 2015, during a public controversy over Jakim's enormous budget, a news portal used figures from the 2016 budget estimates report published by the Ministry of Finance (MoF) to show where Jakim spent its monies (Anisah 2015b). Drawing on this as well as other data from the 2016 MoF report, Table 3.5

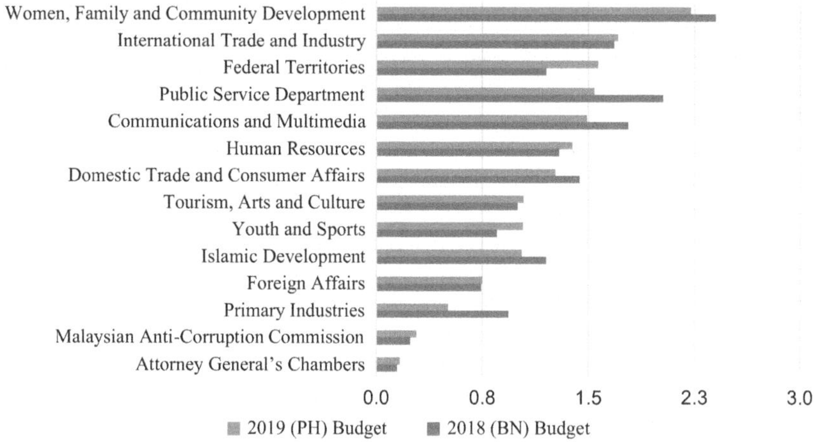

Chart 3.2 Estimated expenditure of federal ministries in comparison to Islamic Development, 2018 and 2019 (RM billion). (Source: Ministry of Finance 2018–2019)

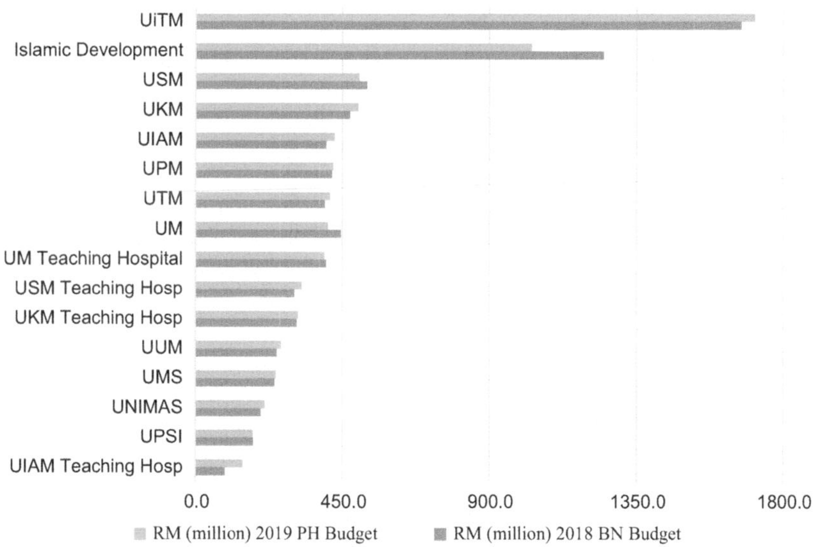

Chart 3.3 Estimated expenditure of public universities in comparison to Islamic Development (RM million) (2018 and 2019). (Source: Ministry of Finance 2018–2019)

Table 3.5 Expenditure of Jakim and other national Islamic institutions (2015)

Type of programme	*Expenditure 2015 (RM)*	*Objectives*	*Outputs*	*No. of staff*
Jakim				
Policy	531,392,000	To thwart attempts to "deviate" Muslims by groups deemed "deviant" and "threatening national security".	6 *negeri*, regional and global-level programmes; 10,000 halal certificates; 2243 research and monitoring efforts; 35 programmes to coordinate the management and development of *fatwa*; 10 programmes to coordinate improvement in the quality of education.	473
Management	125,223,600	To administer payment of staff salaries and coordinate other services.	13,300 processed cash vouchers; 97 per cent officer positions filled; 12 Jakim management meetings; 9000 applications for the *halal* certificate.	181
Jawi	97,374,000	To take charge of Islamic affairs in the FT and prevent Muslims here from flouting religious laws.	60 operations; 500 cases; Management of 88 religious primary schools, 'integrated' primary religious schools, religious secondary schools; 114 quranic and *fardu ain* (essential devotional rules) classes (Kafa).	2141
Human development	24,259,700	To train preachers and scholars; monitor and coordinate Islamic policies; and *dakwah* activities	130 *dakwah* magazines, publications and flyers; 125 programmes on social and Islamic family development.	242

Sabah Jakim	14,934,700	To provide efficient services and administration; boost the quality of human capital, management and administration for society based on Islam's teachings.	135 *dakwah* programmes; 80 Kafa programmes; 60 research programmes; 50 programmes on research and solidifying of *akidah* (faith); 55 programmes at Centre for Islamic Training; 65 publication and public relations programme.	91
Sarawak Jakim	10,593,800	To provide efficient, effective and quality services and management; spread *dakwah*; and strengthen Islam.	270 *dakwah* programmes; 50 secretariat and management programmes; 60 research programmes; 86 Sarawak Training Centre programmes; 44 Malaysian Islamic Skills Institute Sarawak programmes.	57
Darul Quran	8,103,100	To train Malaysian secondary school certificate holders to understand and memorise the Quran, as well as produce preachers and scholars.	559 *huffaz* (memorisers of the Quran); 38 *huffaz* trained in reciting the Quran at undergraduate studies level; 30 participants in a short-term training programme for a *Tarannum Al-Quran* higher certificate; 30 participants in a short-term Basics of *Qiraat* programme open to Malaysian secondary school leavers.	188
Institut Latihan Islam Malaysia (Ilim, Malaysian Islamic Training Institute)	7,194,000	To train civil servants tasked with Islamic affairs to be "religious, competent and courageous in facing challenges".	8000 participants selected for its courses; 160 courses, and one study on the outcome of these courses; One outcome study	129

(continued)

Table 3.5 (continued)

Type of programme	*Expenditure 2015 (RM)*	*Objectives*	*Outputs*	*No. of staff*
Other Agencies				
Jawhar	11,661,500	To ensure planning, coordination and implementation of policy and development programmes of *wakaf*, *zakat*, *mal* and *hajj* institutions in national development remain relevant and monitored more efficiently for the betterment of the *ummah*.	Development of two *waqaf* estates; Three meetings, workshops and seminars; Two international-level sharing and coordinating programmes; Five coordination programmes between Jawhar, SIRCs and other agencies; One published manual.	76
FT Mufti's Office	3,379,200	Serves as advisory to King in all aspects of the Islamic faith, issues "complete and truthful" *fatwa* based on Islamic law and experience, coordinates issuing of *fatwa* with other States, and determines astronomical coordinates for prayers.	19 publications; 11 discussion workshops on current issues; 12 programmes for strengthening of *fatwa*; Meeting with 3000 certificates holders for religious teaching; 4000 participants at serial programme on enlightenment.	45

Maiwp	14,700,000	As a financial institution, to solve problems of Muslim society within the FT through distributive and physical development schemes.	RM518,245,000 *zakat* collected; 157,683 *zakat* payers; 142 skills and guidance training; One youth shelter.	Not available (N.A.)
Islamic training complex/*tahfiz*/Orang Asli Community Centre	4,280,000			N.A.
Construction of mosque/*surau* and repairs and upgrading	6,920,000			N.A.
Construction of religious schools	4,822,700			N.A.
Centre for *halal* research and study	22,400,000			N.A.
Construction of *syariah* courts	9000,000			N.A.
Wakaf asset development	9,923,000			N.A.

Source: Ministry of Finance (2016, 89–132) and adapted from Anisah (2015b)

details Jakim's estimated expenditure for 2015, and that of other federal religious institutions for the same year. Given that subsequent budget reports from the MoF have not itemised government spending, the 2015 figures provide the closest picture of where this body's monies have gone.

Programmes under the rubric of 'Policy', whose stated goal was to prevent and eliminate national security threats like religious 'deviant' groups, spent the largest amount at RM500 million. This funded 6 subnational-level, regional and international programmes, 2243 research and monitoring efforts, 35 programmes for *fatwa* development, issuance of *halal* certificates for businesses and programmes to improve religious education. Staff salaries and management expenses amounting to RM125 million were the next highest expenditure, followed by Jawi which spent just under RM100 million. The latter focused on the enforcement of the *syariah* criminal offences law and the administration and funding of religious schools. The budget also revealed that Jakim, despite being a federal institution, had a presence in Sabah and Sarawak, two *negeri* that do not share the same colonial history and hence religious bureaucracy structures, as their Peninsular Malaysian counterparts. Their estimated expenditure of RM14 million (Sabah) and RM10 million (Sarawak) appears to have gone largely to *dakwah* programmes. Jakim's remaining monies was for training activities by Darul Quran (RM8 million) and the Malaysian Islamic Training Institute (RM7 million).

Besides Jakim, federal Islamic Development funding was also channelled to Jawhar for *wakaf*, *zakat* and *hajj* development, the FT Mufti's Office and the Maiwp. It also supported the construction of mosques, schools, a research centre for *halal* study, *syariah* courts, *wakaf* development, and an Islamic training and community complex for the Orang Asli (indigenous peoples of Peninsular Malaysia). This amounted to between RM3 million and RM22 million.

Courts and the Judiciary

The structures detailed above cover only the non-judicial religious bureaucratic institutions in the country. There are also judicial, religious bureaucratic institutions within the realm of law and courts (Steiner 2018, 39–51). The *syariah* courts system has always been a focus of Malay nationalists, especially to redress what they have perceived as the subordinate status of these courts attributed to the British legacy. Attempts to reform the colonial vestige of 'inferior' and lower-placed religious courts that adjudicated Islamic matters began from the early 1970s, but it was only in 1988 that the Parliament passed an important amendment to the Constitution, resulting in the elevated status of *syariah* courts on par with civil courts. This was largely how the Divine Bureaucracy around *syariah* laws, courts and judicialisation came to be.

Early efforts at scrutinising the status of *syariah* laws emerged from the federal centre. Specifically, MKI and Maiwp formed a special committee in 1974 to study, frame and formulate legislation on the administration of Islamic laws in the FT of Kuala Lumpur. An early mover of *syariah* courts reform was Syed Nasir Ismail, an Umno Member of Parliament from Johor, known for leading efforts to get the Malay language adopted as the medium of instruction in schools and for official business. He headed the MKI committee to study the status of *syariah* and *kadi* (judge) courts in 1972. In 1981, another committee was formed, but at the level of administrators and chaired by a representative from the Attorney-General's Chambers. However, its proposed reforms were limited to simply replicating the civil court structure such that there would be a *syariah* lower court, high court and appeal court.[14] This proposal also required Constitutions of each *negeri* be amended, new enactments passed, and laws on court procedures and evidence applied.

Having more *syariah* laws on the statute books gave greater powers to the *syariah* court in terms of its relevance and scope of judicialisation. The prelude to this goal and concurrent advocacy was demanding that *syariah* courts and judges be upgraded to the same level as their civil counterparts, as well as, importantly, to delimit the jurisdictions of each court system. The *syariah* legal and judicial system was to be the latchkey for Muslim advocates, professionals in government and Umno to further the Malay nationalist agenda (Hussein 1988, 635–634). All that remained was having a crucial moment to elevate the cause. That moment came in 1988. In the late 1980s, the Mahathir-led administration was under pressure by various quarters, not just from the opposition political parties but also from within Umno itself (Shamsul 1988; Funston 1988). More importantly, the judiciary—including the Supreme Court[15]—had been making unfavourable judgements in several key government-related lawsuits. These developments led to a proposed constitutional amendment to limit the powers of the judiciary, which PM Mahathir alleged had overstepped its authority. The collateral beneficiary of this crisis was the *syariah* courts system.

In a move to strengthen the powers of the federal government in relation to the judiciary, this proposed amendment was debated in Parliament in March 1988. A large part of the debate focused on changes to Section 8 of Article 121 pertaining to the powers of the judiciary. This was the most controversial part of PM Mahathir's lengthy speech on the need to amend several articles in the Constitution, as it involved curtailing judicial powers of interpretation. In the same vein, a new section was proposed for inclusion in Article 121; this was Section 1(A), which would remove the jurisdiction of the civil court over all matters within the *syariah* court's jurisdiction (Malaysia 1988a, 1364) The inclusion of this amendment seemed incidental, or perhaps the plan had been in the works for some time. Regardless, this move could not have been timed any better.

Mahathir was tactically planning to weaken the judiciary and would have courted widespread criticism had he not thrown in the 'Islamic' card, which also won him support from Malay-Muslim lawmakers. While there were intense debates on his Section 8 proposal, there was none on Section 1(A), save for one Member of Parliament who supported the move and only expressed concern that there could be a "miscarriage of justice" if *syariah* judges were not given proper training (Malaysia 1988a, 1364).[16] When passed, the amendments served to restrict the jurisdictional powers of all courts in the country. However, crucially with respect to Islam, the High Courts were also stripped of their powers over any matter that fell within the jurisdiction of *syariah* courts (Lee 2017, 85).

The Aftermath of Article 121(1)(A)

On 18 March 1988, the Parliament approved the inclusion of Article 121(1)(A) into the Federal Constitution. The spirit of the constitutional amendment was immediately translated to mean that *syariah* courts would be upgraded and expanded in numbers. It followed that sufficient and more *syariah* laws were needed for use by these courts (Abdul Monir 2016, 78). This in turn necessitated a specialised committee to study and formulate new legislation,[17] leading to the establishment of the hitherto mentioned, Technical Committee on Syariah and Civil Laws. Renowned legal expert, Ahmad Ibrahim, was brought in to lead the committee,[18] with Baheis as its Secretariat.

Syariah law reform was gradual rather than radical, and fully mediated by the structures of the bureaucracy. The Technical Committee studied all laws in relation to the administration of Islam, and prepared drafts of proposed legislation for deliberation by State Legal Advisers and heads of Islamic religious departments. Later, this group was enlarged to include the participation of all *negeri mufti*, *syariah* court chief judges and representatives of the SIRCs.[19] Its proposals had to be first submitted to and approved by the Attorney General's Chambers before being tabled in Parliament or the State Assemblies. Critically, the Technical Committee had suggested that in the determination of authority over Islam, there should be a separation of powers and differentiation of functions between the SIRC, the *mufti* and the *syariah* courts (Abdul Monir 2016, 83).

It took around seven years for the Technical Committee's efforts to start bearing fruit. In 1995, the federal government announced that towards upgrading the status of *syariah* courts and attracting more university graduates to enlist in *negeri* religious bureaucracies, it would review salary scales, monetary benefits and promotion prospects of *syariah* personnel. Furthermore, by placing their service scheme under the federal Public Service Department, their salaries would be higher than that of *negeri*-level officers (New Straits Times 1995a).[20] In 1996, Mahathir declared that *syariah* court administration would be completely revamped to introduce, amongst others, a common-user service scheme for *syariah* court personnel. Federal and *negeri* governments would enter into a formal agreement to decide on provisions for appointments, confirmation, pensions, promotions and disciplinary matters of these officers.

He also announced that a *syariah* justice department would be created and placed under the PM's Department (New Straits Times 1996a).[21] Accordingly, all officers of *negeri syariah* courts—from judges and prosecuting officers to clerks—would come under this department, subsequently named Jabatan Kehakiman Syariah Malaysia (JKSM, Syariah Judicial Department of Malaysia). *Syariah* judges, *kadi* and other court officials had to undergo training at the International Islamic University Malaysia to learn how to adapt civil court procedures to *syariah* court proceedings. On 1 January 1997, Baheis was upgraded into Jakim, a full-fledged federal religious department (New Straits Times 1996b).[22] Policy changes around *syariah* court restructuring appeared to be one of the earliest 'aggressive' moves by the central government to rein in the authority of *negeri* religious bureaucracies and eventually heralded the vast growth and strengthening of federal Islamic institutions.

Following Cabinet approval in July 1996, JKSM was officially established in March 1998. A joint scheme was required because the *syariah* judiciary lacked the necessary trained personnel, particularly judges, to fill the positions of the now expanded courts system. Many may have had the prerequisite religious qualifications, but not what was needed to perform duties as judges based on the new protocol and evidentiary procedures that were almost wholly adopted from civil law (Moustafa 2018, 45–46; Abdul Monir 2016, 99). Nevertheless, not all *negeri* agreed to be part of the joint scheme. Johor, Kedah, Kelantan, Perak, Pahang, Terengganu and Sarawak opted to retain their *syariah* courts and employment of their own officials for protecting *negeri* rights and autonomy.

JKSM's stated mission was to standardise the administration of the Islamic justice system and laws associated with it and ensure that all *negeri* used the joint service scheme for *syariah* administrators. It also had to oversee the running of the Syariah Appeal Court and employ the wide usage of information technology to smoothen administration.[23] In its later years, JKSM focused only on the various *negeri* under the joint scheme. Nevertheless, it is symbolically associated with the centralisation of the *syariah* judiciary, akin to a "pseudo-Federal mechanism" that allowed for centralisation of Islam to occur (Hamayotsu 2003, 62). The advancement of the *syariah* judiciary is almost always identified as the epitome of state Islamisation.

Significantly, although *syariah* judicial institutions have been elevated through federal efforts, most of these actions were not directly related to the original mission of upgrading the status of the *syariah* courts system. Instead, this system has relied on plentitude of resources and material symbols to make its presence known. There are now, for instance, grandiose *syariah* court complexes in all *negeri*, with many outdoing the appearance of civil court complexes. Moreover, JKSM's main function was to coordinate the hearing of all appeal cases, but the number handled each year has been very small compared to that of civil courts.[24] To be sure, the main outcome of this exercise of augmenting the *syariah* courts system has been the multiplication of these religious courts and their locations, outstripping the number of civil courts which have a longer history (see Table 3.6). Also, criminal cases registered with the *syariah* courts only comprise 1 per cent of the number of criminal cases handled by its civil counterparts (Table 3.7); while *syariah* civil (*mal*) cases constitute 10 per cent of all civil cases (Table 3.8).

A noteworthy initiative of JKSM has been its formation of the Bahagian Sokongan Keluarga (BSK, Family Support Division). This was introduced in 2008 to enhance the enforcement of *nafkah* (maintenance) court orders in family or marital cases. There was, however, no proposal to deal with

Table 3.6 Number of civil and *syariah* courts by *negeri*

	Civil courts	Syariah *courts*
Perlis	2	9
Kedah	16	17
Penang	9	16
Perak	25	44
Selangor	25	23
Federal Territories	7	25
Negeri Sembilan	12	15
Melaka	7	12
Johor	22	15
Pahang	16	20
Terengganu	11	16
Kelantan	15	17
Sabah	38	18
Sarawak	45	20
Total	**250**	**267**

Source: Lower courts: http://www.kehakiman.gov.my/ms/mahkamah/mahkamah-rendah/lokasi-dan-alamat-mahkamah-rendah-di-seluruh-malaysia; High Courts: http://www.kehakiman.gov.my/ms/mahkamah/mahkamah-tinggi/lokasi-dan-alamat-mahkamah-tinggi-di-seluruh-malaysia; Appeal and Federal Courts: http://www.kehakiman.gov.my/ms/mahkamah/mahkamah-rayuan/pejabat-pendaftaran-mahkamah-rayuan-malaysia

Table 3.7 Criminal cases registered in civil and *syariah* courts

Year	*Civil courts*	*Syariah courts*	*Syariah criminal cases as % of criminal cases in civil court*
2014	1,741,667	18,148	1.04
2015	1,626,623	19,531	1.20
2016	1,267,176	24,531	1.94
2017[a]	1,970,612	20,859	1.06

Source: For civil cases, 'Monthly statistics report on civil and criminal cases', http://www.kehakiman.gov.my; for Syariah cases, http://www.data.gov.my/data/ms_MY/dataset/statistik-daftar-kes-jenayah-mahkamah-syariah-seluruh-malaysia-2013-2017, 6 April 2019

[a]Figures for the months of February to April were not recorded on the official portal

such criminal breaches committed by errant husbands, despite the law imposing a prison sentence for those guilty of contempt of court.[25] Besides managing the above-mentioned *nafkah* fund, the BSK acts as the executing agency to ensure compliance with court orders. It has been introduced in all *negeri*, and compiles *nafkah* statistics to monitor its collection suc-

Table 3.8 Civil cases registered in civil and *syariah* courts

Year	*Civil courts*	Syariah *courts*	Syariah *civil cases as % of civil cases in civil court*
2014	466,223	94,993	20.4
2015	464,836	100,773	21.7
2016	395,759	104,770	26.5
2017	435,525	105,372	24.2

Source: For cases in civil courts, 'Monthly statistics report on civil and criminal cases', http://www.kehakiman.gov.my; for Syariah cases, http://www.data.gov.my/data/ms_MY/dataset/statistik-pendaftaran-kes-mal-mahkamah-syariah-seluruh-malaysia, 6 April 2019

cess rate. It also provides family counselling and legal advice (JKSM 2011, 50). In 2011, the BSK resolved 55.2 per cent of such cases that it managed in this manner (JKSM 2011, 56), and improved this figure to 70.2 per cent in 2014 (JKSM 2014, 83).

The payment of advance *nafkah* required a revolving fund to be established, and this was dependent on grants as well as payments collected from errant parties. The repayment record, however, has not been impressive. For example, in 2011, BSK collected only 6 per cent of the amount it disbursed as advance *nafkah* (JKSM 2011, 60); while this collection rate increased to 15 per cent in 2014 (JKSM 2014, 80–81), overall it is still very small. Its enforcement unit has had a mixed record across *negeri* where compliance is concerned. The best performer was Pahang (62.5 per cent), and the worst, Johor (2.7 per cent) (JKSM 2011, 61). It would seem that, overall, male negligence in relation to maintenance payments has remained a problem and the question is whether, even as the BSK has been formed to benefit Muslim women, this may also be transferring private male responsibility to the state.[26]

Corporatisation of Religious Resources

As Islamic scholars, policymakers and bureaucrats trained their focus and knowledge on the holistic Islamic system as the ideal condition for Muslims, they also became aware of the fiscal potential of Islam. Sloane-White (2017) first introduced the notion of "corporate Sharia" as a space for "religion making", a "third space" that is neither "fully 'public' nor in any way 'private'" (17). *Zakat,* the obligatory tax for Muslims, for example, has been found to be not only a simple tithe collection for charitable purposes, but also an elaborate form of lucrative taxation based on multiple categories of assets. Other resources for monetisation are *wakaf*, a concept where believers bequeath land and other assets as a trust to fulfil some of Islam's altruistic goals, and *baitulmal* (Islamic treasury), which reinforces the notion that in the name of Islam, a pool of funds and wealth can also be accumulated to benefit Muslims.

While *zakat*, *wakaf* and *baitulmal* are traditional areas within the jurisdiction of the religious bureaucracy, dating from precolonial and colonial times, another emerging corporate Islamic bureaucracy feature is the monopoly, control, certification and capitalisation of the *halal* economy. Hence, the far-reaching bureaucratisation of Islamic affairs did not just begin or end with civil administration and the judicial system, but has extended too into areas of Islamic monetisation, potentially a veritable movement towards 'Islam Incorporated'. These four areas of Islamic economic administration were substantially reformed and restructured in post-1980s Malaysia to reflect a corporatisation model of money wealth around Islam. While the *zakat*, *wakaf* and *baitulmal* domains have remained within the purview of the *negeri* Islamic bureaucracy, *halal*-isation has been dominated by the federal Islamic bureaucracy as well as various other federal institutions not directly connected with Islam.

Zakat

One of the five pillars of Islam is the mandatory payment of *zakat*. Traditionally, this is made to mosques officials during festivities, most commonly during the *Aidul Fitri* celebrations at the end of Ramadan, the fasting month. Muslims grow up with the idea that *zakat* is an essential component of the Islamic faith. The giving of alms or charity is considered an act of worship and thus most Muslims pay their annual *zakat* at the end of Ramadan. This level of knowledge and practice of *zakat* is considered minimal and rudimentary by present-day *syariah* specialists.

Under their direction, *zakat* is now considered "obligatory charity" (Azman et al. 2012, 36) and seen as an essential part of an "Islamic fiscal policy" (Nik Mustapha 1987, 48). It has aspects of purification as one's possessions are donated as a social justice contribution. There is obligatory taxation on one's wealth (*zakat mal*) and a form of individual gifts extended to the poor (*zakat fitrah*). There are two economic aspects of *zakat* to consider and administer. Collection must be done by a designated collector (*amil*); disbursement must go to only eight categories of recipients (*asnaf*), people regarded as deserving of the *zakat*.[27] These categories relate to the poor and needy (or in Arabic, *fuqara, wal masakin)*, including those in debt (*al-gharimin)*, slavery or bondage (*al-riqab*), stranded travellers (*ibnu sabil*), converts to Islam (*muallaf*) and those who serve in the path of Allah to defend and uphold the religion (*fisabilillah*). A portion of *zakat* can also go to the *amil* themselves.

The task of administering *zakat* in every *negeri* lies solely with the respective SIRCs. Traditionally, the designated *amil* or village *imam* (head of prayer) collected payment during Ramadan. During the early years, *zakat* categorisation was not consistent, with most *negeri* collecting only *zakat fitrah* or *zakat* based on paddy harvest (*zakat padi*). In Kedah and Perlis, *zakat padi* comprised almost 100 per cent of *zakat* collection (Suhaili et al. 2013, 41), where only those who worked the land—usually poor tenants and not landowners—contributed (Nik Mustapha 1987, 54–58). Such unfairness made collection problematic and led to under-declarations or other means of protest to get around the system, which was inefficiently managed and burdened the poor rather than letting them benefit from such charity (Scott 1987, 424–437). These flaws were blamed on public ignorance of what *zakat* entailed, administrative inefficiency and a shortage of staff, all which led to a disproportionate amount of the collection going to *zakat* administration rather than to the needy (Azman et al. 2012; Suhaili et al. 2013, 42).

After the 1990s, efforts to make *zakat* collection more efficient and to raise the number of *zakat* payers took a more serious and determined turn, coinciding with the *Penerapan Nilai-Nilai Islam* phase that began in 1985 and Mahathir's corporatisation policy that was introduced in 1991. The idea of specifically corporatising *zakat* has been credited to the then Pahang Chief Minister Abdul Rahim Abu Bakar[28] and Minister-in-Charge of Islamic Affairs, Mohd Yusof Noor (Suhaili et al. 2013, 43). A sum of RM1 million was allocated for a feasibility study by an accounting firm, Coopers and Lybrand, and as paid-up capital to start a company called Hartasuci Sdn Bhd that would become a *fatwa*-sanctioned *amil* (Abdul Rahim Bakar 2006, 115). Unsurprisingly, this model proposal came from Maiwp after the feasibility study it endorsed projected that *zakat* collection in FT could be increased to RM60 million among 45,000 payers if the institution underwent a corporatisation exercise (Abdul Rahim Bakar 2006, 115).

The *Pusat Pungutan Zakat* (PPZ, Zakat Collection Centre) formed in 1990 was the earliest corporation to collect *zakat* for the FT SIRC. The Penang SIRC followed in 1994 with its *zakat* company, Pusat Urus Zakat, which was, in turn, followed by the Selangor's Pusat Zakat Selangor. Melaka set up its corporatised Pusat Zakat in 2001 (Azman et al. 2012, 38). Perlis, Perak, Johor, Terengganu and Kelantan chose to retain control of *zakat* collection and distribution within their SIRCs. FT, Melaka, Negeri Sembilan and Pahang partially corporatised with private companies undertaking only *zakat* collection. The rest of the *negeri*, Selangor, Penang, Sabah, Sarawak and Kedah, privatised both the collection and distribution of *zakat* by companies owned by their respective SIRCs (PPZ-Maiwp 2017, 80). These variations reflect again the importance and degree of rights and autonomy exercised by those in power within each *negeri*.

The differentiation in *zakat* classification is now less ambiguous and the sources of *zakat* payment more extensive. There was a shift from the predominance of *zakat fitrah* and *zakat padi* to income and business earnings *zakat*, collectively known as *zakal al-mal* (Nik Mustapha 1987, 54). By 2008, *zakat fitrah* contributed only RM83.87 million—a mere 1 per cent—out of the almost RM1 billion total *zakat* collected nationally (Suhaili et al. 2013, 44–45). In terms of *zakat* collection, the FT PPZ lists eight mandatory *zakat* sources: income, business, savings, stocks and shares, employees provident funds, gold, silver and agricultural produce.[29]

The increased collection of *zakat* in every *negeri* has been impressive, reaching a combined total of almost RM3 billion by 2017 (Chart 3.4). Selangor's collection was the largest, increasingly rapidly from less than

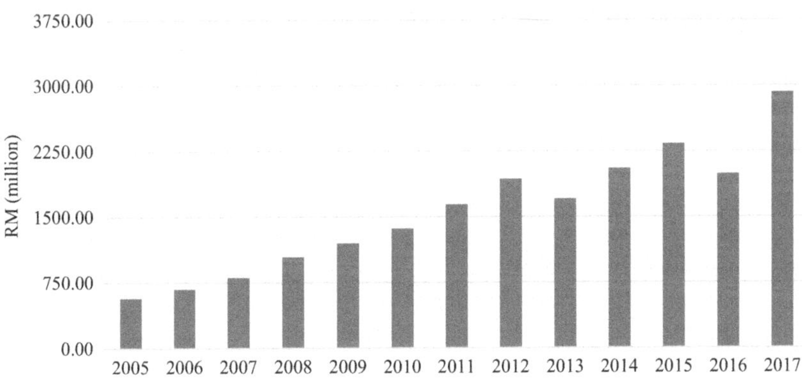

Chart 3.4 *Zakat* collection for all *negeri* (2005–2017). (Source: PPZ-Maiwp 2011, 2017)

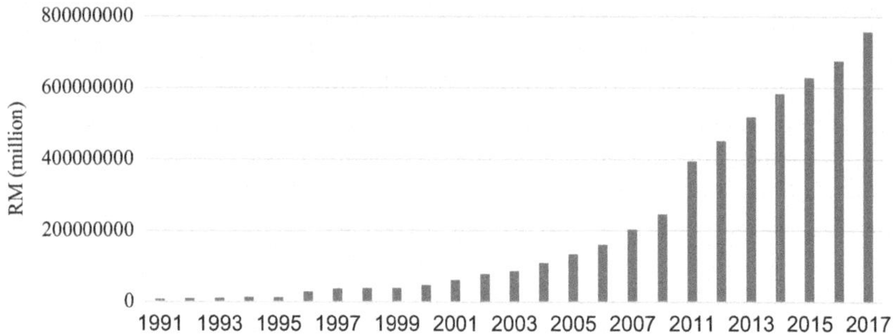

Chart 3.5 *Zakat* collection in Selangor by year. (Source: Data for 1991–2008 from Wan Marhaini (2012, 327–330); data for 2011–2017 from Lembaga Zakat Selangor (2015, 2016, 2017, 2018))

RM10 million in 1991 to over RM700 million in 2017 (Chart 3.5). Besides Selangor, the highest collection came from two other urban *negeri*: FT and Johor. As a comparison, the federal government collected RM11.7 billion in individual taxes in 2007 (Narayanan 2007, 14), while total *zakat* collection for all *negeri* was RM0.81 billion, that is, about 7 per cent of total individual income tax revenue. There is a large difference between government taxation and *zakat* payment as the former is purpose-based (to promote socio-economic development), while the latter (at RM1 billion in 2008) is beneficiary-based (only to the designated eight groups of *asnaf*).

The disbursement pattern of *zakat* is another feature that has raised concern among those following the trajectory of this institution in Malaysia (Hairunnizam et al. 2009; Md Hairi 2009; Wan Marhaini 2012, 258–263). The principles of disbursing *zakat* are quite strict. Besides limiting the *asnaf* to the eight categories mentioned, the funds must be disbursed immediately. Furthermore, *zakat* collected from one area should preferably be spent on *asnaf* living in the same area, disbursement must be maximised to deliver both spiritual and economic benefits and *zakat* should be used to ultimately eradicate economic inequality (Nik Mustapha 1987, 59). To what extent these principles are followed is unclear, but it would appear that allocations are not distributed equally to all eight groups, administration costs remain high and a substantial amount of funds collected are undistributed (Md Hairi 2009, 13–22; Wan Marhaini 2012, 241–263).

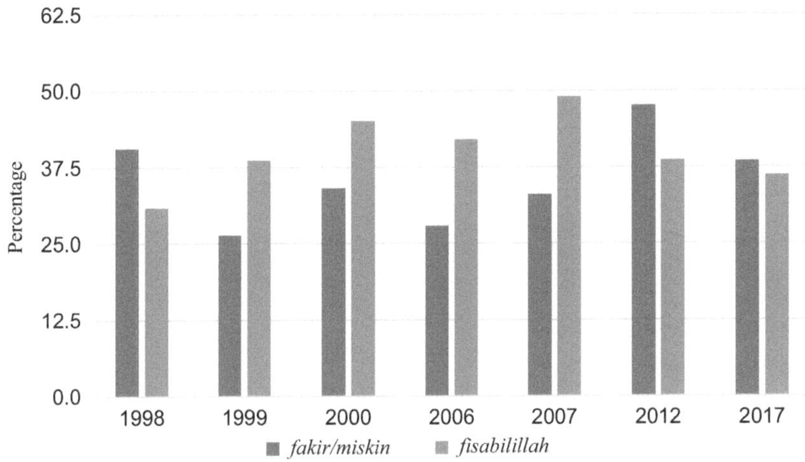

Chart 3.6 Percentage distribution of *zakat* between the poor (*fakir/miskin*) and those in the cause of Islam (*fisabilillah*) in FT (various years). (Source: PPZ-Maiwp Annual Reports, 1998–2017)

In terms of allocation, the group *fisabilillah*—not the poor (*fakir* and *miskin*, or *al-fuqara* and *al-masakin*)—receives the largest share of disbursements in at least five *negeri*, while the *amil* (the *zakat* collection company) also gets a significant share (Md Hairi 2009, 21). This is justified on grounds that *fisabilillah* advances the cause of Islam through many ways, one of the most important being the innovative and precise use of capital for schools, universities and Islamic economic development foundations (Sloane-White 2017, 157). The poor appear to be competing with those in the cause of *jihad* as far as *zakat* distribution funds are concerned. Charts 3.6 and 3.7 indicate how funds under corporatised *zakat* of Maiwp and non-corporatised *zakat* of the Kelantan SIRC have been distributed between the *fakir/miskin* and *fisabilillah*. *Fisabilillah* recipients appeared to receive proportionately more of the funds under Maiwp from 1999, though this amount dipped slightly in 2012 and 2017 (Chart 3.7). The *fakir/miskin* are the bigger beneficiaries under the Kelantan SIRC, especially from the year 2007 onwards (Chart 3.7).

The channelling of money to the *fisabilillah* category is controversial. It covers a wide and somewhat questionable category of recipients, as these could include *dakwah* activities by organisations and individuals, *dakwah*

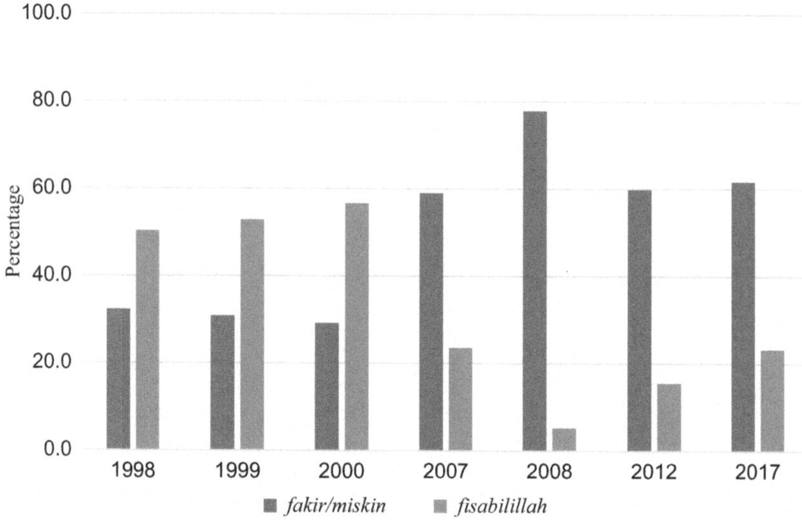

Chart 3.7 Percentage distribution of *zakat* to the poor (*fakir/miskin*) and those in the cause of Islam (*fisabilillah*) in Kelantan (various years). (Source: PPZ-Maiwp Annual Reports, 1998–2017)

seminars and publications (PPZ-Maiwp 2005, 117) and in the most extreme case, '*jihad*', the Islamic call to war (Patmawati 2007, 150). A more controversial outfit that received funds from the Maiwp *zakat* funds was the Institute of Strategic Islamic Research Malaysia (Iksim). This outfit was apparently established in 2012 to redress the LGBT issue as well as attack those whom it claimed to be liberals and pluralists or those whom it considered to be a threat to the Muslim *akidah*. A member of the G25 called for its disbandment in 2018, as the institution had allegedly been mainly maligning other Muslims "as apostates and liberals" and brainwashing students and government officers to its extremist thinking (Arfa 2018).

In 2000, the *fisabilillah* in FT received 45 per cent of its *zakat* disbursement and, in 2017, it received 36 per cent of the *zakat* collection of Maiwp, making it the recipient with the highest proportion of *zakat* allocation (PPZ-Maiwp 2001, 78; 2017, 83). In Selangor, RM14 million of its *fisabilillah* allocation went to salaries of religious teachers and officers, RM6 million to the construction and refurbishment of religious institutions and RM12 million to the Kolej University Islam Antarabangsa Selangor (Wan Marhaini 2012, 355–358). Perlis, the smallest *negeri* in the country, had the largest *zakat* allocation for *fisabilillah* at 59 per cent, followed by Johor at 43.2 per cent. The largest allocation in Kelantan (40 per cent), on the other hand, went to the *amil* (Wan Marhaini 2012, 341–345).

Wakaf

Another area for capital accumulation in the administration of Islam is *wakaf* (Ar. *waqafa*). This is a type of gift, usually in the form of physical assets for specific usage by an intended beneficiary. A property given as *wakaf* cannot be passed on, inherited, transacted, mortgaged, rented or gifted in any form (Asmak 2009, 115–118). It must go to a beneficiary in its existing form, and be used for charitable purposes to receive divine blessings (Ashraf and Abdullaah 2014, 160–1). Anyone aged 18 and above can endow their property as *wakaf* in accordance with the Selangor Wakaf Enactment 1999, and gifts can either be as '*wakaf am*' or '*wakaf khas*'. *Wakaf* is not mentioned in the Quran, but believers still consider this as an obligation given that Islam continuously emphasises the principle of redistributing wealth.

Etymologically, the Arabic word for *wakaf* relates it to the concept of 'prevention' and 'avoidance' (Asmak 2009, 114), or if transliterated from Arabic, 'pausing'. These metaphors can be associated with the idea of controlling greed by giving a permanent endowment under Allah's possession for charity and the good of Islam. Although *wakaf* traditionally involved bequeathing immovable properties—as moveable properties do not last forever—there have been theological debates on this with some now agreeing that movable properties may also be contributed as *wakaf* (Fathullah and Jasni 2017). In Malaysia, this idea is accepted, having been endorsed via a *fatwa* issued by the National Fatwa Committee in 2007 (Asmak 2009, 120).

The sole trustee of *wakaf* endowments is the SIRC of each *negeri*. As with *zakat* management, *wakaf* management has also been thought to suffer from the meagre capacity of the SIRCs such that the potential of its untapped wealth remains under-maximised. Among the problems that have been identified with *wakaf* management and capitalisation are (1) improper conduct of *wakaf* registration, ownership and classification,[30] (2) the lack of capital for its development, and an absence of a system to generate revenue from its rentals, (3) most *wakaf* assets are located in rural areas which have little potential for development, (4) the shortage of personnel for its management and development, (5) the absence of a comprehensive database and (6) the illegal occupation of many *wakaf* lands (Che Zuina et al. 2015, 615–617).

In Malaysia, *wakaf* is conventionally classified as lands for building mosques, *surau* (community prayer hall), cemeteries, religious schools, charity institutions and orphanages. In Selangor, most registered *wakaf* lands (72 per cent) are used for mosques and *surau* (Shabbir 2018, 41). Newer thinking around *wakaf* land use has moved away from conventional notions to more productive purposes such as income-generating initiatives, residential and even commercial projects, not just as "a form of worship" but as "vital tools to increase wealth" (Shabbir 2018, 52–53). This explains the three types of *wakaf* accepted here today: physical, corporate and cash.

In addition to land for schools, mosques and other buildings, physical *wakaf* encompasses lands on which commercial buildings are situated, and then rented out to generate earnings that are channelled to qualified recipients. A newer concept, '*wakaf korporat*' (corporate wakaf) (Abd Shakor 2011), refers to moveable assets as in cash, shares and dividends managed by corporate entities or in collaboration with companies and *wakaf* authorities (Ashraf and Abdullaah 2014, 161–162). Here, *wakaf* are moveable assets held by trustees in the form of private companies, which also act as the beneficiary of such *wakaf*. Cash *wakaf* is the most recent and possibly the most feasible form of endowment best suited to today's economic contexts. It allows funds to be contributed to an account managed by a representative who oversees its uses for religious and charitable purposes (Farhanah et al. 2015, 102). Moreover, the introduction of cash *wakaf* has widened the possibility for *wakaf* to be used as a financial investment instrument in the form of *sukuk* (Islamic bonds), *syariah*-compliant equities, unit trusts and the whole gamut of financial products made available through the promotion of an Islamic economy (Securities Commission Malaysia 2017).

The corporatisation of *wakaf* asset management took longer to take root compared to that of *zakat*, which started being privatised in the early 1990s. The enactments on *wakaf* that specifically recognised the validity of cash *wakaf* were only passed in the late 1990s. Selangor was the first to have such a law in 1999, allowing for *wakaf* to be in the form of immovable or movable assets, and *wakaf* shares to be offered in exchange for personal endowment of *wakaf* to the SIRCs. This means that the donor buys *wakaf* shares to be endowed to the beneficiary (usually the SIRCs) and allows these shares to be invested in perpetuity. Melaka and Negri

Sembilan adopted similar legislation in 2005, followed by other *negeri* via *fatwa* approving these enactments (Fathullah and Jasni 2017, 236–241).

Plans to institutionalise *wakaf* as a corporate conglomerate at the national level were first raised in 1995, when it was proposed that all SIRCs yield their *wakaf* lands to this national corporation for development.[31] This called for yet another federal agency to be created to coordinate these efforts, in anticipation that the Islamic wealth pool could be maximised to its advantage for the trustees, namely the SIRCs. Jawhar, the Department of Wakaf, Zakat and Hajj, was launched in 2004 and tasked with "ensuring that the administration of *wakaf*, *zakat* and pilgrim's affairs [would] be orderly, systematic and impactful" (Jawhar 2017, 8). The Ninth Malaysia Plan (2006–2010) identified a total of 23 projects for *wakaf* development, with a considerable allocation of RM256.4 million given for the construction of hotels, business complexes, shophouses, residences and offices (Jawhar 2009, 24–30). The projects were meant to have smart-partnerships with government agencies, Government-Linked Corporations (GLCs) and the private sector to develop the institutions of *wakaf*, *zakat*, *mal* and *hajj*/*umra*h, as well as to plan and coordinate the 'uniformisation' (*penyeragaman*) of laws (Jawhar 2017, 9–10). Although a federal agency, Jawhar functions like a corporation with its core activities being real estate development of *wakaf* land assets.

The entity has undergone three phases. Phase one involved 16 projects to enlarge its real estate. Phase two focused on forming another corporatised entity, the Yayasan Wakaf Malaysia (YWM, Wakaf Foundation of Malaysia) and its subsidiary the Perbadanan Wakaf Nasional Bhd (PWNB, National Wakaf Corporation Bhd). Phase three saw it collaborate with the Ministry of Higher Education and the private sector to explore developing educational *wakaf* and affordable housing on *wakaf* lands (Jawhar 2017, 29).

If Jawhar is the federal agency for *wakaf* development, there are *negeri*-level corporate entities that are similarly engaged in *wakaf* capitalisation. A prime example is the *negeri*-owned Johor Corporation (JCorp). It was the first to launch what it calls 'Corporate Wakaf' in 2006 when it transferred its equity in various companies[32]—with a net worth of RM200 million—to its own *wakaf* endowment scheme. Through this it built a '*wakaf* hospital' and a chain of clinics.[33] To manage these *wakaf*-centred activities, JCorp created its own management company, the Waqaf An-Nur Corporation Berhad, whose income derived from the dividend payouts of the transferred shares. The mission of maximising the returns to *wakaf* assets and land banks was termed 'Business Jihad' (Johor Corporation 2007).

Establishing this *wakaf* scheme under the sole trusteeship of JCorp was a departure from the stipulation that SIRCs be given this role. Nevertheless, this was resolved with a Memorandum of Agreement with the Johor SIRC, which officially recognised the role of JCorp in initiating the 'Corporate Wakaf' and its status as *mutawwali* (management trustee) for this project (Johor Corporation 2009, 23). It is worth highlighting the enthusiasm of the then Chair of JCorp following the corporatisation of the *wakaf* assets of the *negeri*:

> [T]he defining feature of a Corporate Wakaf must be its appointment as Mutawwali that is fully empowered to exercise all the powers that goes [*sic*] with ownership… the fastest way to set-up such a Corporate Waqaf… would be to 'implant' the Corporate Wakaf 'head and face' into the body framework or corporate structure established under the provision of the prevailing (Malaysian) company legislation… Corporate Waqaf's most formidable inherent appeal is therefore its 'immortality' as a legal entity, sanctioned by Islam.[34]

Another case of how the 'explosion' of cash *wakaf* opened up many possibilities to monetise religion was the collaboration between the commercial Bank Muamalat Malaysia Berhad (BMMB) and the Selangor SIRC's Perbadanan Wakaf Selangor (PWS) (Ashraf and Abdullah 2014). After BMMB and PWS entered into a joint venture in 2012 to introduce their cash *wakaf* scheme, Wakaq Selangor Muamalat, one could purchase *wakaf* share certificates at any BMMB branch, or through internet banking or standing instructions for deductions to be made from their account. These share certificates are then considered as *wakaf* donation to the SIRC. The Joint Management Committee (JMC) between BMMB and PWS subcontracted another company, a subsidiary of BMMB, the Muamalat Invest Sdn Bhd (MISB), as its fund manager. Under this arrangement, profits from investment of *wakaf* funds are split 75 per cent to activities determined by the JMC, while the remainder goes to funding activities of the PWS. In 'religious' terminology and functions, the JMC assumes the role of the trustee of the *wakaf* (*mutawwali*); the MISB is the party mandated to manage the funds through the concept of *wakalah bi al-istithmar* (to be given proxy to act on someone else's behalf) and receives no profits from this venture (Ashraf and Abdullaah 2014, 165).

As was noted earlier, SIRCs own the properties developed on *wakaf* land such as the case of Bank Islam in Kuala Lumpur. From the mid-1990s, *wakaf* (and *zakat*) usage was expanded beyond traditional religious activities—mosque building and charitable contributions to the poor and needy—into financing commercial enterprises and real estate development. This has also been the source of bitter contentions between SIRCs as the developer and inhabitants of *wakaf* lands, displaced by such 'uncharitable' actions.[35] Regardless, the drive towards monetising *wakaf* assets has stimulated calls for more centralisation, standardisation and consensual agreement about what constitutes '*syariah* compliance' as well as, importantly, what accounting, reporting and auditing methods are to be used, as not all *negeri* religious authorities are in agreement (Nori Yani et al. 2018).

Baitulmal

As an institution under the management of the SIRCs, the *baitulmal* is legally empowered to receive money and property, movable or immovable, contributed by any person to this entity. In 2008, the total land possession by all *negeri baitulmal* combined was around 40,000 hectares, along with funds worth about RM316 million (Jawhar 2008). Different to *zakat*, which refers to a collection derived from wealth and involves a collector (*amil*) and recipients (*asnaf*) as well as income and wealth tax, *baitulmal* is a general Islamic treasury. Its revenues are sourced from various forms of taxation and penalties, and hence has a wider revenue base. In Kedah, for example, this extends to include unclaimed *faraid* or Muslim inheritance in the form of land, buildings and cash where there is (1) no legitimate heir, (2) balance remaining after all inheritance has been disbursed, (3) unclaimed money or goods of value, (4) leftover bank deposits that are not '*syariah* compliant', including unclaimed debts and (5) public donations.[36] Money and property that are not derived from *halal* sources can also be donated to the *baitulmal*.[37]

Unlike *zakat* and *wakaf*, *baitulmal* has not progressed in the same upbeat tempo beyond proposals to elevate its status to a full treasury. To date, Jawhar has created the Jawatankuasa Penyelarasan Baitulmal Kebangsaan (JPBK, National Committee for the Coordination of Baitulmal), which is chaired by the de facto Minister of Islamic Affairs, and whose membership comprises all the SIRCs. It has also created a database system (*e-Bayanat* and *e-Wakaf*) and published a management manual, in addition to coordinating the legal aspects of *wakaf*, *zakat* and *mal* (Norhazimah 2009). In line with the drive to corporatise, there is greater demand for the *baitulmal* to be used as a repository for more wealth in the benefit of Islam. Some of the suggestions include seeking new sources of funds such as real estate development of *baitulmal* lands and using Islamic financial instruments like *sukuk* and *ijarah* (leasing contract). Another idea involves collaborating with GLCs and international sources of finance such as the Islamic International Development Bank. In 2015, the National Baitulmal Convention proposed that the *baitulmal* be restructured into a similar entity as the Ministry of Finance. Jawhar was tasked to undertake this study for a transformation plan of the *baitulmal*, with funds coming from the SIRCs and the federal government (Berita Harian Online 2015).

Halal-isation

State regulation over *halal* or permitted foods is a postcolonial development in Malaysia. A committee on Halal-Haram Food was established under Baheis in 1982. Then, food companies obtained the official *halal* logo directly from the Director of Baheis. This changed in the late 1990s after a member of the Halal-Haram Food Committee, Abdul Salam Babji, advocated for a more systematic protocol and use of scientific methods to verify the *halal*-ness of products. Concepts about "science and processing technologies of food", "*halal* verifications and auditing", "HACCP" and "Isi-2020-Fi certification" were introduced to promote more accountability as well as raise the commercial potential of institutions built around *halal*-isation (Babji 1998).

Charges for getting *halal* certification were costly, even in 1998. For instance, the fast food chain KFC paid RM400,000—reportedly a discounted rate—to get *halal* certification for its 250 outlets. The minimum charge for restaurants was otherwise RM250 and the maximum, RM10,000 (Mimi 1998). The high cost has been attributed to the allegedly complex process of auditing to credibly certify that products comply with global *halal* standards, thus enabling them to be marketed worldwide (Long 1999). Indeed, *halal* certification is a big business, with even the United States and Europe venturing into the industry. As the Jakim-issued logo gained popularity, Abdul Salam Babji proposed creating the Malaysian Institute of International Trade and Industry for Halal Food under the Ministry of International Trade and Industry (Miti) (Babji 2000). The certification of *halal* products was privatised to a company called Ilham Daya Sdn Bhd, which was to operate following Jakim's guidelines (New Straits Times 2000).

This certification process came under the spotlight following news that Ajinomoto, a popular flavour-enhancing additive, had been banned in Indonesia in 2001 after it was discovered to have contained pork enzymes. Lobby groups like the Muslim Consumers Association of Malaysia demanded that the government do more than just inspect food outlets to provide certification, by conducting scientific tests on the food products themselves (New Straits Times 2001a). Under pressure, the government eventually replied a question by an opposition Pas Member of Parliament confirming that the product was indeed *halal* (New Straits Times 2001b). This led to increased calls for *halal* verification involving "evidence-based standardisation, certification and auditing procedure", as policymakers were seeing the spinoff business potential around this, from sourcing to packaging to advertising (New Straits Times 2001c). By 2002, *halal* certification appeared to be a sought-after commodity in and of itself when Jakim was tasked to work with the Australian government to certify their meat exports to Muslim countries (New Straits Times 2002).

Responding to the practice of each *negeri* using its own procedures to issue *halal* logos, there was a proposal for a centralised privatised body to implement a standardised and single certification process (New Straits Times 2003a). Jakim played an important role in this move by introducing a new, standardised logo for *halal* certification across all *negeri* in 2003.[38] The annual cost of this logo was RM100 for industries with less than RM500,000 in fixed assets, RM400 for small and medium industries, and RM700 for multinational companies (New Straits Times 2003c). The *halal* injunction would only grow when, in 2004, Selangor designated 988 acres of land on the island of Pulau Indah for the *halal* products industry to cater not just for the local but for global investments too (New Straits Times 2004a).

Despite these measures, *halal* policing by authorities continued and affected even large establishments like Ikea. Following a controversy over the content of its sausages, the global furniture and household goods chain was forced to shut down one of its restaurants and cafés in Kuala Lumpur for a few days (New Straits Times 2005a). It also had to place newspaper advertisements to announce that it was undertaking a religious cleansing process of its utensils and had to verify the validity of its food suppliers' *halal* certificates (New Straits Times 2005b). This demand for *halal* regulation resulted in the Ministry of Domestic Trade and Consumer Affairs forming a *halal* unit within its Enforcement Division to monitor and inspect *halal* logos in business premises (New Straits Times 2005c). Yet this was still deemed insufficient, particularly after a few incidences of products being falsely labelled came to light. Further pressure from Muslim consumer advocates (New Straits Times 2005d) eventually led to the introduction of microchip features in *halal* labels (New Straits Times 2005e) and an International Global Standard 1 (GS1) barcode in which customers could verify a product's *halal*-ness by texting the code numbers to Jakim (New Straits Times 2005f).

All this paved the way for the large-scale corporatisation of *halal*-isation seen today, which has been aided by the establishment of the Halal Industry Development Corporation (HDC) under Miti in 2006.[39] The HDC's coordination reportedly spans across at least 18 government agencies, including Jakim, the Malaysian Industrial Development Authority (Mida), the Royal Malaysian Customs, Department of Chemistry, Department of Veterinary Services, Biotechcorp, the Malaysian Palm Oil Board and various research centres and local universities.[40] Features of *halal* standardisation and auditing (Fischer 2016) or the *halal*-isation mechanisms of law, control, management, inspection and enforcement, laboratory, and information, education, communication and training (Anis Najiha et al. 2018) go towards the amplification of a religious injunction in a market-driven industry, and attest to the arrival of the corporate Islamic bureaucracy.

Conclusion

This chapter has detailed the contemporary features of an augmented Islamic bureaucracy, which, in Malaysia, can be distinguished through its sites of operation, namely in *negeri* or subnational governments, the federal government and the corporate world. Straddling the domains of civil administration, courts and corporations, this correlates with the *negeri* Islamic bureaucracy, federal Islamic bureaucracy and corporate Islamic bureaucracy. Collectively, this Divine Bureaucracy is multilevelled, multi-differentiated and multifaceted. The proliferation and multiplication of its institutions, their duplication and overlap of functions via countless government 'bureaus', sections and departments, together with the utilisation of managerial, technological and scientific standards of modernisation, constitute some of the outstanding features of this Islamic entity.

The enlargement of Islamic matters in the civil administration as seen in the ubiquitous role and dominant presence of Jakim in almost all regulatory aspects of public and private lives has rendered it as the main face of a state-driven "Islamic Leviathan" (Nasr 2001). The upgrading and expansion of *syariah* laws, personnel and courts have also given rise to the phenomenon of 'syariahtisation' (tan 2012, 41) or 'shariatization' (Ahmad Fauzi 2018), the foremost driver of Islamisation in contemporary Malaysia. Corporations that have grown around the capitalisation of Islamic assets, Islamic injunctions and the cleansing of Islamic values have added to the picture of Islamisation as a civilisational alternative to the 'secular-Western' order, yet inevitably imbibing the method and character of capitalism, and its close associate, secularism (Sloane-White 2017).

Through bureaucratisation, Islam is now a faith that is meticulously managed, regularised, systematised, impersonalised and calculable. The explicit goals of these bureaucratic edifices are couched in technocratic language—to 'uniformise' laws and procedures, 'set standards', 'manage efficiently' and 'create economic value'—within the parameters of the greater good of Islam. The rationalisation of religion through bureaucratisation is heavily dependent on a textualist tradition, as legal rational sources are sought to justify plans and programmes. The substantive sources are grounded upon a corpus of sacred as well as antiquated scriptures, but the practice is implemented through organisational principles that are quintessentially modern, technocratised and secularised.

This, in sum, lays down the basis for the disenchantment of Muslim social life, in which every expression of devotion appears to be driven, captured and moulded by a bureaucracy which seeks to maximise the political, social and economic leverage of a belief system that is rich in both symbolism and substance for its valorisation through a rationalisation process. The power and authority of the Divine Bureaucracy has been key to this process.

Notes

1. See Chaps. 4, 5 and 6 for a detailed discussion on Muslim-non-Muslim relations.
2. Definitions taken from dictionary.com.
3. The Malayan Union was ostensibly meant to unite by merging the nine Malay States into one administrative and centralised unit. Due to Malay opposition, this plan was shelved and in place of it was a federation system

(The Federation of Malaya), which was officially established on February 1948. This entity maintained the individuality of each Malay *negeri* (State, subnational unit of governance) including the territories under the Straits Settlements (Zakaria 2006, 30–35).

4. Compare the contents of and reference to these in Selangor's Administration of Muslim Law Enactment 1952 and the Administration of the Religion of Islam Enactment 2003.
5. See Section 45 on "Functions of the Mufti" in The Administration of the Religion of Islam (State of Selangor) Enactment 2003.
6. A fuller explanation and analysis of the roles and implications of a corporate Islamic bureaucracy is the subject of Chap. 7.
7. The MKI's formation was approved by the Council of Rulers at its meeting held in October 1968, but was officially established in 1969.
8. This will be further discussed in Chap. 6 on 'Perfecting Family'.
9. The Council of Rulers is also referred to as the Conference of Rulers. This was introduced by the British as the Durbar (court of a native ruler) and was a way to convene all the Malay sultans from the nine States in one meeting. Filled with pomp and ceremony, the first Durbar was held in 1897 in the Perak royal capital of Kuala Kangsar (see Teh 2018 for a lively account of the Durbars). The website of the Conference of Rulers notes that it was officially established in 1948, the year the Federation of Malaya was formed (http://www.majlisraja-raja.gov.my/index.php/en/organization-info/peranan-majlis-raja-raja-en, accessed 1 February 2019).
10. See http://www.pmo.gov.my/dokumenattached/Dasar/10DASAR_PENERAPAN_NILAI.pdf, accessed 11 January 2019.
11. There were 12 bodies listed as of January 2019. See 'Senarai Agensi YB Menteri di JPM', http://www.islam.gov.my/senarai-agensi-yb-menteri-di-jpm, accessed 24 April 2019. However, in a document produced by Jakim (n.d.) titled '*Kejayaan Institusi-Institusi Agama di bawah Menteri di Jabatan Perdana Menteri*', 14 agencies were listed under the de facto Minister-in-Charge of Islamic Affairs, the two additions being the Yayasan Taqwa Wilayah Persekutuan (under Maiwp) and the World Zakat Organisation.
12. See "Carta Organisasi: Bahagian Penyelidikan", http://www.islam.gov.my/bahagian-penyelidikan/742-carta-organisasi, accessed 24 April 2019.
13. It is interesting to note that Islamic Development under the PM's Department had 3616 staff compared to the University of Malaya, a premier university, with 5878 academic and non-academic staff and an enrolment of 21,055 students. See "UM Fact Sheet 2017", https://www.um.edu.my/about-um/um-fact-sheet, accessed 5 May 2019.
14. In this new structure, the *Syariah* Lower Court would adjudicate early trials and deal with civil and criminal cases, the *Syariah* High Court would

hear cases brought up from the Lower Court and other cases falling within its jurisdiction, and the Court of Appeal would deal with cases forwarded from the High Court.

15. The Supreme Court had delayed the signing of a deal for the construction of the North-South Highway between the federal government and an Umno-owned corporation on grounds of alleged corruption (Lee 2017, 82–85). This ruling had angered Mahathir and many saw his proposal to amend the Constitution as a means to keep the judiciary's powers in check (Crossette 1988).
16. To this the PM replied that *syariah* court judges were already being trained and ready to take on their new roles (Malaysia 1988b, 1582).
17. Prior to this, another committee to study *syariah* and civil laws had already been formed in May 1988, chaired by Mohd Yusof Noor, a minister in the PM's Department.
18. He was also serving then as the Dean of the Faculty of Law at the International Islamic University.
19. This structure of a 'technical' committee to study and formulate laws was later replicated in some *negeri* such as Selangor and Pahang (Abdul Monir 2016, 81).
20. In 1981, there was already a proposal to elevate and expand the status and scope, respectively, of *syariah* courts' jurisdiction. This meant creating a special service and salary scheme for *syariah* judges and officials (Abdul Monir 2016, 83).
21. Along with this, four Syariah Appeal Court judges were appointed under the federal system.
22. There was speculation that these announcements were timed to leverage on political schisms in Kelantan—the only *negeri* not led by BN—between Pas and its coalition partner Semangat 46, in the hope of recapturing it at the next subnational election (Stewart 1996).
23. The goal of 'standardisation' and getting all *negeri* to agree to a joint scheme was presented in some of the earlier JKSM Annual Reports as its stated vision, mission or objectives (see, for example, JKSM 2003, 4–5). However, these have since been revised given not all *negeri* have agreed to the joint service scheme. The vision of 'standardisation' is now only applied those under the scheme.
24. In 2004, there were only 28 appeal case hearings (JKSM 2004, 28) while, in 2011, there were 100 appeal cases registered with JKSM, with only 55 resolved (JKSM 2011, 28). In 2012, the number of such cases heard totalled 101, with 73 resolved (JKSM 2012, 17). In 2018, there were only 72 scheduled hearings for appeal cases. Data downloaded from website of government data (data.gov.my), http://www.data.gov.my/data/ms_MY/dataset/jadual-sidang-mahkamah-rayuan, accessed 3 February 2019.

25. Under Section 133(2) of the 2004 Penang Islamic Family Law, for instance, the penalty for not complying with a court order is one month in jail for each month of unpaid payment or one year for any amount that remains unpaid.
26. The notion of a flawed axiom of 'masculine protectionism' in relation to these issues will also be explored further in Chap. 6, 'Perfecting Family'.
27. See "Recipients and acceptance criteria for *zakat*" in the Lembaga Zakat Selangor website, https://www.zakatselangor.com.my/recipients-and-acceptance-criteria-for-zakat/?lang=en, accessed 7 February 2019.
28. Abdul Rahim Bakar subsequently became the first chairman of the Pusat Pungutan Zakat (PPZ, Zakat Collection Centre), the corporatised *zakat* collection body of Maiwp.
29. Website of PPZ-Maiwp, "Syarat wajib zakat", https://www.zakat.com.my/info-zakat/syarat-wajib-zakat/, accessed 28 January 2019.
30. There is lack of clarity, including legally, as to whether a particular endowment is for specific or general purpose.
31. At the time, there was an estimated 1600 hectares of *wakaf* land in the country worth between RM500 million and RM1 billion (New Straits Times 1995b).
32. This comprised 75 per cent of JCorp's shares in Tiram Travel Sdn Bhd, 12.35 million unit shares of its subsidiary JCorp Kulim, 18.6 million unit shares in KPJ and 4.32 million shares in JLand.
33. The hospital and chain of clinics carry the same name, *Waqf An-Nur*. The clinics, which expand beyond Johor, are equipped with dialysis machines, located near mosques, and patients have access to *baitulmal* funds of the Johor SIRC.
34. From a paper by Muhammad Ali Hashim "The Corporate Waqaf: A Malaysian experience in building sustainable business capability", which was delivered at the Dubai International Conference of Endowments, 17 February 2010, Dubai, and reproduced in Johor Corporation (2009).
35. This issue which will be further discussed in Chap. 7, 'Purifying Money'.
36. See 'Baitulmal' on the website of Majlis Agama Islam Kedah, http://www.maik.gov.my/ms/Page?type=zByNQuF9FYw=&pid=Aic6x6AERv0=, accessed 8 February 2019.
37. See "Pengurusan wang tidak patuh syariah" on the website of Majlis Agama Islam Selangor, http://www.mais.gov.my/perkhidmatan/perkhidmatan-baitulmal/pengurusan-wang-tidak-patuh-syariah, accessed 8 February 2019.
38. That same year, 79 of its officers were also recruited to assist the Ministry of Domestic Trade and Consumer Affairs to monitor the labelling of *halal* products in business premises (New Straits Times 2003b).

39. As of 2019, this agency has been housed within the newly created Ministry of Economic Affairs, though it is still wholly owned by the Ministry of Finance Incorporated. See its website, http://www.hdcglobal.com/publisher/bhi_why_hdc, accessed 8 April 2019.
40. Additionally, the *halal* value-chain is listed as encompassing at least seven elements: feed and farm management, ingredients, manufacturing and processing, logistical services, research and development and innovation, Islamic finance and advertising and promotions.

References

Abbott, Jason P and Sophie Gregorios-Pippas (2010) "Islamization in Malaysia: Processes and dynamics", *Contemporary Politics*, Vol. 16, No. 2, 135–151.

Abd Shakor, bin Borham (2011) "Pelakasanaan Pembangunan Wakaf Korporat Johor Corporation Berhad (JCorp): Satu tinjauan", *International Conference on Humanities,* 1–13.

Abdul Monir, Yaacob (2016) *Perkembangan Pentadbiran Undang-Undang Islam di Malaysia*, Cyberjaya: Universiti Islam Malaysia.

Abdul Rahim, Abu Bakar (2006) "Teks Syarahan Seminar Budaya Pengurusan Zakat di Malaysia: Profesionalisme berbanding tradisionalisme", *Laporan Zakat 2006*, Kuala Lumpur: Pusat Pungutan Zakat, 113–120.

Abdullah Alwi, Haji Hassan (1996) *The Administration of Islamic Law in Kelantan*, Kuala Lumpur: Dewan Bahasa dan Pustaka.

Ahmad Fauzi, Abdul Hamid (2018) "Shariaization of Malay-Muslim Identity in Contemporary Malaysia", *Journal of the Malaysian Branch of the Royal Asiatic Society*, Vol. 91, Part 2, No. 315, December, 49–78.

Ahmad Ibrahim (1965) *Islamic Law in Malaya*, Singapore: Malaysian Sociological Research Institute Ltd.

Ahmad Sarji, AH (1995) *The Civil Service of Malaysia: Towards Vision 2020*, Kuala Lumpur: Government of Malaysia.

Aina, Nasa and Fairuz Mohd Shahar (2015) "Ignorant people fall for IS", *New Straits Times*, 28 February.

Anis Najiha, Ahmad, Ungku Fatimah Ungku Zainal Abidin, Mohhidin Othman and Russly Abdul Rahman (2018) "Overview of the halal food control system in Malaysia", *Food Control*, Vol. 90, 352–363.

Anisah, Shukry (2015a). Anak kepada Tun Dr Ismail mahu Jakim dimansuhkan. *The Malaysian Insider*, 9 November. http://www.theinsiderarchived.com/bahasa/article/anak-kepada-tun-dr-ismail-mahu-jakim-dimansuhkan, accessed 5 April 2019.

——— (2015b), "How Jakim spent nearly RM1 billion this year", *The Malaysian Insider*, 22 November, http://www.theinsiderarchived.com/malaysia/article/how-jakim-spent-nearly-rm1-billion-this-year, accessed 22 November 2015.

Aniza, Damis (2008) "It's to prevent lesbianism", *New Straits Times*, 23 November 23.
Anwar, Ibrahim (1992) *The Asian Renaissance*, Singapore: Times Books International.
Arfa, Yunus (2018) "G25 Urges Reforms of Agencies", *New Straits Times*, 1 June.
Ashraf, Mohd Ramli and Abdullaah Jalil (2014) "Model Perbankan Wakaf Korporat: Analisis wakaf Selangor *muamalat* (Banking Model of Corporate *Waqf*: An analysis of *wakaf* Selangor *muamalat*)", *Jurnal Pengurusan*, Vol. 42, 159–167.
Asmak, Ab Rahman (2009) "Peranan Wakaf dalam Pembangunan Ekonomi Umat Islam dan Aplikasinya di Malaysia" *Jurnal Syariah*, Vol. 17, No. 1, 113–152.
Azman, Ab Rahman, Mohammad Haji Alias, and Syed Mohd Najib Syed Omar (2012) "Zakat Institution in Malaysia: Problems and issues", *Global Journal Al-Thaqafah*, Vol. 2, Issue 1, 35–41.
Babji, Abdul Salam (1998) "Need for clear policy in *halal* certification", *New Straits Times*, 21 November.
——— (2000) "Form body to protect *halal* hub aspiration", *New Straits Times*, 14 April.
Berita Harian Online (2015) "Mentransformasi baitulmal mantapkan ekonomi ummah", 8 December.
Che Zuina, Ismail, Nor Jana Salim and Nor Jawanees Ahmad Hanafiah (2015) "Administration and Management of *Waqf* land in Malaysia: Issues and solutions", *Mediterranean Journal of Social Sciences*, Vol. 6, No. 4, 613–620.
Crossette, Barbara (1988) "Malaysia leader tightens his hold on the courts", *The New York Times*, 20 March.
Farhanah, Mohd Mokhtar, Emira Mad Sidin and Dzuljastri Abd Razak (2015) "Operation of Cash *Waqf* in Malaysia and Its Limitations, *Journal of Islamic Economics, Banking and Finance*, Vol. 11, No. 4, 100–114.
Farrah Naz, Karim (2006) "Rules on khalwat raids to be revised", *New Straits Times*, 16 November.
Farrah Naz, Karim and Sukhbir Cheema (2013) "Mama's alternative maid deal", *New Straits Times*, 11 January.
Farrah, Naz and June Ramli (2003) "Let religious body vet documents first", *New Straits Times*, 23 May.
Fathullah, Asni and Jasni Sulong (2017) "Wakaf Tunai dan Applikasinya dalam Undang-undang di Negara Asean", *Jurnal Syariah*, Vol. 25, No. 2, 217–246.
Firdaus, Abdullah (2003) "Consult Jakim, says Abdullah", *New Straits Times*, 19 March.
Fischer, Johan (2016) "Manufacturing halal in Malaysia", *Contemporary Islam*, Vol. 10, 35–52.
Funston, John (1988) "Challenge and Response in Malaysia: The Umno crisis and the Mahathir style", *The Pacific Review*, Vol. 1, No. 4, 363–373.

Hairunnizam, Wahid, Sanep Ahmad and Radiah Abdul Kader (2009) "Pengagihan Zakat oleh Institusi Zakat di Malaysia: Mengapa masyarakat Islam tidak berpuas hati?", *Jurnal Syariah*, Vol. 17, No. 1, 89–112.

Hamayotsu, Kikue (2003) "Politics of Syariah Reform: The making of the state religio-legal apparatus", in Virginia Matheson Hooker, Norani Othman and Clive S. Kessler (eds), *Malaysia: Islam, society, and politics*, Singapore: ISEAS, 55–79.

Hamidah, Atan (2005) "Jakim guidelines for performers", *New Straits Times*, 9 May.

——— (2006) "Jakim won't wait for decency guidelines", New Straits Times, 19 April.

——— (2008) "Fatwa on yoga this week", New Straits Times, 19 November.

Hariz, Mohd (2011) "Fatwa panel to discuss the use of indelible ink", *New Straits Times*, 21 December.

Harun, Hashim (1999) "Towards codification, uniformity of Islamic law", *New Straits Times*, 14 October.

Hussein, S Ahmad (1988) "Islam and Politics in Malaysia, 1969–1982: The dynamics of competing traditions, PhD thesis submitted to Yale University.

Jakim (n.d.) *Kejayaan Institusi-Institusi Agama di bawah Menteri di Jabatan Perdana Menteri* (Successes of Religious Institutions under the Prime Minister's Department).

Jawhar (2008) *Laporan Tahunan Jabatan Wakaf, Zakat dan Haji 2008* (Jawhar Annual Report 2008).

——— (2009) *Laporan Tahunan Jabatan Wakaf, Zakat dan Haji 2009* (Jawhar Annual Report 2009).

——— (2017) *Pelan Strategik Jawhar 2017–2020* (Jawhar Strategic Plan 2017–2020).

Jayasankaran, S (2010) "'Allah' ruling applies to 3 states", *The Business Times Singapore*, 19 January.

JKSM (2003) *Laporan Tahunan Jabatan Kehakiman Syariah Malaysia* (JKSM Annual Report 2003).

——— (2004) *Laporan Tahunan Jabatan Kehakiman Syariah Malaysia* (JKSM Annual Report 2004).

——— (2011) *Laporan Tahunan Jabatan Kehakiman Syariah Malaysia* (JKSM Annual Report 2011).

——— (2012) *Laporan Tahunan Jabatan Kehakiman Syariah Malaysia* (JKSM Annual Report 2012).

——— (2014) *Laporan Tahunan Jabatan Kehakiman Syariah Malaysia* (JKSM Annual Report 2014).

Johor Corporation (2007) *Annual Report 2007*.

——— (2009) *Annual Report 2009*.

Lee, HP (2017) *Constitutional Conflicts in Contemporary Malaysia*, Second Edition, Oxford: Oxford University Press.
Lee, Koi Kye (2012) "Indelible ink halal, says fatwa council", *New Straits Times*, 12 January.
Lembaga Zakat Selangor (2015) *Laporan Pengurusan Zakat Selangor 2014* (Selangor Zakat Management Report 2014).
——— (2016) *Laporan Pengurusan Zakat Selangor 2015* (Selangor Zakat Management Report 2015).
——— (2017) *Laporan Pengurusan Zakat Selangor 2016* (Selangor Zakat Management Report 2016).
——— (2018) *Laporan Pengurusan Zakat Selangor 2017* (Selangor Zakat Management Report 2017).
Long, Hui Ching (1999) "*Halal* label too costly, say manufacturers", 19 January.
Looi, Elizabeth (2011) "100 couples nabbed in Valentine's raid; Crackdown in Malaysia on Muslims defying ban on marking lovers' day", *The Straits Times*, 15 February.
Mahadeva, Sheridan (2003) "Jakim to stress women's rights", *New Straits Times*, 25 March.
Malaysia (1988a) *Parliamentary Debates, House of Representatives, Seventh Parliament*, 17 March, Vol. II, No. 8, 1256–1450.
——— (1988b) *Parliamentary Debates, House of Representatives, Seventh Parliament*, 18 March, Vol. II, No. 9, 1457–1662.
Malaysiakini (2014a) "No forgiving, punish pat-a-dog organisers", 27 October, https://www.malaysiakini.com/news/278706, accessed 13 May 2019
——— (2014b) "Eminent Malays urge PM to show leadership", 8 December, https://www.malaysiakini.com/news/282833, accessed 13 May 2019
——— (2015a) "'K-Pop fiasco is why Islam forbids such concerts", 12 January, https://www.malaysiakini.com/news/286088, accessed 13 May 2019
——— (2015b) "Facing sedition probe, Tawfik stands firm on view of Jakim", 24 November, https://www.malaysiakini.com/news/320772, accessed 13 May 2019
——— (2015c) "G25 to study where Jakim's money went", 30 November, https://www.malaysiakini.com/news/321531, accessed 19 January 2020.
Malaysian Insider (2015) "Johor sultan wants Jakim to explain RM1 billion budget", 27 December.
Mauzy, Diane K and RS Milne (1983) "The Mahathir Administration in Malaysia: Discipline through Islam", *Pacific Affairs*, Vol. 56, No. 4, 617–648.
Md Hairi, Md Hussain (2009) "Keberkesanan Sistem Agihan Zakat: Suatu pandangan awal", Laporan Kajian, Fakulti Perakaunan, Universiti Utara Malaysia.
Mimi, Syed Yusof (1998) "Megat Junid: Charges for halal certs reasonable", *New Straits Times*, 28 December.

Ministry of Finance (2009) *Anggaran Perbelanjaan Persekutuan 2009* (Estimated Federal Expenditure 2009).
——— (2010) *Anggaran Perbelanjaan Persekutuan 2010* (Estimated Federal Expenditure 2010).
——— (2011) *Anggaran Perbelanjaan Persekutuan 2011* (Estimated Federal Expenditure 2011).
——— (2012) *Anggaran Perbelanjaan Persekutuan 2012* (Estimated Federal Expenditure 2012).
———(2013) *Anggaran Perbelanjaan Persekutuan 2013* (Estimated Federal Expenditure 2013).
——— (2014) *Anggaran Perbelanjaan Persekutuan 2014* (Estimated Federal Expenditure 2014).
——— (2015) *Anggaran Perbelanjaan Persekutuan 2015* (Estimated Federal Expenditure 2015).
——— (2016) *Anggaran Perbelanjaan Persekutuan 2016* (Estimated Federal Expenditure 2016).
——— (2017) *Anggaran Perbelanjaan Persekutuan 2017* (Estimated Federal Expenditure 2017).
——— (2018) *Anggaran Perbelanjaan Persekutuan 2018* (Estimated Federal Expenditure 2018).
——— (2019) *Anggaran Perbelanjaan Persekutuan 2019* (Estimated Federal Expenditure 2019).
Moustafa, Tamir (2018) "The Judicialization of Religion", *Law and Society Review*, Vol. 52, No. 3, 685–708.
Narayanan, Suresh (2007) "The Challenges of Raising Revenues and Restructuring Subsidies in Malaysia", *Kajian Malaysia*, Vol. XXV, No. 2, 1–28.
Nasr, Seyyed Vali Reza (2001) *Islamic Leviathan: Islam and the making of state power*, Oxford, New York: Oxford University Press.
New Straits Times (1995a) "More posts, incentives for syariah law officers", 16 March.
——— (1995b) "Wakaf assets to become economic force", 22 March.
——— (1996a) "PM announces plan to revamp syariah court administration", 24 July.
——— (1996b) "Syariah courts to come under Federal department", 2 November.
——— (2000) "'Halal' food investigator named" 14 April.
——— (2001a) "Conduct tests to confirm Ajinomoto is halal", 9 January.
——— (2001b) "Ajinomoto is halal", 12 April.
——— (2001c) "New focus on halal concept", 30 May.
——— (2002) "Jakim working with Aussies on 'halal' certs", 22 September.
——— (2003a) "Centralised body to issue halal certs", 16 February.
——— (2003b) "Halal labels: 79 to be made enforcement officers", 28 August.
——— (2003c) "New standardized halal certification logo for all states", 1 October.

——— (2004a) "Pulau Indah to be a trade hub", 19 June.
——— (2004b) "Pilot Quranic project to start in 10 primary schools", 22 February.
——— (2005a) "Jakim raids food outlet over sausages", 15 March.
——— (2005b) "Cleansing process at outlets", 19 March.
——— (2005c) "Enforcement division to have 5,000 men", 20 March.
——— (2005d) "Ppim to submit memorandum", 21 March.
——— (2005e) "Halal logo with microchip soon", 30 March.
——— (2005f) "Consumers can verify status of halal products vis SMS", 23 September.
——— (2007) "Jakim monitors websites", 28 May.
——— (2010) "Medical scholarship for religious school students", 27 May.
——— (2013) "IGP: Jakim officers can carry guns", 17 November.
——— (2014) "IGP: No syariah unit for cops", 30 January.
——— (2015) "March tabling for law on terror", 20 January.
Nik Mustapha, bin Hj Nik Hassan (1987) "Zakat in Malaysia – Present and Future Status", *Journal of Islamic Economics*, Vol. 1, No. 1, 47–75.
Norhazimah, Che Hassan (2009) "Memperkasa institusi baitulmal", *Utusan Online*, 7 January.
Nori Yani, Abu Talib, Radziah Abdul Latiff, Aini Aman and Mohd Rizal Palil 2018) "An Exploratory Study of Accounting and Reporting Practice for Waqf Among State Islamic Religious Councils in Malaysia", *International Journal of Islamic Thought* 13, June, 90–104.
Nurris, Ishak (2005) "Draft on sex education ready for Cabinet study", *New Straits Times*, 11 April.
Patmawati, Haji Ibrahim (2007) "Peranan agihan zakat dalam meningkatkan tahap ekonomi ummah", Pusat Pungutan Zakat-Maiwp, *Laporan Tahunan 2007*, 148–157.
PPZ-Maiwp (2001) *Laporan Zakat 2001* (Zakat Report 2001).
——— (2005) *Laporan Zakat 2005* (Zakat Report 2005).
——— (2011) *Laporan Zakat 2011* (Zakat Report 2011).
——— (2017) *Laporan Zakat 2017* (Zakat Report 2017).
Radzi, Sapiee (1998) "Uniform Syariah law taking shape", *New Straits Times*, 7 October.
Rahmah, Ghazali (2012) "Government bans Irshad's book", *New Straits Times*, 25 May.
Reme, Ahmad (2002) "UMNO-owned paper lists 99 names of Allah", *The Straits Times*, 7 September.
Schottmann, Sven Alexander (2011) "The Pillars of "Mahathir's Islam": Mahathir Mohamad on being-Muslim in the modern world", *Asian Studies Review*, Vol. 35, No. 3, 355–372.

Scott, James C. (1987) "Resistance Without Protest and Without Organization: Peasant opposition to the Islamic *zakat* and the Christian tithe", *Comparative Studies in Society and History*, Vol. 29, No. 1, 417–452.
Securities Commission Malaysia (2017) *Securities Commission Malaysia Islamic Fund and Wealth Management Blueprint*, Kuala Lumpur: Securities Commission Malaysia.
Shabbir, Malik Shahzad (2018) "Classification and Prioritization of Waqf Lands: A Selangor case", *International Journal of Islamic and Middle Eastern Finance and Management*, Vol. 11 Issue 1, 40–58.
Shamsul, AB (1988) "The 'Battle Royal': The Umno elections of 1987", *Southeast Asian Affairs*, 170–188.
Sloane-White, Patricia (2017) *Corporate Islam: Sharia and the modern workplace*, Cambridge: Cambridge University Press.
Steiner, Kerstin (2018) "Branding Islam: Islam, law, and bureaucracies in Southeast Asia", *Journal of Current Southeast Asian Affairs*, Vol. 37, No. 1, 27–56.
Stewart, Ian (1996) "Mahathir to modernise Islamic courts and laws", *The Weekend Australian*, 27 July.
Suhaili, Sarif, Nor 'Azzah Kamri and Azian Madun (2013) "The Impact of Malaysian Islamic Revivalism on Zakat Administration", *International Journal of Nusantara Islam*, Vol. 1, No. 1, 36–53.
Syed Nadzri (2006) "Of Sex, Snooping and Open Minds", *New Straits Times*, 19 December.
tan, beng hui (2012) "Sexuality, Islam and Politics in Malaysia: A study on the shifting strategies of regulation", PhD thesis, National University of Singapore.
Teh, Alan Leam Seng (2018) "Conference of Rulers: How it all started", *New Straits Times*, 1 July.
The Edge Markets (2015) "Defiant Tawfik Ismail says Jakim funds better used on Mat Rempit, urban poverty", 24 November, https://www.theedgemarkets.com/article/defiant-tawfik-ismail-says-jakim-funds-better-used-mat-rempit-urban-poverty, accessed 5 April 2019.
The Straits Times (2002) "Movie actor, director can face charges for nude scene", 30 August.
Wan Marhaini, Wan Ahmad (2012) "Zakat Investment in Malaysia: A study of contemporary policy and practice in relation to Shari'a", PhD thesis, University of Edinburgh.
Zakaria, Haji Ahmad (ed) (2006) *Government and Politics (1940–2006)*, Singapore: Editions Didier Millet.

CHAPTER 4

Standardising Faith

Introduction

As Muslims in Malaysia increasingly fall under the purview of the state and its Divine Bureaucracy, the character of religious expression becomes almost wholly subjected to a codified and official definition of what being Muslim means. The terrain of bureaucratic authority has considerably widened in the strictures delineated for Muslim social life. Two processes have gone hand in hand in this exercise. One is the standardisation and regulation of the Muslim subject, as much as possible, on all elements of difference, digression and variation deemed forbidden. The other process is ring-fencing, which includes the subjugation of the civil rights of Muslims to an almost exclusive purview of *syariah* rather than the Federal Constitution, as well as outlawing any exit of Muslims from the *syariah* sphere of control. The standardisation of faith is the subject of this chapter. The ring-fencing of constituents will be examined in Chap. 5.

As illustrated in the previous chapter, by the 2000s, all aspects of social life related to Islam had effectively been taken over by the state. This occurred via the reorganisation and strengthening of religious bodies at the federal and *negeri* (State, subnational units) levels, as well as the corporate Islamic bureaucracy,[1] the expansion and elevation of the *syariah* courts system, the inordinate funding of all forms of Islamic-related institutions, and the corporatisation of any potentially 'monetisable' Islamic commands and practice. Far from adopting an 'old-school' traditionalist

M. Mohamad, *The Divine Bureaucracy and Disenchantment of Social Life*, Contestations in Contemporary Southeast Asia,
https://doi.org/10.1007/978-981-15-2093-8_4

stance, this large-scale movement had in place strategic and pragmatic plans and programmes, orchestrated through the legal, administrative and technocratic infrastructure of a modern, Weberian bureaucracy.

The main argument advanced in this chapter and the next is that standardisation and ring-fencing are the dominant tools of homogenising Muslim identity and demonising all others not within what is defined as acceptable. It was through standardisation and ring-fencing, instruments made possible by bureaucratic ubiquity, that an "Islamic Leviathan" used in the title of a book about the state in Malaysia and Pakistan (Nasr 2001) has been able to relentlessly grow with few obstacles in its way.

What have been the structural channels for the standardisation of Muslim identity? The imposition of *syariah* laws and *fatwa* (legal opinion), a key judicial means, is one such channel. Another is the mobilisation of a Muslim civil society whose role is to continuously purvey the narrative of a dominant ideology of Islam at the level of everyday-defined social practice.[2] The national state also accords enforcement powers of coercion and compliance to the Divine Bureaucracy, with its homogenisation project being one of the most crucial foundations of uniformisation, originally applied to Islamic laws and court systems. Gradually, this has become above all the standardisation of faith. *Negeri* and federal Islamic bureaucracies have played a critical role in this exercise, asserting their moral, legal, shaming and coercive powers to proscribe and delimit competing voices and discourses that potentially threaten the 'legitimacy' dividend amassed through the enlargement of control over Muslims in the country. The case studies in the following section, of proscriptions and prohibitions, reveal why and how the standardisation of faith has become the sine qua non of a Divine Bureaucracy.

Establishing the Official Islam of Ahli Sunnah Wal Jamaah

The standardisation of Islam as a monolithic and at the same time non-ambivalent system of belief and rituals requires all semblance of plurality to be minimised as this would allow for a more rules-based and unambiguous religious practice. However, the legalisation of only one Islam, Sunni Islam, and the banning of Syiah Islam or any variant of even Sunni Islam apart from that which is officially accepted are fairly recent moves. The identification, definition and refinement of what has come to be construed as 'correct' Islam was a process of objectification that only a bureaucratic structure could have made possible. One of the ways was the issuance of *fatwa*, the legal instrumentality used by a rising class of bureaucrat-*ulama* (Islamic scholars) to establish their mark and strength within the sea of competing state authorities, such as secular-trained *syariah* lawyers, scholars, administrators, technocrats, corporate managers and elected public officials who are also staking their claim in the promotion of Islamisation in society. This section begins by clarifying the growing importance of *fatwa*—what used to be 'legal opinions' issued by religious leaders and scholars—which did not have the same power of enforcement of common law.

Following new enactments passed in the 2000s, the separation of powers between three central authorities in Islam—the *negeri* or State Islamic Religious Council (SIRC), *syariah* court and the Mufti's Office—resulted in new dynamics within the *negeri* Islamic bureaucracy. The creation of the Mufti's Office, for example, elevated the process of *fatwa*-making and turned it into an extensive part of bureaucratic Islam. Although there is also a National Fatwa Committee which can issue its own *fatwa*, this federal body does not have enforcement powers nationally except in the Federal Territories (FT). Each *negeri* also has its own *fatwa* committee and the issuance and enforcement of these *fatwa* reside with their respective religious authorities.

Since the mid-1990s, the number of *fatwa* issued has increased tremendously, and now touches upon every aspect of life. *Fatwa* typically falls under the category of the profession of faith or creed (*akidah*), worship (*ibadah*), transaction and economy (*muamalat dan ekonomi*), medicine (*perubatan*), tithes (*zakat*), marriage and family (*munakahat*), food and drinks (*makanan dan minimum*), clothing (*pakaian*), animals (*haiwan*) or social and *syariah* (*sosial dan syariah*) issues (Jakim 2012). *Fatwa*-making can be initiated by anyone—from the central government to the private sector to NGOs, and also through private requests by individuals. Once an application is received, the Mufti's Office conducts its own research on the subject in question. Its recommendation on whether a reported action, behaviour, activity, organisation, book or practice should be *haram* (prohibited), *harus* (allowable) or given *panduan* (guidelines) is then submitted to the *fatwa* committee of each *negeri*. Once agreed upon here, the recommendation then goes to the SIRC before being sent to the sultan for his assent. Following this, the draft for the gazette is submitted to the State Legal Adviser and, when finalised, gets printed as a Government

Gazette. Any *fatwa* adopted in this manner is deemed valid and applicable to all Muslims residing within the same *negeri*, and is recognised by all courts, *syariah* and civil. On the latter, it used to be ambiguous if a *negeri*-based *fatwa* could be subjected to judicialisation by a national institution such as the civil court. The case of a *fatwa* against a women's organisation, Sisters-in-Islam (Sis), which was challenged at a civil court, showed that even a subnational *negeri* fatwa could take effect beyond the boundaries of the *negeri*. More on this is discussed below.

The procedural actions in the legalisation of a *fatwa* is modern but non-democratic as it is not subjected to legislative deliberation. In contrast, *syariah* bills that are formalised into statutes need to be considered and debated by elected representatives of the national Parliament and sub-national State Legislative Assemblies. A bill is passed only when there is a majority vote, and it then becomes legislation upon royal assent. *Fatwa*-making is the preserve of select religious elites where there is little room for participatory input from other parties. There are *fatwa* on just about every aspect of individual conduct, ranging from whether a Muslim is allowed to wear black armbands, consume wine vinegar (*cuka wain*), breed garden snails (*siput babi*) or practise yoga, to the correct ways and limits of investing in gold (Jakim 2012, 66–74, 137). The number of *fatwa* issued by the National Fatwa Committee during Mahathir Mohamad's 22-year rule (1981–2003) was 131, while during only 6 years of Abdullah Ahmad Badawi's tenure as Prime Minister (2003–2009), 104 *fatwa* were issued (Norshahril 2018, 79). It is within this wide and extensive ambit of *fatwa* that little of Muslim social life remains untouched by rules of the Divine Bureaucracy.

Islam was the foundation of the Malay monarchical system and formed the core of its ruling identity for hundreds of years before. However, it was only in the late twentieth century, in 1996 to be precise, when the first *fatwa* by the National Fatwa Committee decreed that the *Ahli Sunnnah Wal Jamaah* (ASWJ) (followers of Sunni Islam) should be the basis of Islam for Malaysian Muslims. How can the concept of ASWJ be understood? Was it a consistent template used to differentiate between authentic and false Islam or between 'correct' and 'incorrect' Muslims? The discussion below is not meant to imply that the concept of the ASWJ was a completely new notion in Islamic history and civilisation. The beginning of divisions within the followers of Muhammad (pbh) had already begun soon after his death in the seventh century. The long and complex struggles between the two main factions were ultimately recognised to be that between the Sunni and Syiah sects. The Sunnis installed Abu Bakar as the first caliph after the death of Muhammad (pbh) in opposition to the Syiahs who wanted Ali, the son-in-law of the Prophet, as his successor. Accordingly, '*sunni*' is a popular term, while the correct technical phrase is '*ahl al-sunnah wa al-jama'ah*', and has a close reference to a sense of being 'orthodox'. '*Bid'ah*', a term that is also used in the rejection of non-Sunni practice, is associated with 'heresy' or translated as 'deviation' (Smith 1957, 20). In the Malaysian context, the term ASWJ was popularised through official discourse only recently.

A book entitled *Ahli Sunnah Wal-Jammah*, written in Arabic by Ahmad Izzuddin Al-Bayanuni, was translated and published by Jakim in 2009 (Al-Bayanuni 2009). However, the hefty two-volume book does not seem to contain any explanation as to what the term ASWJ means, at least not to the unversed ordinary Muslim. An article by the founders of the Institut Ahli Sunnah Wal Jamaah, of Universiti Tun Hussein Onn Malaysia (UTHM), attempts to provide some simplified pointers.[3] The article explains that *ahl* (Mal. *ahli*) means family, followers, group, members, and *al-Sunnah* means anything based on the Prophet in words, deeds, claims, attributes and life history, as well as the path he took together with his disciples (*para sahabat*). *Bid'ah* (heresy, deviation) is thus considered the antonym of practices based on *al-Sunnah*. The term *Ahli Sunnah* was first used during the Abbasid caliphate in the ninth century to differentiate followers of ASWJ from those who used *akal* (reasoning) as advocated by the Muktazilah[4] group (Abd Razak et al. 2018, 73–74).

This form of authority-defined Islam is also established through legal pronouncements or *fatwa* and is sanctioned by powers at the *negeri* level. The National Fatwa Committee issued its first *fatwa* in relation to ASWJ in 1996 primarily with the intention of banning the spread of Shi'ism in the country, rather than to specify what ASWJ meant. However, even the banning of Shi'ism was a move that began in the 1990s (Norshahril 2014, 366). Before 1996, not only was Shi'ism not illegal, but it was also recognised by a national *fatwa* and by at least two *negeri* enactments on Islamic Family Law. In 1984, the National Fatwa Committee recognised Syiah as legitimate Islam provided that it emanated from the Zaiydiyyah and Jaafariah sects. The Malacca Islamic Family Law Enactment of 1983 and Selangor Islamic Family Law Enactment of 1984 both contain a provision that recognises '*Hukum Syara*' (*syariah* law) to be the "laws accepted by the Syafie, Hanafi, Maliki, Hambali and Syiah (Zaidiyyah and Jaafariyah) sects". By 1996, after the issuance of the national *fatwa*, all *negeri*-level legislation removed their clauses for Syiah recognition and subsequently issued new *fatwa* to ban Shi'ism. The background and issues behind the prohibition are discussed below.

To forbid Syiah practice and teachings meant that ASWJ had to be the only legitimate stream of Islam. In Kelantan, various wrongful teachings, not limited to Shi'ism, were banned through its *Fatwa Mengenai Ajaran Sesat* (On Deviant Teachings) issued in 1997. In the same year, Terengganu gazetted a *fatwa* specifically decreeing that only the ASWJ stream would be permissible and that any dissemination of other streams of Islam outside of this, including their teaching, learning, production and sharing of related materials in any form, was forbidden. Kedah also issued a specific *fatwa* on *Membendung Pengaruh Syiah di Malaysia* (Curtailment of Syiah Influence in Malaysia) in 1998. However, this too did not clearly spell out what constituted being ASWJ.

Much earlier, the Perlis *fatwa* committee had already made one of the first mentions of ASWJ in its 1970 *fatwa* entitled, *Pengertian Ahli Al-Sunnah Wal Jamaah* (The Meaning of Ahli Sunnah Wal Jamaah). It contained a line stating that in upholding Islam,

> [T]he Majlis [SIRC] is not tied to any one *mazhab*. In considering the opinions of [different] *mazhab* which are clear and obvious and derived from Allah's book and the Sunnah of his prophets or the companions of Prophet Muhammad (pbh), the Majlis is prepared to accept and derive practices from them.[5]

The *fatwa* mainly stressed that it recognised the Hanafi, Maliki, Syafie and Hanbali *mazhab* as the legitimate schools of Islamic jurisprudence according to the meaning of ASWJ, though what ASWJ construes was not specified, only that the Perlis SIRC would be guided by these various *mazhab*.

Jakim subsequently issued a more elaborate definition of ASWJ after it convened a special workshop on this matter in 2010: "The group which understands and upholds the al-Qur'an and Sunnah of the Prophet (pbh) conveyed through his companions, *tabi'in* and *tabi' tabi'in* loyal to themselves on the principles of *aqidah* (faith), *syariah* and *akhlak* (morals)".[6] In 2012, the FT *fatwa* committee issued a *fatwa* that provided a list of 80 practices represented to be "false teachings", as a way of differentiating the ASWJ from these beliefs.[7] Not until 2016 did a *fatwa* from Negeri Sembilan offer the most succinct and simplest interpretation to ASWJ; the most correct form of Islam is based on the Quran and guidance of Prophet Muhammad (pbh), his companions and *ulama muktabar* (legitimate) as well as upholding (1) *akidah* (faith) and *tauhid* (oneness of God) based on the conviction of Imam Abu Hasan al-Ash'ari and Imam Abu Mansur al-Maturidi, (2) *Fiqh* and *syariah* based on the Shafii *mazhab* while celebrating the Hanafi, Maliki and Hanbali *mazhab*, and (3) *Tasawwuf* (Sufism) based on the *manhaj* (method) of authoritative Sufi *ulama* such as Imam Junaid al-Baghdadi and Imam al-Ghazali.[8] Sabah followed suit in 2017. Its *fatwa* titled *Pegangan dan Akidah Ahli Sunnah Wal Jamaah* (Conviction and Faith of Ahli Sunnah Wal Jamaah) reproduced almost verbatim the contents of the Negeri Sembilan *fatwa*.

The movement to specify and standardise a singular official Islam was thus a gradual one and not without ambiguities. It was started as a defence against "unwanted Islamic practices", notably Shi'ism, and only much later did this official Islam take on a more definitive language with categorical specifications of what it was, or rather what it was not. By the 2000s, scholars within the *negeri* and federal bureaucracies had delved deeper into the basis for the ASWJ to lend justification and legitimacy for the standardisation of Malaysian Islam (Aminudin and Faisal 2010; Zakaria 2011; Adam 2015).

Following this standardisation effort were serious steps in implementation. The aforementioned Institut Ahli Sunnah Wal Jamaah was established to dignify and empower ASWJ (*pembertabatkan dan memperkasakan Ahli Sunnah wal Jamaah*), as well as to address the spread of Shi'ism and other deviant religious practices and counteract thoughts on liberalism, pluralism and al-Arqam (*liberalisme, pluralisme dan al-Arqam*) (Abd Razak et al. 2018, 74). This, as the founders of the Institute argued, was in line with the state's goal of prohibiting false teachings that were increasingly widespread (*semakin menular*) in Malaysia (Abd Razak et al. 2018, 74).

In 2013, Jakim published its first comprehensive book, written by one of its officers in the Seksyen Aqidah, Bahagian Perancangan dan Penyelidikan (Aqidah Section of the Department of Research and Planning). It detailed influences and thinking that are incorrect and false by ASWJ standards (Mohd Aizam 2015). The definition of *aqidah* is defined as embodying the idea of a firm and absolute faith (*kemuktamadan, keyakinan, pegangan, keutuhan dan kepercayaan*) (Mohd Aizam 2015, 22). It also identified four classifications of practices and thinking around Islam considered to be the threat to *akidah*: (1) deviant teachings of Ilmu Hakikat, al-Arqam and Syiah, (2) liberal Islam and religious pluralism, (3) *bid'ah* (innovation) and anti-*mazhab* and (4) mysticism and superstitions. The notion of *akidah* or the Arabic *'aqa'id* refers to the professions of creeds, as formulated by various scholars in Islamic history. The earliest ones were traditionalist scholars against the rationalist camp, speculative theology and certain Sufi interpretation, hence relying exclusively on the Quran and the *sunna*: "[p]rofessions of faith thus became a way for the adherents of orthodoxy to express their doctrine and to distance themselves from divergent groups" (Schmidtke 2001). In Malaysia, these ideas of 'creeds of faith' were only brought into Muslim consciousness in recent times and only through a well-resourced bureaucracy. Jakim's own Aqidah Section of the Department of Research and Planning is a striking example of the mission to stamp the orthodoxy of *akidah* in Muslim social life.

By 2014, more funds were allocated to strengthen promoters and propagandists of ASWJ. The then Deputy Prime Minister Muhyiddin Yassin said that the government would channel funds to *ulama*, *dakwah* (propagation) institutions and NGOs to expand their *dakwah* and establish Malaysia as the regional centre for the development of ASWJ knowledge (Utusan Online 2014). In 2016, a second ASWJ institute was created, this time under the auspices of the Johor SIRC, which allocated four hectares of land at the newly developed Pagoh Higher Educational Hub for this purpose (Utusan Online 2016). Negeri Sembilan also declared in 2016 that it would be building its own ASWJ institute modelled after the Institut Tadbiran Awam Negara (Intan), the national civil service training institute, and make it compulsory for state-sponsored students returning from overseas to undergo a three-month training course there (Yadim 2016). To date, there is no confirmation if this plan has been realised.

To persist with the notion of only one dominant Islam, in one of the Friday prayers in June 2012, a sermon prepared by the Jabatan Agama Islam Selangor (Jais, Selangor religious department) was delivered at all mosques across the *negeri* to stress the need to adhere to ASWJ. The text for another Friday sermon for all mosques in FT, also on the topic of AWSJ, was disseminated by Jakim in February 2016, stating that the path of ASWJ was a catalyst for Islamic civil society (*aqidah ahli sunnah wal jamaah pemangkin masyarakat Islam Madani*). The use of ASWJ as the only path of Islam has been steadfastly employed as well to criticise and denigrate groups who are labelled as 'liberals', tarred as also being anti-ASWJ, although arguments supporting this claim are short of being incredulous.[9] In 2017, for example, the then Dean of the Institute of the Malay World and Islamic Civilization, Sidek Baba, emphasised that besides Syiah, groups which are "liberal pluralists"—Sis and G25 were the ones he singled out—had also deviated from ASWJ as they were interpreting the Quran purely based on rationality (*berdasarkan rasional semata-mata*) (Utusan Online 2017).

Here it is important to explain the significance of the ASWJ as it is related to several narratives of exclusion and standardisation. The term 'Muktazilah' or 'Mu'tazilah' is frequently associated with liberals and pluralists and their use of rationality, reason and logic in critical discourse against mainstream, state or traditionalist Islam. What is the background to this and why is ASWJ invoked to denigrate a legion of social movements besides those traditionally labelled as practising *ajaran sesat* (deviant teachings)?

The Islamic school of thought known as the Mu'tazilah developed from the eighth to the early ninth centuries during the Abbasid caliphate. The main feature of the Mu'tazilah philosophy is rationalism in addressing physics, metaphysics and ethics (Rudolph 2011). Mu'tazilites have felt "that, under God, destiny was in their own hands" (Smith 1957, 111). The Mu'tazilites prospered in Basra and Baghdad, during the reign of the Caliph al-Ma'mun, who was supportive of this school of thought including towards Shi'ite influence. When he was replaced by the more conservative Caliph al-Mutawakkil, Mu'tazilite philosophy waned and so did the political rapprochement of the Sunnis with the Shi'ites (Martin 1980, 17–178). This conflict of philosophical views was set against a political background of the Abbasid caliphate attempting to create a government involving the uneasy alliance of Arab leaders (Sunnis) and the Persian nobility (who were Shi'ites). Besides Shi'ism, Mu'tazilites were influenced by Greek philosophy, and tried to reconcile revelation with reason, which was in opposition to the school of thought led by al-Ash'ari, who "made revelation primary" and that as far as public opinion was concerned, the "Qur'an and the Sunnah were to be supreme". In this conflict, the Sunni school of thought prevailed (Watt 1963, 52).

In present-day theological debates in the Malaysian-Indonesian world, Imam al-Ash'ari is revered as the founder of the Asha'irah theology and the main pillar of ASWJ (Muhammad Rashidi, and Syed Hadzrullathfi 2013). Always in contrast to the Mu'tazilite, 'rationality' is considered the nemesis of ASWJ: "Imam al-Ash'ari acted to leave the Mu'tazilites after discovering faults in the methodological reasoning of the Mu'tazalites which is excessive in terms of its prioritisation of logic as opposed to using the essence of al-Quran and hadith" (Muhammad Rashidi, and Syed Hadzrullathfi 2013, 68). According to an online blog, the emphasis on the use of 'rationality' was in opposition to ASWJ: "Mu'tazilah appears to be the *mazhab* that uses a lot of arguments based on reason within the (*i'tiqad)* school of thought…The [Mu'tazilah] school of thought continued to wane with the rise of two notables Abu Hassan Al-Asy'ari and Abu Mansur Al-Maturidi, from the *mazhab* Ahli Sunnah Wal Jamaah".[10]

The standardisation movement among the Divine bureaucrats excavated from the Islamic historical past something that could be usefully reinvented to thwart challenges coming from contemporary adversaries. Social movement groups such as Sis, G25 and the Islamic Renaissance Front (IRF) have been 'homogenised' by the authorities and critical scholars led by those proclaiming to belong to the neo-Muktazilah stream (Ahmad Fauzi 2018, 33). In line with this analysis, the divide among the *ulama* has been characterised as hovering between the modernist Salafi stream with the traditionalist ASWJ, the latter also associated with Wahhabism, on account of funds flowing from Saudi Arabia to Malaysia (Mohamed Nawab 2014; Ahmad Fauzi 2016). However, this divide has become more complicated with the rise of an even newer stream, labelled as the Salafi-Wahabbi faction, resulting from the co-optation of Salafism by Wahhabis, and later the Salafi-Jihadi stream taking hold over members of Umno (United Malays National Organisation), Pas (Pan-Malaysian Islamic Party) and even mainstream religious establishment figures (Ahmad Fauzi 2018, 35; Mohamed Nawab and Arosoaie 2018).

William Cantrell Smith had presciently observed when he wrote his book, *Islam in the Modern World*, some six decades ago, intellectualism was to be more feared than mysticism among modern Islamic religious leaders (1957, 57). He was also correct to observe that philosophy and Sufism could also bolster another challenging ideology—liberalism:

> There are two major elements from within the past Islam tradition from which a contribution to liberalism could be drawn: philosophy and Sufism. The intellectualism of the former and humanism of the latter could provide important bases for reinterpretation. This was precisely the reason, of course, for which the conservatives had throughout distrusted them – and still distrust them today. The resurgence of classical Islam involves, in fact, a newly invigorated repudiation of these two liberating forces (55).

Clearing the Path to One Islam

The existence of Islamic groups that irk proponents of official Islam is not new. Names such as Ajaran Taslim (kumpulan Matahari), Tarikat Mufaridah, Crypto, Ajaran Mohammad Al-Mashor, Ilmu Laduni, Tarikat Naqshabandiah, Kumpulan Pecah Kuil, Tarikat Mohammad Mahadi,[11] Golongan Rohaniah, Angkatan Revolusi Islam, Angkatan Sabillullah, Golongan Usrah, Tarikat Mohtar Hassan, Ajaran Bahai, Mutaridin, Ekhwan and Taslim have been identified as some of the many 'deviant' formations that emerged from the 1970s onwards. Almost all have centred around a charismatic leader, have cult-like features, indulge in devotional practices that are heavily infused with mysticism and defy aspects of Islam's conventional rituals like daily prayers, with some veering towards militancy (Hussein 1988: 185–190). From 2009 to 2014, Jakim identified 95 such groups which it considered to be following *ajaran sesat*, including those allegedly hiding behind the "principles of intellectualism and human rights freedom" (Jakim n.d., 25).

Starting from the 1980s, such groups were simply outlawed by *fatwa*. Many of them evinced blind loyalty and devotion to a leadership purported to wield magical powers, with some exhibiting elements of Sufism, supernaturalism, mysticism and occultism. For example, one of the proscribed groups was led by a Hj Khahar b Hj Ahmad whose book called *Al-Furqaan-Pembeda*[12]—banned by a *fatwa*—maintained that the Quran was merely a written form of the holy scripture, which was literally up in the clouds, and that the pilgrimage need not be in Mecca but could take place anywhere on God's earth.[13] Yet another example was a cult led by a woman by the name of Tijah @ Khatijah bt Ali and said to carry the teachings of *Wahdatul Wujud* and *Martabat Tujuh*. Among its practices involved adherents reciting the *zikir* (incantations) till losing themselves in a trance (*tidak sedarkan diri*), and adding the name of Fatimah, the daughter of Prophet Muhammad (pbh)[14] to the *Syahadah* (pronouncement of faith).[15] It would appear that most of these banned 'deviant' groups were Sufistic circles, with many adopting Syiah elements in their practices, though by and large they were syncretic in nature.

The Case of Shi'ism

The establishment of a dominant Malaysian Islam was gradually spelt out as ASWJ or the Sunni branch of Islam. This was ultimately propelled by global events. In their everyday life, Muslims of the Malay World did not know that there was Sunni, as opposed to Syiah Islam. The ASWJ was the objectification of an identity spurred by external developments. Widespread campaigns to curb the spread of Shi'ite beliefs were first related to the fear of the aftermath and repercussions of the 1979 Iranian Revolution. Although this event occurred in the late 1970s, it was only after a *fatwa* was issued in 1996 against Shi'ism that the state crackdown against its followers was set in motion (Faizal and tan 2017, 314). Even the Prime Minister, Mahathir Mohamad, was compelled to issue a warning to university staff members to refrain from propagating Shi'ite teachings once the *fatwa* was issued (The Straits Times 1996). The notion of the Iranian Islamic State based on the concept of *Wilayatul Faqih* (leadership by the clerics) and recurrent tensions in the Middle East due to the Syiah-Sunni schism related to the geopolitics of the region were perceived as national security concerns by the Malaysian government (Halim et al. 2018, 6; Norshahril 2014, 371–374). On a personal everyday level, the prosecution in 1995 of a Singaporean man, living in Johor with his ten wives, on the basis of their Syiah beliefs contributed to some moral anxiety among ordinary Muslims.[16] There are also other reasons proffered to explain the origin and nature of state enmity against Shi'ism and the ruthless discrimination against its followers. Malaysia's close ties to Saudi Arabia and the spread of Wahhabism and Salafism through external influences and funding are some of the more credible reasons to explain state violence against Shi'ites as derived from external influence rather than local traditions (Norshahril 2014, 366–367; Mohd Faizal and tan 2017: 310–313).

Selangor was the first to issue a *fatwa* calling for a total ban on Shi'ism in 1996. Even so, there was no clear explication what Shi'ism was. To help, Jakim, in 1998, translated a book written in Arabic and published in Egypt. This was reprinted in 2016 (Al-Musawi 2016). By 2017, every *negeri* had gazetted *fatwa* outlawing all forms of Syiah practices and teachings. Additionally, 803 alleged followers of Shi'ism were arrested from 2010 to 2017 (Halim et al. 2018, 11–12). Although a proposal to specify ASWJ as the only legal Islam in the Federal Constitution was not adopted in 1996, this call re-emerged in 2013. The then Deputy Prime Minister Zahid Hamidi claimed that Shi'ism had become a national security issue and would be placed under the purview of the Home Ministry rather than the religious authorities. He also reiterated that the Federal Constitution would be amended to only recognise Sunni Islam (New Straits Times 2013a). However, this plan failed to transpire even before Umno lost the

2018 general election, and this could also be why the proposal has not been carried through since.

The persecution of the Syiah community continued unabated and turned even more vigorous under the administration of Najib Abdul Razak. It is believed he buckled under the pressure of demands by both governmental and non-governmental groups in exchange for raising his Islamic credentials (Mohd Faizal and tan 2017, 323–324). The number of Syiah followers in Malaysia as stated in a memorandum presented to the agong (king) by the unregistered National Shia Council in 2011 was between 200,000 to 300,000. The Home Ministry also identified ten of the most active Syiah centres in various *negeri*, including Kelantan (New Straits Times 2013b). The Syiah story bears a familiar pattern where a new movement—or one that is old but emboldened—of Islamic expression surfaces, and while its numbers may be far from massive, the phenomenon is still construed as a threat to dominant Islam, that is, an Islam that is securely under the control of the Divine Bureaucracy. In the 2013 reporting of the Syiah security threat, the Home Ministry created a special position for a Public Order and Safety (Religious Affairs) officer whose job was to monitor the activities of this group, alleged to have an extensive business network to the extent of funding a RM20 million mosque (New Straits Times 2013b).[17] Shi'ism as an Islamic faith or political movement is not special in terms of its experience of persecution by the state, as this too had been the case of Darul Arqam in the early 1990s and the Jemaah Al-Quran Malaysia (JAM) in the mid-1990s. The Divine Bureaucracy tightly guards its domain, as it cannot afford to have competing sources of appeal, enchantment and, ultimately, legitimacy. It seems too much may be at stake if a monopoly power over Islam can be chipped away and, at the end of the day, challenged by the diverse and plural expressions of Islam.

The Case of Jemaah Al-Quran and Kassim Ahmad

While the overwhelming majority of the aforementioned groups were led by unknown and obscure spiritual leaders in the fringes of cities, and, most importantly, were not threats to national security, there were still others considered more dangerous to the burgeoning Divine Bureaucracy. In the late 1990s, Kassim Ahmad, a scholar, writer and ex-chairman of Parti Sosialis Rakyat Malaysia (PSRM, People's Socialist Party of Malaysia), became the centre of a major controversy, which evoked the ire of the Islamic authorities. He was among those accused of leading an anti-*hadith* movement, called the Jemaah Al-Quran Malaysia (JAM), said to be in contravention of Sunni Islam and ruled deviationist by the FT *fatwa* committee and the FT SIRC (Maiwp) (New Straits Times 1995a). The group was even referred to the police and the Home Ministry for action (Juhaidi 1995). Kassim's call for an open dialogue with state Islamic authorities and other Islamic scholars was not welcomed (Juhaidi 1995). There was intense pressure from Yadim (Malaysian Missionary Foundation), Abim (Malaysian Islamic Youth Movement), Umno Youth and other Islamic scholars who claimed it was creating divisions among Muslims (Juhaidi and Ramlan 1995; New Straits Times 1995b). The group was refused registration and the then de facto Minister of Islamic Affairs, Abdul Hamid Othman, accused the group, which included intellectuals and university lecturers, as not having a strong foundation in Islam, and out to confuse Muslims (New Straits Times 1995c). *Muftis* nationwide also declared the group *murtad* (apostates) (The Straits Times 1995).

Its presence in Penang, Kuala Lumpur, Johor Bahru and Terengganu was a source of anxiety among those running Yadim and Pusat Islam (also known as Baheis, the precursor to Jakim)—functioning under the Prime Minister's Department (PM's Department hereon)—and they were able to direct the cooperation of all SIRCs to look into the matter (New Straits Times 1995d). Yadim, under the chairmanship of Dusuki Ahmad (a former Deputy Minister of Information), was one of the most vociferous in calling for JAM's ban along with another 50 movements deemed 'deviant' (Juhaidi 1995). Among the reasons given were that JAM in particular could turn out to be as large a threat as the banned Darul Arqam movement, and that it would cause disunity, chaos and confusion among Muslims. Even more worrying for the authorities was that JAM was led by scholars, which meant that an 'intellectual' and 'non-confrontational' approach had to be used against it (New Straits Times 1995c). A 'turf-war' had been ignited. Yadim, Baheis and all other state Islamic institutions, functionaries and academics were on one side of the divide (the nascent Divine Bureaucracy), while those not in the circle of religious elites were on the other 'threatening' side. Representatives of 'government-sponsored Islam' were determined to put a closure to this contestation, especially since Kassim Ahmad's group, though small in influence, harked back to an unwanted remnant of Islamic civil society's struggle in earlier decades, and of the unfinished business of the state co-opting expressions of Islam among middle-class Muslims.

A high-powered meeting held in July 1995 to discuss the course of action against Kassim Ahmad's JAM seemed to be a gathering of the who's who of an embryonic class of new Islamists comprising bureaucrats rather than politicians. Besides the chair and representatives from Yadim and Pusat Islam, state officials present at this meeting included the Perak *mufti*, Harussani Zakaria, Penang *mufti* Sheikh Azmi Ahmad and FT *mufti* Abdul Kadir Talip. The academicians among them were heads of the respective Islamic Studies faculties of public universities, Mohamed Hashim Yahya, head of the Akademi Pengajian Islam (Islamic Studies Academy) in University of Malaya (UM); Mohamed Mokhtar Shafie of the International Islamic University Malaysia (IIUM); Abdul Shukor Hussin of the Islamic Studies faculty, and Hudah Mohsin of the Usuluddin department, both at the National University of Malaysia (UKM); and Rodhi Osman of the University of Science Malaysia (USM) (Juhaidi and Ramlan 1995).

In 1996, Pusat Islam mustered 500 people, including 40 leaders of 'deviationist' groups, to undergo a rehabilitation programme, with the purpose of preventing them from spreading their teachings to civil servants, *penghulu* (village heads) and community leaders (New Straits Times 1996). It was around this time that the government announced its intention to amend the Federal Constitution to deem all forms of Islamic teachings other than ASWJ to be illegal (New Straits Times 1996).

It is worth nothing that PM Mahathir was not always on the same page as the officials under him. On the Kassim Ahmad issue, he was circumspect on the need for detention as a solution and was quoted saying, "We have to go deeply into this because it is a matter concerning religion. Islam allows certain differences in the interpretation" (New Straits Times 1995b). His opinion was not heeded. It would seem that this was the precursor to the extraordinary ability of the religious bureaucrat to act independently of the highest-ranking politician and Executive of the government. In these matters, the Islamic bureaucracy at the *negeri* level was able to exert its independence best. In 1995, Selangor issued a *fatwa* banning the anti-*hadith* group JAM, including a book by Rashad Khalifa,[18] claimed to be JAM's source of influence. The same *fatwa* also banned the group's translation of the Quran into Malay, *Bacaan* (Reading), Kassim Ahmad's *Hadis: Satu Penilaian Semula* (*Hadith*: A Reassessment) and *Hadis Jawapan Kepada Pengkritik* (*Hadith*: Answers to Critics) as well as several other books by JAM's members.[19]

Kassim Ahmad died in October 2017. A few years prior, in 2014, he was arrested and charged in the Syariah High Court with three counts of deriding Islam and for breaching a *fatwa* in one of the talks he gave. He was detained by Jawi, the FT religious department, at his home in Kedah and brought to Putrajaya to be charged. In 2017, a few months before his death, the Federal Court declared the arrest and charges illegal. He won the appeal on the basis that Jawi had violated its jurisdiction by arresting him in Kedah (Hafiz 2017a). Kassim's lawyer, Rosli Dahlan, who was also representing several other Malays similarly prosecuted for going against the 'correct' Islam, remarked that, "it is as if the religious authorities [were] trying to curb free thinking among Muslims, including academicians. They seem to want to control the Malays and Muslims" (Hafiz 2017b). Former premier then, Mahathir, said that the Malays had lost a figure who had sharp insight into their problems and that, in his view, Kassim was not "accorded justice, as required by Islam" (Malaysiakini 2017).

The Case of Muslim Women in Beauty Pageants

The signs of a growing Divine Bureaucracy and its new-found authority in the tangential determination of Islamic faith, as well as its rights and wrongs, presented themselves over the arrest of three Muslim women participating in a beauty pageant. This issue was also the precursor of Mahathir's inability as Prime Minister to have much clout over Islamic matters, now firmly in the hands of a growing *negeri* and federal Islamic bureaucracy. In 1997, the religious authorities of Selangor arrested and convicted three Muslim women for taking part in a beauty contest, on grounds that they had contravened a 1995 *fatwa* banning Muslim women from partaking in such events,[20] even if this was the norm previously. This *fatwa* was inspired by a call in 1995 by a student-based Islamic group, the National Union of Malaysian Muslim Students, to ban beauty pageants. After the group submitted its memorandum to Baheis, the federal Islamic agency, and the National Fatwa Committee, as well as to respective ministers in charge of law, information, home affairs and education (New Straits Times 1995d), only the Selangor *fatwa* committee responded with its *fatwa*.

The 1997 arrests were carried out by religious officers who had sat through the contest and only arrested the three women at the end of the event, in full view of the entire audience. Mahathir responded by calling all *negeri* to stop gazetting[21] *fatwa*, in particular the 1995 Selangor *fatwa*, before consultation and clearance by the National Fatwa Committee that came under the PM's Department (New Straits Times 1997a; The Straits Times 1997a). Not only did he fail in his attempts, his statements and sentiments over the controversy also provoked a backlash. His planned reform of Islamic laws to reflect the moderate stance of the federal government was not to be. After his condemnation of the arrest, several mosque groups held meetings to attack his administration for its interference in the matter, arguing that Islam was constitutionally under the powers of individual *negeri* (The Australian 1997a; South China Morning Post 1997). This was almost akin to an open war between Mahathir's vision of Islam and that of religious functionaries who had emerged out of official Islamisation efforts since the 1970s. Among these adversaries were various *mufti* and *ulama*—they mobilised their local followers through speeches in mosques and widely distributed taped recordings of these—and Pas, which also capitalised on the schism (The Straits Times 1997b).

The above issue and repercussions sparked one of the first forceful debates and divides between moderate and liberal Muslims—coincidentally, prior to then unknown and un-demonised labels—and the increasingly emboldened Islamic bureaucracy, which was beginning to be fully aware of its own enormous powers (The Australian 1997b). Four women's groups—Women's Aid Organisation, All Women's Action Society, Association of Women Lawyers and Sisters in Islam—jointly issued a statement condemning the arrest, based on the approach used, that is, publicly humiliating the women by arresting them at the end of the contest and before a hall of audience. They also criticised the undemocratic nature of *fatwa* for their wide and arbitrary notion of what constitutes "contempt of religious authority" (New Straits Times 1997b). Conversely, women's groups aligned to the Islamic authorities and Muslim civil society and called for a total ban of all beauty contests on grounds that such activities were degrading and exploitative of women (The Straits Times 1997c).

These debates and divergent point of views raised the issue of whether the law, particularly the Federal Constitution, could guarantee unconditional civil liberties to citizens when some of its provisions were not applicable to *negeri* laws on Islamic affairs. The fact that *fatwa* were legally binding without having to go through consultative and democratic debates in national and subnational Parliaments was realised for the first time (New Straits Times 1997c).

The outcome of the 'beauty pageant' arrests demonstrated that even without the support, approval and backing of a federal authority, power over Islam could unequivocally be vested with *negeri* religious authorities. Various parties were drawn into the debate, but the single most significant battle was between Mahathir, who had envisioned a modern, moderate Islam through his Islamic centralisation reform on the one hand and the Divine Bureaucracy backed by unassailable legal, juridical, moral and spatial authority on the other. The old, traditional and simple infrastructure provided by the everyday mosque was used to great effect in mobilising support over to the side of the Divine Bureaucracy, against the remote but seemingly powerful central leadership and urban-based NGOs upholding the language of 'rights' instead of 'faith'. The controversy also laid bare the legal conundrum of Muslim civil liberties, guaranteed by the Federal Constitution but denied by *negeri* legal enactments on Islam. The convergences of new and old bureaucracy, diffused structures of power, ambiguous constitutional provisions and new-found leverage of legal contestation between *negeri* and federal Islamic authorities made for a new turning point in the capture of the Muslim subject.

The Case of Sisters in Islam

In 2009, the homogenisation mission of bureaucratic Islam was extended to Sisters in Islam (Sis). Initially taking root in 1993 before being formally established as a non-profit company in 1998, Sis was formed to advance the rights of Muslim women by going back to the doctrinal sources of the faith, namely the Quran and the *hadith*. According to co-founder Zainah Anwar, the movement was formed to critically re-examine and reinterpret Islamic texts so that an Islamic tradition advocating women's rights, human rights, democracy and modernity could be invoked (Ng et al. 2006, 98). Attitudes towards Sis among those who profess to be defenders of Islam range from being reticently disapproving to openly disdainful and, on several occasions, the resentment has been quite vehement. In 2006, the author was a member of the audience as well as privy to the organisation of a public forum on women held at a public university, in which members of Sis were invited as panellists. Several days before the event took place, banners publicising the event around the campus were removed. During the forum itself, hecklers and representatives from unidentified Islamic groups tried to unsettle the event by posing questions and comments which alleged that Sis had a Western-led agenda and displayed ignorance about Islam. The coordinator of the forum later received a letter from some Muslim students who rebuked her for organising the event. To these groups, Sis was considered unqualified to speak about Islam, and by doing so was close to being heretical.

In 2008, the Home Ministry banned the book *Muslim Women and the Challenge of Islamic Extremism*, edited by another co-founder of Sis, Norani Othman. As with 'deviant' Muslim groups, censorship including book bans came under the purview of the Home Ministry and not the religious authorities. However, Jakim was party to this action as the Ministry had used Jakim's guidelines in making its decision. The book, published in 2005, was a compilation of essays on religious fundamentalism and written by an international group of scholars. According to the government's counsel, the book was banned because it was "prejudicial to public order" that the authors were inviting Muslims to be rid of gender when in fact "Islam did not differentiate (between) [*sic*] men and women" and that the "contents of the book contravened guidelines of the Islamic Development Department and touched on the purity of Islam" (New Straits Times 2009a). The ban was overturned by the court in 2010 when the judge ruled that there was no basis to the argument that the book would disrupt public order. As he noted, it had already been in circulation for a few years without any untoward incident; therefore, it was illegal and irrational for the Minister to ban it (New Straits Times 2010; International Herald Tribune 2010).

Despite the above examples of 'persecution', there was no overt pressure to call for Sis to be banned—not until 2009. This was when Pas passed a resolution at its 55th General Assembly calling for the group to be investigated and outlawed if found to be contravening Islam. Its resolution urged the National Fatwa Committee to investigate if the organisation had gone against the teachings of Islam, and, if so, for Sis members to undergo a rehabilitation programme (New Straits Times 2009b).

In 2014, five years after this call, religious authorities in Selangor issued a *fatwa* declaring that Sis had "strayed and deviated from the teachings of Islam" (*sesat dan menyeleweng daripada ajaran Islam*) because it upheld belief in liberalism and religious pluralism (*berpegang kepada fahaman liberalisme dan pluralisme agama*).[22] By this time, Pas was a component member of the subnational government in Selangor, having been part of the coalition (Pakatan Rakyat, People's Alliance) that won *negeri* elections in 2008 and 2013. The *fatwa* did not explicitly ban the organisation but served to dissuade others from associating with the group it had labelled as 'deviant', and, for those already involved, to repent and return to the right path of Islam.

In 2016, Sis challenged the *fatwa* at the High Court, but the case was dismissed on grounds that only a *syariah* court could determine the validity of *fatwa* (New Straits Times 2016). In 2018, after an appeal before a Federal Court bench of seven leading judges and headed by then Chief Justice Richard Malanjum, the case was sent back to the High Court to be reheard (New Straits Time 2018). In August 2019, the Kuala Lumpur High Court dismissed Sis's judicial review application against the Selangor *fatwa*, ruling that, in accordance with *syariah*, the Selangor *fatwa* committee was well within its jurisdiction to pronounce the organisation as 'deviant' (Alyaa 2019).

Even before the court decision, the *fatwa* against Sis had been used against the organisation. In March 2019, Deputy Minister of Women, Family and Community Development, Hannah Yeoh, was chided in Parliament for giving a grant of RM20,000 to support the legal clinic operated by Sis. A Pas parliamentarian argued that the Deputy Minister had gone against the Selangor *fatwa* and the Selangor sultan, by extending this allocation to the organisation. The Deputy Minister responded that she did not imagine an act of helping Muslim women in need could be construed as being against the religion (Malaysiakini 2019a).

The pursuit of legal redress by Sis against its persecution in the name of Islam is one of many intra-Muslim contestations brought about by the expansion of *syariah* laws, regulations and *fatwa* pronouncements. Nevertheless, it is not legislation per se that has made this happen but rather the worldview of those who have been able to use these laws, regulations and *fatwa* to exacerbate a manufactured 'official Islam' versus 'deviant group' fracture. By providing an alternative approach to Islam, Sis also unsettled an authority-defined identity of the Malay-Muslim subject. The Divine Bureaucracy's project of standardising faith finds its sustainability in the reinvention of a past Islamic history, involving orthodoxy (as in the ASWJ faction) and heresy (as in the rationality stream of the Mu'tazilah). A full-blown fingering of 'liberals', 'pluralists', 'feminists' and eventually 'LGBT' as belonging to the latter stream in a new context occurred in the early 2000s.

The Threat of Liberals, Pluralists, Feminists and Others

A heightened demonisation of alleged Islamic adversaries—painted as liberals, pluralists, feminists and LGBTs—appears to have started in the early 2000s. With a further movement towards the standardisation of faith, these new targets of prohibition were first identified and collectively demonised under the administration of PM Abdullah Ahmad Badawi (2004–2008). Previously, there was scant literature or online posts related to 'liberalism and pluralism' as a subject worthy of Islamic condemnation. At most, it was the label 'secularism' that was predominantly used to distinguish the non-Islamic West from a postcolonial revivalist Islam, the latter being a total living system—and hence imagined to be 'superior'—and an alternative to the former.[23]

In 1996, Anwar Ibrahim, Malaysia's former Deputy Prime Minister, published his book *The Asian Renaissance*, which included the espousal of multiculturalism, humanism and cultural pluralism. At the time, these ideas were clearly not associated with Islamic deviancy. There is some evidence that the above trend of demonising liberalism and its purported implications and derivatives in Malaysia could have originated from Indonesia. Jakim officials writing on this subject cite the Indonesian case as a background to their own reactions (Mohd Aizam 2015, 238–242; Ahmad Yumni and Mohd Fairuz 2016). In Indonesia, post-Suharto democratisation and decentralisation provided transitional moments during which debates and dissension around Islam were considered almost *de rigueur*. Consider the Network of Liberal Islam (Jaringan Islam Liberal, JIL) of Indonesia, which drew on the thoughts of Nurcholish Majid and Abdul Rahman Wahid (Gus Dur) and was founded in 2001. The aims of JIL, according to one of its founders Ulil Abshar Abdaila (2008), was to "critique the interpretations of Islam by fundamentalists, radicals and proponents of violence" and to "spread the understanding of an Islam through a rational, contextual, humanist and pluralist basis". In espousing such principles, JIL very soon met with virulent opposition from other Islamic camps, which pronounced that this movement had gone against the grain of traditional or orthodox Islam. In attacking JIL's philosophical stance, these groups claimed that Islam placed no premium on freedom, rational reasoning (*ijtihad*), multifaith engagement, gender equality or tolerance for same-sex relations (Ahmad Bunyan 2006). By 2005, the

Majlis Ulama Indonesia (Mui, Fatwa Council of Indonesia) issued a *fatwa* declaring that liberalism, pluralism and secularism were un-Islamic.

The denouncement of JIL was also the time during which a debate over liberal Islam appeared in Malaysian religious discourse. Jakim provided the argument by publishing an article in its journal, which called for the ban of the book *Fiqh Lintas Agama* (Legal Principles on Bridging Religion) written by those associated with the liberal Islam camp in Indonesia, including Nurcholish Madjid and Kauthar Azhari Noer (Mohamad Nordin 2005). In 2006, the National Fatwa Committee appeared to have followed Mui's act when it issued a similar *fatwa* denouncing liberalism, pluralism and secularism in Islam. The Malaysian *fatwa* proclaimed that religious pluralism would put all religions on an equal standing, which was unacceptable because this involved lowering the status of Islam (Mohd Aizam 2015, 238). The liberal thought movement was also accused of harbouring beliefs that would make Muslims question and deviate from their faith—the persistent reference to the use of rationality by the Mu'tazilites is favoured—and hence needed to be ruled as *haram* (Ahmad Yumni and Mohd Fairuz 2016).

In Malaysia, a most vocal NGOs at the forefront against 'liberals' or those it labels as the 'enemies' of Islam is Ikatan Muslimin Malaysia (Isma, Alliance of Malaysian Muslims), an organisation founded in 1997. The group's original aim was to develop "total Islamic living and culture" among "middle-class Muslims". However, by the early 2000s, it seemed to have refocused its goals on combating what it called the surge of liberalism, pluralism and secularism in Muslim society. Isma runs an active website that functions as an online news portal, *Portal Islam dan Melayu* (Islamic and Malay Portal).[24] It appears to be non-partisan, though the group's causes are inseparable from Malay ethnocentric interests, hence in support of both Umno and Pas. At the same time, Isma has also been critical of the present Pakatan Harapan (PH, Alliance of Hope) government. Its mode of attack is to present the PH government as supportive of liberalism and women's rights, both of which are portrayed as a threat to Islam (Athirah Huda 2017; Riduan 2018; Siti Fatimah 2018). This development of liberalism-bashing by an NGO seems to be coordinated and conducted in concert with the agenda of the Divine Bureaucracy, which is meant to deal a blow to the sustenance of civil society actors such as Sis and IRF,[25] just as what JIL had been subjected to in Indonesia.

Isma and its women's wing, Wanita Isma, have also been behind efforts to oust inclusivist Muslim women's groups. Specifically, they are very vocal and pervasive in their condemnation of Muslim feminists whom they also associate with the LGBT movement. A study of how women in Isma countered feminism lays down the absolutism of opposition between 'feminism/liberalism' and Islam, the former being a movement from the West. This asserts that while feminism seeks freedom from religion and the ways of Islam, Islam seeks the oneness of Allah and submission to Allah by obeying his commands. Moreover, feminism and liberalism are the "enemy's" plan to destroy the identity and character of Muslim women (*Feminisme dan liberalisme adalah agenda terancang musuh bagi merosakkan jatidiri dan identiti wanita muslimah*) (Norsaleha 2015, 13). The list of 'un-Islamic' stances of feminists include "questioning the justness of *hudud* law", "objecting against whipping as a punishment for women", and "[saying] that veiling is not a religious obligation but an influence of Arab culture". If these are not countered, these viewpoints would dissuade society away from appreciating the "true beauty of Islam" (Norsaleha 2015, 8).

Another organisation marked as 'liberal' by Islamic exclusivists is the IRF. In September 2017, Jawi detained one of its invited speakers, Mustafa Akyol, a renowned Turkish writer residing in the United States. This was justified on grounds that the speaker did not have the *tauliah* (authorisation) from the religious department to deliver his Islamic-related talks in Malaysia.[26] Akyol's book, *Islam Without Extremes: A Muslim case for liberty*, had been translated into Malay, but was immediately banned after this episode. Prior to his scheduled talk, the writer had spoken about the "suppression of rational theology by dogmatists in early Islam" and on "apostasy from Islam" whilst he was already in the country (Akyol 2017). Thereafter, his talk on "The Commonalities Between Judaism, Christians and Islam" was cancelled. In detention, he was told by the arresting authorities that they had acted "to protect Islam". Those who supported his arrest justified it on social media, claiming that he was spreading the dangerous idea of liberalism, and dismissed his talk as an example of a new lifeline given to the orientalist movement (*gerakan orientalis yang diberi nafas baru*).[27]

This agenda to demonise the liberal 'Other' has even included an extensive and concerted educational programme to inform and teach students in universities about the dangers of deviant ideologies. A whole set of courses in the curricula of Islamic Studies is now devoted to unpacking and debating what is known as the Liberal Islam stream, with the purpose of stemming its overt presence. The narratives of gender equality, human rights and interfaith dialogue are particularly singled out as some of the dangers emanating from liberalism, as seen in the following unsubstantiated description in English, and reproduced in its original:

> They have the tendency to go beyond the boundaries of Islam when they claim a pluralist interpretation of Islam, including a controversial look at Allah's laws based on Muslim theology with rational views and dismissing the enforcement of religious moral laws. The Liberal Islam movement in Malaysia is inclined towards copying what had existed earlier in the Middle East and Indonesia. For example, the controversial issues pertaining to the women's rights of today as forwarded by the Sisters in Islam (Sis) organization [*sic*]. (Jaffary et al. 2011, 432)

The Standardisation of Faith Through Women's Dressing

The properly covered self (not just with a veil) is taken as the most potent symbol and commitment of a Muslim woman's submission to Islam. Debates and pressure for women to *menutup aurat*, to cover their forbidden bodily parts, have intensified over the years. Without even conducting any survey on the subject, it is common knowledge that almost all adult Muslim women in Malaysia now don the veil. Nevertheless, the depth, layers and complexity of this act, symbolic or otherwise, have provided fertile ground for many observations and analyses. Even though the *tudung* (headscarf or veil, *hijab*)[28] may be seen as a successful symbol of an advancing and extensive Islamisation to the outsider or non-Muslim eye, the purveyors and monitors of the religion believe otherwise.

For one, they apparently have a much higher standard for judging what constitutes correct veiling. Increasingly, there are more remarks about incorrect veiling than about veiling at all. Views on whether the veil covers the head, hair, face or body adequately, or whether it is so fashionable that it detracts from its 'true' religious purpose, have all been aired publicly and via social media. Even graphic illustrations have been produced to drive home the point about the definitive, correct and authentic way of donning the *hijab*.[29] Although not representative of the mainstream or moderate school of thought, it is worth reproducing parts of a passage from a blog called "*Kami Sayang* Ulama: Ulama *penyambung pejuangan Nabi*" (We Love *Ulama*: *Ulama* as carriers of the Prophet's struggle). According to one of its entries that describes a gruesome punishment for women who do not cover their *aurat* (hair and other bodily parts), those who refuse to do so would be "hung by their hair above the fires of hell until their brains boiled over", while those who accentuated their breasts to look sexy would also be "hung above the fires of hell" but "by suspending them with the chains of hell tied to their navel and breasts".[30]

Concern over Islamic dressing has also been raised by Puteri Umno, the young women's wing of Umno. At its 2015 Annual Meeting, this body passed a resolution that called on all women Umno members to wear the headscarf. However, this call was not made public purportedly because it was a closed-door session. Instead the news leaked only because a senior male member of the Umno Supreme Council who was present—coincidentally the de facto Deputy Minister of Islamic Affairs in the PM's Department—posted his account of this news on Facebook. His post mentioned how the resolution not only received a resounding approval from the 900 delegates, but that they also apparently gave its proposer a standing ovation. His post attracted almost 1000 likes and 150 comments, almost all of which were in support of the resolution.[31]

Another episode as part and parcel of efforts to homogenise the Islamic faith was one which involved a prominent woman politician. Such an incident reveals how the determined parameters of women's dressing do not need to be enforced by the religious bureaucracy since this role has been adeptly undertaken by private actors disguised as dress vigilantes. After the culmination of Malaysia's most recent election in May 2018, which saw the 61-year-old Barisan Nasional government overthrown for the first time, Nurul Izzah Anwar, daughter of Anwar Ibrahim, Malaysia's one-time Deputy Prime Minister and leader of the reform movement, gave an interview at a radio station as a freshly re-elected Member of Parliament. The programme invited people to call in with questions. One of the callers was a man whose interest was not in talking on the topic at hand but in berating Nurul Izzah about her 'indecent' way of wearing the *tudung*. The conversation on air went this way:

Caller:	I want to share a bit with the Honorable Member, sometimes your *tudung* can be out of place and will show things that are not meant to be revealed.
Host:	Oh, ooh, ok.
Nurul Izzah:	Ok, thank you.
Caller:	This is dangerous because what is meant to be concealed must be concealed.

Host:	Thanks a lot.
Caller:	Er, your bra and your breasts can be seen.
Host:	Is that all Azrul? Ok thank you, Assalamuallaikum.[32]

Although this was a radio show, it was also shared on live video feed. This possibly contributed to the reactions of the host and Nurul Izzah—being polite and thanking the caller for his comments and advice—which were somewhat incongruous, perhaps because they were taken aback. It took only a few minutes before Twitter messages went abuzz. Early reactions showed that people were confused. Here was a notable Member of Parliament being humiliated by comments from an unknown caller over her supposedly indecent dressing.[33] Those who condemned the caller's actions put it down as act of religious extremism. That he was imposing his misogynistic worldview in the guise of religion, on a woman many would imagine was adequately veiled and modestly dressed, was shocking. Only later were his actions appropriately named sexual harassment, though Nurul Izzah herself refrained from commenting on this episode.

The veil has continued to be the subject of male and scholarly gaze, and this can be colourfully provided by the controversy over the launch of a Muslim women's headwear in a well-known Kuala Lumpur nightclub, Zouk. The entrepreneur behind this was Neelofa, formerly an actor and TV personality before becoming a successful entrepreneur; she was named one of Asia's top 30 entrepreneurs below the age of 30 by Forbes magazine in 2017. Neelofa's main business was selling fashionable *tudung* through the online medium catered to a younger cohort of women, where she herself would model her products. When a video recording of some *tudung* women clad in tight-fitting pants gyrating to music at the product's nightclub launch went viral over social media in 2018, it drew numerous reactions, from the supportive to the defensive to the offensive. The incident caught the attention of major authoritative guardians of Islam, among whom was the FT *mufti*. In his open letter to Neelofa posted on his webpage, he pointed that,

> [T]he veil is a symbol of shyness and modesty for a woman, a symbol of moral conduct which should be protected, which is a symbol of Islamic pride… what has happened recently will potentially bring about a phenomenon of normalising veiling [where] anything goes as long as the wearer is veiled.[34]

The incident did not go unnoticed by women in Isma either. Active in their roles as defenders and protectors of Islam, they periodically issue statements to address religious transgressions committed by women. In this instance, Dr Fatimah Zaharah Rosli and Dr Nadiah Norudin proffered advice to Neelofa on the sanctity of the veil (Nadiah 2018; Fatimah 2018). Nadiah (2018) averred the following,

> Today Muslim women have been fed the ideology that the veiled woman can do anything she pleases, even with a veil she can sing and dance in front of the public, even with a veil she can smoke a cigarette, and the latest, with a veil one can even enter the nightclub and do dances which titillate.[35]

The never-ending fascination of policing women through the symbolism and enforcement of the *tudung* will be felt for a long time. In April 2019, after Maryam Lee launched her book, *Unveiling Choice*, at a public forum, Jais called for her to be investigated, while Pas wanted her book banned (Malaysiakini 2019b; Nuridah 2019). The book is a personal and intellectual narrative of her journey to remove her veil, which she had worn since the age of nine. She puts the *tudung* question as one bereft of 'choice' as, "[T]he only way that Muslim women, as a collective, have real choice over the hijab is when nobody cares whether we wear the hijab at all!" (Maryam 2019, 57). The wishful "nobody cares" is most unlikely, not when the standardisation of faith is extended to principally include 'care' and control over the body too.

Conclusion

The bureaucratisation of religion added new challenges to being and becoming 'Muslim'. As various groups of Muslims can attest, they have found themselves designated as being incorrect, improper, impure and in contravention of the official creed defined by *negeri* and federal institutions of the Divine Bureaucracy. This bureaucracy has become a force of salvation and deliverance. Only one version of Islam, ASWJ or Sunni Islam, is accepted as the official expression of faith, even though its definitions remain vague if not perplexing and abstruse to the common everyday understanding of being Muslim. Nevertheless, even if this objectification of the ASWJ had been painstakingly refined, the template definition has not been the only means to discriminate between the 'wrong' and 'right' groups of Muslims.

The Divine Bureaucracy did not stop at persecuting groups who were anti-Sunni, namely the Syiah or the anti-*hadith* group. The power of the *fatwa* has also been used to sanction everyday 'immoral' acts such as participation in a beauty contest. Newly identified group labels were added to the gamut of those deemed threatening to the *akidah*. If 'liberalism', 'pluralism' and 'feminism' were identifiers of social movements brought about by the expansion of liberal democracy and human rights discourses, those perceived as their advocates have now been explicitly named as the enemies of Islam, by reducing, simplifying and reinventing an ancient ninth-century philosophical discourse into a binary division of rationalism versus revelation. No meticulous arguments that they have strayed from the ASWJ stream need to be proffered, only the suggestion that there is some historical connection to past contentions. Characteristics of those not conforming to official Islam and *aqidah* can be arbitrarily expanded and used as disciplinary measures to standardise religious expressions.

Cases analysed in this chapter, involving injunctions imposed by the Divine Bureaucracy on the anti-*hadith* movement, Shi'ism, beauty contestants, feminist organisations, liberals, pluralists and women's dressing, can be read as the necessity and outcome of standardisation and its antecedent, the objectification and disenchantment of social life. The contentions around these issues show the unassailable and expansionary strength of the Divine Bureaucracy in its ability to attack, condemn, vilify and malign personalities and act with impunity. Even so, in its use of disproportionate measures to curb competitors and challenges to its moral authority, these actions also reveal deep insecurity. As the Divine Bureaucracy disenchants and objectifies the Muslim subject through the rational and copious uses of law, *fatwa* and sacred texts, it also bares its vulnerability as an overbearing autocrat, which depends on a vicious cycle of domination with a no-exit rule for the dominated. The following chapter will continue with this argument in discussing the condition of ring-fencing Muslim constituents.

Notes

1. This subject will be delved into more fully in Chap. 7.
2. See Shamsul (2001, 365) for an explication of the difference between 'authority-defined' and 'everyday-defined' social practices; in his case it was the idea of identity.
3. The Institut Ahli Sunnah Wal Jamaah was set up in 2013 as a research and consultancy unit at the Universiti Tun Hussein Onn Malaysia (UTHM) in

Johor (see http://iaswj.uthm.edu.my/index.php/tentang-kami/pengenalan, 9 April 2019).

4. A discussion of the significance of the 'Mu'tazilah' narrative will be discussed in the later section of this chapter.
5. It says, "*Majlis tidak terikat kepada mana-mana satu mazhab tertentu. Di dalam Mazhab mana pun yang jelas dan nyata pendapat mereka itu dari kitab Allah atau Sunnah Rasulnya atau Jemaah Sahabat Rasulullah s.a.w. maka Majlis sedia menerima dan beramal dengannya.*; *Adapun Mazhab-mazhab seperti Hanafi, Maliki, Syafie dan Hanbali pada pandangan rasmi Majlis adalah terhitung di dalam Mazhab-mazhab yang muktabar yang tergolong di dalam istilah Ahli Sunnah Wal Jemaah*", from "Pengertian Ahli Al-Sunnah Wal Jamaah", Perlis *fatwa* committee, issued in 1970, http://e-smaf.islam.gov.my/e-smaf/fatwa/fatwa/find/3, 21 February 2019.
6. "Golongan yand memahami dan berpegang kepada al-Quran dan Sunnah Nabi SAW menerusi para sahabat, *tabi'in* dan *tabi' tabi'in* yang setia bersama mereka dalam prinsip-prinsip aqidah, syariah dan akhlak" (Mohd Aizam 2015, 19).
7. Fatwa on "Ciri-Ciri Ajaran Sesat Yang Menyalahi Pegangan Ahli Sunnah Wal Jamaah", Federal Territory, 2012, http://e-smaf.islam.gov.my/e-smaf/fatwa/fatwa/find/3, accessed 21 February 2019.
8. "Tafsiran Pegangan dan Aqidah Ahli Sunnah Wal Jamaah" not gazetted but decided by Negeri Sembilan *fatwa* committee on 25 February 2016, http://e-smaf.islam.gov.my/e-smaf/fatwa/fatwa/find/3, accessed 21 February 2019.
9. More on this will be discussed in Chap. 5.
10. From: "Tinta Seorang Da'ie", http://aqidah-falsafah.blogspot.com/2011/05/mutazilah-dan-ahli-as-sunnah-wal-jamaah.html, 29 April 2019.
11. Kumpulan Pecah Kuil and Tarikat Mohammad Mahadi, respectively, are infamous for their involvement in the Kerling Temple desecration incident and the attack on the Batu Pahat police station. See also Chap. 2.
12. This is translated as the sense of the Quran as 'providing the difference'.
13. From Government of Selangor Gazette, 29 August 1991 (*Fatwa Ilmu Salah*).
14. This was a veneration of the descendants of the Prophet as the rightful heir to Islamic continuity. It was the source of the split between the Sunnis who installed the Abu Bakar as the first caliph after the death of Muhammad and the Syiahs who wanted Ali (husband of Fatimah) as the Prophet's successor.
15. From Government of Selangor Gazette, 24 September 1998, (*Fatwa Tentang Ajaran Tijah @ Khatijah bt Ali*).
16. See Chap. 6 for an elaboration on this case.

17. The application for a construction permit to build the mosque was rejected by the government.
18. Dr Rashad Khalifa was an Egyptian-born American scientist who was associated with an Islamic reform group. He interpreted the Quran based on a mathematical structure and disavowed the *hadith* as being corrupt. His teachings have been rejected by traditionalists. He was killed inside a mosque in Arizona in 1990. The book banned by the Selangor *fatwa* was "The Computer Speaks – God's Message to the World".
19. Government of Selangor Gazette, 12 November 1995, Vol. 48, No. 4 (*Fatwa Tentang Golongan Anti-Hadith*).
20. Government of Selangor Gazette, 11 May 1995, Vol. 48, No. 10, (*Fatwa Tentang Penyertaan Wanita Islam Dalam Pertandingan Ratu Cantik*).
21. *Fatwa* has the status of being gazetted, which means it is formalised by the *negeri* government. It can also remain un-gazetted, as a decision of each *fatwa* committee. There are grey areas all around and whether an un-gazetted *fatwa* can be enforced.
22. Government of Selangor Gazette, 31 July 2014, Vol. 67, No. 16 (*Fatwa Pemikiran Liberalisme dan Pluralisme Agama*).
23. The book *Islam and Secularism* by Syed Muhammad Naquib Al-Attas (1993), first published in 1978, was one of the most popular and influential guideposts for Islamic resurgence activists searching for an alternative postcolonial order in Malaysia.
24. See https://www.ismaweb.net, 10 April 2019.
25. The IRF was launched by Tariq Ramadan in 2009 and describes itself as "an intellectual movement and think tank focused on youth empowerment and the promotion of Muslim intellectual discourse". As well, it is "committed to liberating the Muslim mind from rigid orthodoxy and conservatism". See https://irfront.net/about-irf/introduction/, accessed 9 April 2019. More is said on the IRF below.
26. Under the Syariah Criminal Offences (Federal Territories) Act 1997, any speaker on Islamic religious matters must receive a *tauliah* (authorisation in the form of a license) before he can proceed with his speech. The failure to do so will subject the person to a fine not exceeding RM5000 or imprisonment up to three years, or both.
27. See "Mustafa Akyol, IRF dan Wacana Islam Liberal", 29 September 2017, https://www.ismaweb.net/2017/09/29/mustafa-akyol-irf-dan-wacana-islam-liberal/, accessed 14 March 2018. The statement was signed by Associate Professor Dr Rafidah Hanim Mokhtar, International Women's Alliance for Family Institution and Quality Education (Wafiq).
28. The *tudung* is literally "cover" in Malay. The *hijab* (in Arabic) is also used to mean the veil.

29. See “Menutup aurat dengan betul”, *Kosmo Online*, xx, http://www.darulkautsar.net/darulkautsar-net/pemurnian-syariat/wanita/kesalahan-kesalahan-di-dalam-menutup-aurat.html http://ww1.kosmo.com.my/kosmo/content.asp?y=2013&dt=0531&pub=Kosmo&sec=Pesona&pg=ps_04.htm, [date accessed?]; and “Kesalahan-Kesalahan Menutup aurat”.
30. *Balasan wanita yang membuka rambut kepalanya selain suaminya akan digantung dengan rambutnya di atas api neraka sehingga menggelegak otaknya, berterusan selama ia tidak menutupnya…dada yang sengaja dibuka atau ditonjolkan supaya kelihatan seksi akan digantung atas api neraka dengan pusat dan buah dadanya diikat dengan rantai neraka sebagai penggantungnya*, from website of *Kami Sayang Ulama*, which seems to be affiliated with or in support of the political party Pas, https://kamisayangulama.wordpress.com/?s=menutup+aurat&submit=Search, accessed 15 March 2018.
31. See Facebook of Asyraf Wajdi Dusuki, https://www.facebook.com/116331768396879/photos/a.148660531830669.27045.116331768396879/1210819208948124/, accessed 15 March 2018.
32. “*Nak share sikit… kadang kadang YB pakai tudung terselak, ternampak yang tak sepatutunya* (Host: *Oh, ooh, ok*; Nurul Izzah: *Baik terima kasih*). *Macam itu bahaya supaya ketup tu mesti nampak ketuplah* (Host: *Terima kasih banyak*). *Erh nampak baju dalam, nampak buah dada* (Host: *Itu sajakah Azrul. Ok terima kasih Asmk*)”.
33. Ironically too, this was far from the truth given that Nurul Izzah is known to dress ‘modestly’ and dons a conventional *tudung*.
34. In the *mufti*’s post he wrote, *[T]udung adalah simbol sifat malu seorang wanita, simbol akhlak Muslimah yang perlu dipelihara dan simbol kemegahan Islam… apa yang terjadi baru-baru ini bakal membawa satu fenomena normalisasi dalam bertudung. Apa sahaja boleh dan dibenarkan asalkan bertudung*. See http://muftiwp.gov.my/ms/sumber/berita/pejabat-mufti-wilayah-persekutuan/2318-qalam-mufti-2-surat-terbuka-kepada-hajjah-neelofa, accessed on 11 March 2018.
35. *Hijab, bukanlah sarung kepala. Hijab, bukan aksesori pakaian anda. Hijab adalah mahkota yang memelihara kemuliaan wanita. Hari ini, wanita Islam khususnya disogok dengan ideologi wanita bertudung juga serba boleh untuk lakukan apa sahaja. Bertudung, masih boleh menyanyi dan menari di khayalak ramai. Bertudung, masih boleh hisap rokok. Dan yang terbaru, bertudung masih boleh masuk ke kelab malam dan membuat tarian menggiurkan*. See Nadiah Noruddin (2018), “Usah gadaikan maruah hanya untuk berfesyen”, 28 February, https://www.ismaweb.net/2018/02/28/usah-gadaikan-maruah-hanya-untuk-berfesyen/, accessed 15 March 2018.

References

Abdul Razak, Omar, Nur Zainatul Nadra Zainol, Halimi Mohd Khalid and Abdullah Sulaiman (2018) "Institut Ahli Sunnah Wal Jumaah UTHM: Peranan dan tanggungjawab", *Jurnal Penyelidikan Jabatan Agama Islam Negeri Johor*, Edisi khas (Special edition), 71–84.

Adam, bin Badrulhisham (2015) "Ahli Sunnah Wal Jamaah dan Pemakaiannya di Malaysia: Isu dan cabaran", paper presented at Simposium Aqidah dan Tasawuf, Malacca, 7 March.

Ahmad Bunyan, Wahib (2006) "Questioning Liberal Islam In Indonesia: Response and critique to Jaringan Islam Liberal", *Al-Jami'ah,* Vol. 44, No. 1, 23–51.

Ahmad Fauzi, Abdul Hamid (2016) "The Extensive Salafization of Malaysian Islam", *Trends in Southeast Asia*, No. 9, 1–41.

——— (2018) *Islamisme dan Bahananya: Cabaran besar politik Malaysia abad ke-21*, Penang: Penerbit USM.

Ahmad Yumni, Abu Bakar and Mohd Fairuz Jamaluddin (2016) *Menjawab Islam Liberal: Pendedahan Jaringan Islam Liberal (JIL) dan Sisters in Islam (Sis)*, Kuala Lumpur: PTS Publishing House.

Akyol, Mustafa (2017) "A Proposal for Islam", *The New York Times*, 28 September; https://www.nytimes.com/2017/09/28/opinion/mustafa-akyol-detention-malaysia.html. Accessed 14 March 2018.

Al-Attas, Syed Muhammad Naquib (1993) *Islam and Secularism*, Kuala Lumpur: International Institute of Islamic Thought and Civilization.

Al-Bayanuni, Ahmad Izzuddin (2009) *Ahli Sunnah Wal-Jamaah: Petunjuk akidah 1 dan 2*, Jabatan Kemajuan Islam Malaysia.

Al-Musawi, Musa (2016) *Dedah Fahaman Syiah*, Putrajaya: Jakim.

Alyaa, Alhadjri (2019) "Sis fails to challenge 'deviant' fatwa", *Malaysiakini*, 27 August.

Aminudin, Basir @Ahmad and Faisal Ahmad Shah (2010) "Kedudukan Golongan yang Menyeleweng (al-Firaq): Satu analisis dari perspektif al-Quran dan al-Sunnah", *Al-Bayan: Journal of al-Quran and al-Hadith*, Vol. 8, 171–188.

Athirah Huda, Zalhe (2017) "Dua darjat fahaman liberal tapi tujuan tetap mahu melemahkan Islam", *Isma Web*, 28 August, https://www.ismaweb.net/2017/08/28/dua-darjat-fahaman-liberal-tapi-tujuan-tetap-mahu-melemah-kan-islam/. Accessed 15 March 2018.

Fatimah Zahrah Rosli (2018) "Teguran Doktor Hafizah buat Neelofa", 3 February, https://www.ismaweb.net/2018/03/01/teguran-doktor-hafizah-quran-buat-neelofa/. Accessed 15 March 2018.

Hafiz, Yatim (2017a) "Federal Court dismisses Jawi's appeal in Kassim Ahmad case", *Malaysiakini*, 10 March.

——— (2017b) "Kassim Ahmad was a great Malaysian, says his lawyer", *Malaysiakini*, 10 October.

Halim, Daud, Zarina binti Othman and Nor Azizan Idris (2018) "Fahaman Syiah dan Keharmonian Agama Islam di Malaysia: Perspektif pendeketan keselamatan negara", *Journal of Social Sciences and Humanities*, Vol. 13, No. 3, 1–19.

Hussein, S Ahmad (1988) Islam and Politics in Malaysia, 1969–1982: The dynamics of competing traditions, PhD thesis submitted to Yale University.

International Herald Tribune (2010) "Ban on book is overturned by court in Malaysia; Government had said that the publication might confuse Muslim women", 26 January.

Jaffary, Awang, Mohamad Zaid Mohd Zin, AA Sakat and MRM Nor, (2011) "Islamic Studies in Malaysia in Confronting Liberalism", *Advances in Natural and Applied Sciences*, Vol. 5, No. 5, 432–439.

Jakim (2012) *Keputusan Muzakarah Jawatankuasa Fatwa Majlis Kebangsaan Bagi Hal Ehwal Ugama Islam Malaysia*, Jabatan Kemajuan Islam Malaysia.

——— (n.d.) *Pelan Strategik Jakim 2015–2019*, Jabatan Kemajuan Islam Malaysia.

Juhaidi, Yean Abdullah (1995) "50 more anti-hadith people identified", *New Straits Times*, 11 July.

Juhaidi, Yean Abdullah and Ramlan Said (1995) "Yadim advised against staging dialogue", *New Straits Times*, 18 July.

Malaysiakini (2017) "Dr M mourns the passing of 'sharp, brave' Kassim Ahmad", 10 October.

——— (2019a) "PAS accuses Yeoh of going against S'gor sultan and fatwa", 10 March.

——— (2019b) "Why fear intellectual discourse on de-hijabbing, ask forum panelists", 17 April.

Martin, Richard C (1980) "The Role of the Basrah Mu'tazilah in Formulating the Doctrine of the Apologetic Miracle", *Journal of Near Eastern Studies*, Vol. 39, No. 3, 175–189.

Maryam, Lee (2019) *Unveiling Choice*, Petaling Jaya: Gerakbudaya Enterprise.

Mohamad Nordin, bin Ibrahim (2005) "Pengaruh Fahaman Liberal dalam Buku *Fiqh Lintas Agama*", *Jurnal Penyelidikan Islam*, 157–172.

Mohamed Nawab, Mohamed Osman (2014) "Salafi Ulama in Umno: Political convergence or expediency?", *Contemporary Southeast Asia*, Vol. 36, No. 1, 206–231.

Mohamed Nawab Mohamed Osman, Aida Arosoaie, (2018) "Jihad in the Bastion of "Moderation": Understanding the Threat of ISIS in Malaysia", *Asian Security*, 1–14

Mohd Aizam, bin Mas'od (2015) *Diskusi Isu Akidah dan Pemikiran Semasa Di Malaysia*, Putrajaya: Jabatan Kemajuan Islam Malaysia

Mohd Faizal, Musa and tan beng hui (2017) "State-backed Discriminiation against Shia Muslims in Malaysia", *Critical Asian Studies*, Vol. 49, No. 3, 308–329.

Muhammad Rashidi, Wahab and Syed Hadzrullathfi Syed Omar (2013) "Peringkat Pemikiran Imam al-Ash'ari dalam Akidah" (Stages of Imam al-Ash'ari Thought in Theology), *International Journal of Islamic Thought, Bangi*, Vol. 3, 58–70.

Nadiah Noruddin (2018) "Usah gadaikan maruah hanya untuk berfesyen", 28 February, https://www.ismaweb.net/2018/02/28/usah-gadaikan-maruah-hanya-untuk-berfesyen/. Accessed 15 March 2018.

Nasr, Seyyed Vali Reza (2001) *Islamic Leviathan: Islam and the making of state power*, Oxford, New York: Oxford University Press.

New Straits Times (1995a) "Writer Kassim Ahmad named anti-hadith movement leader", 4 July.

——— (1995b) "Kassim's group application with PM's department", 19 July.

——— (1995c) "Proper information on Islam necessary, says Abdul Hamid", 9 August.

——— (1995d) "Call for beauty contest ban", 14 February.

——— (1996) "Move to weed out deviant teachings", 26 March.

——— (1997a) "States get order on Islamic rulings", 9 August.

——— (1997b) "Why JAIS action is wrong-headed", 7 July.

——— (1997c) "Questions raised on enactment on fatwa", 22 July.

——— (2009a) "SIS book ban challenge for Jan 25 decision", 22 December.

——— (2009b) "Women's rights Sisters slammed, PAS urges ban", 8 June.

——— (2010) "High Court lifts ban on SIS book", 26 January.

——— (2013a) "No Place for Shia", 8 December.

——— (2013b) "Shia followers exceed 250,000, says ministry", 6 August.

——— (2016) "Court throws out Sisters in Islam's fatwa challenge", 25 June.

——— (2018) "Challenge against fatwa sent back to High Court", 26 September.

Ng, Cecilia, Maznah Mohamad and tan beng hui (2006) *Feminism and the Women's Movement in Malaysia: An unsung (r)evolution*, London: Routledge.

Norsaleha Mohd Salleh (2015) *Penolakan Terhadap Agenda Feminisme aan Liberalisme Di Malaysia*, Research Gate, https://www.researchgate.net/publication/287232617. Accessed 13 May 2019.

Norshahril, Saat (2014) "'Deviant' Muslims: The Plight of Shias in contemporary Malaysia", in Bernhard Platzdasch and Johan Saravanamuttu (eds), *Religious Diversity in Muslim-majority States in Southeast Asia: Areas of toleration and conflict*, Singapore: ISEAS Publishing, 359–378.

——— (2018) *The State, Ulama and Islam in Malaysia and Indonesia*, Singapore: ISEAS Publishing.

Nuridah, Mohd Salleh (2019) "Provokasi Syariah: Apa tindakan selepas JAIS siasat?", *Harakah Daily*, 19 April.

Riduan, Mohd Nor (2018) "Ancaman Islam Liberal di Malaysia", *Ismaweb*, 21 May, https://www.ismaweb.net/2018/05/21/ancaman-islam-liberal-di-malaysia/. Accessed 10 April 2019.

Rudolph, Ulrich (2011) "Muʿtazilah", *Religion Past and Present*. Leiden: Brill Online Reference Works.
Schmidtke, Sabine (2001). "Creeds", in Jane Dammen (ed.) *Encyclopaedia of the Qurʾān*. McAuliffe, Georgetown University, Washington DC et al. Brill Reference Online. https://referenceworks-brillonline-com.libproxy1.nus.edu.sg/entries/encyclopaedia-of-the-quran/creeds-EQSIM_00099?s.num=0&s.f.s2_parent=s.f.book.encyclopaedia-of-the-quran&s.au=%22Schmidtke%2C+Sabine%22&s.q=aqida. Accessed 14 May 2019.
Shamsul, AB (2001) "A History of an Identity, an Identity of a History: The idea and practice of 'Malayness' in Malaysia reconsidered", *Journal of Southeast Asian Studies*, Vol. 31, No. 3, 355–366.
Siti Fatimah Ishak (2018) "Makin hari makin hak Islam, Melayu ditarik satu demi satu", *Ismaweb*, 15 September, https://www.ismaweb.net/2018/09/15/makin-hari-hak-islam-melayu-ditarik-satu-demi-satu/. Accessed 10 April 2019.
Smith, Wilfred Cantwell (1957) *Islam In Modern History*, Princeton: Princeton University Press.
South China Morning Post (1997) "Top Islamic chiefs 'sparks racial unrest'", 16 October.
The Australian (1997a) "Defiant muftis polarise modern Malaysia", 15 August.
——— (1997b) "Pageant arrests polarise Malaysia", 15 July.
The Straits Times (1995) "Anti-hadith groups called apostates by Muslim authority", 10 September.
——— (1996) "Varsity Staff warned against promoting Shi'ism", 26 May.
——— (1997a) "KL to review Syariah laws and Islamic officials' powers", 9 August.
——— (1997b) "Ulamas criticising govt from pulpit, MP warns", 30 October.
——— (1997c) "Ban beauty contests for all, say women leaders", 19 July.
Ulil, Abshar-Abdalla (2008) "Menjadi Muslim dengan perspektif Liberal", 25 August, http://islamlib.com/gagasan/islam-liberal/menjadi-muslim-dengan-perspektif-liberal. Accessed 13 March 2018.
Utusan Online (2014) "Perkasakan Ahli Sunnah Wal Jamaah langkah tepat", 22 May.
——— (2016) "Institut Ahli Sunnah Wal Jamaah ditubuh", 18 February.
——— (2017) "Manhaj ASWJ perlu dipertahankan", 4 April.
Watt, Montgomery W (1963) "The Political Attitude of the Mu'tazilah", *The Journal of the Royal Asiatic Society of Great Britain and Ireland*, No. 1/2, 38–57.
Yadim (2016) "Negeri Sembilan cadang tubuh Institut Ahli Sunnah Wal Jamaah", 20 August, http://www.yadim.com.my/v2/negeri-sembilan-cadang-tubuh-institut-ahli-sunnah-wal-jamaah/. 20 February.
Zakaria, Stapa (2011) "Kedudukan pemikiran al-Ash'ari dan al-Maturidi dalam Mazhab ahli Sunnah Waljamaah", *Jurnal Antarabangsa Pengajian Islam (International Journal of Islamic Studies)*, Vol. 33, 37–44.

CHAPTER 5

Ring-Fencing Constituents

Introduction

In addition to the standardisation of faith, the second imperative of the Divine Bureaucracy is ring-fencing the Muslim subject. Under more vigorous state-led Islamisation, both *syariah* and civil laws delineate the boundaries of group identity by playing a gatekeeping function, defining who should be taken in as legitimate members of the group—adjudged as Muslims—and who should be precluded from it. The following are some of the ways by which this function has been instituted: (1) no Muslim can opt-out of being subjected to *syariah* laws; (2) exiting Islam is dependent on the legal permission of the *syariah* court; and (3) cultural (Islamic) identity supersedes citizenship as one's primary identity. Essentially, Muslims can be ring-fenced as subjects under religious law with the corollary consequence of the diminution of their civic identity. This is attained by having laws that affix the identity of Islam on all identification papers for Muslims; criminalise all conversions out of Islam; prohibit Muslim-non-Muslim marriage and legally negate all non-heteronormative identities.

To capture the essence of the above, this chapter will examine three domains of social life, which demonstrate how ring-fencing is used as a con-

The original version of this chapter was revised. Text has been updated. Correction to this chapter can be found at https://doi.org/10.1007/978-981-15-2093-8_9

M. Mohamad, *The Divine Bureaucracy and Disenchantment of Social Life*, Contestations in Contemporary Southeast Asia,
https://doi.org/10.1007/978-981-15-2093-8_5

cept to outline the sphere of domination and influence of the Divine Bureaucracy. Most of the contentions between members of society and the Divine Bureaucracy have involved court litigations, with the former as plaintiff and the latter as defendant. The Divine Bureaucracy as represented by *negeri* (State, subnational level) religious departments is the enforcer of *syariah* law and *fatwa* (legal opinions), while those on the receiving end are the 'offenders'. Two groups of 'offenders' are discussed here; one, 'apostates' persecuted for 'false teachings' and those entrapped in reverse conversions[1] or 'forbidden marriages'; and two, those who commit sexual offences as contained in the *syariah* statutes, and specifically, sexual and gender marginals. While these groups of 'offenders' are considered as having deviated from Islam, they have also been prevented from leaving the faith that they have allegedly transgressed, hence the syndrome of ring-fencing.

Accordingly, this chapter examines three case studies to elucidate how ring-fencing operates. The first involves the Divine Bureaucracy's encapsulation and destruction of an array of religious enchantment movements, through the legal application of a 'no-exit' rule for apostates. The second relates to litigation and judicialisation of forbidden marriages, which inadvertently became the 'theatre' to legitimise the separation between *syariah* and civil jurisdictions. The third involves how the Divine Bureaucracy imposes upon and engages itself with groups whose sexualities have been marginalised, namely the LGBT community, and whom the religious authorities consider to be deviant, yet salvageable, and hence to be ring-fenced.

Disenchanting the Enchanters: The 'No-Exit' Rule

The legal prohibition to disallow Muslims from opting out of Islam—in effect to reject the one *authoritative* Islam decreed by the state—is the palpable and infallible 'gatekeeping' device of ring-fencing. Not all *negeri* laws on Islam explicitly spell out apostasy as an offence,[2] but the extremely strong public pressure and social norms against *murtad* (apostates) among Muslims have been the best deterrents to those contemplating exiting the religion, even if denial of religious freedom is an infringement of one's constitutional rights (Mohamed Azam 2007). Negeri Sembilan is the only one with an explicit and elaborate provision on the renunciation of Islam, essentially 'allowing' Muslims to convert out of the faith after all avenues for repentance have been exhausted.[3] It approved 16 such applications out of 84 received from 1994 to 2003 (Mohamed Azam 2007, 17). To apply for a renunciation is not in itself unlawful. However, it is an offence if a

'Muslim' declares themselves to be non-Muslim to avoid being subjected to *syariah* laws. This somewhat tautological predicament is punishable by a fine of up to RM5000 or imprisonment of up to three years.[4] Regardless, using the 'apostasy' argument to escape being convicted under *syariah* law has now been made an offence in enactments of most *negeri*.

How have Muslims intending to leave Islam navigated through such legislation? First, not all who have been caught in the dragnet of these laws were intending to leave Islam; most were merely trying to elude the draconian strictures of the Divine Bureaucracy. The legal struggles of litigants Mohamed Ya, his wife Kamariah Ali, Md Yaacob and Mamat Daud are not just academic case studies. They also show ring-fencing at work, at the same time illustrating the limits of constitutionalism, and how the ring-fencing of Muslim subjects has become an unyielding mission of those in control of official Islam.

From 1986 till 2005, a number of litigants endured a long and laborious process involving imprisonment and court room battles to obtain freedom to practise a religious expression of their choice. They were not seeking to renounce Islam. The four mentioned above were followers of a *tarekat* (Sufi sect), which had a large following nationwide from the early 1970s. What can be pieced together from various accounts about their practice was that they were followers of a sect first founded by Hassan Yaakob, a *silat* (Malay art of self-defence) teacher, popularly known as Hasan Anak Rimau. The group was reported to have 300 followers (New Straits Times 2009). According to a publication of Jakim (Islamic Development Department of Malaysia) (Nawi@Mohd Nawi 2010), its teachings were a mixture of animism and various concepts and practices of Sufi mysticism. In numerous local settings where Hassan was influential, his teachings were referred to by a variety of local names: Tarekat Zikrullah Hassan Anak Rimau, Ratib Kuat Tok Ayah Hassan, Ilmu Isi, Tarekat Batik Pak Chu Hassan, Zikir Kuat Haji Hassan, Ilmu Hakikat and Ilmu Sejati (Nawi@Mohd Nawi 2010, 61).[5]

After Hassan's death in 1998, his son, Yusuf Hassan, and other followers, including Ariffin Mohammad (better known as Ayah Pin) and Ya Haji Yahya, continued his teachings. The latter was the father of Mohamed Ya, husband of Kamariah Ali. Ayah Pin claimed that although he had initially followed the sect under Hassan, he subsequently left owing to differences in principles (Lim and Tong 2005). The religious department of Kelantan had already been monitoring the activities of Hassan Yaakob from 1980 (Nawi@Mohd Nawi 2015, 63). It was later revealed by the religious authorities of several *negeri* that Ayah Pin's sect, which appeared to be an offshoot of Hassan's, had its beginnings in Kampar and then advanced to Malim Nawar, both in Perak. It even had a base in Butterworth, in the adjacent *negeri* of Penang, before Ayah Pin moved to Pahang, and finally to Terengganu in 1975 (New Straits Times 2005a, b; The Age 2005). Ayah Pin gathered followers not just among Malays but also from among Orang Asli, Chinese and Caucasians (New Straits Times 2005a). His teachings, which were said to have originated from Hassan's, apparently took root in many small villages in Kelantan, Terengganu and Pahang, including in some government land settlements under the Federal Land Development Authority (Felda). He had up to 2000 followers.[6]

In 1983, the National Fatwa Committee issued a *fatwa* advisory for *Ajaran Hasan Anak Rimau* to be monitored by the *negeri* or State Islamic Religious Councils (SIRCs) of Kelantan and Terengganu. Kelantan subsequently produced a *fatwa* in 1986 to declare Hassan's teachings wrong, but it did not deem this an offence for his followers.[7] More than ten years later, the Terengganu *fatwa* committee issued a *fatwa* specifically against Ayah Pin's teachings in 1997.[8] In the early 2000s, Sky Kingdom, a commune of Ayah Pin's followers in Hulu Besut, a remote area in Terengganu, came under the limelight (Malaysiakini 2004), even though its symbolic monuments—a giant teapot, vase and umbrella—had already been built since 1994 (The Age 2005; Malaysiakini 2005b).

In 2001, Ayah Pin submitted a statutory declaration that he was no longer Muslim. He was subsequently charged for insulting Islam and jailed 11 months and fined RM2900 (New Straits Times 2005c; Lim and Tong 2005). In July 2005, in what appeared to be state-sanctioned vigilantism, 50 men wearing masks and headbands arrived in 20 vehicles in the early hours of the morning to burn down the concrete structures within the Sky Kingdom commune (New Straits Times 2005d). None of the trespassers and arsonists were arrested. Instead, 3 days later, a party of 70 police and religious officials from Terengganu arrived in 20 vehicles, including 4 police trucks, to raid and arrest 59 people at the commune (New Straits Times 2005e). On 31 July 2005, the commune and its monuments were completely demolished by authorities from the *negeri* Land Office, Public Works Department and electricity and water agencies (New Straits Times 2005f). Ayah Pin himself escaped the arrest and purportedly went into hiding in an unknown location (Malaysiakini 2005a, c). Fearing backlash against any support shown towards the sect, no *syariah* lawyer came forth to defend those charged (New Straits Times 2005g). Ayah Pin, who was never found, could not be arrested nor charged.[9]

So far there has been no comprehensive and objective account and history of the numerous small religious sects (outside of the larger and more well-known ones like Darul Arqam) or Sufi-mystical *tarekat* led by charismatic personalities in the geographical fringes of the country. However, Jakim has compiled a few studies on why some of these groups, such as the Kumpulan Tal Tujuh (Zamri 2007), Ajaran Hj Kahar (Jakim Cawangan Akidah 2005) and Nur Muhammad (Udah 2005), which were largely unknown to the general public, were considered 'deviant' and subsequently banned. In fact, there were many such religious sects as Ajaran Subud and Ajaran Martabat Tujuh (famous in the 1950s); Tarikat Mufarridah and Tarikat Samaniah Ibrahim Bonjo (1960s); and Tarikat Naqsyabandia Kadirun Yahya and Ajaran Nordin Putih (1970s), before the emergence of better known contemporary ones like the Syiah, anti-*hadith* movement, Darul Arqam and Aurad Muhammadiyah from the 1980s onwards (Siti Zubaidah 2010, 250; Mohd Aizam 2015, 57–188).

While many sects have been in existence since early times, they remained obscure. This was until their membership expanded to include urbanites, the middle class and even foreigners (as in the case of Ayah Pin's Sky Kingdom), or when their unusually 'abundant' material resources caught the state's attention (as was the case with Darul Arqam in the 1990s and Sky Kingdom in the 2000s). In Selangor alone, 70 deviant teachings (*ajaran sesat*) were identified or proscribed by its religious department, Jais, up till 2009. Of these, 25 had been banned by *fatwa* rulings, 23 were under investigation, while the remaining 22 cases were said to have been resolved. However, out of the 25 banned, eight were reported as still active (Siti Zubaidah 2010, 251). In 2000, false teachings and prohibited publications were the target of the most number of *fatwa*, amounting to 118 out of 150 gazetted *fatwa* in the country (Ahmad Hidayat 2011, 33–35). What could be the appeal and attraction of these sects and groups, which the Divine Bureaucracy deemed as 'false' Islam?

There was an enchantment of sorts, a return to the magical allure of religion. A common element was the feature of being guru-centred and being led by a *Syeikh Mursyid* (Abdul Hayei 2005), considered the absolute teacher and guide to followers, even to the point of deification. Their practices typically combine various elements of Islamic rituals while subsuming others, and a deep immersion in devotional prayers in the form of communal *zikir* (or *dhikr*). The practice of *zikir* is a spiritual technique and ritual of Sufist *tarekat*. It is a rapturous-like prayer ceremony performed as a central activity of these groups and involves the repetitious chanting of the name of Allah and recitation of *quranic* verses. It would be led by the *Syeikh Mursyid* of the order or its 'spiritual director', to the point where participants reach some sort of spiritual ecstasy, sometimes achieved with the aid of music and dance (Hillenbrand 2014, 157).

The purpose is to be close to God, to seek his pleasure, to remember him from all aspects, to purify, to honour, to believe in his oneness, to worship him, to give thanks and to glorify him (Thahirah et al. 2014, 62). The *Sheikh Mursyid* appears to be a person endowed with some supernatural and mystical powers. Although the practice of *zikir* is acceptable in official Islam, as are some *tasawwuf* (Sufi belief and practice), the line between what is argued by Jakim scholars to be appropriate and conforming to the Ahli Sunnah Wal Jamaah (ASWJ), and what is deemed 'false' and 'deviant' is somewhat very fine. The reasoning is often too abstruse for a common understanding of what is the 'correct' or 'wrongful' *tasawwuf* (see, for example, Abdul Fatah 2006).

With respect to the prominent sects of the 1980s, the example of the Sky Kingdom's followers Mohamed Ya, Kamariah Ali, Md Yaacob and Mamat Daud provides some important observations. Mohamed Ya and his wife Kamariah originated from Kelantan and were both religious teachers in secondary schools in Kampar, Perak. Mohamed Ya was educated in a *madrassah* in Kelantan, and then at Darululum, Deoband, India, before going to Egypt. Kamariah herself qualified from Egypt's Al-Azhar University. They were both thus educated in Islamic knowledge. Mohamed Ya was convicted in Ipoh, Kota Bharu and Besut (Siti Zubaidah 2010, 266). The first court case included Mamat Daud and others, likely some of whom were also followers of Ayah Pin. They were charged under Section 298A of the Penal Code for acting as unauthorised *bilal* (caller to prayer), *khatib* (*quranic* reciter/orator) and *imam* (head of prayer) at Friday prayers in Kuala Terengganu in 1983, without appointment under the Terengganu Administration of Muslim Law Enactment 1955. They were also alleged to have adopted unacceptable Islamic practices. Since there were no provisions under *syariah* law to prosecute them for this offence of unacceptable practices, the authorities resorted to using the Penal Code instead. In 1986, the Supreme Court (now the Federal Court) allowed the litigants to challenge this ruling. Two years later, the court pronounced that because only *negeri* authorities had the power to legislate on the subject of religion, the Penal Code could not be used on the petitioners.[10]

In 1995, Mohamed Ya, Kamariah Ali, Md Yaacob and Mamat Daud were tried at the *syariah* court of Kota Bharu, Kelantan, on charges of contravening a *fatwa* against their practices. The four were sentenced to imprisonment. A statutory declaration that they were no longer Muslims was submitted to the Kelantan *syariah* court but this was rejected, as the judge was of the view that they had done this to escape from being subjected to Islamic law. In 1996, the *Kadi*'s Office ordered them to repent. They refused and were subsequently charged again at the *Syariah* High Court in 2000 for false teachings, and sentenced to three years in jail.

After her release, Kamariah Ali joined Ayah Pin's commune in Terengganu, but was rearrested with several others from the sect in 2005. To evade charges under Terengganu's *syariah* provisions, she again declared herself to be non-Muslim. This resulted in her being charged under Section 7 of the 2001 Syariah Criminal Offence Enactment (*Takzir*) of Terengganu for being an apostate (Murali 2008). In 2006, she contested this decision by applying to the Court of Appeal, asking it to rule if she had the right to freedom of religion under Article 11(1) of the Federal Constitution.[11] Six years later, the court dismissed the appeal,

> by virtue of Article 121(1A) of the Federal Constitution and section 11(3)(b)(x) Enakmen Mahkamah Syariah (Terengganu) 2001 and also section 205(2) of the Administration of Islamic Religious Affairs Enactment 1986, matter [*sic*] pertaining to apostasy in the state is within the sole domain of the Syariah Court of the state.[12]

The 'no-exit' rule was applied brutally in Kamariah's case despite her tireless dependence on a judicial solution to her persecution.

The case of *Soon Singh a/l Bikar Singh v Pertubuhan Kebajikan Islam Malaysia (Perkim) Kedah & Anor, 1999*, is another ring-fencing example but about those who convert into Islam, and the challenges they face in trying to exit from the faith. Having been converted to Islam at the age of 17, Soon Singh petitioned the High Court in 1992 to recognise that he was no longer a Muslim since he had reconverted to Sikhism at the age of 21. At this hearing, his counsel relied on two constitutional arguments. The first, that Article 12(4) of the Federal Constitution empowers a parent or guardian to determine the religion of a person under 18 years of age—in this case, his client was converted when he was a minor, and without parental approval; and the second, that Article 11(1) of the same Constitution provides for every person to have the right to profess and practise their religion. Despite these arguments and proof that he had undergone a Sikh baptism ceremony, thereby renouncing the religion of

Islam, the High Court rejected Soon Singh's application as it ruled that only the *syariah* court had jurisdiction in this matter. None of the judges were convinced that he had valid constitutional grounds to revert back to his original faith. The civil courts would not decide on whether a Muslim's constitutional right to freedom of belief was within their jurisdiction. The Soon Singh judgement provided a precedent for the subsequent cases discussed below.

Forbidden Marriages

Muslim-non-Muslim intermarriage attempts were similarly thwarted in an ultimate show of ring-fencing. The case involving Nor'aishah Bokhari, a Malay-Muslim woman, and Joseph Arnold Lee, a Chinese Christian, created a media and public furore in 1997. In short, Nor'aishah had decided to convert to Christianity to marry Joseph.[13] She prepared a statutory declaration renouncing Islam before a Commissioner for Oaths in October 1997 but when her family learnt about this, they disapproved and kept her under house confinement. Through her lawyer, Nor'aishah then filed a habeas corpus action seeking the court's assistance in obtaining her release. The hearing was postponed three times within a month before it was finally heard. In the interim, a media frenzy had built around this case, and it took on a political dimension with both government and opposition parties keen to intervene in the course of events. Nor'aishah's conversion had rocked the communal and religious sensibilities of Muslims, putting enormous pressure on her to withdraw her intention to convert out of Islam.

On 30 December 1997, Nor'aishah escaped from her parents' house before her trial began. Her family lodged a police report alleging that Joseph Arnold Lee had kidnapped her.[14] The police conducted extensive investigations and ultimately produced Leonard Teoh, Nor'aishah's lawyer, before the Magistrate's Court of Pontian, Johor. Teoh was remanded for seven days for refusing to release information on Nor'aishah's whereabouts. He invoked the argument of solicitor-client privilege and challenged the remand order at the High Court. Holding that legal privilege did not extend to the furtherance of a criminal act, the court dismissed his challenge. In delivering this judgement, Justice Abdul Malik Ishak peppered his words with quotes from popular pop songs and romance literature.[15]

Despite this, Nor'aishah was determined to renounce Islam and embrace Christianity. She retained Leonard Teoh to advise her on her conversion process and, on her instructions, he prepared her a statutory declaration to renounce Islam, which she affirmed before a Commissioner for Oaths on 22 October 1997. Around this time, the judicial process was overtaken by the Executive, given the potentially divisive outcome of the whole proceedings. Muslim and non-Muslim anger over this case was defused through a top-down media directive. Almost overnight news coverage on this case seized, removing the Nor'aishah issue from public view. Little more was heard of Nor'aishah and her whereabouts. Presumably, her renouncement of the Islamic faith through the statutory declaration could not be legally rejected.

The cases of Priyathaseny[16] and Tongiah Jumali[17] are also about marriage, conversion and ring-fencing. Priyathaseny and Tongiah were both born Muslim but had converted and married Hindu and Christian spouses, respectively. In the legal proceedings they initiated, they sought for formal recognition of their conversion out of Islam and also for the civil court to validate their marriages to their non-Muslim husbands. Priyathaseny, ethnically Malay and born Muslim, renounced Islam five years before the trial and adopted Hinduism as her religion.[18] She married her husband, an ethnic Indian and lifelong Hindu, and they had two children. Despite this, the Islamic authorities continued to treat her as a Muslim, and had her arrested on grounds of cohabitation and having children out of wedlock, both offences under *syariah* law. A similar predicament confronted Tongiah Jumali, who sought the High Court to declare that she was a Christian, hence not subject to the religious provisions of Johor, and to consider her marriage to a non-Muslim as valid under Malaysian law.

The High Court struck down both applications for the women to be recognised as non-Muslims, claiming that it had no jurisdiction to hear cases involving conversions out of Islam. In Priyathaseny's case, the judge reminded that there was already a precedent, to which he was bound,

> [T]he central and substantive issue is whether the first plaintiff remains a Muslim despite her so-called renunciation of the Islamic faith and professing now, the Hindu faith and practice… I am now guided by and bound by the pronouncement of our apex court in Soon Singh that the jurisdiction of this court is now ousted from determining the merits of this application.[19]

The judge in Tongiah's case was no different, taking a firm view that "the Syariah Court [was] the only forum qualified to answer whether a Muslim [had] renounced Islam".

The conundrum of these verdicts is summed up in the argument by Priyathaseny's lawyers,

> To send this case to the Syariah Court would be to give the Syariah Court powers over persons who do not profess Islam in Malaysia – a country comprising people professing and practicing so many different religions. This cannot be right, particularly as the Federal Constitution expressly provides that the Syariah Courts shall have jurisdiction 'only' over persons 'professing' the religion of Islam.[20]

Priyathaseny and Tongiah were no longer practising and professing Islam by virtue of the fact that they were married as a Hindu and Christian, respectively. Yet, the civil court, using Article 121(1)(A) of the Federal Constitution, had submitted to the seemingly greater powers of the *syariah* court to determine the identity and faith of citizens.

Lina Joy's application to renounce Islam in the early 2000s was at one level the apotheosis of Muslim anxiety and, at another, the height of non-Muslim concern for the rising climate of Islamic dominance within the judiciary. Lina Joy, whose name was originally Azlina Jailani, was born in 1964 to Malay parents, and hence born a Muslim. In *Lina Joy vs Majlis Agama Islam Wilayah Persekutuan & Ors, 2005*, it was recorded that she was 26 years old when she began practising Christianity and was baptised in 1998. Since being a Muslim in Malaysia carried with it obligations that are legally enforceable as well as a different set of personal laws, Lina no longer wished to be considered Muslim. Although the National Registration Department (NRD) approved her application to change her name, it refused to accept Lina's repeated requests to modify her national identity card to reflect her change of religion. The NRD felt it had no jurisdiction to do so without confirmation from the *syariah* court or an appropriate Islamic authority, that she had renounced Islam.

Lina commenced legal proceedings at the High Court in May 2000 to seek declarations that would establish her status as a Christian. Following the dismissal of her suit at this level in April 2001, she took her case to the next stage, the Court of Appeal. Four years later, in September 2005, the Court of Appeal dismissed her application, by a 2-to-1 majority decision. The two judges with the majority opinion decided that the NRD's policy of requiring an Islamic religious authority to confirm Lina's assertion was reasonable. The dissenting judge, Justice Gopal Sri Ram, however, held that since the NRD's reason for questioning Lina's change of religion was to ascertain the truthfulness of that assertion, her baptism certificate, and not a *syariah* court order, was the relevant documentary evidence.[21]

Lina persisted with taking her case further, culminating in it being heard in the Federal Court in 2007.[22] In the lead-up to and course of the court proceedings, protesting Islamic groups threatened that were the judgement to go in her favour, there would be public disorder. The exaggerated fear of such a decision opening the floodgates to an imagined exodus of Muslims out of Islam was vociferously expressed by protesting Muslims in their private circles as well as by those in high positions of authority. One example of the highly charged atmosphere at the time can be seen in the following passage that was shared with fellow Muslims on an online discussion group:

> What happens if this Murtad issue goes out of hand, then what power can the sultans wield, and what's to prevent them from being shown the door? And with the exit of the sultan, gone are the special rights of the Malays. We will be "*penumpang di Bumi Melayu*", as are the Malays in Singapore...My dear friends, **we have to realise that any erosion of our rights as a Muslim is an erosion of our rights as a Malay,** so we really need to wake up and defend this right in whatever way that we can [emphasis added in bold].[23]

A notable figure in the *negeri* religious bureaucracy, the *mufti* of Perak appeared to concur with the above views:

> If Lina Joy wins in this case, Islam will be destroyed. It will bring about these implications, (i) The powers of Malay rulers over Islam will be usurped (ii)The powers of the Syariah Court will be made redundant (iii) Muslims cannot force their children to perform prayers, will have no right to collect tithes and everyone will be able to interpret Islam according to their whims and fancies. That will be the result.[24]

On 30 May 2007, with more than 100 Muslims holding vigil outside the Federal Court, the presiding judges delivered the ultimate conclusion to the Lina Joy case by upholding the Court of Appeal decision, again by a majority of 2-to-1. With that, the final stage of Lina Joy's appeal to remove the word 'Islam' from her identity card came to an end. In the public eye, this case had confirmed "the *syariah* court as the sole judicial institution in the country in regard to all things Islam" (New Straits Times 2007). The renunciation of Islam by Muslims cannot now be decided by any other court except the *syariah* court. Even though Malaysia is a signatory to the United Nations Universal Declaration on Human Rights—which includes a provision on freedom of religion—this has not deterred the national courts from pronouncing such a decision, as it has been argued that such international conventions merely serve as "persuasive authority", and are only used where there is a lacuna in national laws, according to the Attorney General in *Kamariah Bte Ali dan Lain-Lain Lwn Kerajaan Negeri Kelantan Dan Satu Lagi, 2005.*

These arguments were to have far-reaching implications on the status of human rights in Malaysia and formed the basis of heated public debates, setting the stage for the ever widening divide between those supporting regulated or restricted freedom of religion and those supporting freedom of religion as a constitutional and basic human right. Whether it be Nor'aishah Bokhari, Priyathaseny, Tongiah Jumali, Soon Singh, Lina Joy or Kamariah Ali, all would have to seek licence from the *syariah* court to determine their personhood, a move that would criminalise their applications in any case.

Casting the Ring-Fencing Net Wider: Sexual and Gender Marginals

While the ring-fencing of those involved in false teachings and practices of Islam was an exercise which started much earlier, the condemnation, control and closing of safe havens for those with sexual and gender expressions outside the norm of official Islam has been a more recent phenomenon.

It is not that acts of bodily and sexual conduct were not regulated before; they have been since ancient times. There were precolonial injunctions against sex outside marriage, sodomy and bestiality, offences punishable by whipping, stoning or death (tan 2012, 57–59). When or if these were enforced, or even how many individuals were subjected to such punishment, is harder to ascertain. Under British rule, the notion of sexual mores, impropriety and transgression was recognised to be within the ambit of local customs and subjected to the power of Malay rulers. There were thus laws around this but tempered and modified in accordance with British 'civilisational' sensibility in that any punishment for these offences was limited to a fine or imprisonment. With the British codification of laws, these offences also derived more specificity. For example, adultery was only an offence if it was committed between two married persons. Incest was outlawed, and women who were suspected of being 'prostitutes' and cohabiting with other men were punished as well. *Khalwat*, an offence related to illicit sex though not tantamount to it, was a peculiarly Malay preventative approach to *zina* (fornication between unmarried persons). This offence made it into the statute books from the early twentieth century onwards and was fully adopted by all Malay *negeri* by 1938 (tan 2012, 60–61). *Khalwat* is a more 'prosecutable' offence partly because the onus of proving *zina* is difficult, whereas convicting a couple who are in close proximity, without the presence of others, and "likely to commit *zina*" is legally uncomplicated (Maznah 2016, 66).

In 1995, the National Fatwa Committee produced a *fatwa* to provide clarity and guidance on the meaning of *maksiat* (sinful acts). The preamble to this rejected the viewpoint that for something to be considered an offence, it must bring harm to others. It disputed that private consensual acts such as *berpesta* (partying), *minum arak* (drinking alcohol), *berbogel beramai-ramai* (group nudity), *mengadakan majlis tari menari* (having dance functions), *berzina* (sex outside marriage) or *berkhalwat* (close proximity) were not *maksiat*. In defining this term, it specified two categories of offences: one against Allah and the Prophet, the other against worldly-beings (humans, animals, nature). As far as the committee was concerned, moral and sexual transgressions were forbidden acts that went against the word of Allah and the Prophet. Among others, these included illicit sex, rape and sodomy (Jakim 2011, 69–76). Nevertheless, in accordance with Malaysian constitutional limits, the list of Islamic offences codified as transgressions against Islam can only be those that are not covered by the existing Penal Code of the country. Some offences in the two *hudud* enactments in Kelantan and Terengganu (such as theft and murder) overlap with those found within the Penal Code, as well in other *syariah* criminal offences law or *takzir*, and have led to a situation of constitutional discord (Faruqi 2016, 70–75).

A variation of terms, meanings and forms of punishment in each *negeri* is extensively discussed by tan (2012, 62–66), where newer infractions—pimping, preparation to have illicit intercourse, sodomy, lesbianism, posing as the other sex and public indecency—have been added into the list of *syariah* criminal offences throughout the country starting from

Kelantan in 1985. It is not coincidental that this period also saw the seeds of a vigorous move to upgrade and expand the *syariah* courts system. Legislation had to be commensurate with this new status of the *syariah* judicial institution. While there was much political and social clamour for 'more Islam' in society, it was in fact the substantive swelling of the body of laws that provided the strongest rationale for the elevation and spread of institutionalised Islam.

Table 5.1 contains *syariah* provisions criminalising offences related to sexuality as found in selected *negeri* enactments. Pahang's laws in this regard appear confounding as its list of sexuality-related offences is the most extensive. These are enumerated in two enactments, namely the Pahang Syariah Criminal Offences Enactment 2013 and the Administration of the Religion of Islam and the Malay Custom of Pahang Enactment 1982. In Terengganu, the *syariah* criminal offences legislation divides sexuality-related offences into two parts, Part IV on 'Offences relating to Decency' and Part V on 'Offences Relating to Public Justice and Security'.

Despite the seemingly comprehensive regulation on all aspects of Muslim sexual conduct, it is difficult to determine if these laws have also been extensively enforced, or if it has even been possible to do so. While there are statistics on the number of cases registered under these offences, there is little basis to compare the relative scale or prevalence of 'sexual crimes' to other offences that are found in the Penal Code. For example, from 2005 to 2009, the highest number of cases in the *syariah* courts was *khalwat*, which comprised 66 per cent of all religious offences in the country (see Table 5.1 in tan 2012, 146). Table 5.2, which displays a similar dataset but from 2009 to 2012, shows an unchanged pattern, the highest offence remains *khalwat* at 64 per cent for this duration. By *negeri*, *khalwat* comprised 82 per cent of all *syariah* offences in the Federal Territories between 2000 and 2010; in Selangor, this constituted 89 per cent of offences from 2003 to 2010, and in Negeri Sembilan, it was 84 per cent of all offences between 2000 and 2010 (computed from Daniels 2017, 83–87). With regards to the 'newer' *syariah* offences, the highest number registered from 2011 to 2014 was "man posing as woman", which accounted for 97 per cent of all offences (See Table 5.1 in Mafudzah 2015, 30). It is obvious that both these types of outlawed conduct are also the easiest to prosecute, based on certainty of evidence. Nevertheless, the power of *syariah* or divinely ordained prohibitions against selective sexual infractions should be thought of not just in terms of the scope of

Table 5.1 *Syariah* offences related to sexuality[a]

State enactments	*Titles and sections*	
Syariah criminal offences (Federal Territories) act 1997	**Part IV Offences relating to decency** *Sections* 20. Incest 21. Prostitution 22. *Muncikari* [pimping] 23. Sexual intercourse out of wedlock 24. An act preparatory to sexual intercourse out of wedlock 25. *Liwat* [sexual relations between men] 26. *Musahaqah* [sexual relations between women] 27. *Khalwat* [close proximity] 28. Male person posing as woman 29. Indecent acts in public place	
Syariah Criminal Offences (Takzir) (Terengganu) Enactment 2001	**Part IV Offences relating to decency** *Sections* 24. Incest 25. An act preparatory to prostitute 26. An act preparatory to prostitute wife and child under his care 27. Prostituting wife and child 28. *Muncikari* [pimping] 29. An act preparatory to sexual intercourse out of wedlock 30. *Musahaqah* [sexual relations between women] 31. *Khalwat* [close proximity] 32. Sexual intercourse other than with human 33. Male person posing as woman 34. Indecent acts in public space 35. Exposing body in public 36. *Watie* [intimacy, not involving penetration with non-spouse]	**Part V Offences relating to public justice and security** *Sections* 42. Encouraging vice 43. Enticing a married woman 44. Preventing married couple from cohabiting 46. Enticing a female person 53. Disturbing female in public space
Kelantan Syariah Criminal Code (II)(1993) (amended in 2015)	**Part 1 Hudud offences** *Sections* 12. Adultery 14. Sodomy 17. *Qazaf* [unsubstantiated accusation of adultery or sodomy] 19. *Al-li'an* [accusation of adultery by oath by husband against wife] 22. Syurb [drinking liquor]	

(*continued*)

Table 5.1 (continued)

State enactments	*Titles and sections*	
Pahang Syariah Criminal Offences Enactment 2013	**Part IV Offences relating to decency** *Sections* 28. *Muncikari* [pimping] 29. Sexual intercourse out of wedlock 30. An act preparatory to sexual intercourse out of wedlock 31. Pregnant or giving birth out of wedlock 32. *Khalwat* [close proximity] 33. Man posing as woman 34. Woman posing as man 35. Indecent acts or words in public place	**Part V Miscellaneous offences** *Sections* 43. Disturbing the marriage of others 44. Taking away a married woman 45. Preventing a married couple from cohabiting 47. Taking away a woman 53. Indecent clothing in public space
Administration of the Religion of Islam and the Malay Custom of Pahang Enactment 1982	**Part IX Offences** *Sections* 145. Lovemaking or *khalwat* 146. Adultery 147. Incest 148. Illicit intercourse between divorced persons 149. Adultery with non-Muslims 150. Carnal relations between females 176. Offer oneself to prostitution 177. Husband forcing or allowing wife to prostitution 178. Wife offering herself for prostitution 183. Exposure of body 184. Immoral act	

[a]These statutes are in English, although many Arabic terms are used without their translations. The translations in square parentheses are the author's

its dragnet, but rather the sense of moral anxiety that it is able to elicit, and protract, for the benefit of a network of *syariah* "moral entrepreneurs" as referred to by Shanon (2018, 10), along with a well-resourced surveillance bureaucracy.

The case for further widening the ring-fencing to enclose Muslims through sexuality and gender norms prohibited by *syariah* law demonstrates both the entrepreneurial and innovative capacity of the Divine Bureaucracy and its network of vigilantes and supporters. The role of 'moral entrepreneurs', the use of *negeri* funds (including *zakat* or religious tithe) and the extension of bureaucratic surveillance have reined in

Table 5.2 *Syariah* criminal offences (2009–2012)

Offence/year	*2009*	*2010*	*2011*	*2012*	*Total*	*%*
Gambling	711	1190	1288	1463	4652	7.7
Alcohol consumption	471	909	496	531	2407	4.0
Incest	3	3	4	5	15	0
Prostitution	33	4	4	5	46	0.1
Pimping	1	1	0	0	2	0
Sex outside marriage	1638	1335	1462	1032	5467	9.0
Complicity in prohibited sex	565	0	35	173	773	1.3
Unnatural sex	0	0	0	0	0	0
Pregnancy out of wedlock	91	105	85	331	612	1.0
Sodomy	2	0	8	0	10	0
Lesbianism	3	1	6	3	13	0
Khalwat	10,700	9932	9129	8970	38,731	63.7
Cohabitation	2	1	60	842	905	1.5
Man posing as woman	114	218	131	199	662	1.1
Indecent behaviour in public	1486	3249	242	1513	6490	10.7
Total	**15,820**	**16,948**	**12,950**	**15,067**	**60,785**	**100.0**

Source: Jakim (n.d., 23)

yet another group of Muslim constituents, those the Divine Bureaucracy names as 'LGBT'. The vehemence and hostility against same-sex relations and sexual and gender marginals, defined as "gay men, lesbian women, transsexuals and transgenders", have set "new benchmarks" for deviancy (tan 2012, 4). This seemed to have found its beginnings from 2010 onwards. Previously, the vocabulary for same-sex relations within the *syariah* lexicon was limited. In contrast, the axiom or acronym "LGBT" is now pronounced and written with ease among *syariah* scholars, bureaucrats and *ulama* (Islamic scholars). LGBTs are now an identifiable group, a 'them' that is to be demonised, but also among Muslims, an 'us' to be cleansed. This naming of another 'ring-fenceable' constituency also enlarges the sphere of control. The offences associated with this group, though vaguely codified, are already in the statutes, and there may be benefits to the dominant paradigm having them enforced. However, the strongest impulse driving this persecution and cleansing movement may well be the fear of an imagined Malay-Muslim cohesiveness and of a "heteronormalized Malay-Muslim masculinity" breaking down (Goh 2015, 1–5). Masculinism is also the bedrock of Islamism, hence the disproportionate attention given to salvaging Muslim males from the 'abyss' of non-normative sexuality. This is not to say that punishment executed on women 'offenders' has been less harsh, as the decision of the Terengganu *syariah* court, which meted out six lashes of the cane on two women accused of attempting to have sex, amply demonstrated (Fitri 2018; Ramzy and Tan 2018).

Events around the 'outing' of two highly educated young Malay-Muslim males from 2010 to 2011 have been analysed as the peaking of a moment of moral panic (Goh 2014, 2015). The first involved the appearance of Azwan Ismail in a YouTube video sometime in December 2010, and the second, the marriage of Ariff Alfian Rosli to an Irish man in December 2011. Both events became pivotal in triggering a rancorous, yet methodical, reaction from the *syariah* purveyors.

After the December 2010 YouTube confession of Azwan of being gay, Pas Youth leader Nasrudin Hassan issued a statement urging the government to increase its scrutiny of social media, particularly those of gay Muslim men, and specifically calling on Jakim to act against gay activities amongst Muslims (Star Online 2010). This was immediately taken up by the government, which pledged to monitor such activities, particularly that of NGOs behind the production and release of the video. The clip with Azwan was in fact part of a video series produced by Seksualiti Merdeka (Independent Sexualities), a little-known organisation among Muslims, which had prior to this incident organised an annual sexuality festival in Kuala Lumpur since 2008. In November 2011, while the festival was underway, police issued a ban preventing it from continuing after its second day, on the basis of "protests from non-governmental organizations, including Islamic and non-Islamic organizations, which feared the programme could create disharmony, enmity and disturb public order" (Star Online 2011). The women's wing of Pas was one of the first to call for this ban, claiming that Seksualiti Merdeka aimed to make same-sex relations *halal* (permissible) in Malaysia (Utusan Online 2011a). Immediately after the ban, an investigation was conducted into the initiative, with police calling in 50 people for questioning, including organisers, supporters and participants of the event (Utusan Online 2011b). Even Mahathir, then not yet re-elected as Prime Minister, echoed the numerous calls to reject the activities of Seksualiti Merdeka (Utusan Online 2011c).

In December 2011, a month after the frenzied condemnation of Seksualiti Merdeka, this moral panic[25] was further aggravated after pictures of the marriage of a Malay student to an Irish man were circulated over the internet. Ariff Alfian Rosli was a medical student in Dublin under the sponsorship of Petronas (Malaysia's oil corporation). The 'spectacle' of Ariff—the epitome of the exemplary, high achieving Malay male with a prime scholarship—being involved in a gay union created a veritable panic among defenders of Malay and Islamic rights. A Malay NGO, Jaringan Melayu Malaysia (JMM), immediately proclaimed itself to be one of the key NGOs opposing LGBT activities, which it insisted were forbidden by Islam and which also went against the moral and natural inclination of human beings (Utusan Online 2012a). In March 2012, this same NGO claimed its research on LGBTs showed that they were a "danger", and that the public should reject them on grounds that upholding the sanctity of religious faith trumped the political interests backing the group (Utusan Online 2012b). A Muslim counsellor interviewed urged the government to take firm and immediate action as LGBTs had become "a social disease that had spread like cancer". Those who practised *budaya songsang* (perverted culture) were mentally unstable, had split personalities and were constantly in a flux while adhering to liberal principles (Utusan Online 2012c).

In 2013, the Chairperson of Yayasan Dakwah Islamiah Malaysia (Yadim) questioned if Jakim had the capacity to monitor the numerous websites said to contain materials on same-sex relations, hence hinting at more government resources to be channelled for this purpose (Aziz 2013). A year later, a writer from a government-owned Islamic television channel TV Al-Hijrah also warned of the dangers of homosexuality since those promoting this included Muslims who were *munafik* (traitors), and those who subscribed to the ideology of pluralism and liberalism (Rokiah 2014). This demonisation of LGBT—often conveniently lumped together with liberalism and pluralism—as totally against Islam has been aggressively pursued in recent years, and so too has the reach of the Divine Bureaucracy over the lives of sexual and gender marginals, in terms of public messaging, media coverage and organised programmes largely of a 'rehabilitative' nature.

From 2011, Jakim with the cooperation of religious departments of the different *negeri* embarked on a distinct programme or what it termed the support and rehabilitation of LGBTs. The bureaucratic, managerial and technical nature of this agenda was guided by Jakim's Strategic Plan for 2015–2019 (*Pelan Strategik Jakim* 2015–*2019*), which had a specific anti-LGBT thrust, the *Pelan Tindakan Menangani Gejala Sosial Kecelaruan Gender* (Action Plan for Handling Gender Disorder Social Ills). Jakim also established a Focal Point Action Committee consisting of academics and religious officials who met in October 2015 to draw up this action plan (Jakim 2015, 68–69).

A signature programme of this Strategic Plan is the *Program Mukhayyam*, a 'religious bootcamp', held over several days at different points of time in a year. In 2015, Jakim sponsored and organised nine programmes on "LGBT Well-being". These included seven *Program Mukhayyam*, four targeting "Man Sex with Man [*sic*] (MSM)", four for "Transgender (TG)" and one for "Lesbian" (Jakim 2015, 68–70). In 2016, there were 15 programmes altogether, four of which were the *Program Mukhayyam*. New activities included seminars, breaking of fast (*iftar*) dinners with the community, one study visit to Yayasan Peduli Sahabat in Tangerang, Indonesia, two publications and one video production (Jakim 2016, 78–79). The next year, six camps were held in Sabah, Kelantan, Pahang, Perak, Melaka and Penang; three targeted the "Transgender (TG)" group, two for the "Man Sex With Man [*sic*] (MSM)" group and one for the "Woman Sex With Woman [*sic*] (WSW)" group. A workshop to design a module for the Treatment and Rehabilitation of Lesbian and Gay Groups (*Modul Rawatan dan Pemulihan Golongan Lesbian dan Gay*) was also held in the same year. The panel for the module comprised mainly academics, together with religious department officials and two Islamic NGOs (Jakim 2017, 132–134).

By 2015, up to 500 participants were recorded as having gone through the *Program Mukhayyam* and related activities. The core of this programme was religious immersion, but this was interspersed with various sporting activities from snorkelling to jungle trekking. By this stage, Jakim was offering funds to NGOs to run its "rehabilitation modules", and it had also announced plans to establish 'Ilaj Home', a treatment centre for those with HIV among the Muslim LGBT community (Berita Harian 2015a). Some transgenders received allowances and had the rental of their business premises paid for by Jakim and the SIRCs. In 2015, reportedly 30 of them voluntarily attended a religious programme organised by Jakim (Berita Harian 2015b).

During this time too, at least two Jakim-sponsored NGOs headed by former transgenders were established. Mohamed Bakri Abu Bakar became the chairman of the Persatuan Insaf Pahang (Pahang Society for the Repented), and Mohd Khairi Mohd Ramli headed the Persatuan Kebajikan Darul Modahish (The Amazing Welfare Organisation).[26] Jakim, Jawi (FT religious department) and the SIRCs were credited as supporters of these groups (Berita Harian 2015c). By 2017, Jakim reported that it had 900

Muslim volunteers registered in training programmes to rehabilitate Muslims with social problems (drug addicts, juvenile delinquents and LGBTs) (Berita Harian 2017).

A former transgender, Mohd Khairi Mohd Ramli, was one of the speakers at a 2017 convention for officials of Jakim's Centre for Family, Social and Community Development, where he praised Jakim for its compassionate rather than coercive approach, adding that the negative perceptions of its programmes needed to be corrected: "It is not true because the contents are full of loving elements, teaching prayers and to get to know Allah The Almighty (*Ia tidak benar kerana pengisiannya penuh dengan elemen kasih sayang, mengajar solat dan mengenal Allah SWT*)" (Berita Harian 2017). As president of the Persatuan Kebajikan Darul Modahish, Mohd Khairi was also quoted saying that Jawi was successful in rehabilitating 3000 individuals including transgenders, lesbians, gays and bisexuals (Berita Harian 2018b). According to him, religious departments in all *negeri* had an allocation for the LGBT group if they were willing to change and lead new lives.

Jakim's increased yearly budget allocation spurred calls among Islamic scholars for a larger portion of its budget to be used for more activities, especially the *Program Mukhayyam* to guide, rehabilitate and engage (*menyantuni*) the LGBT community. In relation to this, it was proposed too that other NGOs be roped in to work with government agencies to advance *syiar Islam* (the calling of Islam) (Berita Harian 2018c). In 2018, a Friday sermon in Selangor reminded those present of the 'dangers' LGBTs posed, and what measures would be taken to stem its tide. The mosque *khatib* (orator) presented statistics from the Ministry of Women, Family and Community Development which claimed that in 2013 there were 173,000 people, or 3 per cent of the total population in the country, involved in "*gejala* LGBT" (ills of LGBT). However, he also said that the community would be showered with love and charity so that they may repent.

The above message of 'compassion' was made possible since earlier, the Selangor *fatwa* committee had decreed that this group was eligible for *zakat* under the *Asnaf Al-Riqab* recipient category it gazetted in 2012.[27] The *fatwa* was careful to specify that the *zakat* in Selangor would not be given directly to these recipients but through an intermediary, whether institutions, centres, Islamic NGOs or even individuals, that is those who function to rehabilitate the group to the path of Islam (Berita Harian 2018a). Originally meant for slaves or people in captivity deserving of *zakat*, the modern twist to this *fatwa* is that 'in captivity' now meant people "enslaved in perverted lifestyles" (*terbelenggu gaya hidup songsang*). This included "prostitutes, lesbians, transgenders, gays, homosexuals, gigolos, bisexuals, *pengkid*, tomboys and those cohabiting with non-Muslims".[28] The *fatwa* specified two categories of *Al-Riqab*—those with social problems (*masalah sosial*) and those with faith 'problems' (*masalah akidah*). Within these two categories, there are also various subcategories of people "shackled and bonded" in accordance to their identity (as "transsexual", "tomboy", "pengkid") or their activities (as in "prostitutes" or "gigolo"), all specified in the *fatwa*. *Zakat* allocations are not given directly to these groups and individuals but are instead channelled to those (institutions or individuals) who are involved in work and programmes to rehabilitate them. As a result of this, the Majlis Agama Islam Selangor (Mais, Selangor Islamic Religious Council) had given more powers to its Bahagian Pemulihan Al-Riqab (Al-Riqab Rehabilitation Division) to facilitate the distribution of this category of *zakat* to the appropriate agencies.[29] It needs to be emphasised here that although they are considered *asnaf* (eligible for *zakat*), funds do not go to them, which invited some uneasiness as to the legitimacy of this *fatwa*, or even if *zakat* should be used for the purpose of their rehabilitation (Bernama 2018). It is an extensive list, worth detailing in Table 5.3.

Table 5.3 List of *Asnaf Al-Riqab* eligible for *zakat* to be used for their rehabilitation (Selangor *fatwa* under Section 47)[a]

Social problems	*Faith problems*
1. **Shackled by drugs**	1. **Shackled by problems of *syirik* [idolatry] and *khurafat* [superstitious beliefs]**
i. Drug addicts	i. False doctrine
ii. Former drug addicts	ii. Claiming to be a prophet
2. **Shackled by *syariah* offences**	iii. Insulting Islam
i. Alcohol drinking	iv. Wrongful worship
ii. Zina	v. Denigrating Al-Quran and Hadis
iii. Khalwat	2. Purifying the faith of Muslims who have strayed
iv. Gambling	i. Those intending to become apostates, or leave the religion
v. Baby dumping	ii. Those in the proses of *istitabah* [repentance]
vi. Pregnancy out of wedlock	

(*continued*)

Table 5.3 (continued)

Social problems	*Faith problems*
vii. Denigrating Al-Quran and Hadis	
viii. Incest	
ix. Illicit sex	
x. Muncikari (ibu ayam) [pimping]	
xi. Selling or giving away a child to a non-Muslim	
xii. Any other offences contained in the Selangor *Syariah* Criminal Offences Enactment 1995	
3. **Shackled by wrongful Islamic practice**	
i. Not praying	
ii. Not fasting	
iii. Baby dumping	
iv. Suicidal	
v. Cohabiting with a prostitute	
4. **Shackled by perverted lifestyle**	
i. Prostitute	
ii. Lesbian	
iii. *Mak nyah* (transsexual) [transgender]	
iv. Gay	
v. Homosexual	
vi. Gigolo	
vii. Bisexual	
viii. *Pengkid*	
ix. Tomboy	
x. Cohabiting with non-Muslims	
5. **Shackled by juvenile delinquency**	
i. Gangster	
ii. Property-related crimes	
iii. Fights involving injury	
iv. Robbery	
v. House break-ins	
vi. Rape	
vii. Crimes related to dangerous weapons	
viii. Blackmail involving violence	
6. **Shackled by chronic disease**	
i. HIV/AIDS	
ii. Cancer	
iii. Tibi [TB, tuberculosis]	
iv. Hepatitis	
v. Others	

[a]Translated version, with some terms retained in their original as in document

Selangor has two other *fatwa* that are related to prohibiting the 'lifestyles' of LGBT. A 1993 *fatwa* forbids a man from marrying a transgender person who has undergone a sex-change operation to become a woman, while a 2009 *fatwa* prohibits the *pengkid* identity, defined as "a woman acting and representing herself as a man and with the sexual urges of one" (*wanita Islam yang berpenampilan dan mempunyai gerak laku serta naluri seksual seperti lelaki adalah*). Back in 1982, the National Fatwa Committee had also issued a *fatwa* stating that whoever was born in the sex he/she had been registered as at birth should remain in that sex even after undergoing a sex-change procedure. All sex-change procedures are thus considered *haram* (prohibited).

Conclusion

The traditional and long-standing adversary of the Divine Bureaucracy has always been the religious enchanters and re-enchanters who have been labelled *sesat* (lost, gone astray), and the challenge of ring-fencing them has had to be continually performed through *fatwa*, law, detention, rehabilitation, enforcement, even harassment and psychological warfare (Mohd Aizam 2015, 65). Yet, Jakim itself acknowledged that by 1999 there were still hundreds of these groups spread throughout the country, and, in 2011, four main ones were considered the most resilient: the reconfigured Darul Arqam in the form of the Rufaqa Corporation and later Global Ikhwan; the Syiah and those following the teachings of al-Mansur and Ilmu Hakikat (Mohd Aizam 2015, 64). Strong elements of enchantment and re-enchantment within these doctrines and practices are still able to draw people towards them.

As for those merely seeking to form unions for love and happiness, but prohibited by law, they too have had to be proscribed through the imposition of a 'no-exit' rule. Those wanting to apostatise as a means of release out of the ring-fence have found no solace through judicial means but only through the route of voluntary 'disappearance', as in the cases of Nor'aishah Bokhari and Lina Joy. In a similar vein, those considered transgressors of acceptable sexual and gender identities were not only disallowed from leaving the faith but also salvaged through a procedure of conditional charity and the ring-fence of 'benevolence' as in the *zakat*-related rehabilitation programme.

This chapter has provided examples of how the ring-fencing of Muslims has occurred over the years. Whether it has been to do with the search for the enchantment or re-enchantment of religion, or of finding love in forbidden unions, or of accepting and living with one's unique sexual or gender identity, these actions have all been subjected to the scrutiny of, and eventually, intervention by the Divine Bureaucracy. Acting as a social behemoth, the Divine Bureaucracy has affected a wide swathe of constituents, rolling out group identity where the Muslim *nomos*[30] takes on the form of a "normative universe in which law and cultural narrative are inseparable" (Shachar 2001, 2).

Notes

1. Conversions from another religion into Islam is part of state policy in that public funds are used in proselytisation programmes, notably on the indigenous Orang Asli tribes (Jamilah et al. 2014). However, conversion out of Islam into another religion is not legally recognised even though they exist as cases in this chapter will show. The idea of 'reverse conversion' is used in the context of conversion out of Islam.
2. Only five *negeri* (State, subnational units of governance) in Malaysia, namely Pahang, Perak, Melaka, Sabah and Terengganu, have legal provisions which make the renunciation of Islam an offence punishable by fines, imprisonment or whipping.
3. Section 119(8) of the Administration of the Religion of Islam (Negeri Sembilan) Enactment 2003 states "If after the expiry of the period ordered under subsection (8) the person still refuses to repent, the person who is responsible for him [*sic*] shall prepare a report as soon as possible and bring him [*sic*] before the Syariah High Court and the Court may make a decision to declare that the person has renounced the Religion of Islam".
4. Section 48 of the Syariah Criminal Offences (Negeri Sembilan) Enactment 1992.
5. It is unclear if leaders of these groups use similar textual sources. The concept of 'Ilmu Hakikat' (Fundamental Knowledge) was also attributed to other banned groups in Kelantan. A book written by Haji Ahmad Laksamana Haji Omar titled *Hakikat Insan* was banned in 1992 by the National Fatwa Committee and in 1996 by the Kelantan State (*negeri*) Islamic Religious Council (Mohd Aizam 2015, 65–96).
6. "Ajaran: Hasan Anak Rimau", https://www.carigold.com/portal/forums/showthread.php?t=392208, accessed 14 February 2019.
7. "Ajaran Ayah Pin", http://mufti.terengganu.gov.my/index.php/home/99-fatwa-diwartakan/138-ajaran-ayah-pin, accessed 14 February 2019.
8. "Fatwa mengenai ajaran salah (Haji Ahmad Laksamana, Hassn bin Yaacub dan Mohamad Nor bin Seman)", http://mufti.kelantan.gov.

my/index.php/component/content/article/125-e-fatwa-kelantan-pentadbiran/akidah/170-fatwa-mengenai-ajaran-salah-haji-ahmad-laksamana-hasan-bin-yaacub-dan-mohamad-nor-bin-seman?Itemid=437, accessed 14 February 2019.

9. He eventually died in 2016, in the same village of Hulu Besut where his Sky Kingdom was formed (New Straits Times 2016).
10. See *Mamat bin Daud & Ors v Government of Malaysia, 1986; and Mamat bin Daud & Ors v Government of Malaysia, 1988.*
11. *Kamariah binti Ali & Anor v Majlis Agama Islam dan Adat Melayu Terengganu & Ors, 2005.*
12. *Kamariah binti Ali & Anor v Majlis Agama Islam dan Adat Melayu Terengganu & Ors, 2011.*
13. In Malaysia, marriage between a Muslim and a non-Muslim is not legally recognised.
14. *Re The Detention of Leonard Teoh Hooi Leong, 1998.*
15. In the words of the judge: "Trouble reared its ugly head when she fell in love with one Joseph Arnold Lee, a Christian Chinese. The cupid arrow must have struck Nor'aishah right smack into her heart so much so that she lost all sense of balance. He must have used love potion number 9, for she seemed to be on cloud nine. As Francis Bacon once remarked: 'It is impossible to love and be wise'. Shakespeare too in 'A Midsummer Night's Dream' once said: 'The course of true love never did run smooth'".
16. *Priyathaseny & Ors v Pegawai Penguatkuasa Agama Jabatan Hal Ehwal Agama Islam Perak & Ors, 2003.*
17. *Tongiah Jumali & Anor v Kerajaan Negeri Johor & Ors, 2004.*
18. The case file did not state how it was legally possible for her to have converted to Hinduism and changed her name.
19. *Priyathaseny & Ors v Pegawai Penguatkuasa Agama Jabatan Hal Ehwal Agama Islam Perak & Ors, 2003.*
20. Ibid.
21. *Lina Joy* vs *Majlis Agama Islam Wilayah Persekutuan & Ors, 2005.*
22. Lina Joy v Majlis Agama Islam Wilayah Persekutuan & Ors, 2007.
23. The passage is as is. The person writing this post was a highly qualified professional not someone many would expect to have such opinions. Nevertheless, the purpose in sharing this excerpt is to show how the understanding (or misunderstanding) of a politicised issue like the Lina Joy case elicited many 'primordial' outpourings of racial, religious and national sentiments. Translation of the Malay phrases used are as follows: *Penumpang di Bumi Melayu* (Squatters in a Malay land); *rezeki melimpah-limpa*h (boundless good fortune); *Alhamdullilah* (God be praised). The author is a member of this e-list.
24. *Jika dalam kes ini Lina Joy menang, maka agama Islam akan hancur. Ia membawa implikasi: (i) Kuasa Raja mengenai agama Islam akan hilang*

(ii) Kuasa Mahkamah syariah tidak boleh dipakai (iii) Orang Islam tidak boleh memaksa anaknya asembahyang, tidak berhak lagi kutip zakat dan tiap-tiap oang boleh mentafsir Islam ikut kehendaknya. Itulah akibatnya. This message was relayed through a wide-reaching electronic mailing list at the height of demonstrations over the Lina Joy case titled "Peringatan Mufti Perak Perlu DiRenungi". Dated 10 August 2006, it was written by Anual Bakhri Haron, who attributed the speech to the Perak *mufti*.

25. On moral panics, this is a much-used concept developed by Stanley Cohen to mean,

> [A] condition, episode, person or group of persons emerges to become defined as a threat to societal values and interests… the moral barricades are manned by editors, bishops, politicians and other right-thinking people; socially accredited experts pronounce their diagnoses and solutions. (Quoted in Wright Monod 2017, 1–2)

26. Another NGO, Pertubuhan Amal Firdausi), had apparently been involved in the rehabilitation of LGBTs through Islam since the late 1990s, and used the Masjid Jamek mosque in the heart of Kuala Lumpur as its operations centre.
27. Government of Selangor Gazette, Vol. 65, No. 12, 7 June 2012 (*Fatwa Jenis Penerima Asnaf Al-Riqab Negeri Selangor dan Apa-Apa Yang Berkaitan Dengannya*).
28. *Antara senarai penerima agihan asnaf Al Riqab yang layak menerima bantuan zakat Al Riqab ialah golongan terbelenggu gaya hidup songsang, termasuk pelacur, lesbian, mak nyah, gay, homoseksual, gigolo, biseksual, pengkid, tomboi dan bersekedudukan dengan orang bukan Islam* (Berita Harian 2018b).
29. See "Apakah yang dimaksudkan dengan *Al-Riqab*?", official portal of Mais, http://www.mais.gov.my/info-mais/informasi/penerbitan/ar-riqab, accessed 14 May 2019.
30. This refers to the concept of law in ancient Greek philosophy, which can be expressed and translated into unchangeable forms of moral conduct (see https://www.britannica.com/topic/nomos-Greek-philosophy, accessed 11 May 2019).

References

Abdul Fatah, Haron Ibrahim (2006) "Syari'at, Haqiqat dan Ma'rifat: Suatu analisa kritis", *Jurnal Penyelidikan Islam*, Vol. 16, 1–30.

Abdul Hayei, bin Abdul Sukor (2005) "Syeikh Mursyid di antara penghormatan dan pendewaan", Vol. 18, *Jurnal Penyelidikan Islam*, 127–142.

Ahmad Hidayat, Buang (2011) "Fatwa ajaran sesat dari sudut undang-undang dan cabaran pembanterasannya di Malaysia", *JFATWA: Journal of Fatwa Management and Research*, Vol. 2, No. 9, 27–47.
Aziz Jamaludin, Mhd Tahir (2013) "Promosi budaya gay: Runtuhnya proses mengadabkan insan", *Utusan Online*, 16 March.
Berita Harian (2015a) "Program Mukhayyam pulih golongan LGBT", 24 July.
——— (2015b) "Dilema LGBT: Dibantu atau disisihkan?", 21 July.
——— (2015c) "Bekas LGBT bantu 'rakan' kembali ke pangkal jalan", 23 July.
——— (2017) "Persepsi negatif jauhkan mak nyah dari jabatan ugama", 1 November.
——— (2018a) "Khutbah Jumaat Selangor sentuh isu LGBT", 24 August.
——— (2018b) "Bimbing insan LGBT ke pangkal jalan", 18 August.
——— (2018c) "Bimbing LGBT, jadikan NGO Islam rakan pembangunan syiar", 2 November.
Bernama (2018) "LZS Cari Golongan Asnaf Dari Rumah ke Rumah", 1 October.
Daniels, Timothy P (2017) *Living Sharia: Law and practice in Malaysia*, Seattle: University of Washington Press.
Faruqi, Shad Saleem (2016) "Shariah Laws, Civil Laws and the Federal Constitution", in G25 Malaysia, *Breaking the Silence: Voices of moderation, Islam in a constitutional democracy*, Singapore: Marshall Cavendish, 55–75.
Fitri, Nizam (2018) "Public caning of lesbian couple first in country", *New Straits Times*, 4 September.
Goh, Joseph N (2014) "Fracturing Interwoven Heteronormativities in Malaysia Malay-Muslim Masculinity: A research note", *Sexualities*, 17, 600–617.
——— (2015) "Peculiar Politics in Malaysia: A queer perspective on non-heteronormative Malay-Muslim men", in Jillian E Cox and Jo Grzelinska (eds), *Ways of Queering, Ways of Seeing*, Oxfordshire, UK: Inter-Disciplinary Press, 3–34.
Hillenbrand, Carole (2014) "Mystical Dimensions of Islam, Past and Present (Keynote 4)", *Journal for the Study of Spirituality*, Vol. 4, No. 2, 149–161.
JAKIM (n.d.) *Pelan Strategik JAKIM 2015–2019*, Jabatan Kemajuan Islam Malaysia.
——— (2011) *Garis Panduan Yang diPerakukan oleh Muzakarah Jawatankuasa Fatwa Majlis Kebangsaan Bagi Hal ehwal Ugama Islam Malaysia (MKI)*, Jabatan Kemajuan Islam Malaysia.
——— (2015) *Laporan Tahunan 2015.*
——— (2016) *Laporan Tahunan 2016.*
——— (2017) *Laporan Tahunan 2017.*
JAKIM Cawangan Akidah (2005) "Penyelewengan ajaran Hj Khahr b Hj Ahmad Jalal", *Jurnal Penyelidikan Islam*, Vol. 18, 1–14.
Jamilah, Mohd Zin Engku Ahmad Zaki, Engku Alwi (2014) "Aktiviti Dakwah Jabatan Kemajuan Islam Malaysia (JAKIM) Terhadap Masyarakat Orang Asli: Pelaksanaan dan cabarannya", *Prosiding Bicara Dakwah kali ke 15: Pengurusan dakwah kontemporari*, UKM, Selangor, 6 May.

Lim, Danny and Tong Yee Siong (2005) "Pie in the Sky", *Sun2Surf*, 8 July.

Mafudzah, Mohamad (2015) "Lesbian, Gay, Biseksual dan Transgender: Perspektif undang-undang jenayah syariah", *Jurnal Undang Undang dan Masyarakat*, Vol. 19, 29–36.

Malaysiakini (2004) "Lo and behold! The Sky Kingdom", 26 July.

——— (2005a) "Followers fear attacks on Sky Kingdom, face Syariah charge", 20 July.

——— (2005b) "Apostate Ayah Pin follower granted bail", 15 August.

——— (2005c) "Ayah Pin follower pleads guilty", 23 August.

Maznah, Mohamad (2016) "Policing and Protecting Women: Some aspects of Malay-Islamic law-making under British colonialism", *Kajian Malaysia*, Vol. 34, 159–78.

Mohamed Azam, Mohamed Adil (2007) "Restrictions in Freedom of Religion in Malaysia: A conceptual analysis with special reference to the law of apostasy", *Muslim World Journal of Human Rights*, Vol. 4, No. 2, 1–24.

Mohd Aizam, Bin Mas'od (2015) *Diskusi Isu Akidah dan Pemikiran Semasa Di Malaysia*, Putrajaya: Jabatan Kemajuan Islam Malaysia.

Murali, RSN (2008) 'Sky Kingdom member jailed for 2 years for apostasy' *The Star*, 3 March.

Nawi@Mohd Nawi bin Haji Ismail (2010) "Ajaran Sesat Hassan Anak Rimau: Satu sorotan", *Jurnal Penyelidikan Islam*, Vol. 23, 61–82.

New Straits Times (2005a) "Mufti: Use ISA to detain Ayah Pin:, 21 July.

——— (2005b) "MC: Demolition legal", 2 August.

——— (2005c) "Dept: Ayah Pin still a Muslim", 23 July.

——— (2005d) "Mob torches sky kingdom", 19 July.

——— (2005e) "59 Sky Kingdom members detained", 21 July

——— (2005f) "End of 'Sky Kingdom;", 1 August.

——— (2005g) "Indefensible behaviour", 6 August.

——— (2007) "Syariah Court Sole Authority on Islam", 7 June.

——— (2009) "'Yahu' fails to make comeback", 2 February.

——— (2016) "Court throws out Sisters in Islam's fatwa challenge", 25 June.

Ramzy, Austin and Sharon Tan (2018) "In Malaysia. Two women are punished with caning", *The New York Times*, 4 September.

Rokiah, Ismail (2014) "Menangani musuh dalam kalangan Islam", *Utusan Online*, 16 November.

Shachar, Ayelet (2001) *Multicultural Jurisdictions: Cultural differences and women's rights*. Cambridge: Cambridge University Press.

Shanon, Shah (2018) *The Making of a Gay Muslim: Religion, sexuality and identity in Malaysia and Britain*, Cham, Switzerland: Palgrave Macmillan.

Siti Zubaidah, Ismail (2010) "Menangani Ajaran Sesat di Kalangan Umat Islam: Perspektif undang-undang dan pentadbiran", *Jurnal Syariah*, Vol. 18, No. 2, 247–276.

Star Online (2010) "Gay man fears for his life after exposing his sexuality on net", 23 December.
——— (2011) "Seksualiti Merdeka movement festival banned", 3 November.
tan, beng hui (2012) "Sexuality, Islam and Politics in Malaysia: A study on the shifting strategies of regulation", PhD thesis, National University of Singapore.
Thahirah, Hassan Basri, Faudzinaim Badaruddin and Abdul Manam Mohamad (2014) "Konsep Zikir Darajah dalam Disiplin Ilmu Tarekat", *Jurnal Islam Dan Masyarakat Kontemporari*, No. 8, 61–72.
The Age (2005) "Muslim leaders use bulldozers to etch the boundaries of religious freedom", 20 August.
Udah, bin Mohsin (2005) "Nur Muhammad dari sudut hadis", *Jurnal Penyelidikan Islam*, Vol. 18, 143–156.
Utusan Online (2011a) "Pas bantah penganjuran program Seksualiti Merdeka 2011", 3 November.
——— (2011b) "Seksualiti Merdeka: Polis jamin siasat secepat mungkin", 12 November.
——— (2011c) "Gerakan seksualiti merdeka wajib ditolak – Dr M", 24 November.
——— (2012a) "JMM dedah ada pihak promosi LGBT, seks bebas kepada pelajar", 16 January.
——— (2012b) "Seks songsang pelajar serius", 11 March.
——— (2012c) "Penyakit rosakkan bangsa", 11 March.
Wright Monod, Sarah (2017) *Making Sense of Moral Panics: A framework for research*, Palgrave Macmillan.
Zamri, bin Abdul Halim (2007) "Kumpulan Tal Tujuh", *Jurnal Penyelidikan Islam*, Vol. 20, 68–82.

CHAPTER 6

Perfecting Family

Introduction

In Malaysia, perfecting the Islamic family can be performed in at least three ways—through contentious male-female *syariah* litigation; the teaching and learning of marriage; and the judicial displacement of Muslim-non-Muslim[1] family units where one partner is Muslim and the other a non-Muslim. Without the formidable strength and presence of the Divine Bureaucracy over a wide swathe of social life, these structures of disruption would not have been possible.

The disenchantment of Muslim marriage and divorce stems from the disintegration of a once-rich, bilateral and multifaceted social phenomenon of Malay family formations involving the intertwining relationships of cognates, agnates and conjugates (see Djamour 1959; Karim 1987, 1992; Peletz 1988). These relationships have been reduced into a modality of rules-based, singular behavioural conduct between men and women. Undeniably, laying down the appropriate rules and norms for marriage and family, and specifically gender relations between the properly married man and woman, had featured as a reform agenda in the earlier centuries in the Malay World. Some prominent early Malay texts played a didactic and prescriptive role in trying to convey variations of the proper (and unequal) gender norms during the nineteenth century (Hijjas 2013). However, at the everyday level, gender relationships were more flexible, as there was a range of applicable *adat* (customs) and Islamic norms and

M. Mohamad, *The Divine Bureaucracy and Disenchantment of Social Life*, Contestations in Contemporary Southeast Asia,
https://doi.org/10.1007/978-981-15-2093-8_6

traditions that tended towards an "ideology of balance and equality" (Karim 1987, 44). Wider socio-economic transformations ultimately changed family demography, but the disenchantment of Islamic marital life was also structured by its objectification through laws, sanctions, instructions, teachable skills and ultimately the displacement of the 'aberrant' family.

This chapter first documents and analyses the evolution of *syariah* family laws over various periods of social reform. This condition culminated in an extensive platform for the judicialisation of male-female marital disputes, at the same time manifesting an emergent ideology of male entitlements and female responsibilities, and template for the new Malay-Muslim family. Perfecting this new Muslim family has also involved more affable routes rather than contentious court disputes. Through the certification of mandatory marriage education courses before a marriage can take place, Muslim marriage is objectified as a set of skills and conduct that is teachable and learnt. I emphasise that contents and orientation of currently mandatory pre-marriage courses are heavily geared towards imparting religious knowledge and rules about male-female behaviour in a marital relationship rather than resolving relationship problems as they relate to lived realities of modern life. The final section discusses the seemingly anomalous Muslim-non-Muslim family, which has appeared as a challenge for the Divine Bureaucracy in its scheme of perfecting the Islamic family. The judicialisation of the Muslim-non-Muslim family has worked towards the unmaking of family rather than its protection, but enhances the (as yet unassailable) authority of the Divine Bureaucracy, the key agent of family-making and unmaking. The notion of 'masculine protectionism' serves as a guidepost on how marital issues and disputes are addressed through a *syariah*-driven bureaucratic and judicial system.

Masculine Protectionism in the Islamic Family

In the realm of worship, devotion and religious duties, women and men are equal in the eyes of God, as noted in numerous *quranic* verses (Roded 2001). However, symbolically the idealisation of the Islamic family suggests a paradigm of protectionism towards those presumed to be weaker, namely women and children in society. Greater rights are accorded to males in accordance with their heavier obligations towards the security and prosperity of the family. The verse from *Surat al-Nisa* (4:34)[2] is commonly quoted and invoked to represent this axiom: "Men are sustainers of women as God has preferred some of them over others, and because they sustain them from their wealth". Another verse, "And We sent Messengers before you, and We assigned to them wives and offsprings",[3] ascribes a gendered starting point within marriage and family relations in Islam. Male entitlements are a representation of Muslim prowess just as female behaviour is about harmonious obedience. The narrative of 'complementarity' is thus widely underscored as the essence of gender relations in Islam. In creating the authentic Islamic family, preachers and religious writers in modern-day Muslim Southeast Asia diligently set out the formula for this; male and female differences should not only be presented 'naturally', but ought to be exaggerated, with women's obedience towards God and husband marking female piety (White 2006, 277–288).

In applying the above suppositions to the analysis of the 'family' under the Divine Bureaucracy, the notion of the masculine protector is borrowed and expanded to mean one who subjects "those protected, paradigmatically women and children, in a subordinate position of dependence and obedience" (Young 2003, 2). The Islamic marriage embodies the notion of 'protectionism', which creates an effective appeal of security, care and benevolence of spiritual guidance. However, the idea of masculine protectionism can also explain some of the disjunctures of Islamic marriage and divorce within the realities of contemporary society (Maznah 2011).

It is beyond the scope of this study to ascertain if Islam, through its foundational texts, the Quran and *hadith*, has some immutable and fixed notions of gender relations. Scholars such as Amina Wadud (1999) and Asma Lamrabert (2018) have persuasively argued that some of the misogynistic worldviews and gender unequal ideologies expressed are due to selective elision or misinterpretation of verses and intentions of the texts. The Quran itself contains many references and mentions of women in multiple roles, with complex character attributes that defy an archetype of what femaleness should mean within the Islamic context (Stowasser 1997).

However, in several verses of the Quran, it is difficult to dispute that a hierarchical social order based on gender is delineated. *Surat al-Nisa* 4:34 is one of the most debated passages within gender and feminist discourse on male dominance and female submissiveness:

> Men are in charge of women, because Allah has made some of them excel the others, and because they spend some of their wealth. Hence righteous women are obedient, guarding the unseen which Allah has guarded. And those of them that you fear might rebel, admonish them and abandon them

> in their beds and beat them. Should they obey you, do not seek a way of harming them; for Allah is Sublime and Great (translated version from Dunn and Kellison 2010, 15).

Since men are *qawwamun* (guardians) over women, they are obliged to provide (financially) for women (Dun and Kellison 2010, 16). Nevertheless, there are both literal interpretations as well as reformist contextualisations of this verse (Dunn and Kellison 2010, 16–33). Verse 18 of Chapter 43 (*Surat al-Zukhruf*) alludes to "someone who is brought up amongst trinkets, who cannot put together a clear argument" and is interpreted as a reference to women's lesser intelligence and in-eloquence (Geissinger 2015, 47).

The idea of masculine protectionism used in this chapter is derived from observations of how Malaysian *syariah* family statutes have been reformed over the years, the nature and trend of judicialisation involving marital disputes as well as cases of Muslim-non-Muslim tussles over parental and children's rights. While the notion can be interpreted as privileging male benefits and rights, underlying this is also the narrative of a contractual male *qawwamun* (guardianship) in exchange for female compliance and submissiveness. This is an idealistic essence of the Islamic family that may not find expression in day-to-day practices.

Objectification of Muslim Marriage

An early purview of the religious bureaucracy was the domain of marriage and the family. If most areas of Muslim social life were not administered under the authority of bureaucratic Islam before, family matters had always been so. Marriage and divorce among Malays were solemnised by the rules of Islam, even if formal requirements of the signed and sealed contract, and state registration and validation were absent. One can say that British colonial administrators first founded a judicial bureaucracy for Islamic matters in response to the need for rules and procedures to govern Muslim marriage. The passage of the 1880 Ordinance on 'Mohamedan Marriages' in the Straits Settlements enabled the registration of marriage and divorce, the appointment of a *kadi* (judge) and the provision of a marriage property law in accordance with *syariah* (Yegar 1979, 173–174). Similar laws were passed two decades later in the Federated Malay States, and, after another 20 years, detailed legislation on Muslim marriage and divorce registration came into being in 1920 (Yegar 1979, 178–179). Even in the Unfederated

Malay States, the legislation of Muslim marriage and divorce was effected gradually between 1911 and 1938 (Yegar 1979, 181–183). Based on this it would appear that the codification of Muslim marriage and divorce laws into English-modelled statutes was a twentieth-century invention, at least for the Malay *negeri* (States, subnational units of governance). The judicial bureaucracy built around this early codification exercise was mainly related to the appointment of a marriage registrar and a divorce mediator, in this case, the institution of the Office—and later the Courts—of the *kadi*.

Syariah *Codification*

Before the above period, Muslim marriage and divorce were also governed by rules, though the extent of their formalisation is uncertain. Around the fifteenth to sixteenth centuries, a set of laws compiled as the Laws of Malacca or the Malacca Digest had at least six sections that dealt with rules on Islamic marriage and divorce (Abdul Monir 2016, 46–49). The first mention of Muslim law of marriage and divorce was said to be in the eighteenth-century *Ninety-Nine Laws of Perak* (Winstedt 1945, 24). Much of these rules were an admixture of *adat* (Malay customs), *syariah* precepts and Hindu practices. There were also *kitab* or books, such as the one written by a Malay World *ulama* (Islamic scholar) Syeikh Daud Abdullah al-Fatani called the *Idhah Al-Bab Li Murid Al-Nikah Bi Al-Sawab*, or translated as "For those of sound mind who wish to be truly married".[4] This text is popularly used in religious schools or *pondok* schools in Kelantan even till today (Zamri 2011, 5–8). Laws on marriage and divorce enacted during colonial times did not comprehensively cover all areas of marriage as specified in these old marriage texts. Marriage was a contract between two people, the groom and a representative of the bride, her *wali*, the terms of the agreement then witnessed by two other adult males of good standing.

Before colonialism too, marriage and divorce rules were the preserve of the *penghulu* (village head), *imam* (head of prayer) or *kadi* of the locality, and for the most part passed on by oral tradition. It is unclear if they kept a register of marriages before the adoption of formal laws, but this was unlikely. Even if they did, the records would not have been officially compiled as record-keeping was an administrative rather than religious requirement. Hence, when the British introduced laws related to marriage and divorce, these officials were largely meant to register and compile such records in a proper and systematic way. The role of the *kadi* was transformed into that of a registrar and the law would only recognise marriages or divorces conducted under licensed *imam*. Under British colonialism, sultans in the Malay *negeri* had the sole authority in the appointment of *imam* and *kadi* and also the final say on the confirmation of any divorce (Yegar 1979, 170–183).

From the 1950s onwards, the codified contents of Islamic marriage and divorce laws became increasingly extensive. During the Federation of Malaya phase (1948–1957), the Selangor Administration of Muslim Law Enactment 1952 only had 19 provisions contained in its 'Part VI: Marriage and Divorce'. Thirty-two years later, when the Selangor Islamic Family Law Enactment 1984 came into force, there were 10 parts in the law with 135 provisions covering sections from marriage to guardianship. When this law was replaced by the Islamic Family Law (State of Selangor) Enactment 2003, the 10 parts were retained, with 137 provisions. The scope of marriage and family judicialisation was thus widened, framing it as an expansive legal domain and responsibility of the *syariah* judiciary and its bureaucracy.

Bureaucratisation of Marriage and Family

Which institutions regulate the Muslim family in Malaysia today? At the highest national level, there is the Ministry of Women, Family and Community Development, established in 2001. However, the Ministry does not have a specific department or division on Islamic family matters. Instead, the purview of the Muslim family sits within Jakim and is called the Family, Social and Community Development Division, formed only in 2009. Its precursor was the Family, Social and Mosque Development Division (Kesuma) formed in 1999. In Jakim's official website, the justification and impetus for the establishment of these divisions was a Cabinet decision in 1998 to address *gejala sosial* (social ills) in society.[5] Besides playing its role in overcoming this, Jakim's family division oversees the management of marriage, divorce and reconciliation (*nikah, cerai dan rujuk*), and other family issues at the national level as well.

With the *negeri* Islamic bureaucracy, there are also divisions dealing with family matters under all the religious departments. Their mission includes the formulation, coordination and administration of matters related to Muslim marriage, divorce and reconciliation, the collection of data on family matters and training of facilitators and volunteers in the Muslim community.[6] The management of the Islamic family includes counselling and arbitration services (*perkhidmatan rundingcara*) aimed at resolving family and marital conflicts (Utusan Online 2015).

Another important bureaucratic institution in Islamic family welfare is the *Bahagian Sokongan Keluarga* (BSK), Family Support Division), which was set up in 2009 under the Malaysian Syariah Judicial Department (JKSM).[7] BSK's formation was largely to address mounting cases of non-compliant maintenance (*nafkah*) orders and unpaid family maintenance payments from errant husbands. While the Family, Social and Community divisions of Jakim and the *negeri* religious departments play their roles in strengthening and upholding the family institution, the BSK upholds the family institution in cases when family disputes are brought to court or end up in divorce.[8] Family has been considered central in the advancement of Islam in the country, although at the same time there is also a realisation that the 'Islamic family' is not a naturalised unit but needs to be structured, regulated and maintained as a social construct, under the tight guardianship of the Divine Bureaucracy.

Perfecting Family Through Contentious, Gendered *Syariah* Litigation

Over several decades, Malaysian laws on the Muslim family have changed from a more pluralist tradition to one with a strong emphasis on male entitlement and female compliance. Revised sets of Islamic family laws shifted towards the absorption of a more pronounced sense of masculine protectionism. As discussed in earlier chapters, the years after independence (1957) until about the late 1980s was also a period of Islamic bureaucratic reorganisation based on the political need to accommodate the interests of more strident agents of Islamisation. The reforms gave some concessions to recognising women's rights in the areas of marriage, polygamy, divorce entitlements and property inheritance.

Most of the advocates of new Islamic family laws at the time were not trained in *syariah* law and theology. Among the main drivers behind the upgrading and modernisation of Islamic family laws were academics like Ahmad Ibrahim, a law professor trained in Western law who was a key player in drafting a model Islamic family law for the Federal Territories (Ahmad 1986). University of Malaya's academics such as a law expert on Muslim women's material entitlements, and a linguistics professor, contributed papers on safeguarding women's rights at various seminars towards upgrading the contents and implementation of *syariah* law (Ahilemah 1981; Asmah 1978). During the 1980s, the Islamisation project directed by the federal government was one that tried to fit in with the image of a progressive and moderate Islamic nation.

In the 1984 legislation, modernists and progressive women seemed to have had an upper hand, ahead of Islamic pressure groups in this project. Islamic family law at the time was generous towards granting women some rights in matters of marriage and divorce, and was even considered to be one of the most progressive in the Muslim world (Zainah Anwar 2008). Through this, Selangor's Syariah Appeals Committee rejected a husband's pronouncement of *talak* (repudiation of marriage) outside of court in *Zainab binti Mahmood v Abd Latif bin Jusoh, 1991*. Likewise, in the case *of Fakhariah bte Lokman v Johari bin Zakaria, 1992*, the court allowed a wife's application to seek divorce by stipulation (*cerai taklik)* on grounds that the husband had failed to provide maintenance. In this case, the court rejected the husband's defence that his wife had committed *nusyuz* (act of disobedience) as it was not considered material to the divorce application she initiated (Horowitz 1994, 545–546, 553–554).

By the 2000s, the somewhat progressive Islamic family legislation of the 1980s was repealed in almost all *negeri* and replaced by a new family law statute, one that would enhance men's entitlements and curtail women's rights. The Technical Committee on Syariah and Civil Laws formed in 1988 drafted this new law. At the time of the Committee's inception in 1988, the 13-member team had an all-male membership (Abdul Monir 2016, 78). Areas of change effected by the new *syariah* family law included revised conditions for polygamy, conditions for judicial divorce (*fasakh*) and conditions for granting an injunction on disposal of assets during matrimonial proceedings (divorce or maintenance orders). Under this new cultural reinvention, men were granted more entitlements in marriage, divorce and property division, while women were subjugated to increased obligations to good behaviour in exchange for maintenance, custody and divorce compensation rights.

In 1996, the Selangor Islamic Family Enactment 1984 was amended to abolish a previous ruling, which required Muslim men to get the consent and signature of their first wives before they could proceed with a subsequent marriage. At the time, Malay women, particularly those within the ruling party Umno, were quite vocal in protesting against this move. The President of the National Council of Women's Organisations, Zaleha Ismail, who was also the then Minister for National Unity and Social

Development, submitted a memorandum of protest to Prime Minister Mahathir Mohamad on this new regulation. The following day, the Prime Minister's wife, Siti Hasmah Ali, appeared on television to express her disappointment with the change of regulation on polygamy. She was responding to a statement by the Deputy Chairman of the Majlis Agama Islam Selangor, the Selangor State (*negeri*) Islamic Religious Council, that the new regulation was meant "to make it easier for eligible men to practice [*sic*] something that was essentially their right under the Syariah law" (New Straits Times 1996a). A Selangor State Executive Councillor was also quoted as saying that though the change in polygamy requirements had angered women, it pleased many men (The Straits Times 1996b). The English newspaper *New Straits Times* (1996b) ran a story to express the displeasure about the new polygamy ruling by featuring the opinions of prominent scholars, politicians and intellectuals. In the end though, even the voices of these highly placed people in government and society were unable to reverse this tide towards a 'masculine protectionist' phase of state Islamisation.

The entrenchment of masculine protectionism depended on the strength of the Divine Bureaucracy. In 2003, 12 women's organisations led by Sisters in Islam (Sis) embarked on a campaign to promote monogamy with the title, 'One Husband, One Wife'. It was launched by Endon Mahmood, wife of Abdullah Ahmad Badawi, the Prime Minister then. Despite the endorsement by the highest leadership, two major Malay newspapers, *Utusan Malaysia* and *Berita Harian*, opposed the campaign with negative publicity through stories that featured disapproving views of several *mufti*, one of whom was quoted as saying, "If nothing is done to stop the campaign, Muslims may in future question other aspects of the law because of their lack of understanding of the religion" (The Straits Times 2003a). The campaign was said to be against Islam as it was the right of husbands to take on more wives, and that monogamy could not be the solution to social ills (New Straits Times 2003a). The *mufti*—conventionally aligned with Umno—and Pas were united on this issue. Women NGOs and women leaders from Umno stood on the opposite side, with the Women and Family Development Minister, Shahrizat Abdul Jalil, defending the monogamy campaign in Parliament (New Straits Times 2003b).

In 2004, more than a dozen NGOs petitioned the government to propose a law against marital rape. It was disclosed that 170 married women had reported being raped by their husbands in 2003 (Kuppusamy 2004).

The Human Rights Commission of Malaysia (Suhakam) also called for the inclusion of marital rape as an offence under the Penal Code (New Straits Times 2004a). On this issue too, Muslim feminists and Suhakam were rebuked by the bureaucratic authority of Islam. The *mufti* of Perak said that Suhakam's proposal was "against God's law" (New Straits Times 2004b). He was also quoted saying that if a wife did not obey to having sex, except when menstruating, she would be punished (Kuppusamy 2004). In 2005, the National Fatwa Committee issued a *fatwa* that declared there was no terminology (*istilah*) for rape or the violation of human rights in a legitimate Islamic marriage (Jakim 2012, 121). The campaign for recognising marital rape has continued, although the government-of-the-day still has no plans to criminalise the offence.

Marriage and Divorce Under Masculine Protectionism

Malaysian *syariah* statutes, multiplied and reformed as part of Islam's growing institutionalisation, have had a profound impact on the reordering of family relations. Family arbitration and reconciliation studies by Sharifah Zaleha and Sven Cederroth (1997) and Michael Peletz (2002) have elucidated the significant role that the *syariah* court plays in defining the parameters and conduct of the Islamic family. These have functioned to "translate Islamic Family Law to the masses", suggesting that Islamic family rules are not necessarily obvious to Malay families who want to conduct themselves appropriately in society (Sharifah Zaleha and Cederroth 1997, 228). Litigation in the courtrooms reiterates a certain hegemonic norm and imposes rewards for compliance and penalties for contravention, reproducing a Weberian disciplinary system based on formal rules and regulations (O'Neill 1986).

Syariah reforms in Malaysia from about the early 2000s reveal the excessive liberty and entitlements given to men within the rules of marriage, divorce and polygamy. In contrast, restrictive stipulations have been enhanced for women in their exercise of rights in marriage and divorce. What is being fashioned is a new Malay-Muslim masculinity, which is based on conferred entitlements rather than responsibility-based, earned authority. Traditional Malay society was previously characterised as bilateral and matrilineal with gender roles seldom divided to starkly favour men as heads of households (Peletz 1988; Karim 1992; Stivens 1996; Ng 1999). However, as well-noted by Nik Noriani (2003, 36–37), more recent trends in *syariah* reforms had strongly emphasised the following:

- The unilateral rights of men to pronounce divorce (*talak*) upon women, anywhere, anytime and under any circumstances. Even though there are legal provisions to prevent this from occurring outside of court—it is considered a *syariah* offence—these have had little deterrence value (see Chart 6.1);
- Enhanced polygamy entitlements with minimal conditions attached to such applications, for example, the necessity to be fair *and* just to all co-wives is now less emphasised by the court as a criterion for these applications to be approved;
- Men's entitlement to a share of women's matrimonial assets to support polygamous marriage;
- Onerous qualifications to women's rights and entitlements to obtain divorce by judicial decree, often requiring that these applications go through the burdensome motion of ineffective counselling and reconciliation exercises.

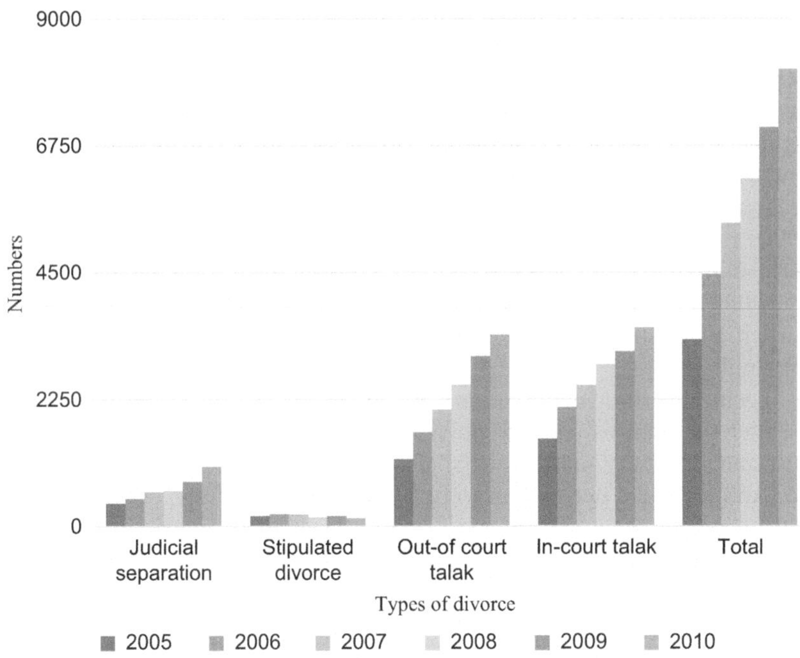

Chart 6.1 Dissolution of marriages by divorce type in Selangor 2005–2010. (Source: Adapted from Siti Zubaidah et al. 2011, 982)

From the above trends, a definition of the Islamised family unit is being performatively outlined through battles over Islamic family law reforms and in court adjudications, with male privilege as its mainstay. In essence, the creation of this new Malay-Muslim family, starkly patriarchal, goes against the grain of what was the norm in male-female relations within traditional Malay family structures. Polygamy, although prescribed in *quranic* doctrinal texts, was not a prevalent cultural practice in traditional Malay societies or under customary law. In fact, the practice of polygyny was only made much easier by the introduction of recent Islamic laws. Before the widespread establishment of Islam in the Malay Peninsula, Malay matrilineal society strongly favoured monogamous rules in marriage (Yegar 1979, 120–121). For example, in Negeri Sembilan, where the matrilineal system prevails, a Malay could not marry a second wife without obtaining the permission of the ruler and the consent of the first wife (Ahmad 1965, 187). This was in the past. Today, *syariah* lobbyists are claiming that their support for polygamy is in line with a purer and authentic Islam, not tainted by indigenous customs.

The conditions to be fulfilled for polygamy used to be that a man had to prove that he should be 'just and necessary' to all co-wives. On this basis, some women were able to overturn, by appealing to a higher body, the decision of religious courts that had allowed their husbands to take on new wives, by asserting that this may not be just even if the marriage was necessary (Horowitz 1994, 546–547). However, starting from the mid-1990s onwards, rules on polygamy were gradually relaxed. The written permission of existing wives to consent to polygamy was removed in 1996. In 2005, further changes were made to the law to lessen the economic burden of husbands in their quest to propagate and maintain multiple families.

Specifically, three new clauses were added in newer legislation to make it easier for men to practice polygamy: (1) removing the justice clause 'just and necessary marriage' to 'just *or* necessary marriage' as a condition and for court permission to be granted for polygamy; (2) allowing a man, upon his new marriage, to stake a claim over matrimonial assets jointly acquired at the point of marriage with his other wife or wives; and (3) allowing a man to maintain his wives either through regular payment of monetary allowances (*nafkah)* or dividing joint matrimonial assets such that he can use proceeds from this as a source of support for his wife or wives. Divorced Muslim women had always been entitled to matrimonial property (*harta sepencarian*), a right that was set in place almost unwaveringly in customary Malay law (Taylor 1937). However, amendments to Islamic family law in the early 2000s allowed a man, upon him taking a co-wife, to stake a claim over jointly acquired matrimonial assets with a previous wife. The proceeds from sale of these assets, for example, would enable the man to maintain his entire family. As remarked by one of the critics to this amendment, "It used to be that a Muslim man had to prove he could provide and treat his wives equitably before taking on a second, third or fourth wife. Now it would seem that the Malay man is to be subsidised by his first wife... with or without her consent" (Nafisah 2005).

A high percentage of divorced men have also breached court orders to pay compensation or maintenance to their former wives. One study by Muslihah (2009) showed how out of the 3005 divorces registered in the Selangor *syariah* courts in 2003, only 432 were cases of successful post-divorce support payments to women, or just 16 per cent of total divorce cases for the year (154). The study also found that 44 per cent of women complained about husbands not complying with court orders to pay for their *iddah* (period of waiting before a divorce is finalised) maintenance; 67 per cent said that their husbands did not pay their *mutaah* (post-divorce gift) and 58 per cent did not pay the arrears on their *nafkah* while 10 per cent did not comply with court orders to pay for child maintenance (Muslihah 2009, 154).[9] The non-enforcement of court orders for maintenance payments had become a mounting national issue such that the state stepped in to intervene, and in so doing, concealed the direness of Muslim male negligence. Between 2000 and 2009, there were 206,000 registered divorce cases, and 12,570 applications for *nafkah*, with BSK tasked to resolve the issue of unpaid maintenance (Siti Nurbaiyah et al. 2011).

In the above cases, it is unlikely that family well-being has been enhanced. Instead, the ability of men to project a new masculinity has been strengthened and bolstered, without even having to go to great lengths—such as proving valour or stewardship—to win the right to be the patriarch of the family. Today, family welfare is seldom placed squarely on the shoulders of male heads of households, and it has become a joint responsibility of the state and women to help husbands and other co-wives. While enjoying the usual privileges of manhood, Muslim men now doubly enjoy being 'subsidised' by the state and their wives. For feminist activists, these developments and grandstanding by Islamists merely justify patriarchal power which has little basis in indigenous traditions—nor for that matter, Islamic values—but conveniently stamped as divine and immutable by *syariah* proponents (Zainah 2001, 237–240).

Men Versus Women: "Heads I Win, Tails You Lose"

Syariah law in Malaysia has now been constructed into a formulaic doctrine for authentic 'Muslimness'. In the process, various social disjunctures have surfaced, particularly when marriages are being dissolved. With successive amendments to the Islamic Family Law, the gap between men's and women's rights and entitlements has widened. Under current *syariah* legal arrangements, marital dissolution—a highly traumatic experience in family life—deals an added blow to Muslim women as their options to exercise the right to sustain or dissolve a marriage as well as their entitlement to a fair, just and equitable post-divorce settlement are restricted. Women, especially those living in poverty, suffer appreciably from these situations as they are not protected by legal provisions or assurance of sustained support in the event of a marital breakup. In a study I conducted in a rural settlement in Kelantan, men in poverty were often unable to live up to their religious obligation as family head and provider, yet were given the court mandate to imagine that they could, that is, via approved applications for polygamy and the small sums and painless terms of payment in which awards to their divorced wives were disbursed through court orders (Maznah 2012).

While modern *syariah* statutes try to imbibe the Islamic tenet of 'masculinist protectionism', their provisions for divorce have not resulted in more family security and protection. What exists is the discrepancy between official ideology about Muslim masculinity—as provider and head of household, and thus worthy of entitlement—and the day-to-day reality of an economically incapacitated male wage-earning partner in a marriage. In most cases, specifically those from the lower socio-economic stratum, a man's wage is hardly adequate to support a family. Hence a wife is likely to work for a wage as well. In rural households, there is enormous sharing and cross-subsidisation of household expenses between married partners, parents, children, siblings and relatives. In this context, conferring a uniform entitlement of rights upon males, regardless of their status, ignores the likelihood that there are those who simply cannot fulfil many of the religious obligations under the Islamic marital contract.

Yet, drawing from Butler (1988), the performativity of Islam entices all Muslim men to imagine that their entitlement is God-given and must be permitted, despite their material inadequacy. The law attempts to reconcile this gap with clauses to sustain the delusion that all men ***should*** be able to provide for the household, while contradictorily reforming selective legal wordings to make these appear gender-neutral such that men can share their wives' property. This reform trend appears inconsistent in intent, such that boundaries between the religious and legal dimensions are often inadvertently blurred to serve the double purpose of sustaining "the patriarchal ideology that informs these rules, and at the same time allowing for their modification" (Mir-Hosseini 1993, 192).

The modern *syariah* may not be too different from secular law where the implicit code of a hegemonic masculinity results in the accruing of a "patriarchal dividend" for those complicit in this control (Connell 2008, 374). Various legal systems are more similar than they are different in terms of gender ideology and the consequences for the family. Nevertheless, the inflexible nature of the Islamic gender divide suffers from an ability to reconcile reality with dogma. As a study of Iran and Morocco has illustrated, no legal system, no matter how divine, can ensure that a man performs the responsibility that accompanies his authority when he "is out of work and incapable of providing his own maintenance" (Mir-Hosseini 1993, 193). Hence, the foundation of the *syariah* which is based on the entitlement of males to head their households is negated by a social reality of the various cases of male incapacity to materially support their families.

Perfecting Family Through Teaching and Learning Marriage

If the 'perfect' Islamic family is somewhat coerced through contentious litigation, it can also be moulded within more congenial and benevolent settings. Masculine protectionism pervades through the enforcement of state-sponsored and organised Islamic marriage education. Around the mid-1990s, 'teaching' and 'learning' the dos and don'ts of marriage began to develop into a burgeoning field of enterprise under the Divine Bureaucracy. Some of the justification for this derived from a common but strong perception of the family as a fragile institution in need of direction and guidance through religious precepts.

Table 6.1 Crude marriage and divorce rates, Muslims and non-Muslims (2016 and 2017)

Year	*Muslim*		*Non-Muslim*	
	2016	*2017*	*2016*	*2017*
Crude marriage rate (%)	7.4	6.8	4.7	4.5
Crude divorce rate (%)	2.1	2	0.9	0.8

Source: Department of Statistics Malaysia, social statistics on marriage and divorce, 2016–2017

There were other interconnected reasons too, including the demographic reality of more 'broken' Muslim families due to higher divorce rates compared to other religious groups (see Table 6.1). This, however, was not necessarily the strongest factor for the change. Justifications to reform family law and the implementation of new regulations and requirements for Muslim marriage have seldom been based on broad demographic trends of Muslim family life, especially in relation to high rates of divorce, remarriage and early marriage. Rather, it was a deep sense of moral anxiety of how sexual and gender relationships were not contained and regulated properly according to Islamic rules of rights and wrongs, as strictly sourced from the Quran, *sunna* and selected authorised *hadith*. These appeared to be the main motivation behind family policies, predicated on Islamic worldviews.

The 'Muslim family' seemingly had to be retaught and reinvented to become a crucial fount of Islamic values and *habitus*, equipped with a set of rules and codes of conduct that would symbolise the perfect Islamic unit of social and biological reproduction. Pierre Bourdieu's concept of *habitus* is referenced here as involving the propagation and internalisation of social structure derived "not primarily as normative values or rules, but as transposable cognitive classifications, 'practical taxonomies', as tastes or preferences, and 'schemes of action', all of which undergird the 'practical sense' or 'feel for the game'" (Friedland 2009, 889). Perhaps one way of simplifying this notion, as applied to the Muslim marriage situation, is that couples, to behave as exemplars, need to be taught all the practical codes of marital conduct. Islamic marriage education—in the form of knowledge dissemination of comprehensive *syariah* prescriptions for the family, and a mandatory instructional programme before marriage—was the means to do so.

Under an enlarged, well-resourced and diligent Islamic bureaucracy, getting married has been transformed into a methodical disenchanting process. Before a marriage can happen, couples, including their family and friends, have to navigate the bureaucratic rigmarole of entering into a legal union. In 2012, Jakim introduced an online portal known as Sistem Pengurusan Perkahwinan Islam Malaysia (SPPIM, the Malaysian Islamic Marriage Management System) "to enable a more efficient and systematic work process" for the use of all Jabatan Agama Islam Negeri (Jain, *negeri* religious departments), and especially Pejabat Agama Islam Daerah (Paid, district religious offices) throughout the country. Among the documents uploaded include forms to apply for the "premarital marriage course", "permission to marry" and "registration of marriage" as well as "processes in relation to divorce, revocation and arbitration".[10] There is also a complete list of addresses of all the district religious offices nationwide, as marriage applications are made here.

As if these were insufficient, Jakim also produced a series of instructional booklets (downloadable through the SPPIM portal) on all aspects of marriage. The following listing and description of these booklets illustrate the nature of bureaucratisation which disenchants the notion of marriage as involving a series of systematised state-ordained prerequisites and procedures.

1. *Garis panduan bagi prosedur pentadbiran perkahwinan, perceraian dan ruju'* (Guidelines on administrative procedures for marriage, divorce and revocation of divorce). Three important requirements need to be fulfilled before official permission for marriage is granted: a certificate of attendance at an authorised premarital course that uses Jakim's common curriculum; HIV test at a government-approved health centre, and finally, after a process of verification, permission from the Registrar of Marriage to proceed with the *akad nikah* (marriage solemnisation) and the registration of marriage. Other forms of marriage as in overseas marriages, polygamy and underage marriages must adhere to other additional procedures.
2. *Fatwa Munakahat* (*Fatwa* on Marriage). This guidebook lists rulings by the various *fatwa* committees on marital and family matters. The 2013 edition contains 30 such *fatwa* ranging from rules on DNA testing to establish the paternity of the child to rules on marrying off a woman who is pregnant outside of wedlock.

3. *Garis panduan bagi prosedur pentadbiran perkahwinan, perceraian dan ruju' di luar* negara (Guidelines on administrative procedure for marriage, divorce and revocation of divorce overseas). This provides instructions on how to apply for permission and registration of marriage for those residing overseas.
4. *Garis Panduan Upacara Akad Nikah di Masjid dan Perkara-Perkara Berkaitan Dengannya* (Guidelines on *Akad Nikah* Ceremony Held in Mosques and Related Matters). As mosques are considered sacred sites, having the *akad nikah* ceremony on their premises necessitates this guideline, which comes with a long list of dos and don'ts for the marrying couple and their accompanying parties when they enter mosque grounds.
5. *Kedudukan Anak Tak Sah Taraf: Dari Kedudukan Undang-Undang* (The Status of Illegitimate Children: From the Legal Standpoint). This booklet emphasises the point that the status and rights of children born out of wedlock are unlike that of other children. Most importantly, they have no right to claim inheritance or *nafkah* from the biological father, and as such cannot inherit or be entitled to *nafkah* from him. The entire care and maintenance of such a child is the responsibility of the mother, and when a female child is to be married, she is not permitted to have her biological father as her *wali* as the status of her father is not recognised. She would need to use a *wali hakim* or a proxy appointed by the court.

Muslim marriage education programmes in Malaysia are religion-centric and promote particular Islamic values, rules and doctrines to sustain and reproduce the model of a sacred 'familism'—something which was already prevalent in the West from the seventeenth century—or the association of "prevailing family principles of marriage, childbearing, motherhood, commitment, and sacrifice for family with a sense of sacredness" (Nock 2005, 22). However, while Muslim marriage education may have a different origin from its Western counterpart, it shares similar demographic contexts and is underpinned by a perceived moral crisis involving the family. Both intend to make good marriages 'teachable'. In Malaysia, the scale and frequency of these programmes are wide-ranging, involving the annual participation of at least 100,000 Muslim cohorts who have reached the 'age-of-marriage' (see Table 6.2 on registered marriages). What could have triggered the panic and anxiety over the

Table 6.2 Muslim marriages and divorces (2008–2017)

Year	*No. of registered marriages*	*No. of registered divorces*
2008	131,053	22,800
2009	135,436	27,891
2010	135,548	28,035
2011	140,535	27,355
2012	148,806	29,253
2014	159,851	33,842
2015	174,321	36,732
2016	142,712	41,030
2017	134,008	39,709

Source: Department of Statistics Malaysia, social statistics for marriage and divorce, 2010–2017. Note that marriage and divorce statistics are not made available for 2013

tenuousness of Muslim marriage and family life for it to be subjected to such earnest interventions?

Moral Panic and Proper Marriage Norms

The general worry over the rise in incidences of marital breakdown among Malays has been a constant feature of religious and social discourse on the family (New Straits Times 1995a, b). At one time, a course on marriage was even offered to secondary school students (The Straits Times 1995a). The desire for a template to produce uniformed 'good marriages' drew its impetus from the apprehension about controlling and ring-fencing 'wrongful' forms of religious expressions. In this regard, it is useful to highlight the example of a 'deviant' Muslim marriage that generated profound unease among the Islamic authorities and acted as trigger for more intervention in Muslim marital life by the bureaucracy.

In 1994, Abu Talib Harun, a Singaporean man living in Johor, was charged in the *Syariah* Court of Johor for multiple offences, one of which was cohabiting with six women and having unlawful sex. He was living with ten women, four of whom he was legally married to under ***nikah daaim*** (regular, permanent marriage), while the other six he married under ***nikah mutaah*** (temporary marriage). Abu Talib claimed in his defence that he was a Syiah Muslim and that this allowed him to have more than four wives (The Straits Times 1994). During their defence in court, one of his wives also testified that they were followers of the ***mazhab***

Syiah *imammiyah*, which recognises *nikah mutaah*, and that two Sunni *ulama* allegedly considered *nikah mutaah* valid as well (The Straits Times 1995b). Interestingly, at this time the prosecutor was unable to argue that these Syiah practices were illegal as there was no law or *fatwa*, which categorically stated that Sunni Islam was the only officially accepted Islam in Malaysia.

Abdul Talib himself made a spirited defence of his case by lecturing the court on the history of Islam. He quoted passages from 14 Arabic books and stressed that Muslim scholars had long supported temporary marriages. Moreover, it was a "divine blessing to help meet the sexual needs of man [*sic*]" (The Straits Times 1995c). All ten wives were in their 20s, and six were employed (New Straits Times 1995c). Abdul Talib also invoked the Constitution as guaranteeing his freedom of religious belief, and claimed that, as a Shi'ite and a Singaporean, he was not subjected to Johor's Islamic administration law. Another wife argued that this law had overridden what the Quran and *hadith* allowed (New Straits Times 1995d). At the end of the trial, Abdul Talib and his wives were found guilty of 16 out of 17 charges under Johor's Islamic administration enactment.[11] He was sentenced to 25 months jail and fined RM14,000; the first 4 'lawful' wives were each fined RM500 and 1 month's jail, and the other 6 were each fined RM3500 and 3-month imprisonment (Visvanathan 1995).

At this time, Shi'ism had not yet been decreed illegal by any law or *fatwa*, and the judge emphasised that the court was "not against any sect but on individuals who went against the Islamic laws enforced in the state" (New Straits Times 1995d). Nevertheless, the case of the *mutaah* marriage of Abdul Talib made waves, especially in providing the justifications for stronger curbs against Shi'ism. Following the trial, the 1995 Umno General Assembly saw various delegates calling for the Syiah ban (New Straits Times 1995e). Not long after, the government expressed its concern over the perceived threat of a growing Shi'ism against Sunni Islam in the country. For the first time there was a call for the Federal Constitution to be amended to reflect and address this anxiety. De facto Minister of Islamic Affairs, Abdul Hamid Othman, maintained that the historical rivalry between the two sects had been too entrenched that if allowed to exist in one place, this would lead to disunity and conflict among Muslims here (The Straits Times 1996).

A Syiah group, Jamiya as-Sirat al-Mustaqim, with 200 followers, had reportedly established itself in Petaling Jaya. Some Malay women had also brought back babies after marrying Iranian students under *nikah mutaah* while studying in the United States. At the same time, religious teachers had complained that some local women were being influenced to enter into such marriages. There were unverified allegations as well that Iran's strategy of spreading Shi'ism to majority Muslim countries outside its own was one way of gaining support for the new Islamic republic. Against this backdrop, the case of Abdul Talib and his ten wives was conveniently used to paint a negative image of Shi'ism (The Straits Times 1996). Not surprisingly, this also redoubled the focus on the Muslim family as yet another constituency to be managed and regulated through the rules and laws of ASWJ.

Justifying Premarital Courses

Before the imposition of mandatory premarital courses, couples could voluntarily attend these programmes and sit for an evaluation test. This way they did not need to go through an interview (introduced in 1992) by the religious authority during which they would be tested on the basic tenets of Islam, including their ability to read the Quran. About 30 per cent of these couples failed the interview on Islamic knowledge in their first attempt (The Straits Times 1995d). Following reports in 1995 that the divorce rate for Muslims was rising—averaging 20 to 30 per cent and with one *negeri* in the East Coast, a traditional Malay belt, hitting 40 per cent compared to 18 per cent nationwide the previous year—the government announced that it would be making it mandatory for all Muslim couples to attend a basic course on marriage before they were permitted to marry (The Straits Times 1995d). An early version of the marriage course was offered as a one-day event at Universiti Sains Malaysia (USM, University of Science Malaysia) in Penang. Titled, 'Towards the Betterment of the Islamic Family Institution', and jointly organised by the USM Muslim Staff Association and the Pos Malaysia Berhad Muslim Welfare Association, it focused on Islamic teaching as a key to solving family problems and instilling family responsibility to create an Islamic society (New Straits Times 1995f).

Around the same time, a similar seminar, titled 'Child, a Gift of God', was held in Negeri Sembilan. Its Chief Minister also announced that the government would increase the duration of marriage courses from one to two days, and that the emphasis would be on creating "Muslim families with good values". These were justified with statistics that showed a breakdown of the family structure: 24 cases of child abuse and 174 cases of juvenile crimes including seven by girls, committed in the first quarter of the year (New Straits Times 1995g). In 1997, a Cabinet Committee on Social Ills was formed and focused on the family unit as its source of resolution. This sense of moral panic could also be understood as a state-generated discourse on the 'Asian values' which sought to counter Western values responsible for the breakdown of family and marriage due to individual drive for selfish and materialistic pursuits over community good (Ng et al. 2006, 140–142). Around the time of this concern, the compulsory marriage course for Muslims had incorporated lessons on parenting skills, and had also been streamlined so that a certificate of attendance issued by any *negeri* would be recognised in all others (New Straits Times 1997).

Some criticised this mandatory requirement for marriage given the inadequacies of the premarital course, including its exclusion of tackling familial social problems like incest and domestic violence, and because it was mainly geared towards inculcating couples only with Islamic tenets and knowledge (New Straits Times 2002). Zainah Anwar (2006), Sis co-founder, related that a premarital course she attended listed the leadership quality of a husband as one who did not listen to his wife. An *ustaz* also gave tips to would-be grooms that they could take a second wife by crossing the border to Thailand to avoid the legal requirements governing polygamy in Malaysia. Even beating one's wife the 'Islamic way' was taught in some classes.

The average number of registered Muslim marriages from 2008 to 2017 was 144,697 (see Table 6.2). In Perak, the number doubled from 10,181 in 2003 to 21,468 in 2008 (Ruhil Hayati 2011, 69). In Johor, almost 30,000 attended state-endorsed courses conducted by 7 private companies and 11 charitable bodies between 2013 and 2014 (Berita Harian 2014). Even higher figures were recorded for FT Kuala Lumpur and Putrajaya—166,128 people registered for the module from 2015 to 2017, averaging around 55,000 a year.[12] In 2019, in just one district (Hulu Langat) in Selangor, there were 40 courses scheduled for the year, each lasting two days. At the time of writing, five of these had been fully subscribed and registration closed.[13] Courses offered by Paid and Jais cost RM80 per person; those by Jawi-licensed private outfits such as Astana Mukmin Enterprise and Baitul Amin Consultancy, and conducted in suburbs of Kuala Lumpur like Wangsa Maju and Taman Tun Dr Ismail respectively, cost RM120 per person. These are held every weekend (Saturday to Sunday) and also Wednesdays to Thursdays.[14] The Kedah religious department appears to have subcontracted the running of its marriage courses to the 18 private companies listed on its website.[15] Additionally, the Perak religious department has a portal for matchmaking (*portal cari jodoh*) called the *CintaSakinah*, operated with a private company called K-Perak INC.[16] The portal also has a flowchart to show how the matchmaking process is done.[17] In 2018, newly elected de facto Deputy Minister of Islamic Affairs, Fuziah Salleh, announced that the marriage modules would be revised to keep up with demands of the times, that is, by including aspects of husband-wife responsibilities and better communication between spouses, thus going beyond what marriage and its rules were, as well as what was considered permissible (Berita Harian 2018).

Gender Differentiation and Masculine Protectionism

Premarital marriage education courses form a socio-legal component of Muslim marriage registration in Malaysia today. Although not mandated by law, a Muslim couple needs to produce a certificate of attendance from a government-approved premarital programme to get married. Throughout the country, these programmes share a common curriculum, the Islamic Pre-Marriage Integrated Modular Course (*Modul Bersepadu Kursus Pra-Perkahwinan Islam*). All course facilitators and participants are also given a manual published by Jakim (2008), titled *Memasuki Gerbang Perkahwinan* ("Entering the Gateway of Marriage", henceforth *Gerbang Perkahwinan*), as a standard reference text. The programmes run by facilitators are organised around three main themes: religious foundation, household management and family conflict management. These cover topics such as faith, worship and morals, spousal communication, health, financial and time management and stress and conflict management. Each rule and justification for a prescribed conduct, as explicated in the manual, is supported by verses from the Quran or the *hadith*, which appear on almost every page of its text.

The facilitated programme based on *Gerbang Perkahwinan* heavily emphasises gender differentiation, in terms of *akhlak* (moral conduct) and responsibilities between men and women. The ideal *akhlak* is referred to as *mahmudah* (good virtues), and elaborated as "pious, wise, firm, prudent, patient, honest, trustworthy, caring of spouses". Loathsome *akhlak* (*mazmunah*) include "spite and resentment, betrayal, deceitfulness, wastefulness, mistrust, anger, laziness, fear, impatience, breach of promise, disobedience" (Jakim 2008, 29). Although some of these traits could be gender-neutral, the manual, based on the interpretation of two *hadith*, also spells out the prescribed *akhlak* and responsibilities as categorically different for husbands and wives.

For a husband's *akhlak*, the *hadith* transmitted by al-Tarmizi, is stated as, "A believing man with impeccable faith is one with good conduct and gentle towards his wife and children".[18] For a wife, the *hadith* as transmitted by al-Nasa'i is used, "The best of women are those whom when you set your eyes upon them, gladdens your heart and when you command them, they will obey and when you swear upon them, they will do good towards you".[19]

In interpreting these *hadith* then, *Gerbang Perkahwinan* introduces and promotes a gender-based definition of desired *akhlak* that is largely different for husbands and wives (Jakim 2008, 29–31). Table 6.3 is a listing of the gender-differentiated *akhlak*.

As for the sharing of responsibilities, *Gerbang Perkahwinan* includes several *hadith* and specifies the following divisions listed in Table 6.4 (Jakim 2008, 48–62).

It is noteworthy that in transmitting the above, Jakim also produced a set of PowerPoint slides, which modified the above-mentioned

Table 6.3 List of *akhlak* for husbands and wives (as contained in *Gerbang Perkahwinan*)

Husband	*Wife*	*Traits to avoid for both husband and wife*
Piousness	Piousness	Exaggerating a trivial problem
Exercise leadership as befitting of a husband	Exercise leadership as befitting of a wife	Neglectful of each other's emotions
Protect secrets of the household	Protect secrets of the household	Not treating religious matters seriously
Responsibility	Obeisance and faithfulness to husband	Not refined in manners and conduct
Socialise in a good manner	Love and adoration towards husband	Demeaning the other partner and his/her lineage
Open and accommodating attitude	Adorning oneself for husband	Extreme jealousy
Practice of wisdom	Safeguarding personal dignity and husband's property	Hurtful of each other's feelings
Consensual	Seeking husband's permission	
Providing a good example		

Table 6.4 Responsibilities between husband and wife (as contained in *Gerbang Perkahwinan*)

Husband	*Wife*	*Jointly/mutually*
To offer *mahar* (dowry) at marriage	To obey husband in all matters except those that are against the teachings of Islam	To provide love
To provide maintenance (*nafkah*)	To safeguard self-dignity and property of husband	Trust and secrecy
To care for wife with kindness and mutual respect		Good family socialisation
To provide guidance and education		Sexual fulfilment
		Respect for each other's kin
		Mutual appreciation of each other's personality
		Control feelings of jealousy
		Self-care to be outwardly presentable
		Property ownership
		Cooperation
		Accommodation and tolerance

differentiations to one version as seen in Table 6.5, for use in the premarital courses such as the one held in Kedah in 2016.

There are also prescribed features to look for in an ideal wife and husband, and these are not the same for both according to *Gerbang Perkahwinan*. The selection of a bride should at best fit the criteria of 'religion', 'lineage', 'beauty' and 'property'; for the selection of a bridegroom, it is listed as 'embracing religion', 'possessing noble morals', having the 'capacity to lead the family' and 'compatibility' (Jakim 2008, 34–35). The module on family management comprises many lessons and instructions on supplications (*do'a*) to be read even when in the act of lovemaking. For instance, participants are taught to read their supplications when first entering the conjugal room, before the start of intercourse and when orgasm and ejaculation are reached (Jakim 2008, 77–80).[20]

Table 6.5 Responsibilities between husband and wife (as presented in Jakim PowerPoint)

Husband	*Wife*	*Jointly*
Fulfil obligations to Allah (pbh)	Fulfil obligations to Allah (pbh)	Love and care
Provide *nafkah*	Obey husband in matters that are not against Islam	Cooperation
Guide wife to do good (*makruf*) and avoid evil (*mungkar*)	Care for husband with goodness	Enjoyment (*istimta'*) of sexual relations
To be fair in polygamous marriage	Adorn oneself for husband	Respect for kin
Care for wife with goodness	Safeguard self-dignity	Joint planning for family well-being
Provide shelter and security	Protect husband's property	Mutual discussions Education of children Household management Protection of reputation

Presented in one of the courses observed in 2016

Marriage Education: Survey Results

Between 2016 and 2017, research was conducted on marriage courses in Johor, Kelantan, Kedah, Penang, Terengganu, Kelantan and Sarawak. This study assessed the effectiveness of marriage education programmes run by Jakim, together with religious departments of the different *negeri* and their collaborative private sector partners. A random survey of 101 course participants was also conducted, together with 26 face-to-face interviews with facilitators and administrators of the courses. The average age of the survey participants was 25 years old, while the average monthly income among those employed was RM1870. Forty-two per cent of them were men, 58 per cent women. The majority (75 per cent) of those surveyed had lower tertiary level qualifications or below (diploma level, secondary and primary schooling).

The curriculum and contents delivered in these courses reveal that they are primarily a conduit for the fashioning of Muslim sexuality, marriage and parenting as a modern but religion-centric way of life. The reframing and reinforcement of gender relations as not equal are touted as based on religious principles, and that the solution to a defective marriage should largely be achieved through the heightening of religiosity—*akidah* (faith/creed), *ibadah* (worship), *akhlak*—rather than through policy change or other means of social intervention. The process of identity refashioning is treated as embodying specific cognitive components that can be learnt towards the making of a new Islamic *habitus*.

Realistically, it is not feasible to undo marriage and divorce trends by merely making it compulsory for those intending to marry to attend a two-day programme of lectures given by a motley set of instructors based on a standardised curriculum provided by a central bureaucracy. Nevertheless, participants of the marriage course in the six *negeri* surveyed thought that it was not a wasted exercise, even if the actual outcomes were uncertain.

The results revealed that an overwhelming majority of those surveyed (83 per cent) felt that the courses were highly useful; none said that they were irrelevant (Table 6.6). However, there was no follow-up or tracer studies done by the course providers to relate what had been learnt in the courses with what was later practised in marriage. The facilitators and course managers also emphasised that the value of these courses was in "the knowledge" gained, and at least one said that it had been beneficial for "those who came to get knowledge, [and] that this was effective, but to reduce the rate of divorce, no, that cannot be achieved by the course attendance".[21]

When asked to choose one factor that could contribute to a successful marriage, both the male and female participants (77 and 80 per cent, respectively) overwhelmingly selected "strong religion as guide", whereas the care and well-being of children was the least popular (5 per cent) (Table 6.7).

In terms of what they thought would potentially lead to the breakdown of marriage (Table 6.8), the majority of respondents (63.3 per cent) selected "domestic violence". The least preferred response to this question

Table 6.6 Assessment of courses attended

Gender	*Very useful and relevant for couples getting married*	*Useful but not necessary to make it compulsory*	*Not useful as I already have enough knowledge on the topics taught*	*Not useful at all*	*Others*	*Total*
Male	31 (74%)	4			1	42
Female	52 (88%)	2	2			59
Total	83 (82%)	6	2		1	101

Table 6.7 Reasons for a good marriage, by gender

Gender	*No of respondents*	*Strong religion as guide*	*Equal division of labour between husband and wife*	*Open and constant communication between husband and wife*	*Good financial management*	*Good housekeeping management*	*Caring and good upbringing of children*	*Sharing of household tasks*
Male	42	32 (76.9%)	6 (14.2%)	20 (47.6%)	18 (42.9%)	24 (57.1%)	3 (7.14%)	19 (45.2%)
Female	59	47 (80.0%)	9 (15.3%)	27 (45.8%)	23 (40.0%)	32 (54.2%)	2 (3.4%)	37 (62.7%)
Total	101	79 (78.2%)	15 (14.6%)	47 (46.5%)	41 (40.6%)	56 (55.4%)	5 (5.0%)	56 (55.4%)

Table 6.8 Reasons for marriage breakdown by gender

Gender	*No of respondents*	*Incompatibility and lack of communication*	*Sexual problems*	*Financial problems*	*Domestic violence*	*Extra marital affairs*	*Disobedient wife*	*Over-domineering husband*	*Interference from in-laws*	*Total (%)*
Male	42 (42%)	22 (52%)	10 (23.8%)	18 (42.8%)	26 (62.0%)	10 (23.8%)	9 (21.4%)	6 (14.3%)	11 (26.2%)	112 (100)
Female	59 (58%)	23 (39.0%)	8 (13.5%)	31 (53.0%)	38 (64.4%)	13 (22.0%)	11 (18.6%)	5 (8.5%)	21 (35.6%)	150 (100)
Total	101	45 (44.5%)	18 (17.8%)	49 (48.5%)	64 (63.3%)	23 (22.7%)	20 (19.8%)	11 (10.9)	32 (31.7%)	363 (100)

was "over-domineering husband", with only 10.9 per cent of respondents selecting this.

About 3 per cent of the respondents were divorced and another 2 per cent were widowed (Table 6.9). Interestingly, all identified "domestic violence" as one of the most important reasons for marital breakdown.

Addressing rising divorce rates and family conflicts needs more than just the learning or unlearning of marriage as there are a whole host of other factors that could be considered as pathways for intervention. For example, rising divorces could also correlate with easy divorce as provided by current Islamic family law. Unequal entitlements between men and women may contribute to disjuncture in marital relations when gender role expectations do not match lived realities where women are also income earners and household providers. Arguably, as seen in the foregoing account, the function of marriage courses has not merely been to solve problems but also to build a captive community that is a repository of the Islamic way of life as defined by the Divine Bureaucracy.

Perfecting Family Through Displacement of the Muslim-non-Muslim

The bureaucratisation of perfecting family ultimately involves displacing or unmaking the 'imperfect' family. In Malaysia, entrenching Islam's dominance within the state supersedes the state's interests in family welfare. In cases where family disputes involve Muslim and non-Muslim parties, state policies on what can be termed the Muslim-non-Muslim family have been inconsistent in prioritising family well-being and productivity. Attaching 'Muslim' and 'non-Muslim' into a word, Muslim-non-Muslim is intended to interrogate a homogenous identity. The Muslim-non-Muslim as applied to Malaysian cases of Muslim and non-Muslim family ties and conflict is an imposed marker that could be used to connote either impurity or uniqueness of family formation. As Miriam Cooke had done in coining the neologism Muslimwoman as noun and adjective, the ascription of any label "reduces all diversity to a single image" (Cooke 2007, 140). The "single image" of a sense of threat and disruption is one which evokes the reaction from the Divine Bureaucracy as discussed below.

It is when upholding the status of Islam as a national obligation, that parents, spouses and children of Muslim-non-Muslim family units are torn apart for the larger 'good' of 'performing' Islam's supremacy. Essentially,

Table 6.9 Reasons for marriage breakdown by marital status

Marital status	*Number of respondents*	*Incompatibility and lack of communication*	*Sexual problems*	*Financial problems*	*Domestic violence*	*Extra marital affairs*	*Disobedient wife*	*Over-domineering husband*	*Interference from in-laws*
Single	81 (80%)	37 (45.7%)	15	39 (48.1%)	51 (62.9%)	21	16	9	23 (28.3%)
Married	14 (13.8%)	7 (50%)	1	7 (50%)	8 (57%)	1	2	1	8 (57%)
Divorced	3 (2.9%)	1	1	2	3 (100%)				
Widowed	2 (1.9%)		1		2 (100%)		1		1
Others	1 (<1%)			1		1	1	1	
Total	101 (100%)	45	18	49	64	23	20	11	32

this is meant to bind the imagined solidarity of the Islamic majority. Performativity as a concept is understood as acts of reiteration, repetition and reification of norms or narratives, which construct the materiality and concreteness of identity, be it of gender (Butler 1988) or the nation-state (Feldman 2005). Sometimes too, their immutability is given a juridical or legal quality. In the examples discussed below, Muslim-non-Muslim families are divided, repetitively and reiteratively, by the reification or sealing of Islam's authority in the national body politic. The phenomenon illustrates the judicialisation of 'displacement', which acts to undo and replace Muslim-non-Muslim families that are deemed imperfect and inappropriate.

The Judicialisation of Displacement

From the 2000s, there were a spate of high-profile cases involving largely male non-Muslim spouses, Hindu men in particular, who converted to Islam in the midst of undergoing divorce. Litigated at Malaysia's highest courts, these include *Subashini a/p Rajasingam v Saravanan a/l Thangathoray, 2008*; *Shamala a/p Sathiyaselan v Jeyaganesh a/l C Mogarajah, 2010*; *Indira Gandhi v Pathmanathan a/l Krishnan, 2014* and *Pathmanathan a/l Krishnan (also known as Muhammad Riduan bin Abdullah) v Indira Gandhi a/p Mutho, 2016*. Their national prominence arose from unravelling some of the complications of having a dual and competing parallel legal system. In all, the children ended as collateral damage because none of the judges were willing to override their sphere of jurisdiction and rule in their favour.[22] As with Muslim conversion, civil court judges have become increasingly unwilling to intervene in family cases that involve at least one Muslim party.

In the above cases, husbands who converted to Islam proceeded to also convert their underage children without the knowledge and consent of their non-Muslim wives. The advantage of becoming Muslim in such instances is the opportunity to use *syariah* provisions to win battles connected to the divorce, foremost of which would be matters involving the custody of children. Under Malaysian *syariah* law, full custody of underage children is given to the father, while only the right to *hadhanah* (childcare) goes to the mother for children below a certain age. There is also no provision for Muslim men to pay any maintenance to their divorced wives. Importantly, once one party comes under *syariah* jurisdiction, the other non-Muslim party has no recourse to any application or orders of the Muslim court. These cases were politically charged because they touched on many issues beyond inter-religious relations, raising imponderables about the dualistic nature of the legal system. Are Muslims and non-Muslims accorded equal rights within the law? Which court is supreme, civil or *syariah*? Can a non-Muslim mother be subjected to *syariah* rulings involving care and custody of her own children who have been 'converted' into Islam without her knowledge by their father? To date, none of these issues have seen any resolution whether in the court system, by the state or civil society.

A heart-rending illustration of the seemingly fused interests of the state and the Islamic bureaucracy is seen in the story of Raimah and Marimuthu. The couple was married for 21 years before the authorities 'caught up' with what they deemed to be an illegal union, as Raimah was still registered as Muslim on her identity card whereas her husband was not. Their marriage was also not legally registered,[23] although the couple already had seven children. In April 2007, seven officers from Jais visited their home and told Marimuthu that his wife of over two decades was born a Muslim—and therefore according to Malaysian law, was still a Muslim—and as such, she and her children aged between 4 and 12 had to be detained and placed in a rehabilitation centre for violating *syariah* law.

The only recourse at the time was for Marimuthu to apply for a habeas corpus to get his wife and family released from forced confinement under Jais, the Selangor religious department. When Raimah appeared at the High Court, husband and wife drew up an agreement based on the religious authority's insistence that as a Muslim, she could not be lawfully married to Marimuthu. To save the family, Raimah surrendered custody of her children to Marimuthu, and was prohibited from living together with them. Under duress, she 'accepted' relinquishing her rights over her children and reportedly "was seen weeping as she confirmed her decision" (The Star Online 2007a). This was a case of "a family ripped apart because of disputes over religion", and some Muslims, distraught by the episode, called it "a disservice to Islam that we merely stand by and watch the agony of families torn apart" (The Star Online 2007b).

This case was a precedent in Malaysian legal history. Never before had the Islamic authorities agreed that the custody of the children would be handed from a Muslim mother to a non-Muslim father. There was not much logic nor justice in this issue, except that the Islamic religious department would not countenance an application for conversion out of Islam for Raimah. The need to ring-fence was too strong and overpowered the best interests of the family. The case was also significant because the non-Muslim father's custodial rights over the couple's children were upheld over that of his wife, the Muslim mother, suggesting that masculine protectionism prevailed. As a senior and well-known local politician succinctly opined, that a family of 7 children and 21 years of marriage, "should be broken up by religious factors" seems to run against family unity and love being "the paramount concern of all religions".[24]

The idea of performativity needs to be reiterated here, as in almost all of the high-profile cases involving Muslim-non-Muslim disputes, the state and the Divine Bureaucracy as its representative take the stance of 'delivering' Islam by continually reiterating, reinforcing and representing itself as the promoter and protector of the faith.

Another example of forced displacement is the case of *Indira Gandhi v Pathmanathan a/l Krishnan, 2014*. In 2009, Pathmanathan converted to Islam and sent official documents to his wife Indira, denoting without her prior knowledge, the conversion of their three children to Islam. At both the High Court and the Court of Appeal, Indira failed to get the conversion of her children renounced. She was also denied access to them throughout the trials. Eventually, the Federal Court ruled the unilateral conversion of Indira's children null and void. The highest court ruled that both Indira and her ex-husband Pathmanathan were bound by the Guardianship of Infants Act 1961, which stipulates that the consent of both parents is required before any formal conversion to Islam can made upon their children.

After converting to Islam, Pathmanathan had approached the *syariah* court to obtain a divorce from Indira and gain custody of their children. The court ruled in his favour in 2009. The following year, the High Court declared that Indira had rightful custody of the children (Malaysiakini 2019). Pathmanathan responded by seizing the youngest child, and converting her to Islam without Indira's knowledge. Her daughter's whereabouts have remained unknown despite a court order for him to produce her. The Inspector General of Police himself appealed for the court to set aside the order compelling him to rescue the child and arrest the errant husband on grounds that "he was caught between two equally valid orders issued by the Syariah High Court and civil High Court" (Malaysiakini 2014). While the court judgements were favourable to Indira, the bureaucracy, especially the police and *negeri* Islamic bureaucracy, appeared to conspire against her and side with her Muslim husband, to the point of 'closing a blind eye' to the plight of the missing child.

> Reading comments on social media, you will discover that while most non-Malays view this kidnapping as a transgression against a mother, there are many Muslims who have no sympathy for Indira. They believe that her young daughter was saved from an idol-worshipping culture and from her race, which they define in the most racist of stereotypes (Thayaparan 2019).

What transpired above was the Divine Bureaucracy displacing the inappropriate and imperfect Muslim-non-Muslim family in its scheme of perfecting the Islamic family. Today, on the payroll of the *negeri* and federal Islamic bureaucracies are 'moral vigilantes' with the resources and legal authority to carry out the job of tracking down families who have strayed from the norms of the official Islam. The Divine Bureaucracy sees its employees as mundanely executing their duties, disciplining and exerting social control in accordance with the written laws, rules and all manner of Standard Operating Procedures, laid down as their job specifications.

In 2018, the Federal Court ruled that the unilateral conversion of a child by one parent is illegal (Hafiz 2018). Soon after this judgement, the discourse of 'Islam first, family second' was reemphasised. Persatuan Ulama Malaysia (PUM, Ulama Association of Malaysia) warned that it did not trust Indira to raise her child as a Muslim, even if the child was to be returned to her (Malaysiakini 2018a). Another Islamic group claimed that the court's interpretation of 'parent' was going against Islam as the right to determine a child's religion is solely the right of the father (Malaysiakini 2018b). Over a year after the judgement, the government remains unable to trace the whereabouts of Indira's disappeared child (Malaysiakini 2018c). Among non-Muslims and other dissenting Muslims, this only reinforced their view that Islam as represented by those in authority is bereft of a compassionate side in the well-being of family (Wong 2016; Mohd Siddiq 2016; Thayaparan 2018). These contestations have led to the undoing of the family. To undo the 'Other' Muslim-non-Muslim family is also to 'make' the Islamic family. The process of manufacturing this 'ideal' family is not without social and cultural costs, but for the state, under the sway of the Divine Bureaucracy, it may well be worth it. For as long as state legitimacy is hinged upon the performativity of reiteration, reification and repetition of norms over Islamic family-making and the constitutional supremacy of Islam, as facilitated by the Divine Bureaucracy, this project will persist.

Conclusion

The Divine Bureaucracy has an important role to play in fashioning the performatively 'perfect' Islamic family. The various examples raised in this chapter—of court litigation and social contestation around the family, and of organised programmes around marital conduct—demonstrate the Divine Bureaucracy's influence over family-making, fashioned around guidelines, prescriptions, proscriptions and symbols of an apparently faultless Islamic religious system. While perfecting the family is usually associated with its social construction, this chapter has demonstrated that it can also be achieved through structural disruptions.

The Islamic family-making project reinforces the adage of masculine protectionism, rather than the prioritisation of family units that aspire to be socially whole and economically productive. The model family being advanced through a narrative and ideology of masculine protectionism can be seen as leading to a complete way of life, and of security, caring and spiritual fulfilment. While this maxim is not always successful in keeping the family intact, it is vital in upholding the conception of Islam as being benevolently protective, yet supreme in a competitively multireligious, multiracial and identity-diverse society.

Within the secular-developmental tradition of nation-making, two imperatives are particularly emphasised as the modern state's mission over the family—moral and social responsibility over its welfare, and managing familial units as sites for social and human capital investment (Quah 2009, 174). Different premises have underscored the quest for the perfection of the Islamic family in this chapter's discussions. These encompass at least three main priorities. The first was in the successive reformulation of *syariah* family laws and regulatory rules to embody a new Malay-Muslim masculinity and femininity and, in so doing, disrupt old forms of bilaterality in Malay family formation. The second was to enable Muslim couples to go through an organised and mandatory religiously focused marriage education programme as entry level tutelage in the making of an exemplary and, supposedly, more authentic, Islamic marriage. Most importantly, the differentiation of male-female conduct in marriage was conveyed as a teachable skill. A third priority was to address what was perceived to be the aberration of emergent Muslim-non-Muslim family units. Displacement was achieved through the use of legal means, the supremacy of Islam as a constitutional entitlement was emphasised, and Islamic masculine protectionism was defended as an inviolable right—all these within the functional duties of the Divine Bureaucracy.

Notes

1. Drawing from Cooke (2007), the intentional combination of 'Muslim' and 'non-Muslim' into a neologism Muslim-non-Muslim is meant to interrogate the imposition of singular and homogenous identities. Combining the two categories here constitutes them as whole families or social circles. A discussion of this as applied to families is discussed in the later section of this chapter.
2. Quranic reference to the name of the chapter and the verse number. There are variations of usage, between *Surah* and *Surat*. *Surat* to denote chapters in the Quran is used in the *Encyclopaedia of the Qur'an* (McAuliffe 2001).
3. The verse from *Surah al-Ra'd:* 38 as presented in Holland (2012, 5). Such verses are extolled by Imam Al-Ghazali, in his philosophical treatise *Adab Al-Nikah: The proper conduct of marriage*, as God's favourable command to marry. Imam Al-Ghazali was a twelfth-century philosopher-saint and one of the most revered in the Sunni tradition. The *Adab Al-Nikah* is widely used as the foundational reference on Islamic marriage. See translations of this by Holland (2012) and Farah (2012), by Malaysian publishers.
4. Translation from: *Inilah Kitab Yang bernama Idhah Al-Bab Li Murid Al-Nikah Bi Al-Sawab: Pada Menyatakan Bagi Yang Berakal Yang Berkehendak Berkahwin Dengan Sebenarnya*. This is one translation of a transliterated version from the Jawi script by Ust. Noriane Abu, published in Selangor in 2013 by the Al-Hidayah House of Publishers.
5. See the Jakim website section 'Bahagian Keluarga, Sosial dan Komuniti', n.d., http://www.islam.gov.my/bahagian-keluarga-sosial-komuniti/1275-profil, accessed 11 April 2019.
6. See again, http://www.islam.gov.my/bahagian-keluarga-sosial-komuniti/1273-visi-misi-objektif-fungsi-dan-piagam-pelanggan, accessed 5 March 2019.
7. This entity is also discussed in Chap. 3.
8. See a Jakim-produced pamphlet explaining the functions of the BSK titled 'Bahagian Sokongan Keluarga: BSK' (n.d.).
9. By Islamic statutes legislated in the country, all divorced Muslim women are entitled to one or all of these forms of payments: (1) *iddah* (temporary) maintenance before formalisation of divorce; (2) arrears on unpaid *nafkah* (material entitlements during duration of marriage); (3) *mutaah* (post-divorce gift) and (4) child maintenance.

10. See website, "Sistem Pengurusan Perkahwinan Islam Malaysia", http://www.sppim.gov.my/sppim/home, accessed 4 March 2019.
11. The judge dropped the charge of unauthorised collection of money for religious purposes on grounds of insufficient evidence (Visvanathan 1995).
12. "Statistik bilangan peserta kursus pra-perkahwinan modul bersepadu kursus pra-perkahwinan Islam (MBKI) di Wilayah Persekutuan", http://www.data.gov.my/data/ms_MY/dataset/statistik-bilangan-peserta-kursus-pra-perkahwinan-mbkpi-di-wilayah-persekutuan, accessed 10 March 2019.
13. "Kursus Pra Perkahwinan dan Kekeluargaan Islam Anjuran Pejabat Agama Islam Daerah Hulu Langat", http://www.kursuskahwinpaid.com/, accessed 20 February 2019.
14. See website of Astana Mukmin, https://kursuskahwin.org/, accessed 20 February 2019.
15. Syarikat Pengendali Kursus Perkahwinan, http://www.jaik.gov.my/?page_id=2413, accessed 20 February 2019.
16. See http://cintasakinahjaipk.perak.my/, accessed 20 February 2019.
17. Carta Alir Cinta Sakinah JAIPk, http://cintasakinahjaipk.perak.my/img/bg-img/carta_alir.jpg, accessed 20 February 2019.
18. In Malay: *Sesungguhnya lelaki mukmin yang sempurna imannya ialah mereka yang baik tingkah lakunya dan lemah lembut terhadap isteri dan anak-anaknya.*
19. In Malay: *Sebaik-baik perempuan (isteri) ialah apabila engkau melihatnya akan menggembirakan hati engkau dan apabila engkau menyuruhnya, dia mengikut perintah engkau, apabila engkau bersumpah atasnya, dia berbuat baik terhadap engkau.*
20. This survey is part of a study titled, "Protecting and Perfecting the Muslim Family: Marriage and parenthood education programmes in Malaysia and Singapore" which the author co-researched with Suriani Suratman from 2016 to 2017. The grant was awarded by the Centre for Family and Population Research (CFPR), National University of Singapore.
21. Interview with course facilitator, Roziah (not her real name) in Kelantan, 19 December 2016.
22. Article 121(1)(A) of the Federal Constitution is interpreted as not allowing the civil court to make decisions that could be construed as the jurisdiction of the *syariah* court. This was effected after a constitutional amendment in 1988 to create a parallel civil and *syariah* legal system.
23. The circumstances of their marriage were not included in the court records sighted. They were likely to be married under customary or religious rites at a Hindu temple without official registration papers.
24. Blog of Lim Kit Siang, "Six children being returned to Marimuthu to be brought up as Hindus – habeas corpus application for Suresh/Revathi case",

posted on 3 May 2007, https://blog.limkitsiang.com/2007/05/03/six-children-being-returned-to-marimuthu-to-be-brought-up-as-hindus---habeas-corpus-application-for-sureshrevathi-case/, accessed 7 May 2019.

References

Abdul Monir, Yaacob (2016) *Perkembangan Pentadbiran Undang-Undang Islam di Malaysia*, Cyberjaya: Universiti Islam Malaysia.

Ahilemah, Jonet (1981) "Aspek Perkahwinan dan Perceraian: Harta, nafkah dan warisan – undang-undang Islam", paper presented at the Seminar Wanita dan Undang-Undang, organised by University Women's Association, University of Malaya, Kuala Lumpur, 24–26 August.

Ahmad, Ibrahim (1986) "Undang-Undang Kekeluargaan Islam Yang Baru", paper presented at Seminar Perundangan Islam, organised by Abim, Muslim Youth Movement of Malaysia, 24 August.

Ahmad Ibrahim (1965) *Islamic Law in Malaya*, Singapore: Malaysian Sociological Research Institute Ltd.

Asmah, Haji Omar (1978) "Poligami", paper presented at *Seminar Pentadbiran Undang-Undang Syariah Jenayah dan Keluarga* in Kedah, 28–30 April.

Berita Harian (2014) "Jaij tidak cadang tambah tempoh kursus praperkahwinan", 16 November.

——— (2018) "Modul baharu kursus perkahwinan akan diperkenal", 3 August.

Butler, Judith (1988) "Performative Acts and Gender Constitution: An essay in phenomenology and feminist theory", *Theatre Journal*, Vol. 40, No. 2, 519–531.

Connell, RW (2008) "Gender as a Social Practice", in Steven Seidman and Jeffrey C Alexander (eds) *The New Social Theory Reader* (Second Edition), London and New York: Routledge, 369–375.

Cooke, Miriam (2007) "The Muslimwoman", *Contemporary Islam*, Vol. 1, 139–154.

Djamour, Judith (1959) *Malay Kinship and Marriage in Singapore*, London School of Economics Monographs on Social Anthropology, No. 21, London: University of London, The Athlone Press.

Dunn, Shannon and Rosemary B Kellison (2010) "At the Intersection of Scripture and Law: Qur'an 4:34 and violence against women", *Journal of Feminist Studies in Religion*, Vol. 26, No. 2, 11–36.

Farah, Madelain (trans.) (2012) *Al-Ghazali: Marriage and Sexuality in Islam*, Petaling Jaya: Islamic Book Trust.

Feldman, G (2005) Development in Theory: Essential crises; a performative approach to migrants, minorities, and the European nation-state. *Anthropological Quarterly*, Vol. 78, No. 1, 213–246.

Friedland, Roger (2009) "The Endless Fields of Pierre Bourdieu", *Organization*, Vol. 16, No. 6, 887–917.
Geissinger, Aisha (2015) *Gender and Muslim Constructions of Exegetical Authority: A rereading of the classical genre of Qur'an commentary*, Leiden: Brill.
Hafiz, Yatim (2018) "Apex court rules in favour of Indira Gandhi in unilateral conversion case", *Malaysiakini*, 29 January.
Hijjas, Mulaika (2013) "Guides for Mrs Nawawi", *Indonesia and the Malay World*, Vol. 41, No. 120, 215–236.
Holland, Muhtar (trans.) (2012) *Adab Al-Nikah: The proper conduct of marriage in Islam*, Kuala Lumpur: Dar Al Wahi Publication.
Horowitz, DL (1994) "The Qur'an and the Common Law: Islamic law reform and the theory of legal change", *The American Journal of Comparative Law*, Vol. 42, No. 3, 543–580.
Jakim (2008) *Memasuki Gerbang Perkahwinan* (Edisi Kedua), Putrajaya: Jabatan Kemajuan Islam.
——— (2012) *Keputusan Muzakarah Jawatankuas Fatwa Majlis Kebangsaan Bagi Hal Ehwal Ugama Islam Malaysia*, Putrajaya: Jabatan Kemajuan Islam Malaysia.
Karim, Wazir-Jahan (1987) "The Status of Malay Women in Malaysia: From culture to Islam and industrialization", *International Journal of Sociology of the Family*, Vol. 17, No. 1, 41–55.
——— (1992) *Women and Culture: Between adat and Islam*, Boulder, Co: Westview Press.
Kuppusamy, Baradan (2004) "Call grow to declare marital rape a crime", *South China Morning Post*, 24 August.
Lamrabert, Asma (2018) *Women and Men in the Quran*, Palgrave Macmillan.
Malaysiakini (2014) "Indira fails to get IGP to execute court order", 17 December.
——— (2018a) "What guarantee Prasana will be a practising Muslim under Indira?", 1 February.
——— (2018b) "Perkasa: Ruling on child conversion not based on Islamic interpretation", 30 January.
——— (2018c) "Indira Gandhi: Dear Harapan gov't, IGP, is my daughter alive?", 17 November.
——— (2019) "No new leads on Indira's child, ex-husband, says Fuzi", 26 February.
Maznah, Mohamad (2011) "The Islamic Divorce Contract and a Flawed Axiom of Masculine Protectionism", *Asian Journal of Social Science*, Vol. 39, 821–844.
——— (2012) "Gender Battles and the Syariah: Translating Islamic marital law into everyday practice In Malaysia", in Gavin Jones, Terrence Hull and Maznah Mohamad (eds), *Changing Marriage Patterns in Southeast Asia: Economic and socio-cultural dimensions*, London: Routledge, 171–184.
McAuliffe, Jane Dammen (2001) (ed) *Encyclopaedia of the Qur'ān*, Brill Reference Online, Leiden: Brill.

Mir-Hosseini, Ziba (1993) *Marriage on Trial: A study of Islamic family law, Iran and Morocco compared*, London: IB Tauris and Co Ltd.

Mohd Siddiq, Azani (2016) "Let Indira hug all her children again", *Malaysiakini* 30 April.

Muslihah Hasbullah @ Abdullah, Najibah Mohd Zin' and Saodah Wok (2009) "Relationships between Satisfaction of Muslim Women on Financial Supports After Divorce and Ex-Husbands' Compliance to the Supports with Post-Divorce Welfare", *Pertanika Journal of Social Sciences & Humanities*, Vol. 17, No. 2, 153–166.

Nafisah, M (2005) "Mystified over law's aim", *New Straits Times Online*, http://www.nst.com.my/Current_News/nst/Friday/Letters/200512300, accessed 30 May 2009.

New Straits Times (1995a) "The main causes of marital break-ups", 16 February.

——— (1995b) "When divorce is inevitable", 16 February.

——— (1995c) "Enforcement chief swore to destroy Talib, says wife", 12 April.

——— (1995d) "Local Syariah court has no right, says accused", 17 May.

——— (1995e) "Be wary of Syiah teachings, says FT delegate", 27 November.

——— (1995f) "Islamic course on family harmony", 8 May.

——— (1995g) "Longer marriage courses to create better Islamic families", 15 May.

——— (1996a) "Dr Siti Hasmah saddened by polygamy ruling", 28 October.

——— (1996b) "For women, a step backwards", 21 October.

——— (1997) "programmes against moral decay to be streamlined", 25 February.

——— (2002) "Don't blame pre-marital courses for rise in incest", 24 April.

——— (2003a) "Campaign provokes objection from religious leaders", 20 March.

——— (2003b) "Campaign not intended to question Syariah", 19 March.

——— (2004a) "Amend code to include marital rape", 22 August.

——— (2004b) "Suhakam under fire over marital rape proposal", 23 August.

Ng, Cecilia (1999) "Gender and the Changing Division of Labour in a Rural Community", in Cecilia Ng (ed) *Positioning Women in Malaysia: Class and gender in an industrializing State*, London: Macmillan Press, 34–60.

Ng, Cecilia, Maznah Mohamad and tan beng hui (2006) *Feminism and the Women's Movement in Malaysia: An unsung (r)evolution*, London: Routledge.

Nik Noriani, Nik Badli Shah (ed) (2003) *Islamic Family Law and Justice for Muslim Women*. Kuala Lumpur: Sisters in Islam.

Nock, Steven L (2005) "Marriage as a Public Issue", *The Future of Children*, Vol. 15, No. 2, Autumn, 13–32.

O'Neill, John (1986) "The Disciplinary Society: From Weber to Foucault", *The British Journal of Sociology*, Vol. 37, No. 1, 42–60.

Peletz, Michael (1988) *A Share of the Harvest: Kinship, property, and social history among the Malays of Rembau*, Berkeley: University of California Press.

——— (2002) *Islamic Modern: Religious courts and cultural politics in Malaysia*, Princeton and Oxford: Princeton University Press.

Quah, SR (2009) *Families in Asia: Home and kin,* London and New York: Routledge (Second Edition).
Roded, Ruth (2001) "Women and the Qur'ān", *Encyclopaedia of the Qur'ān*, Jane Dammen McAuliffe (ed), Georgetown University, Washington DC et al., Brill Reference Online,
Ruhil Hayati, binti M Busra (2011) "Modul Kursus Praperkahwinan Islam: Kajian terhadap keberkesanannya di Jabatan Agama Islam Negeri Perak Darul Ridzuan", MA thesis, University of Malaya.
Sharifah Zaleha, Syed Hassan and Cederroth, Sven (1997) *Managing Marital Disputes in Malaysia: Islamic mediators and conflict resolution in the syariah courts,* Richmond, Surrey: Curzon Press Ltd.
Siti Nurbaiyah, Nadzmi and Adie Suri Zulkefli (2011), "'Catching' men who weasel out", *New Straits Times* (Malaysia), 20 June.
Siti Zubaidah, Ismail, Ilhaamie Abdul Ghani Azmi and Zulfikri Yasoa (2011) "Justice delayed is justice denied?: Divorce case management in Malaysian Shariah court", Proceedings International Conference on Management (ICM), 977–987.
Stivens, Maila (1996) *Matriliny and Modernity: Sexual politics and social change in rural Malaysia*, St Leonards, Australia: Allen and Unwin.
Stowasser, Barbara Freyer (1997) *Women in the Qur'an, Traditions and Interpretation*, Oxford: Oxford University Press.
Taylor, EN (1937), "Malay Family Law", *Journal Malayan Branch of the Royal Asiatic Society*, Vol. XV, Part 1, 1–78.
The Star Online (2007a) "Rubber tapper wins custody", 4 May.
——— (2007b) "Be guided by compassion and wisdom", 10 May.
The Straits Times (1994) "S'porean with 10 wives charged in Johor", April 21.
——— "Cautioned statement allowed as evidence", 25 November.
——— (1995a) "Course on marriage may be resumed in schools", 22 February.
——— (1995b) "Accused says man's 10 wives committed no sin", 14 February.
——— (1995c) "Get to the point, judge tells accused", 24 March.
——— (1995d) "KL may make marriage course mandatory for Muslims", 17 February.
——— (1996) "Sunni-Shi'ite schism in Malaysia: Why?", 12 May.
——— (2003) "Muftis hit out at 'one husband, one wife' initiative", 19 March.
Thayaparan, S (2018) "Indira Gandhi case – how reality conflicts with claims of moderation", *Malaysiakini*, 31 January.
——— (2019) "Those who believe they are saving Indira Gandhi's daughter", *Malaysiakini,* 25 February.
Utusan Online (2015) "Modul kursus kahwin disemak setiap 5 tahun – Jakim", 22 September.
Wadud, Amina (1999) *Qur'an and Woman: Rereading the sacred text from a woman's perspective*, Oxford: Oxford University Press.

White, Sally (2006) "Gender and the Family", in Greg Fealy and Virginia Matheson (eds) *Voices of Islam in Southeast Asia: A contemporary sourcebook,* Singapore: ISEAS, 273–352.

Winstedt, RO (1945) "Old Malay Digests and Malay Customary Law", *The Journal of the Royal Asiatic Society of Great Britain and Ireland*, No. 1, April, 17–29.

Wong, Chee Tuck (2016) "What Indira thinks today, Malaysia shall think tomorrow", *Malaysiakini*, 18 January.

Visvanathan, Thanam (1995) "Jail, fine for man and his 10 wives", *New Straits Times*, 13 July.

Yegar, Moshe (1979) *Islam and Islamic Institutions in British Malaya: Policies and implementation*, Jerusalem: The Magnes Press, The Hebrew University, Jerusalem.

Young, Iris Marion (2003) "The logic of masculinist protection: Reflections on the current security state". *Signs: Journal of women in culture and society*, Vol. 29, No. 1, 1–25.

Zainah, Anwar (2001) "What Islam, whose Islam? Sisters in Islam and the struggle for women's rights", in RW Heffner (ed), *The Politics of Multiculturalism: Pluralism and citizenship in Malaysia, Singapore and Indonesia*, Honolulu: University of Hawai'i Press, 227–252.

——— (2006) "Stemming the 'I divorce you' trend", *New Straits Times*, 6 October.

——— (2008) "Advocacy for Reform in Islamic Family Law: The experience of Sisters in Islam" in Asifa Quraishi and Frank E Vogel (eds), *The Islamic Marriage Contract: Case studies in Islamic family law*, Cambridge, Massachusetts: Islamic Legal Studies Program, Harvard Law School, 275–284.

Zamri, bin Ghazali (2011) "Konsep Perkahwinan Mengikut Syeikh Daud bin Abdullah Al-Fatani Dalam Kitab *Idah Al-Albab*", MA thesis, University of Malaya.

CHAPTER 7

Purifying Money

Introduction

The foregoing account has demonstrated how the tangible corporeal dimensions of identity and family made it possible for *negeri* (State, sub-national unit of governance) and federal Islamic bureaucracies to exercise palpable coercive power over them. The control of money was something quite different, particularly as this was located in a realm dominated by secular agents. In financial matters, *zakat* (religious tithe/tax) collection and *wakaf* (trusts/endowments) and *baitulmal* (Islamic treasury) management were the only areas that traditionally fell within the scope and capacity of *negeri* and federal religious bureaucracies. There came a point, however, when Islam's reach was expanded far beyond these spheres.

The penultimate chapter of this book is organised around three related questions: why, when and how did the sphere of money, finance and ultimately capitalism become enmeshed with Islam in Malaysia? It will show that the empowered postcolonial Divine Bureaucracy was able to capture spheres that were once unreachable by its predecessors. Where *negeri* and federal Islamic bureaucracies reached their limits, state bankers, financial technocrats and managerial industrial capitalists who saw Islam as a resource for advancement joined forces and assumed central roles in the

---

The original version of this chapter was revised. Text has been updated. Correction to this chapter can be found at https://doi.org/10.1007/978-981-15-2093-8_9

M. Mohamad, *The Divine Bureaucracy and Disenchantment of Social Life*, Contestations in Contemporary Southeast Asia,
https://doi.org/10.1007/978-981-15-2093-8_7

corporate Islamic bureaucracy to widen the reach and maximise the yields of Islamic corporatisation. Chapter 3 had earlier shown how this entity fits in as a third arm of the Divine Bureaucracy; here its features and implications will be more comprehensively explored.

Specifically, this chapter focuses on three case studies to explain the emergence and rise of the corporate Islamic bureaucracy. These cover Islamic banking and finance, asset management and *wakaf* development as three areas illustrative of the monetisation of religion. Part one analyses the pivotal and distinctive role of Bank Negara Malaysia (BNM, Central Bank of Malaysia) and its financial technocrats in driving a parallel Islamic economy alongside the larger world of the conventional economy.[1] The BNM with its own *syariah* bureaucracy has not only played a prime national role but has also acted as a leading force in laying down the rules of Islamic finance capitalism on a global scale. The rules of exception it has promoted for Islamic finance, as I argue, contributed to the disenchantment of overall Islamic social life. Part two deals with the confrontation between the traditional Islamic bureaucracy and the country's largest government-owned unit trust corporation (Permodalan Nasional Berhad, PNB), exposing the tensions between spiritual restraint and the path of individual material progress. The chapter closes with a discussion of the multiple and everyday dissensions of those who have yet to benefit from the monetisation of religion. It shows the bewildering character of corporatised trading and exchange that once was only understood as the relationship of transactions between humans (*muamalat*), but has now developed into an inexorable commercialisation of Islamic financial wealth and assets in the name of Islam. For ordinary Muslims, these developments have invariably been disenchanting.

What Constitutes the Corporate Islamic Bureaucracy?

Although there are overlapping and collaborative functions among the three layers of the Divine Bureaucracy, *negeri*, federal and corporate, there are also differences and divergences of purpose. For instance, both *negeri* and federal Islamic bureaucracies have parallel functions, except for their source of funds and use of central power by the latter. Built around administrative templates first established during colonial times, they can be considered the traditional bureaucracy. Importantly, they do not have the monopoly over Islam in the sphere of money. Instead, the Islamisation of banking, finance and business has been pursued by the corporate Islamic bureaucracy whose agenda unleashed new-found monetary value to Islamic institutions, assets and transactions under the cause of 'purifying' money and capital accumulation for Islam's exaltation as a complete societal system. Table 7.1 schematises the corporate Islamic bureaucracy and the Islamisation that has occurred under its authority and regulation.

Table 7.1 Islamic businesses under the authority and regulation of a corporate Islamic bureaucracy

Types of business	Islamic banking, insurance and other financial services	Halal industries	*Zakat* managerial services	*Wakaf* real estate development	Asset management or shares and unit trusts for *bumiputera* advancement
The corporate Islamic bureaucracy (government or government-linked agencies)	Bank Negara Malaysia (BNM) Securities Commission Malaysia (SCM) Lembaga Tabung Haji (LTH, Pilgrims Fund Board)	Halal Industry Development Corporation (HDC) and 14 *halal* parks	Pusat Pungutan Zakat-Majlis Agama Islam Wilayah Persekutuan (PPZ-Maiwp) Lembaga Zakat Selangor (LZ-Selangor)	National Wakaf Corporation Wakaf An-Nur of Johor Corporation (JCorp)	Permodalan Nasional Berhad (PNB)
Notes	BNM and SCM have their respective *Syariah* Advisory Councils; LTH is a corporation under the Prime Minister's Department	The *halal* parks are situated throughout the country as joint ventures between *negeri* government corporations and private companies	*Zakat* collection and distribution; private agencies in partnership with or subsidiary companies under *negeri* or State Islamic Religious Councils (SIRCs)	Development of *wakaf* land banks; government-linked and private companies in partnership with SIRCs	Majority of shareholders are Muslims; shares are expected to be *syariah* compliant

The corporate Islamic bureaucracy's presence and authority can be located in at least five business sectors: Islamic banking, insurance and financial services; the *halal* (permissible) industry; *zakat* managerial services; *wakaf* real estate development; and asset management of unit trusts. The rules on *haram* (prohibited) and *harus* (obligatory though not mandatory)[2] are applied in the finance sector and *halal* industry, while rules based on more elaborate *fiqh* jurisprudence are used in *zakat* and *wakaf* management. Most of the agencies created to regulate and develop Islamic-related businesses are either state-owned or owned by Government-Linked Corporations. A key agent in the monetisation of Islamic assets is the *negeri* or State Islamic Religious Council (SIRC). As *zakat*, *wakaf* and *baitulmal* are under their charge, this entity has been legally empowered to function as a corporation and to own property and conduct businesses. SIRCs have also entered into partnerships with private companies to manage all forms of monetised activities under them. As such, they are an integral part of the corporate Islamic bureaucracy.

'Exceptionalisms' of Islamic Finance Capitalism

Within banking and finance, there are a number of features that set apart Islamisation propelled by the corporate Islamic bureaucracy from that of the religious bureaucracies discussed previously. Chief among these are its global interconnectedness, the employment of Islamic managerial capitalists from outside the sphere of religious theology and its inclusive participation and leadership in terms of gender and ethnicity, besides just religious identity. BNM is the principal institution that governs and regulates the Islamic financial sector in the country, and the growth of this sector has led to a dual financial system—Islamic and conventional—mirroring the Malaysian judicial system with its parallel civil and *syariah* jurisdictions.

Besides the International Financial Services Act 2013, regarded as a paramount legal framework to enhance global 'cross-border transactions' and capital flows (Sim and Roziana 2012), there have been other drivers behind the expansion of Islamic finance in Malaysia. Leading this are two human resource development institutions set up by the BNM. The first is an institution of higher education called the International Centre for Education in Islamic Finance (Inceif), which has been custom-training those expected to work in the field of Islamic banking and finance (or Islamic Financial Institutions, IFI) since 2005 (New Straits Times 2006),[3] and, the second, the International Syariah Research Academy (Isra), which undertakes studies in the area of *syariah* and finance. The Syariah Advisory Council of the Securities Commission of Malaysia (SCM) also embarked on an aggressive programme to train personnel in Islamic finance by initiating the Islamic Capital Market Graduate Training Scheme (Zarinah 2009). These regulatory and educational bodies are governed by a multinational team established in Malaysia whose emphasis is on the globalisation of Islamic finance, its transnational linkages and the role of an international web of *syariah* experts, scholars and practitioners within the field.

A special feature of Islamic finance is that participation is not limited to Muslims, nor is the establishment of IFI confined to Muslim-majority countries. As one study by an international financial advisory and consultancy firm noted, mostly non-Muslims subscribed to Islamic banking in Malaysia (Straits Times 2013). A local Islamic finance house also recorded non-Muslims forming 40 per cent of its depositors and 60 per cent of its borrowers (Arnold 2007). This interest by non-Muslim investors is also seen outside of Malaysia where more than 58 per cent of them surveyed in the United Kingdom regarded Islamic finance as an ethical system (Financial Adviser 2014). At the same time, Islamic banks are being mainstreamed with some indicating their intention to drop the label 'Islam' to expand their customer base. This is premised on a belief that segment of the market which would choose them for their 'Islam' brand has already been optimised. The other growth option for these banks is to move into new markets in Asia, Europe or Africa, in countries with Muslim minorities and where establishing a profitable presence will require attracting large numbers of non-Muslims (Malaysian Insider 2014).

Another inclusive feature of the IFI industry is its 'secularisation', which allows for women to assume key leadership roles within its institutions. One such woman credited for transforming Malaysia into a major international Islamic financial hub is former BNM Governor, Zeti Akhtar Aziz. During her tenure, from 2000 to 2016, she was tenacious in building a tighter governance framework for the IFI sector, not solely because of its 'spiritual' association or its potential to rebrand Islam and dissociate it from terrorism, but also because of its tangible contributions to restructure a better financial system, one that "serves the real economy" (Damodaram 2012). It was through her efforts that BNM established the regulatory and governance structures, and human resource development initiatives mentioned earlier, which helped strengthen the IFI services system.

Besides Zeti, other women head Malaysian IFI or are key players in the industry. They include Rafiza Ghazali, who led Islamic Finance (Asia) at Thomson Reuters in Malaysia; Jamelah Jamaluddin, Managing Director (MD) of RHB Islamic Bank in 2007, and the first woman in the world to head an Islamic bank before being appointed Chief Executive Officer (CEO) and MD of Kuwait Finance House, Malaysia, in 2010 and 2013, respectively; Raja Teh Maimunah Raja Abdul Aziz, former CEO of Hong Leong Islamic Bank and Global Head of Islamic Markets at Bursa Malaysia and Fozia Amanulla, head of Eoncorp Islamic Bank in 2007. In addition, Engku Rabiah Adawiah Engku Ali, the first woman Islamic financial *syariah* adviser registered with SCM, was also the first woman appointed to the apex Syariah Advisory Council (SAC) of BNM (Gooch 2010). In all, there are at least ten such *syariah* financial experts in the country, while the number of women *syariah* scholars has tripled in five years (The Globe and Mail 2010). Women in Islamic finance, in Malaysia particularly, have been featured in studies on gender and political economy, with the nuances of the gendered aspect of their 'empowerment' (Elder 2017).

Extraordinary Exceptionalisms

The growth of IFI can partly be attributed to two salient features of economic neoliberalism: the expansion of foreign trade and the elevation of 'financialisation' (Dumenil and Levy 2011, 36–37). The eagerness to tap into the abundance of Muslim capital occurred from the late 1980s, after the deregulation of banking opened up national markets to international competition and introduced more novel banking products to consumers. With greater yields from investment in mutual funds, the money market, stocks and bonds, investors had more options as they no longer had to depend on interest income from savings. Forced to be more innovative in their product offerings, banks started tailoring these to become *syariah* compliant (Warde 2010, 101–104). After the subprime crisis in the United States in 2008, modern finance was perceived as having been overwhelmed by the detachment of money from its productive value (Mydin Meera 2012, 7–24). In contrast, Islamic finance, grounded in a real and asset-based economy, found much favour among prudent investors, while Islamic banking, rooted in the moral positioning that capital should not be delinked from its productive purposes, also gained popularity.

To be globally competitive, financial institutions require a flexible technology of governance or a "condition of exception", referred to here as 'exceptionalisms' (Ong 2006, 5). A striking exceptionalism regards religion as an ally rather than adversary of capitalism. In this respect, neoliberalism and Islamisation needed to converge and collude to provide the basis for the flourishing of Islamic finance capitalism. This in turn required a new class of financial managers who could mobilise *syariah* and dictate the terms of capital accumulation, in concurrence with the 'purification' of money.

Technocrats from the BNM—the emergent corporate Islamic bureaucracy—were in the best position to play this role though with an important caveat: they would not draw upon the authority of the traditional religious bureaucracy to legitimise their functions. Instead, BNM created its own *syariah* body, the SAC, and put this under the authority of the bank's governing board. It also ensured that since its inception in 1997, the composition of the SAC has never been dominated by *ulama* (Islamic scholars) from the traditional bureaucracy. Instead, it has been mixed and included professionals from various fields and academics trained in the newly emerging disciplines of Islamic commercial law and Islamic finance. The formation, roles and functions of the SAC are legislated by the Central Bank of Malaysia Act 2009, not *syariah* law. This way, BNM has ensured that *syariah* governance over Islamic financial matters remains under its jurisdiction rather than that of any other body. The road to getting the SAC recognised as the sole authority on *syariah* laws relating to Islamic finance, even superseding that of the judiciary, was not straightforward and will be discussed later in this chapter.

Exceptionalisms undergird the authority of the BNM as it conducts its mission of advancing Islamic finance. The first exception involved subordinating the juridical power of the courts to the bank itself, through the SAC. Unlike the traditional bureaucracy that thrives on *syariah* judicialisation, those within the corporate Islamic bureaucracy prefer to be insulated from judicial intervention. The second exception is in the reconciliation of *syariah*'s inflexible precepts with the imperative of flexibility for the expansion of finance capitalism. For the financial bureaucrats, *ijtihad* (rational reasoning) is key. This cannot be too constrained or directed by traditional Islamic schisms over competing *mazhab* (school of thought). While the traditional Divine Bureaucracy cannot have enough of homogenisation and containment, those in the corporate Islamic bureaucracy cannot have enough of *ijtihad*. After all, Islamic finance exists within the free-market sphere of global capitalism, which requires it to be dynamic, innovative, flexible and ahead of the curve to stay competitive. This is another form of

Islamisation, one which is more hinged on the purpose of 'purifying' money for capital accumulation in the present world, rather than for the rewards of the hereafter. This form of Islamisation thrives on the condition of neoliberal exceptionalism.

An early issue plaguing the feasibility of Islamic finance was the question of *riba* (interest) as its avoidance has been the most basic and popularly understood feature of Islamic finance. Yet, there is also confusion over what is really prohibited—is it all forms of interest or only usury or excessive interest? Are Islamic banking and financial matters to be treated as religious matters? Can a *mufti* (jurisconsult) or *ulama* solely be trusted to rule on matters of Islamic finance? These notwithstanding, a widely debated issue has been whether Islamic finance disputes ought to be tried under the *syariah* court given that all matters *syariah* had been the domain of the traditional Divine Bureaucracy (Abdul Hamid 2013; Ahmad Hidayat 2007).

Legally, a number of factors preclude Islamic finance and its related activities from falling under the jurisdiction of *syariah* law and courts. As already noted, *syariah* legislation is passed by *negeri* legislatures, and *syariah* courts can only hear cases within the boundaries of their respective *negeri*. They are thus unable to match the scope of commercial law that governs IFI, which is not only a 'cross-*negeri*' activity but a cross-national enterprise too. More importantly, *syariah* courts can only decide on cases involving parties who are Muslims; Islamic corporate institutions have non-Muslims participating as well. Even though some *syariah* scholars associated with Islamic finance have argued that the term 'Islamic law' can be widely interpreted as to its jurisdiction, the most preferred interpretation is that Islam can only be applied to persons, not inanimate institutions, "Islamic law has no general application to other person or legal persons such as banks and financial institutions, which cannot be construed as professing the religion of Islam" (Hakimah 2010, 4). This interpretation means that laws are only Islamic if they can be imposed on Muslims, and since this is not the case with the mixed client base of Islamic finance and commerce, Islamic laws cannot be used in this sphere. Given such understanding, some disputes with Islamic banks have been denied hearing in *syariah* courts, even if Muslim applicants may have chosen to seek redress here (Hakimah 2010, 5).

Since IFI cases pertaining to commercial law are excluded from being tried in *syariah* courts, and Islamic 'laws' said to govern IFI cannot be legislated as *negeri* statutes, a related conundrum follows—does this mean that disputes of this nature can only be adjudicated within civil courts, and by judges trained in secular not *syariah* law? Such a stream of legal and constitutional issues question if it is at all possible to *syariah*tise finance. If IFI services are to distinguish themselves from similar 'conventional' institutions, should they not be required to be governed by *syariah* principles? According to sceptics and critics of the authenticity of Islamic banking, it is religion or some form of ethics that should distinguish 'Islamic' capitalism from the rest, and clearly, to function outside of the mainstream *syariah* system may not make it morally legitimate (Kuran 2004, 7; Rethel 2011, 75–98). Corporate Islamic bureaucrats, however, would rather have a situation of 'heads I win, tails you lose', where exceptionalisms are used to overcome legal and political roadblocks that lie in the way of advancing Islamic finance capitalism.

As suggested thus far, a key narrative and kernel identity of Islamic finance is *syariah* compliance, which "signifies the essence of maintaining the relationship between the different stakeholders as well as the relationship with God" (Zulkifli 2012, 25). Stated differently, one critical prerequisite for IFI businesses to qualify as 'Islamic' is ensuring that all financial transactions and products are *halal*. The authoritative bodies, which ascertain this compliance, are the *syariah* boards, such as the Syariah Committee, Syariah Advisory Council and Syariah Control Board, formed within finance institutions. It would seem that only these *syariah* boards and the use of classical Arabic terms to label similar products offered by other commercial banks were to be the prime distinguishing marks of an 'Islamic' financial system (Khan 2010, 817–818). Originating in Egypt in 1976, the concept of the *syariah* board is a twentieth-century invention (Kahf 2004). The main *syariah* board in Malaysia is the SAC of the BNM. IFI are also distinguished by a framework of *syariah* governance, defined as "a set of organisational arrangements concerning how the Shari'a board is directed, manages, managed, governed and controlled" (Malkawi 2013, 544). In Malaysia, this has been formalised through the BNM's Shariah Governance Framework document issued in 2011.

The newness of the SAC as the national *syariah* 'overseer' of Islamic finance is evident by how its formation and functions were only legislated and enforced in 2004 after the Central Bank of Malaysia Act 1958 was amended to include a new Section 16(B) regarding its formal establishment (Abdul Hamid and Trakic 2012, 4).[4] Prior to this, the SAC had already been up and running since May 1997 (Abdul Hamad and Trakic 2012, 3). The significance of this entity should be appreciated because it is key to understanding the exceptional conditions propelling the rise of IFI in the country, and why there is also a competitive form of bureaucratic Islam today. The discussion below details the evolutionary role of the SAC.

A Syariah *Sphere Insulated from the Judiciary*

The government first announced that it would establish the SAC of BNM in 1995. At the time, then Deputy Finance Minister, Afifuddin Omar, was reported saying that the body's function was "to issue *fatwa* and oversee the entire operations of banks offering interest-free services" (Azman 1995). When the SAC was eventually established in 1997, its roles were couched in secular and limited terms, and it was given the authority to ascertain "Islamic law for the purposes of Islamic banking business, *takaful* business, Islamic financial business, Islamic development financial business, or any other business which [was] based on Shariah principles and [was] supervised and regulated by Bank Negara Malaysia".[5] The first SAC chairperson was Abdul Halim Ismail, former MD of Bank Islam, Malaysia's pioneer Islamic bank, when it was created in 1983. While the SAC is not a *fatwa*-making body, nor is it entrusted to oversee the operations of Islamic banks, the legitimacy of BNM's vision and mission to develop Islamic finance capitalism solely rests on this body.

The amended Central Bank of Malaysia Act 1958, which legalised the establishment of the SAC in 2004, was repealed and replaced by the Central Bank of Malaysia Act 2009. The new legislation upgraded the status of the SAC and clarified its roles and powers. Its functions were also expanded to include ascertaining Islamic law on all financial matters, and advising BNM on any *syariah* issue related to Islamic financial business. Appointments would be made by the King "on the advice of the Minister, after discussion with the Bank". Two crucial additions to this new legislation—Section 57, "Effect of Shariah rulings",[6] and Section 58, "Shariah Advisory Council ruling prevails"—decreed that SAC decisions on *syariah* matters in Islamic financial business were binding before any court or arbitrator, and that the rulings of the SAC would prevail over any *syariah* body formed by other IFI. This move provided the SAC with "semi or quasi-judicial power" and caused some uneasiness on the part of the civil court (Mohammad Azam et al. 2015, 340).

As suggested earlier, there have been many legal conundrums in establishing an Islamic financial regime within the national system. Though the SAC did not receive undue resistance from the traditional bureaucracy, including the *syariah* judiciary, there were recurring instances when the civil courts provided formidable resistance to the expansion of Islamic finance. For example, the decision to grant the SAC extraordinary powers, which allowed it to dictate decisions of the civil court, made for the uneasy relationship between Islamic finance advocates and the civil judiciary.

In the initial years of Islamic financialisation, the *bai' bi thaman ajil* (BBA) contract was one of the most controversial instruments offered by Islamic banks. BBA was used in transactions that involved borrowing for the purchase of properties or assets. Unlike conventional banks where the borrower would receive the loan and repay it based on an agreed-upon interest rate and time schedule, Islamic banking practice required them to enter into a trade transaction. As a prominent *syariah* scholar explained, with this, "the sale format [was]... used to legalize the profit earned by the bank in the form of a markup price in the second sale which would otherwise be a loan with interest" (Ahmad Hidayat 2007, 336).

During this time, litigation over the validity of the BBA comprised the largest number of Islamic finance institution cases brought before the court (Apnizan and Hakimah 2012, 54). Questions raised were typically around the basis of its distinctiveness, including whether IFI were interest-based, non-interest-based or interest-bearing, just form rather than substance or justified merely by use of Arabic nomenclature. In the case of *Bank Islam Malaysia Berhad v Azhar bin Osman, 2010*, Justice Rohana Yusoff was not convinced by the bank's insistence on treating *ibrar*, an instrument to retrieve default payments, as unconnected to profit-making. She even noted that "in [her] view using Arabic terminology *per se* does not make any transaction a Shariah transaction". In the case of *Arab Malaysian Finance Bhd v Taman Ihsan Jaya Sdn. Bhd & Ors, 2008*, the BBA contract was ruled to be contrary to the Islamic Banking Act 1983 and the Banking and Financial Institutions Act 1989 in that it had an interest component and was therefore not Islamic. In *Arab-Malaysia Merchant Bank Berhad v Silver Concept Sdn Bhd, 2008*, the judge also ruled that the SAC was "an organ of the executive bench of government, and not a judicial authority" and therefore its recommendation was not binding.

Judgements such as these were likely what pushed BNM to attempt to minimise the role of civil court judges in Islamic finance cases. For these corporate Islamic bureaucrats, the operationalisation of Islamic finance should undoubtedly come under the unilateral control of bankers together with their chosen *syariah* board members, rather than leaving the field open for judicial assertion. High Court rulings that deemed BBA contracts—whose architects were bankers—as invalid seemed to be a 'reprimand' of the system, which was not living up to its own ethical standards. Nevertheless, as a whole, the Malaysian judiciary was not one to rock the boat, especially when it came to a highly strategic project of the state. It was little surprise when High Court judgements on the invalidity of the BBA were eventually overturned at the Court of Appeal level. For example, in *Bank Islam Malaysia Berhad v Lim Kok Hoe and Anor, 2009*, the Court of Appeal judges appeared to have eschewed their judicial independence to collude with the Islamic banking technocrats when deciding on what should be construed as an Islamic transaction. They ruled that such responsibility should be transferred to the SAC as it was assumed that "the Syariah Advisory Council under the aegis of Bank Negara Malaysia, would have discharged their statutory duty to ensure that the operation of the Islamic banks [were] within the ambit of the Religion of Islam".

Understood this way, the introduction of the Central Bank of Malaysia Act 2009 appeared to be a way to resolve a jurisdictional conundrum or, more likely, to rein in the powers of the judiciary particularly through the new Sections 56, 57 and 58 that made it mandatory for courts to refer to the SAC whose decisions on IFI matters were also binding upon them. These provisions not only rendered the SAC the final authority on all matters related to IFI, but also made the validity of Sections 56 and 57 retroactive, which, according to one legal opinion, was an "infringement of the constitutional right to be heard [and hence] a breach of natural justice" (Apnizan and Hakimah 2012, 59). To silence these protests, Malaysia's Court of Appeal in *Tan Sri Abdul Khalid Ibrahim v Bank Islam Malaysia Bhd, 2012,* ruled that these sections were not unconstitutional. It maintained that the SAC's role was not to determine *syariah* laws but to identify the best rules that could be applied to Malaysia, as well as standardising these rules to stabilise the Islamic banking industry in Malaysia. With this, the SAC of BNM became the apex authority on Islamic finance superseding all other *syariah* institutions and judicial bodies (Mohamed Hadi 2011, 196–197).

Since this ruling, the SAC, under tight supervision of BNM, has acted as the super as well as supra-'rules-determining' body of IFI, much like the *fatwa* committees that make decisions on emerging cases within this field. SAC now publishes its rulings as the *Resolusi Syariah Dalam Kewangan Islam* (Syariah Resolutions in Islamic Finance), currently in its second edition (Bank Negara Malaysia 2010). Like *fatwa*, there are numerous rulings on various aspects of banking and financing the Islamic way: from the conditions of Islamic car loans through the *al-ijarah thumma al-bai* (use of two contracts, one for lease and another sale and purchase), to whether a debt security can be used as collateral in a collateral-based (*rahn*) contract, to the prohibition of joint contributors (*musahamah*) in *takaful* insurance contracts where bonus or refunds are given to holders if they do not make any claims. Almost all of the decisions in the BNM-published book of 'Syariah Resolutions' (Bank Negara Malaysia 2010) are supported by *quranic* injunctions, *hadith* (words of the Prophet) or *sunna* (ways of the Prophet) or *fiqh* principles of select jurists (*fuqaha*). Among the corporate Islamic bureaucracy's strongest proponents is Abdul Hamid Mohamad, former Chief Justice of Malaysia, who only had praise for this system.

> Bank Negara and the Securities Commission are in a position to ensure that the rulings are complied with. No other religious department, religious council or fatwa committee has such power and expertise. (Abdul Hamid and Trakic 2012, 38)

His position is not entirely surprising given that Abdul Hamid has been a member of SACs in both BNM and the SCM. The above notwithstanding, the validity of the SAC's judicial powers continued to be challenged by parties not satisfied with its rulings. This was until the Federal Court convened a nine-person bench to finally put this matter to rest in April 2019. In a 5-4 majority decision, the country's highest court deemed that any ruling by BNM's SAC was constitutional and binding on civil courts, even though it was not a judicial body. The four judges who held the dissenting view argued that Section 57 of the Central Bank of Malaysia Act 2009—which gave SAC its judicial power—was unconstitutional, but to no avail. With this judgement, SAC's role and powers could no longer be legally contested in any court (Star Online 2019).

Even before the uncertainty over the SAC's role and terms of Islamic finance's legal engagements with the judiciary were fully resolved, BNM had already adopted its own '*syariah* governance' in 2011, when it produced the "Shariah Governance Framework" document and required that all *syariah*-compliant financial institutions be subjected to this (Business Monitor Online 2011). The document determined "Shariah principles" through the operation of a "two-tier Shariah governance infrastructure"—one a centralised entity, SAC, and the other, various internal bodies such as the *syariah* committees of each Islamic Financial Institution.[7] The document is devoid of *quranic* or prophetic *hadith* and *fiqh* texts but contains a long list of detailed instructions and dictates on what constitutes the roles and functions of IFI within the *syariah* governance framework of the BNM.

All members of IFI *syariah* committees have to be Muslim, and the majority are also expected to have a bachelor's degree in *syariah*, including "*usul fiqh* (the origin of Islamic law) of *fiqh muamalat* (Islamic transaction or commercial law)".[8] Together they verify and ensure that IFI products comply with *syariah* principles. As can be seen, compared to the everyday social life of a Muslim, the determination of what is Islamically 'correct' or 'wrongful' goes through a vastly different route in the IFI world: less 'red tape', less bureaucratic divisions, no enforcement units and no involvement of *negeri* or federal Islamic bureaucracies. The functional outcome of the corporate Islamic bureaucracy is thus perhaps the most disenchanting of all the divisions of the Divine Bureaucracy.

Ijtihad *as the Cornerstone of Islamic Finance*

Rich and global institutional investors have typically been the market base of Islamic banks. Already in 2007, Islamic bankers in Malaysia noted that there was around USD300 billion of surplus petrodollars coming from the Middle East (New Straits Times 2007). The euphoria over the success of Islamic banking continued when BNM officials encouraged more conventional banking institutions to establish Islamic banks as their subsidiaries. More incentives were given, including allowing these subsidiaries to have foreign partners with a 49 per cent stake, unlike conventional banks whose foreign equity was capped at 30 per cent (The Edge Malaysia 2007). Given the global success of the industry, banking technocrats were anxious that banking principles be as flexible as possible to attract a diverse group of investors. Why and how the IFI industry in Malaysia has been able to move ahead of other Islamic countries is explained by one banker below,

> We do not limit the application of syariah in the market to a particular school of thought as it is against syariah. This huge debate about the Malaysian approach, the GCC (Gulf Cooperation Council) approach or whatever approach is irrelevant to Malaysia. To my mind, it is a total waste of time. We allow all the approaches all interpretations of syariah. What is also important is that syariah management is fully governed by the Malaysian regulator and

> is enshrined in the Islamic Banking Act 1983. You can see the GCC Islamic banks licensed in Malaysia benefiting from this framework. That is why in Malaysia, the market is vibrant and active. (Goh 2009)

The notion of *syariah* compliance is fundamental to Islamic finance, but whether there is a method to determine this and who has the last say remains unclear. Prohibitions against usury (*riba*), risks and speculative behaviour (*gharar*) and gaming and gambling activities (*myasir*) ultimately need to be translated into measurable indices to determine the *halal*-ness of products that have gone beyond consumable food and drinks. How can seemingly incorporeal and intangible commodities like bonds, shares, stocks, deposits or insurance be *halal* certified, or in current technocratic lexicon, '*syariah* compliant'? Globally, there is yet to be a single, absolute authority for this, and there will likely not be any, at least not one, universally accepted by all national authorities (Syed Farhan et al. 2012, 1018–1026).

Malaysian and Middle Eastern Islamic authorities have often taken divergent views in their *syariah* interpretations of *halal* banking and finance. Malaysian bankers have been anxious to craft innovative financial products through a more liberal interpretation of the *syariah*, but their Arab counterparts have been less forthcoming. The SAC of BNM approved instruments such as "Islamic real-estate investment trusts, structured dual-currency derivatives, Islamic stock-index funds and *syariah*-compliant single-stock futures" ahead of its equivalent counterparts in the Middle East. Determined to be a leader in bridging the gap between orthodoxy and creativity, Malaysia was "eager to educate oil-rich Gulf investors about such financial novelties", leading BNM to spend some USD57 million on a "Shariah dialogue" with international Islamic scholars so that a diversity of interpretations could help boost Islamic finance internationally (Trofimov 2007).

In many cases, *syariah* compliance has been largely reflexively determined within a notion of a 'post-secular' reasoning and argumentative methodology in the interpretation of *quranic* texts and other traditions (*ijtihad*) executed by a new breed of non-theologian Muslim scholars. Scholars and researchers at BNM's Isra mentioned earlier, and the government-owned International Institute of Advanced Islamic Studies (IAIS), have contributed actively to these debates through their respective journals, the *Isra International Journal of Islamic Finance* and *Islam and Civilizational Renewal*. The core philosophical or doctrinal issue revolves around the notion of the higher goals and objectives of Islamic law, the "*maqasid al-Shari'ah*" or an approach generally defined as the attainment of a greater good for society rather than a narrow focus on unbendable rules (Kamali 2008).

Muhammad Hashim Kamali, a renowned *syariah* scholar who currently heads IAIS in Kuala Lumpur, calls for a "broad", "rational" and "comprehensive" appreciation of transactions and exchange (*muamalat*) so that it will not be merely approached through a literalist and mechanical standpoint as anything forbidden based on speculation and rigidity will be a violation of freedom (2013, 4). His reasoning would facilitate the establishment of Islamic finance within a free-market system. Scholars affiliated to IAIS argue that contracts should not merely be based on legality but also on their *maqasid* aspects (Sheila Ainon and AlHarthy 2014, 127). They recommend making a finer distinction between a product being merely '*syariah* compliant' as opposed to '*syariah* based' (Habib 2011, 150). Here two aspects are emphasised: one, while legal requirements must be fulfilled in form and substance, the use of ruses or legal stratagems to facilitate transactions should be prohibited (Ahmed 2011, 152) and, two, Islamic finance needs to fulfil Islam's social requirements by serving the needs of all market segments, from the rich to the middle and poorer sectors (Ahmed 2011, 150–154). There are also questions around accountability, responsibility, independence and competency and hence the need for risk management, review and audit functions (Abdul Rahim 2011, 137–138). Others would like more innovation to take place, since according to them there "is nothing sacrosanct about these instruments… In fact, some of these modes represent pre-Islamic practices, which were subsequently adopted simply because they were in conformity with the principles of Islam" (Ariff and Rosly 2011, 316–317).

Syariah-compliance specifications as determined by corporate Islamic bureaucrats, the regulators of Islamic finance, are not considered absolute or doctrinally unambiguous. While the definition of what is *halal* or *haram* can be explicitly spelt out, there are different configurations or delineations of what is allowable and prohibited, subject to debate. For instance, should a company be delisted from a roster of *syariah*-compliant companies when one of its smaller subsidiaries is involved in a *syariah*-prohibited economic activity (Securities Commission of Malaysia 2009, 13–26)? There is also concern that some products may be less competitive and less appealing to Muslim consumers, hence the attempt to simplify their terms (Mydin Meera 2012). This was not a route free of unexpected adverse reactions from the traditional bureaucracy, as the following section of this chapter shows.

The goal for the corporate Islamic bureaucracy is clear: creating a *syariah*-based governance and regulatory framework that provides the ethical-philosophical foundation of Islamic finance, but on its own terms rather than that of its traditional counterparts. Ultimately, this group seeks to make *syariah* compliance consonant and competitive with the specifications of a neoliberal, global capitalist order. The growth of Islamic finance has thus drawn on a *syariah* narrative but flourished outside the domain of the traditional Divine Bureaucracy. Had this not happened, it would have been difficult to promote an openness and pluralism of perspectives, necessary for the competitiveness demanded of capitalist enterprises. The creation and rise of Islamic finance capital enabled BNM-endorsed technocrats to control and amass resources to dictate their own pathways of Islamisation, involving both purification and accumulation of money. Federal IFI technocrats are the foremost representatives of the corporate Islamic bureaucracy, and their contribution to an 'other' Islamisation, even a resurgent Islam, should not be undervalued.

Corporate Islamic Bureaucracy Versus Traditional Bureaucracy

The distinguishing markers of money transactions in Islam are premised on the prohibition of *gharar*, *myasir* and *riba*. Previously, these were either not developed as sanctions, or were simply interred by the colonial authorities, which selected other areas of Islamic life to be bureaucratised. Perhaps this was not to detract from the overall imperial goal of advancing capitalism. Having played little or no role in the Islamic financial sector up to then, government religious authorities, namely the National Fatwa Committee, issued a ruling in 1993, ten years after the country's first Islamic bank (Bank Islam) was established. The *fatwa* decreed that unless forced by circumstances to fulfil a basic need, it was *haram* for Muslims to borrow from commercial banks as this involved *riba*. They could still deposit their money with these banks, but all interest earned had to be surrendered to the *baitulmal* (Islamic treasury). This *fatwa* also pronounced it *haram* for Muslims to lease their property to commercial banks as this involved *riba*. Furthermore, while Muslims could still receive gifts and other offerings such as scholarships from these banks, they were barred from owning their shares (Jakim 2009a, 11–15). Initially, not many Muslims took notice of this *fatwa* let alone heeded any of its calls. It would seem that their awareness about *halal* and *haram* monetary transactions was largely muted in this period before the advent of the corporate Islamic bureaucracy-led Islamic finance. These concepts only became extensively projected onto Muslim public consciousness thereafter.

In 2011, the Selangor *fatwa* committee issued a *fatwa* to declare that Muslims could not invest in stocks offered by Amanah Saham Nasional Berhad (ASNB), a federal government unit trust agency. This *negeri fatwa* directly contradicted another one issued three years earlier by the National Fatwa Committee, which ruled that these shares were obligatory but not mandatory (*harus*) for Muslims. Penang and Pahang also put out similar decrees, but Selangor's had the most comprehensive justifications for its decision. The most important was that these shares were tied in a mixture of investment companies, *halal* and *haram*, and therefore were *syariah* non-compliant (Muhammad Hafiz et al. 2017, 196–197).

The ASNB was launched in 1981 as part of the New Economic Policy (NEP) that sought to uplift the socio-economic status of *bumiputera* (sons of the soil, *lit.*) in the country. Its management was placed under Permodalan Nasional Berhad (PNB), the largest investment company in Malaysia established in 1980. In 2017, ASNB had RM279.2 billion in assets and 13.2 million account holders (Permodalan Nasional Berhad 2017, 12). PNB has investments in more than 200 companies, the strategic and largest ones in government-linked banking, industrial and plantation corporations such as Malayan Banking Berhad, Sime Darby Berhad and Sime Darby Plantation (Permodalan Nasional Berhad 2017, 56–76). As of 2017, there were around 9 million *bumiputera* subscribers to the Amanah Saham Bumiputera (ASB), one of the largest of the ASNB unit trust schemes (Permodalan Nasional Berhad 2017, 132).

The ASNB controversy demonstrated the paradoxical twist in the entrenchment of the 'Islamic economy' that has mainly been driven by the growth of Islamic finance capitalism. When the Selangor *fatwa* committee issued its *fatwa* in 2011 to declare investments in ASNB as *haram*, it did not use the classical method of relying on *quranic* and prophetic texts. Rather, it used the guidelines on *syariah* compliance of financial products issued by the SCM. Prior to this, state finance technocrats did not need to seek the expertise or participation of the traditional Islamic bureaucracy in their push to grow the Islamic finance sector. The agenda and design for the Islamic economy relied instead on experts with skills in finance over and above *syariah* training. To carve out distinctive Islamic financial products, commonplace commercial notions were given sacred identities with Arabic phraseology or new concepts were introduced.[9] This was how the traditional *syariah* bureaucracy found itself learning concepts like 'conventional banking' (code for non-*halal* banking) and *syariah* compliance (code for *halal* business that is measurable, including its quantitative value). It was technocrats—to whom the traditional religious bureaucrats would either gladly give their support or concede to because it was too complex (even convoluted) a field to engage—who invented this method of drawing a 'scientific' separation between permissible and prohibited monetary transactions.

The SCM criteria to determine *syariah*-compliant shares and stocks involve a fairly tedious process. There are different benchmarks and thresholds for 'non-permissible' activities and 'permissible' businesses before stocks can be declared '*syariah* compliant'. For severely prohibited activities—those involving businesses in pork, alcohol and gambling—the threshold is set at 5 per cent, meaning that if these activities contribute more than 5 per cent to the overall business of a said company, then its stocks are deemed *syariah* non-compliant. Those with businesses in hotels and resorts may have a higher threshold of 25 per cent. If conscientious Muslim investors discover that their shares are *syariah* non-compliant, they may dispose of these within a specified period, and any dividends or capital gains obtained from ownership of the shares must be channelled to the *baitulmal*. There can be variations in the benchmark levels in different time periods,[10] given that this is determined through *ijtihad*.

The ASNB controversy started in February 2009 when the SCM routinely informed Maybank, Malaysia's largest financial group, that it was not fully *syariah* compliant due to its 'over the threshold' investments in many conventional IFI. Since Maybank's shares comprised one of the largest of PNB's holdings, some within the traditional bureaucracy interpreted that the ASB unit trust scheme, together with another called Amanah Saham Nasional (ASN), was also not *syariah* compliant according to this SCM benchmark. This led the Selangor *fatwa* committee to infer that ASB and ASN unit trusts were *haram*. The response of the committee—that the benchmark was to be considered an unequivocal measure of *halal* and *haram*—was unexpected by SCM and PNB. Conventional banks are not thought to be *haram*, although they are not fully *syariah* compliant. This finer distinction between being *haram* and non-*syariah* compliant can sometimes be lost. However, the episode reinforced doubts among the traditional bureaucracy about trading contracts (*mudarabah*) involving multiple parties. It highlighted Maybank as one of the largest conventional (read *haram* to some) investment counters of ASB and ASN, and that Maybank as a financial group was not an Islamic bank (Muhammad Hafiz et al. 2017, 190–195). Reactions such as that of the Selangor *fatwa* committee could perhaps be interpreted as symptomatic of Islamic bureaucrats at the *negeri* level wanting to have more say within the burgeoning field of Islamic money matters. Why would the field of *hukum muamalat*—laws regulating economic exchange, transactions and contracts—not be within their scope of authority? Even Jakim was slow to realise that *muamalat* matters could well be under its purview, and only established a web portal *e-Muamalat* to "compile *fiqh* debates ... in the field of finance, contract, businesses" in 2010.[11] Significantly, this was one of the earliest signs of Islamic intra-elite disagreement, between the tradition-based religious authorities (comprising the triumvirate of *mufti*, *syariah* judiciary and *ulama*) versus a new class of finance-driven state technocrats.

To dispel the 2011 Selangor *fatwa* and the circulation of viewpoints doubting the *halal* nature of ASB and ASN investments, the PNB-managed ASNB published a 112-page booklet to justify why investments in these funds were *harus* and not *haram* (Amanah Saham Nasional Berhad 2016). While it is doubtful if Muslims heeded the 2011 Selangor *fatwa*—the number of ASB unit holders rose from 7.3 million in 2011 to 8.8 million in 2015 and 9.3 million in 2017[12]—this issue still needed addressing to prevent other forms of dissension from igniting. Additionally, Jakim produced its own clarification on its *e-fatwa* website, affirming that the 2008 national *fatwa* allowing for investments like ASB should not be disputed.[13] Mainstream media articles and Facebook postings[14] were also deployed to assert the *harus* dimension of ASB investments, particularly highlighting the viewpoints of select *mufti* in support of this position (see Berita Harian 2014; Berita Harian 2015; Harian Metro 2015; New Straits Times 2015).

The PNB booklet itself contained strenuous arguments in support of ASB investments, again, backed by all the right religious sources, especially the opinion of the *mufti* of Kelantan. Its main point was that even if there was a mixing of *halal* and *haram* elements in these investments, the ratio was low. Moreover, since the majority of Muslims were still living in poverty and occupying the lower end of the socio-economic scale, ASB and ASN investments were a means to redress this situation. Hence, they were deemed permissible on the basis of serving the greater good of the community (*maslahah ummah*), as well as being in line with the Islamic principle of *maqasid syariah* (Amanah Saham Nasional Berhad 2016, 20–25). In 2014, the National Fatwa Committee also saw it fit to issue further clarification on its 2008 *fatwa*, this time on the role of Maybank in PNB investments. The committee decided that to drop the bank from the PNB list where Muslims were the largest shareholders would not only cause the economy to collapse and bring dire effects on other Islamic bodies, but would deny employment to the over 16,500 *bumiputera* Muslims serving at the bank as well (Amanah Saham Nasional Berhad 2016, 47–48).

The booklet avoided any mention of the dissenting Selangor *fatwa* and instead focused on *fatwa* from other *negeri* that approved the practice of unit trust investments. It also explained the differences between the role of the SCM and the role of a *fatwa* committee. The former's main function was to "classify securities for Syariah compliance without being influenced by various other elements such as *syar'iyyah*, needs and common *maslahat* [good]", while the latter was "not tied to the benchmark of the Securities Commission" when it came to making decisions. The SCM's benchmarking was supposedly based on arguments derived from the methods of "*fiqhiyyah* to arrive at a ruling, with *ijtihad* and consensus in evaluating securities that are mixed with non-*Syariah* compliant activities as in the case of ASB and ASN" (Amanah Saham Nasional Berhad 2016, 47).

In 2017, the Selangor Mufti's Office was 'persuaded' to issue a revised opinion not tantamount to a new *fatwa*, although coming across as rescinding the 2011 *fatwa*. This was in the form of a letter from the *mufti* addressed to the Chairman of PNB, dated 11 May 2017 (Astro Awani 2017). The letter conveyed the outcome of the *negeri fatwa* committee meeting, which decided that ASB and ASN investments were *harus* in accordance with the SCM's latest standards. One reason given was that the percentage of PNB's investment in *syariah*-compliant companies had exceeded the 66 per cent benchmark. The letter, however, added a *proviso* that the ruling would be revised after three years, with the expectation that the *syariah*-compliance benchmark would exceed 75 per cent by then.[15] By the end of 2017, all *negeri fatwa* on the *harus* ruling of investment in PNB shares had been standardised (Berita Harian 2017). Table 7.2 lists the progression of *fatwa* approvals or written decisions by each State in chronological order.

Table 7.2 *Fatwa* or written consent approving Muslims investing in ASB and/or ASN and year issued

Year	*States/body*
1992	Perak, Kedah
1993	Terengganu
2002	Sarawak
2008	National Fatwa Committee, Malacca, Johor, Sabah, Federal Territory
2009	Kelantan
2012	Negeri Sembilan, Pahang
2016	Perlis
2017	Selangor, Penang

Source: Adapted from Permodalan Nasional Berhad (2017, 88)

Table 7.3 *Zakat* payouts by PNB to SIRCs in 2017

State	Zakat *payouts (RM)*
Pahang	9,384,000
Negeri Sembilan	7,376,800
Federal Territory	17,265,600
Selangor	27,013,600
Melaka	5,384,000
Sabah	19,365,600
Kedah	11,386,400
Kelantan	11,867,200
Perak	5,865,600
Sarawak	15,631,200

Source: Amanah Saham Nasional Berhad (2016, 120)

PNB also had to align itself more to the agenda of the Islamic finance industry by sponsoring major conferences such as the International Islamic Fund and Wealth Management Forum, Kuala Lumpur Islamic Finance Forum, the World Islamic Economic Forum and the Shariah Governance and Assurance Forum (Amanah Saham Nasional Berhad 2016, 90). PNB's own Shariah Advisory Committee declared that a list of PNB products "conform[ed] to the requirements of Shariah, based on *Maqasid Shariah* and *Siyasah Syar'iyyah* principles" (Amanah Saham Nasional Berhad 2016, 106). The body went so far as to tout itself as one of the largest *zakat* contributors to the SIRCs (Amanah Saham Nasional Berhad 2016, 120) (Table 7.3).

Everyday Dissensions Against Corporate Islam

The corporatisation of assets under an Islamic religious guardianship inevitably inflamed some degree of discontentment among those on the 'adverse' receiving end of such 'game-changing' transformation. To date, these expressions of dissent have been sporadic and relatively muted. The power of the Divine Bureaucracy is not an easy edifice to crack. SIRCs particularly had become a wealthy body with their control over *zakat*, *wakaf* and *baitulmal*, and although SIRCs as representing the traditional bureaucracy did not have formal working arrangements with the corporate Islamic bureaucracy, there were potentially many areas that would draw them closer to each other. The need to commercially develop *wakaf* land banks and *halal* industrialisation through financialisation brought the IFI technocrats nearer to the traditional Islamic bureaucracy. Jakim and Jawhar were already organising meetings between banking and financial services technocrats to discuss means of raising the market potential of *wakaf*.[16] Such a frenzied pace of commercialisation also affected pockets of Muslim society who were either unimpressed with such materialistically 'calculating' developments or were victims of them. This last section of the chapter highlights some of these episodes of dissension.

In 2012, the Persatuan Pengguna Islam Malaysia (PPIM, Muslim Consumer Association of Malaysia) urged the National Fatwa Committee to review the terms of Islamic banking. This was in response to a case where home loan borrowers of Bank Islam had continued paying their mortgages despite the housing project being abandoned by the developer. They demanded to know why there was no profit and loss sharing with the bank when this was supposed to be part of the *mudarabah* contract to which they had agreed. According to PPIM, which represented the house buyers, the bank should not have sought repayment as the product (the abandoned housing project) was 'non-existent' and that doing so went against the BBA Islamic banking concept (Astro Awani 2014). A video of the angry house buyers showed some of them protesting that there was no concept of profit and loss sharing—claimed to be the main distinction from conventional banking—in Islamic financing after all.[17] They argued that if the promised housing did not exist, the bank had no right to reap any profits from the transaction.[18] In this way, Islamic banking was criticised for not only being unjust but also for operating without the soul of Islam (Utusan Online 2015).[19]

On the PPIM website, there was a link to a videoclip titled "The Islamic banking deceit".[20] It showed a former CEO of Bank Muamalat giving a speech in Indonesia in 2015 where he exposed why the Islamic banking system as currently practised was deceitful and concealed the making of *riba* by disguising transactions as trading. He concluded that a genuine Islamic banking system had to exist outside the present global monetary system, which thrives on profit and had failed to meet the social justice and distribution of wealth goals of Islamic banking. PPIM further claimed that *syariah* committees in banks had "conflicts of interest", were not independent and were not performing their duties as demanded of them (New Straits Times 2012a).

Following these criticisms, a Malay daily, *Utusan Malaysia*, published an opinion piece by the Dean of the Institute of Islamic Banking and Finance of the International Islamic University of Malaysia. He pointed out that the emphasis on profit-maximisation rather than risk-sharing was due to the current practice of Islamic banking, which prioritised debt financing rather than equity financing. He argued that the line separating conventional banking's usurious and speculative activities from the avoidance of such activities by their Islamic banking window was merely illusory (Ahmadi 2016). Another scholar from the Institute of Islamic Understanding (Ikim—Institut Kemajuan Islam Malaysia) highlighted that while Islamic finance was growing globally at a fast pace, poverty and maldistribution of wealth among Muslims were still high (Nizam 2018). Islamic finance was censured for emulating conventional banking by serving the rich. A prominent scholar of Islamic law was also quoted in the article (Nizam 2018) as saying that *syariah* advisers were dependent on classical *fiqh* texts without contextualising them in accordance with *quranic* and *hadith* principles. Islamic banking products purportedly built on principles derived from *fiqh* texts that were hundreds of years old, and were in actual fact imitations of contemporary conventional banking products, according to the quoted scholar.

Wakaf commercialisation, the features of which had been discussed in Chap. 3, is another striking site of discontentment. A highly controversial area of religious monetisation is developing the commercial potential of *wakaf*—land and assets bequeathed for religious and charitable purposes—not least of all because it has displaced the symbols of spirituality and the goodwill of donors. In 1995, the first national *wakaf* corporation, the Malaysian Wakaf Development Corporation (MWDC), was formed under Yayasan Pembangunan Ekonomi Islam Malaysia (Yapeim, Islamic

Economic Development Foundation). Yapeim and the MWDC were to collaborate with the SIRCs to convert *wakaf* land banks into money-generating projects (New Straits Times 1995a).

In 2007, Prime Minister Abdullah Ahmad Badawi pronounced that it would be in the interest of Muslims for *wakaf* lands to be commercially developed, even if these were originally donated for religious or charitable purposes. He said this when he launched a 34-storey building for Maiwp, the FT SIRC at a half-acre site in the heart of Kuala Lumpur. The project was a joint venture between Lembaga Tabung Haji (LTH, Pilgrims Fund Board), TH Technologies Sdn Bhd and Bank Islam (New Straits Times 2007). In 2009, another piece of *wakaf* land belonging to Maiwp was jointly developed by LTH and Bank Islam into a RM151 million office complex in the 'Golden Triangle' of Kuala Lumpur. Bank Islam's own building sits on this land (New Straits Times 2009). *Wakaf* development also involved increasing the pool of movable assets in the form of cash and investment donations in stocks. Twenty years on, the National Wakaf Corporation was launched to undertake more determined *wakaf* commercialisation (Fazleena and Fairuz 2015). By 2015, other banks and financial institutions were teaming up to embark on a full-scale and comprehensive development of *wakaf* into high value real estate. Uda Waqf Sdn Bhd, a subsidiary of the government corporation Urban Development Authority (Uda), partnered with Bank Muamalat for this purpose, with the latter injecting RM100 million into the venture. Through such corporatised partnerships, *wakaf* became a land bank with at least 120 hectares (Muhammed 2015). The various periods of this commercialisation exercise have been fraught with controversies and resistance.

Already in 1995, the Majlis Agama Islam Negeri Pulau Pinang (Mainpp, Penang SIRC) had developed a *wakaf* endowment land to site a multistoried commercial building. This involved tearing down an old three-storey building owned by the United Malays National Organisation (Umno), which stood on a piece of *wakaf* land in the heart of Georgetown, the capital city of Penang, to make way for a RM35 million, 21-storey new Umno building, later named Menara Umno. Penang Umno leaders had been concerned that although the market value of some *wakaf* land was around RM11.4 million, they produced paltry rental returns (New Straits Times 1995b). This project was one of the first joint ventures between Mainpp and a private company called the South East Asia Development Corporation Bhd. The *wakaf* land, which is legally under the trustee ownership of Mainpp, used to site the first Umno building in the country, built in 1953. By 1995, it was reported as being 'offered' to Umno by the chairman of the Umno Penang division, simply on account of the old Umno building being there and also that the first Umno Tanah Melayu conference was held on the site in 1955 (New Straits Times 1995c).[21] Anwar Ibrahim, then Deputy Prime Minister, was one of the strongest advocates of *wakaf* land development and officiated the groundbreaking ceremony of this project. He was quoted as saying, "Some feel *wakaf* land must not be changed. This attitude must go. In the middle of the city, some *wakaf* land can become an eyesore if not developed or improved" (Kathirasen 1995). Subsequently, the building changed ownership three times, and it is unclear if Umno ever owned the building, but in 2013, it was only renting two of its floors (New Straits Times 2013). That this building would house Penang's Umno headquarters, that is, using religious assets for partisan interests, raised questions over the propriety of such usage of *wakaf* land and property.[22]

Around the same time, there was also a plan to demolish a small mosque on another piece *wakaf* land adjacent to the Umno headquarters. It was shelved after a descendant of the testator who declared the land as *wakaf*, and the mosque committee, sued Mainpp over its proposal to replace the mosque with a five-storey commercial complex. The plaintiffs of the suit claimed that the property could only be used for the purpose of "Muslims gathering to pray and for no other purposes" as stated in the agreement signed back in 1900 (New Straits Times 1995d).

Another protracted case of displacement in Penang involved the Masjid Abdul Cauder *wakaf* land in Seberang Perai. In 2010, the federal authority Jawhar allocated a sum of RM50 million to develop this land, which had 46 settlers with homes on it. Fourteen of them refused to move despite being promised compensation (Buletin Mutiara 2018). In 2019, they were forcibly evicted in an incident that led to injuries of a policeman and a religious enforcement worker. Even in 2018, newly elected Prime Minister Mahathir's attempts at resolving the issue came to nought. The eviction cost Mainpp RM3 million and took four court orders over a period of nine years to regain the 2.7 acre land for the development of a 22-storey apartment building with 470 low-medium cost units (Malay Mail 2019).

In Kedah, there was also a plan to commercialise a piece of *wakaf* land into a shopping and business centre to the tune of RM50 million (New Straits Times 1995e). Contention over this plan, which included the demolition of a 100-year-old mosque of heritage value, continued throughout the 2000s (Tunku Yusuf 2012; New Straits Times 2012b). The decision to tear down the mosque to make way for the commercial buildings had, however, been approved by the Kedah *fatwa* committee (Star Online 2011). During the construction, a committee member of the mosque filed a suit against the Majlis Agama Islam Kedah (Maik, Kedah SIRC) and the Kota Setar District Land Administrator for the demolishment of the old mosque (Nadia 2012). Despite this court challenge, and a court order in favour of the plaintiff (New Straits Times 2012c), the project went ahead in 2014. The Kedah government had apparently paid RM1.48 million to Maik for the *wakaf* land and planned to build a new *surau* (community prayer hall) in the mall to replace the old Madrasah Salihiah that was demolished (Star Online 2011).

The shopping mall eventually opened in 2016, but dissent around it swirled (Star Online 2016). During the period of controversy, a *negeri*-level law was enacted to prevent anyone from questioning the decision of the *mufti* and the *fatwa* committee in this matter. Before the completion of the mall, and in anticipation of challenge against the earlier decision of the *fatwa* committee allowing for the development of the *wakaf* land, the Kedah legislature passed an amendment to the Mufti and Fatwa (Kedah Darul Aman) Enactment 2008. The inclusion of Section 22A in this enactment bars people from challenging any *fatwa* enacted by the government, in any civil or *syariah* courts (Malaysiakini 2012). The Malaysian Bar Council issued a press statement on the unconstitutionality of this new enactment (Malaysian Bar 2012), and a member of the Kedah royal family also lodged a police report against its passage (mStar 2012). Even the *mufti* of the neighbouring *negeri* of Perlis opined that the law was against Islamic principles as it prohibited legal challenges to any *fatwa* (Perak Today 2012).

An opinion piece in a newspaper urged politicians to listen to the enchantment and offerings of good *do'a* (prayers and supplication) given by the ordinary people for their political success (Noor Adzman 2011). To be headstrong about *wakaf* commercialisation and going against the people's wishes may have contributed to the failure of politicians like Anwar Ibrahim who was associated with *wakaf* land development in Penang, who was sacked as Deputy Prime Minister in 1998.[23] A warning was also sounded to Azizan Abdul Razak, the then Kedah Menteri Besar (Chief Minister), to be cognisant of his political future over the Kedah shopping mall and *wakaf* controversy (Noor Adzman 2011). In the 2013 general election, Azizan and his party Pas failed to be re-elected as the government. In 2013, a freak thunderstorm dislodged a 15-metre lightning arrestor pole on top of the aforementioned 21-storey Penang Menara Umno building, causing it to plunge to the street and claim two lives. Anwar, one of the initiators of *wakaf* development in Penang, was indirectly implicated in the questionable status of the building.[24]

Conclusion

The participation of a new class of managerial capitalists using religiously based precepts and knowledge has given rise to the corporate Islamic bureaucracy. Its pursuit of the agenda of monetising the market worth of religious assets resembles an Islamic resurgent movement, but one that is entangled with economic neoliberalism and its secular tenets. The disenchantment entailed in 'purifying' money lies in its plethora of rules, regulations, standards, benchmarks, indexes, audits and certification. *Syariah* compliance has now crept into the vocabulary of 'doing' and 'practising' religion, and as a way of distinguishing *halal* from non-*halal* conventional finance. Likewise, the creation of *syariah* boards and *syariah* governance are relatively new institutions and procedures underwriting the architecture of Islamic finance, which distinguishes them from their conventional counterparts. The instruments and expertise that go into standards and compliance verification is a form of technocratisation, which has enabled the supposed purification of money. At the same time, it allows for the continuance and desirability of capital accumulation.

This chapter has discussed the distinctive role of BNM in introducing exceptionalisms for Islamic financial practices, where its technocrats and *syariah* bureaucracy have been instrumental in developing Islamic finance capitalism. The process of subjecting Muslim social life to monetary exchanges replete with regulations and standards of prohibitions and permissibility disenchants a spiritual life that would otherwise be more vibrant and indeterminate. This, however, has given rise to a different set of challenges as seen in the confrontation between the traditional Islamic bureaucracy and its corporate counterparts, represented by the country's premier investment institution, PNB. The controversy analysed pitted the spiritual enchantment of religious restraint against the disenchantment that followed the emphasis on individual material progress of the Malay-Muslim *bumiputera*. The latter, imbued as a national goal, was put to the test when the State Islamic bureaucracy questioned this teleological approach to development. By exploring everyday dissension of those uncomfortable with monetising religious assets or left out as beneficiaries of such enterprises, this chapter has also revealed the lack of clarity and often unfulfilled notions of social justice and distribution in Islamic finance. Coupled with the persistent drive for the commercialisation of marketable religious assets, all these have contributed to the disenchantment of ordinary Muslims.

The domain of Islamic finance bears little similarity to the traditional bureaucratic sphere led by religious administrators, *mufti* and *syariah* judges within *negeri* and federal bureaucracies. Corporate Islam is marked by its extensive global interconnectedness and inclusivity in terms of agents, leaders and clients. However, the rise of Islamic finance driven by corporate Islamic bureaucracy was helped along by several exceptionalisms that gave BNM and state-owned asset management corporations an extraordinary advantage in valorising the commercial worth of religious assets. Islamic finance facilitated by *syariah* technocrats has been insulated from judicial intervention and, unlike the traditional Islamic bureaucracy, is based on *ijtihad*-centric Islam. Innovation and flexibility in the competitive world of banking and finance capitalism has been a necessity. Instead of limiting precepts to a singular *mazhab* or one that is prescribed by a *negeri* religious authority, a variety of doctrines are now accepted. This need to accommodate Islamic finance to the interests of the free market has necessitated a plurality of viewpoints. Where certain money matters were declared *haram* by other domains of the Divine Bureaucracy, as in the case of the *fatwa* against the ASB unit trust scheme, the corporate Islamic bureaucracy used its superior resources and expertise to swiftly overcome this depiction as a misrepresentation. Pockets of criticisms within Muslim civil society, disgruntled bank customers, critical scholars and those displaced by the commercial development of *wakaf* land have added voices of dissent to the cosy association of Islam with capitalism. To the surprise of few, the divine goal of 'purifying' money has come with social costs.

Notes

1. An earlier article on the subject of Islamic banking and finance in Malaysia stressed its crucial role in creating an alliance of Muslim technocrats and capitalists, thereby contributing to an emergent global multipolar financial and regulatory space (Maznah and Saravanamuttu 2015).

2. There are several categories of allowable consumption in Islam, *haram* is absolutely forbidden, *makruh* is permissible though there will be a loss of merit in the afterlife if these items are consumed. *Harus* is obligatory though not mandatory. Outside of food consumption, the activity of gambling or risk-taking is also *haram*.
3. See the International Centre for Education in Islamic Finance website, http://www.inceif.org/, accessed 15 July 2014.
4. Under this new law, the Central Bank of Malaysia (Amendment) Act 2003, Section 16(B)(2) also provides that the Minister, "on recommendation of the Bank", can appoint members of this body.
5. BNM's Syariah Advisory Council website, http://www.bnm.gov.my/index.php?ch=en_about&pg=en_thebank&ac=439&lang=en, accessed 14 March 2019.
6. All of BNM's documents, including other institutions conducting Islamic banking, use the spelling 'Shariah' instead of 'Syariah'. This is only a speculation without substantiation—it could be that most of the documents were drafted by an international group of advisers and consultants who were not cognisant of the local spelling, '*syariah*'.
7. The document 'Shariah Governance Framework' is available at the BNM website, http://www.bnm.gov.my/guidelines_old/05_shariah/02_Shariah_Governance_Framework_20101026.pdf, accessed 14 March 2019.
8. This passage is from page 30 of the 'Syariah Governance Framework', http://www.bnm.gov.my/guidelines_old/05_shariah/02_Shariah_Governance_Framework_20101026.pdf, accessed 9 May 2019.
9. Jakim (2009b) has published an extensive glossary of Arabic phrases used in *muamalat* transactions.
10. See, for instance, an early benchmark for Syariah-compliance in 2010 (Securities Commission of Malaysia 2010, 4–17) versus the later standards contained in the 2018 guideline (Securities Commission of Malaysia 2018, 11–15), which have variations in the threshold levels of similar activities.
11. In Malay, *memuatkan perbahasan* fiqh *muamalat sebagai rujukan berautoriti bagi umat Islam khususnya yang melibatkan penentuan hukum -hakam dalam bidang kewangan, kontrak, perniagaan dan sebagainya.* See Portal Rasmi Muamalat dan Kewangan Islam, Jakim, http://e-muamalat.islam.gov.my/ms/info-korporat/pengenalan, accessed 15 March 2019.
12. Statistics for 2011 from Rozita et al. (2015, 59) and for 2015 and 2017 from Permodalan Nasional Berhad (2017, 132).
13. See "Pelaburan dalam ASN, ASB dan seumpamanya", http://e-muamalat.islam.gov.my/ms/bahan-ilmiah/fatwa-muamalat/117-pelaburan-dalam-asn-asb-dan-seumpamanya, accessed 12 March 2019.
14. The Facebook posting by Asyraf Wajdi Dusuki, a former Deputy Minister, was featured in the ASNB booklet (Amanah Saham Nasional Berhad 2016, 61–64).

15. To date, there is no official or gazetted Selangor *fatwa* on this new position. The PNB issued its own press statement on 16 May 2017 to affirm the decision of the Selangor *fatwa* committee as conveyed by the *mufti*, http://www.asnb.com.my/pdf/media/berita/20170516_PR_Fatwa_Harus_Mufti_Selangor_Department_BM.pdf, accessed 1 May 2019.
16. For example, two papers were presented on this at a Jakim conference which brought together *syariah* bureaucrats from the finance institutions in 2015. A Council of Syariah Finance Institution Advisers had already been established. See papers by Md Nurdin (2015) and Anan (2015).
17. Youtube video, "Berita kezaliman perbankan Islam", http://www.ppim.org.my/18511342014-kezaliman-perbangkan-isla/, accessed: 11 March 2019.
18. See website of PPIM, http://www.ppim.org.my/1102-rakyat-news-1012014-kementerian/, accessed 11 March 2019.
19. "'Perbankan Islam' hanya nama, tapi zalim dan menekan?", http://www.ppim.org.my/perbankan-islam-hanya-nama-tapi-zali/, accessed 11 March 2019.
20. See www.ppim.org.my/2442-video-perbankan-islam-fikir/, 11 March 2019.
21. There was a lot of grey area in this episode. All *wakaf* lands are under the ownership of SIRCs as these are properties bequeathed by benefactors for Islamic charity and religious purposes. At the time of the construction, Umno, being very powerful in the government, was able to 'collaborate' with Mainpp to see through the development of the land. Umno was to have only occupied several floors of the commercial building and was not necessarily the owner, although the building was named Menara Umno, and gave the impression that the party owned the property. See subsequent development below for the unravelling of all of these misrepresentations.
22. See some criticisms on this, "Menara Umno Pulau Pinang—Menimbulkan banyak tanda tanya", July 2013, http://kudaranggi.blogspot.com/2013/07/menara-umno-pulau-pinang-menimbulkan.html, accessed 14 April 2019.
23. Anwar was sacked as Deputy Prime Minister in 1998 by then Prime Minister Mahathir, then charged and imprisoned for sodomy, which led to a lengthy setback in his political career.
24. One of the victims was buried in the crater created by the impact of the pole hitting the ground; his body has never been found (Chow 2013). When asked about the status of Umno with regards to the building, an Umno committee member said that the party did not own the building and that it was Anwar Ibrahim who named the building after Umno. Hence, it was he who should be queried if the project was given special approval (New Straits Times 2013).

References

Abdul Hamid, Mohamad (2013) "Malaysia as a Hub for Islamic Finance: On choice of law and forum for settlement of disputes" in Mohammad Hashim Kamali and Sheila Ainon Yussof (eds), *Islamic Transactions and Finance: Principles and developments*, Kuala Lumpur: Malaysian Current Law Journal Sdn. Bhd and International Institute of Advanced Islamic Studies, 103–104.

Abdul Hamid, Mohamad and Adnan Trakic (2012) "The Shari'ah Advisory Council's Role in Resolving Islamic Banking Disputes in Malaysia: A model to follow?", Isra Research Paper No. 47, Kuala Lumpur: International Shari'ah Research Academy for Islamic Finance, 1–43.

Abdul Rahim, Abdul Rahman (2011) "Enhancing Integrity of Islamic Financial Institutions in Malaysia: The case for the Shari'ah audit framework," *Isra International Journal of Islamic Finance,* Vol. 3, Issue 1, 137–138.

Ahmad Hidayat, Buang (2007) "Islamic Contracts in a Secular Court Setting? Lessons from Malaysia", *Arab Law Quarterly*, Vol. 21, No. 4, 317–340.

Ahmadi, Khaliq (2016) "Islamic banking's challenges and goals", *New Straits Times*, 18 April.

Ahmed, Habib (2011) "Maqasid-al-Shari'ah and Islamic Financial Products: A framework for assessment," *Isra International Journal of Islamic Finance,* Vol. 3, Issue 1, 49–60.

Amanah Saham Nasional Berhad (2016) *Kompilasi Panduan Hukum Pelaburan ASB & ASN Harus* (Edisi Pertama), Kuala Lumpur: Amanah Saham Nasional Berhad.

Anan, C Mohd (2015) "Pembangunan wakaf menerusi pendanaan kerajaan dan kerjasama institusi kewangan dan korporat: Hala tuju, cabaran dan harapan", paper presented at Muzakarah Wakaf, held at Bank Negara Malaysia, 12 November.

Apnizan, Abdullah and Hakimah Yaacob (2012) The Trend of Legal Suits Involving Islamic Financial Transactions in Malaysia: Evidence from the reported cases, Research Paper No. 48, Kuala Lumpur: International Shari'ah Research Academy for Islamic Finance, 1–73.

Ariff, Mohamed and Saiful Azhar Rosly (2011) "Islamic Banking in Malaysia: Uncharted waters", *Asian Economic Policy Review*, Vol. 6, No. 2, 301–319.

Arnold, Wayne (2007) "Adapting finance to Islam", *The New York Times*, 22 November.

Astro Awani (2014) "Bank Negara urged to resolve loan issue of abandoned projects", 13 April, http://english.astroawani.com/malaysia-news/bank-negara-urged-resolve-loan-issue-abandoned-projects-33782. Accessed 11 March 2019.

——— (2017) "Mufti Selangor putuskan hukum pelaburan ASNB harus", 16 May, http://www.astroawani.com/berita-bisnes/mufti-selangor-putuskan-hukum-pelaburan-asnb-harus-142847, accessed 14 May 2019.

Azman, Ahmad (1995) "Plan for more takaful licences", *New Straits Times*, 22 December.

Bank Negara Malaysia (2010) *Resolusi Syariah dalam Kewangan Islam,* Kuala Lumpur: Bank Negara.

Berita Harian (2014) "Hukum pelaburan ASB, AS harus", 4 July.
——— (2015) "Tak perlu pertikai harus melabur ASB", 6 March.
——— (2017) "Kesepakatan syariah dalam pelaburan ASB", 29 September.
Buletin Mutiara (2018) "Mainpp teruskan tawaran kepada penghuni enggan pindah di tanah wakaf Masjid Abdul Cauder", 6 December, https://www.buletinmutiara.com/mainpp-teruskan-tawaran-kepada-penghuni-enggan-pindah-di-tanah-wakaf-masjid-abdul-cauder/. Accessed 16 March 2019.
Business Monitor Online (2011) "Islamic, mortgage products to maintain growth amid monetary tightening", 31 March.
Chow, Melissa Darlyne (2013) "Coroner visits storm mishap site", *New Straits Times*, 29 October.
Damodaram, Rupa (2012) "Zeti: Islamic finance doesn't need rebranding", *New Straits Times*, 21 September.
Dumenil, Gerard and Dominique Levy (2011) *The Crisis of Neoliberalism*, Cambridge, Massachusetts: Harvard University Press.
Elder, Laura (2017) "Gendered Accounts of Expertise Within Islamic Finance and Financialization in Malaysia", in Timothy P Daniels (ed), *Sharia Dynamics: Islamic law and sociopolitical processes*, Palgrave Macmillan, 171–201.
Fazleena, Aziz and Fairuz Mohd (2015) "Najib launches National Wakaf Corp, Wakaf Corporate Programme" *New Straits Times*, 14 July.
Financial Adviser (2014) "Sharia finance popular among non-Muslims", 13 February.
Goh, Joyce (2009) "50 Year of Central Banking in Malaysia: Unexpected catalyst for Islamic Banking", *The Edge Malaysia*, 9 February.
Gooch, Liz (2010) "High Achievers in High Finance: Malaysian women find acceptance as leaders in Islamic banking sector", *The International Herald Tribune*, 27 September.
Habib, Ahmed (2011) "Maqasid-al-Shari'ah ad Islamic Financial Products: A framework for assessment", *Isra International Journal of Islamic Finance*, Vol. 3, No. 1.
Hakimah, Yaacob (2010) "The New Central Bank of Malaysia Act 2009 (Act 701): Enhancing the integrity and role of the Shariah Advisory Council (SAC) in Islamic finance", Research Paper No. 6, Kuala Lumpur: International Shari'ah Research Academy for Islamic Finance (Isra) 1–29.
Harian Metro (2015) "Hormati keputusan fatwa—Hukum pelaburan ASB harus kerana maslahah ummah serta pelbagai faktor lain", 12 March.
Jakim (2009a) *Himpunan keputusan Muzakarah Jawatankuasa Fatwa Kebangsaan Berhubung Dengan Isu-isu Muamalat*, Putrajaya: Jakim.
——— (2009b) *Glosari Muamalat*, Putrajaya: Jakim.
Kahf, Monzer (2004) "Islamic Banks: The rise of a new power alliance of wealth and sharia scholarship" in Clement M Henry and Rodney Wilson (eds), *The Politics of Islamic Finance*, Edinburgh: Edinburgh University Press, 17–36.
Kamali, Mohammad Hashim (2008) Maqasid Al-Shari'ah Made Simple, Occasional Papers Series 13, London, Washington: The International Institute of Islamic Thought.

——— (2013) "Permissibility and Prohibitions in Islamic Transactions and Contracts", in Mohammad Hashim Kamali and Sheila Ainon Yusoff (eds) *Islamic Transactions and Finance: Principles and development,* Kuala Lumpur: Malaysian Current Law Journal Sdn. Bhd. and International Institute of Advanced Islamic Studies.

Kathirasen, A (1995) "Anwar's Advice to Penang Malays", *New Straits Times,* 22 December.

Khan, Feisal (2010) "How 'Islamic' is Islamic Banking?", *Journal of Economic Behavior and Organisation,* Vol. 76, No. 3, 805–820.

Kuran, Timur (2004) *Islam and Mammon: The Islamic predicaments of Islamism,* Princeton: Princeton University Press.

Malay Mail (2019) "For Penang Islamic Council, a costly RM3m and nine years to regain *wakaf* land", 11 March.

Malaysiakini (2012) "Kedah passes fatwa bill barring challenges in courts", 18 April.

Malaysian Bar (2012) "Press Release: Amendment to Mufti and Fatwa (Kedah Darul Aman) Enactment 2008 is unconstitutional and goes against separation of powers", 7 June, http://www.malaysianbar.org.my/press_statements/press_release_amendment_to_mufti_and_fatwa_kedah_darul_aman_enactment_2008_is_unconstitutional_and_goes_against_the_separation_of_powers.html. Accessed 28 January 2019.

Malkawi, Bashar H (2013) "Shari'ah Board in the Governance Structure of Islamic Financial Institutions", *The American Journal of Comparative Law,* Vol. 61, No. 3, 539–577.

Maznah, Mohamad and Johan Saravanamuttu (2015) "Islamic Banking and Finance: Sacred alignment, strategic alliances", *Pacific Affairs,* Vol. 88, No. 2, 193–213.

Md Nurdin, Ngadimon (2015) "Pembangunan wakaf: Pendanaan melaui Sukuk *Sustainable and Responsible Investment* (SRI)", paper presented at Muzakarah Ahli Majlis Penasihat Institusi Kewangan Di Malaysia Kali ke 11, held at Bank Negara Malaysia, 12 November.

Mohamed Hadi, Abd Hamid (2011) "Majlis Penasihat Syariah: Nasihat yang mesti dipatuhi", *Jurnal Muamalat,* No. 4, 187–198.

Mohammad Azam, Hussain, Rusni Hassan and Aznah Hasan (2015) "Analysis on the Development of Legislations Governing Shariah Advisory Council of Bank Negara Malaysia", *Jurnal Syariah,* Vol. 23, No. 2, 352–342.

MStar (2012) "Tunku Laksamana Kedah buat laporan polis mengenai pindaan enekmen", 22 April, https://www.mstar.com.my/lokal/semasa/2012/04/22/tunku-laksamana-kedah-buat-laporan-polis-mengenai-pindaan-enakmen. Accessed 14 May 2019.

Muhammad Hafiz, Muhammad Isa and Ahmad Azam Sulaiman@Mohamad (2017) "Polemik Skim Amanah Saham Bumiputera (ASB): Tinjauan terhadap perbezaan pandangan hukum", *Jurnal Muamalat,* No. 10, 181–206.

Muhammed, Ahmed Hamdan (2015) "Uda, Bank Muamalat ink *wakaf* land pact", *New Straits Times,* 21 January.

Mydin Meera, Ahmed Kameel (2012) "A Critique of the Diminishing Balance Method of Islamic Home Financing", *Isra International Journal of Islamic Finance*, Vol. 4, No. 2, 7–24.

Nadia, Badarudin (2012) "Feb 21 hearing of madrasah suit", *New Straits Times*, 7 February.

New Straits Times (1995a) "Experts to head Malaysian Wakaf Development Corporation", 26 September.

——— (1995b) "Plan to re-develop wakaf' land for benefit of Muslims", 19 April.

——— (1995c) "Menara Umno set to be the latest landmark in State", 22 December.

——— (1995d) "Court declines to rule on wakaf issue", 14 October.

——— (1995e) "Council told to speed up wakaf land development", 29 April.

——— (2006) "INCEIF Conferred University Status", 16 December.

——— (2007) "RM250m shot in the arm for wakaf land projects", 9 June.

——— (2009) "Bank Islam eyes new role in developing wakaf land", 17 December.

——— (2012a) "AIBIM: Islamic banks not reaping excessive profits", 22 February.

——— (2012b) "Kedah should review mall project", 21 January.

——— (2012c) "Madrasah panel gets order against council", 15 May.

——— (2013) "Menara Umno's Proud History", 19 June.

——— (2015) "ASN and ASB put priority on harus elements", 30 March.

Nizam, Yatim (2018) "Perbankan Islam menekan pengguna?", *Utusan Online*, 19 October.

Noor Adzman, Baharudin (2011) "Save the surau and get plenty of good 'doa'", *New Straits Times*, 18 November.

Ong, Aihwa (2006) *Neoliberalism as Exception: Mutations in citizenship and sovereignty*, Durham and London: Duke University Press.

Perak Today (2012) "Undang-undang 'fatwa' Kedah tidak ikut prinsip Islam, kata Mufti Perlis", 19 April, https://peraktoday.com.my/2012/04/undang-undang-'fatwa'-kedah-tidak-ikut-prinsip-islam-kata-mufti-perlis/. Accessed 28 January 2019.

Permodalan Nasional Berhad (2017) *Annual Report 2017: 40 years of nation building—Enhancing the wealth of Malaysians*, Kuala Lumpur: Permodalan Nasional Berhad.

Rethel, Lena (2011) "Whose legitimacy? Islamic Finance and the Global Financial Order", *Review of International Political Economy*, Vol. 18, No. 1, 75–98.

Rozita, Abu Bakar, Anuar Nawawi and Ahmad Saiful Azlin Puteh Salin (2015) "Determinants of lower bumiputera participation in the variable-price unit trust investments", *International Academic Research Journal of Social Science*, Vol. 1, No. 1, 58–66.

Securities Commission of Malaysia (2009) *Senarai Sekuriti Patuh Syariah oleh Majlis Penasihat Syariah Suruhanjaya Sekuriti Malaysia* (List of Shariah-Compliant Securities by the Shariah Advisory Council of the Securities Commission of Malaysia), 30 November.

——— (2010) *Senarai Sekuriti Patuh Syariah oleh Majlis Penasihat Syariah Suruhanjaya Sekuriti Malaysia* (List of Shariah-Compliant Securities by the Shariah Advisory Council of the Securities Commission of Malaysia), 26 November.

——— (2018) *Senarai Sekuriti Patuh Syariah oleh Majlis Penasihat Syariah Suruhanjaya Sekuriti Malaysia* (List of Shariah-Compliant Securities by the Shariah Advisory Council of the Securities Commission of Malaysia), 25 May.

Sheila Ainon, Yusoff and Abdullah Masoud Humeid AlHarthy (2014) "Malaysia's Governance Framework for Islamic Institutions", in Mohammad Hashim Kamali and Sheila Ainon Yusoff (eds) *Islamic Transactions and Finance: Principles and development,* Kuala Lumpur: Malaysian Current Law Journal Sdn. Bhd. and International Institute of Advanced Islamic Studies.

Sim, Bak Heng and Roziana Hamsawi, "New Islamic Banking Law," *New Straits Times*, 7 December 2012.

Star Online (2011) "PAS-led govt accused of practising double standards", 19 December.

——— (2016) "Mall reigns as largest in Kedah", 29 March.

——— (2019) "First 'super bench' of nine judges decides Bank Negara Council supercedes civil courts on syariah matters", 10 April.

Syed Farhan, Shah, Mohammad Wajid Raza and Malik Rizwan Khurshid (2012) "Islamic Banking Controversies and Challenges," *Interdisciplinary Journal of Contemporary Research Business,* Vol. 3, No. 10, 1018–1026.

The Edge Malaysia (2007) "Islamic Banking More Dynamic", 9 March.

The Globe and Mail (2010) "Wanted: Female financial advisers who know Sharia principles", 4 November.

The Malaysian Insider (2014) "What's in a name? Islamic banking rebrands in attempt to go mainstream" 2 July, http://www.themalaysianinsider.com/business/article/whats-in-a-name-islamic-banking-rebrands-in-attempt-to-go-mainstream. Accessed 3 July 2014.

The Straits Times (2013) "Recognizing Potential of Islamic Banking", 14 June.

Trofimov, Yaroslav (2007) "Malaysia blazes a trail in global Islamic finance", *The Wall Street Journal Asia*, 4 April.

Tunku Yusuf, Jewa (2012) "It is termite-riddled, let it go", *New Straits Times,* 6 January.

Utusan Online (2015) "Perbankan Islam tiada 'roh Islam', zalim?", 23 October.

Warde, Ibrahim (2010) *Islamic Finance in the Global Economy*, Edinburgh: Edinburgh University Press.

Zarinah, Anwar (2009) "Preface", *Islamic Equity Market*, Kuala Lumpur: Securities Commission of Malaysia.

Zulkifli, Hasan (2012) "Menilai Semula Pelaksanaan Kewangan Islam", *Journal Muamalat,* No. 5, 97–109.

CHAPTER 8

The Power of Disenchantment

Introduction

To date there has been an extensive body of scholarship to explain the growing intensity of religiosity among Muslims in Malaysia. Some have attributed this to a vigorous adoption of Islam by the state in its move to neutralise other religio-political competitors, as well as in the use of religion as its source of legitimacy and national identity (Nasr 2001; Liow 2009; Ahmad Fauzi 2007; Norshahril 2018). Other studies have focused on understanding why and how the extensive use and application of *syariah* as formal statute and living law for the governance of Muslims and Muslim matters have been the driving force for greater Islamisation and its ensuing conflicts in society (Moustafa 2018; Daniels 2017). Beyond politics and law, the concept of *syariahtisation* has been recognised as contributing to 'corporate Islam' in the understanding of Islamic religiosity in finance, economy and modern work life (Sloane-White 2017). Equally on the obverse side, some scholars question if a monolithic Islam is not in itself constantly subverted at the everyday level, since Islam is also being interpreted, performed or inhabited in multiple and plural ways (Hoffstaedter 2014). The act of piety at the individual, gendered, non-

The original version of this chapter was revised. Text has been updated. Correction to this chapter can be found at https://doi.org/10.1007/978-981-15-2093-8_9

M. Mohamad, *The Divine Bureaucracy and Disenchantment of Social Life*, Contestations in Contemporary Southeast Asia,
https://doi.org/10.1007/978-981-15-2093-8_8

state collective level also defies the stark dichotomy of submission, passivity on one side and empowerment, autonomy on the other (Frisk 2009). The Divine Bureaucracy is but one of many lenses in the understanding of social life infused with religiosity. The interface between religiosity and bureaucratisation as reflective of the "shift in the balance of Muslim piety from an other-worldly towards a this-worldly focus" (Robinson 2004, 47) deserves to be more adequately explored as a crucial focus of studies on the transformation of Islam.

This book has introduced a different framework of analysis to explain similar questions around the rise, prominence, ubiquitousness and vigour of Islam in Malaysia today. Its main postulation is that the expanding visibility and palpability of Islamic piety has been due to the proliferation, enlargement and accretion of institutions of religious governance funded and facilitated by the state. This immense sense of reorganisation is not only driven by piety or cultural ideology but also by the instrumentalist goals of "administration, social control, ethnicity and modernisation" (Benjamin 2014, 310). These institutions, once enlarged in magnitude and interlocking in their interdependence, became akin to a Divine Bureaucracy with religious attributes and power conjoined through a secular modality. However, this is far from saying that the outcome of such secularising exercises or the disenchantment they generate has not been a powerful force in and of itself. In a paradoxical twist, people can even be enchanted by the option of a disenchanted religious life; rules, laws and methods towards the achievement of ordered behaviour, conduct, disposition, deportment, mien and style are agential in themselves (Mahmood 2005). Hence, the domination of the Divine Bureaucracy would have been routinised in a normal sense, with the subjects enchanted by the spell of disenchantment—the Foucauldian implication of being disciplined without noticing it, even enfolding it.[1]

Nilai, *Syariah*, *Akidah and Syariah* Compliance

To recapitulate, this study has demonstrated that the postcolonial state's Islamisation project in Malaysia traversed several successive discursive fields to bolster the Divine Bureaucracy's expansion and modernisation. The case studies in Chaps. 4, 5, 6 and 7, respectively on standardising faith, ring-fencing constituents, perfecting marriage and purifying money, showed that there were four major narratives which ran throughout the motivations and features of practice the Divine Bureaucracy. The first was the superiority of Islamic ethics and values (*nilai*); the second, of Islamic law as the pillar of religious identity (*syariah*); the third, of the indefinable notion of creed or *akidah* as the ultimate test of Islamic personhood; and fourth, of the calculable translation of Islamic permissibility through the yardstick of *syariah* compliance. These narratives have marked the expansionary stimulus and moments in the rise of bureaucratic Islam in Malaysia.

The first period of postcolonial Islamisation, starting from the government under the first Prime Minister (PM), Tunku Abdul Rahman, until the late 1990s under the Mahathir administration, saw Islamisation being elevated on the basis of its compelling sense of ethics, effect and emotional appeal. Islamic values of moral restraint and discipline, and time-honoured rituals of devotion provided the stabilising essence of the Malay identity. The second period under the premierships of Abdullah Ahmad Badawi and Najib Abdul Razak saw a peaking of the Divine Bureaucracy's presence in social life through the standardisation of faith and ring-fencing of Muslims as Chaps. 4 and 5 showed. In Chap. 6, *syariah* legal reform and judicialisation were revealed as enabling the family as a site of Islamic performativity. Finally, the infusion of capital in Islamic finance introduced the technocracy of *syariah* compliance as another calculable marker of Islamicness.

The postcolonial state's involvement in developing Islam as a governmental priority began as early as 1962 when the Pilgrims' Savings and Deposits Bank was established to support the financial needs of pilgrims for their *hajj*. To go on a pilgrimage was a necessary devotional ritual for Muslims and creating a financial institution for this purpose was one of the first significant Islamisation projects undertaken by the postcolonial government. Even before the challenge of Islamic revivalist movements began to influence policy directions on Islam from about the late 1970s, the federal government had already established various Islamic institutions. The significance of Islamic development as the foundation of ethics culminated in the government policy of *Penerapan Nilai-Nilai Islam Dalam Pentadbiran* (The Integration of Islamic Values in Administration) launched in 1985.

The second narrative of *syariah* law as the pillar of Islamisation gained strength from 1988 onwards. This was the year that Parliament passed the constitutional amendment to separate the jurisdiction of the *syariah* court from the civil court. The formation of the Technical Committee on Syariah and Civil Laws in 1988 was key to the multiplication of *syariah* legislation and the expansion of the *syariah* court system. The professed goal of this exercise was to standardise, uniformise and elevate *syariah* as the pillar of Islamisation and to institutionalise Islamic justice. Although Islamic matters were under the jurisdiction of each *negeri* (State, subnational unit of governance), the expansion of *syariah* through central coordination was thought to be the only feasible way to achieve such an objective. Centralisation meant that the development of Islamic institutions had to be decided by the national leadership, specifically through the PM's Department. This role was entrusted to the Jabatan Kemajuan Islam Malaysia (Jakim, Department of Islamic Development Malaysia), the de facto Ministry of Islamic Affairs. Under Jakim, the Technical Committee on Syariah and Civil Laws was a critical body in drafting almost all the new or revised *syariah* laws after the 1980s (Norhashimah 1996, 218–219). The groundwork for the Islamisation of laws was laid out in publications by those like Ahmad Ibrahim and Mahmud Saedon Awang Othman (1988). In this manner, the intellectual force behind early *syariah* law reforms emanated from the centre.

Early efforts to elevate the *syariah* court took the shape of revising its powers to mete out punishment. Under the Muslim Court (Criminal Jurisdiction) Act 1965, the maximum penalty that a *syariah* court could impose was six months' imprisonment and a fine of RM1000. In the 1980s, through pressure from the Islamic lobby, this act was amended with the passing of the Muslim Courts (Criminal Jurisdiction) Act 1984, to give the *syariah* court powers to impose a punishment of imprisonment of up to three years, a maximum fine of RM5000 as well as six strokes of the cane (Norhashimah 1996, 213). Still, this enhancement of court powers was not considered sufficiently severe by the Islamic lobby, since according to some scholars on Islam the punishment for illicit sex (*zina)* is purportedly stoning till death; for apostasy, also death (Mohd Izani 2005, 160), and for drinking alcohol, 100 strokes of the cane (Mahmood Zuhdi 2001, 179).

A bill proposed in Parliament in 2017 to amend the Syariah Court (Criminal Jurisdiction) Act, popularly known as RU355, sought to increase punishments that could be meted by *syariah* courts to 30 years' imprisonment, a fine of RM100,000 and up to 100 strokes of the cane, equivalent to the criminal sentencing limits of the Sessions Court. So severe were the moral crimes of Muslims that they were thought to deserve such extreme punishment (The Star Online 2017a). Even though the bill was proposed by the leader of Pas, Umno, the ruling party before May 2018, appeared to back this as a means of winning the Malay vote for the upcoming general election (Zulkifli et al. 2017). This bill was not passed before the election, and since then has not been raised under the new government.

Jakim, whose main role during its inception was the coordination of *syariah* centralisation, subsequently grew to become the dominant and omnipresent face of Islam in the public eye. The strength and ubiquity of

Jakim were not only facilitated by the *syariahtisation* of laws but in various other areas of social life regulation. While its role in the reinforcement and expansion of *syariah* laws has been the most important source of its legitimacy, there have also been other pivots of authority on which it could pull its weight. As analysed in Chap. 3, there were numerous episodes and spheres of everyday life that saw Jakim's presence and intervention as the overseer of Islamic rules and conduct. Jakim does not have the power to enforce laws or *fatwa* (legal opinion), but it has ample resources to implant, spread and entrench certain dominant narratives about Islamisation into society. By doing so, it is able to activate the Islamic bureaucracy of each *negeri* to use powers of *syariah* enforcement to its maximum effect. Jakim's role in standardising faith, in streamlining and refining the bounds of as well as the threats to *akidah* was one aspect of its powers that surfaced in the early 2000s. It was not a case of only *syariahtisation*. It was about applying *akidah* as the 'blue chip' or 'gold standard' benchmark of Islamic subjectivity. The most correct and absolute Islam was declared to be *Ahli Sunnah Wal Jamaah* (ASWJ). This, however, was only defined in a national *fatwa* in 2012 after Jakim held a workshop in 2010 on *Definisi Ahli Sunnah Wal Jamaah* (The Definition of Ahli Sunnah Wal Jamaah) (Mohd Aizam 2015, 19). The *fatwa* was deliberate in specifying who did *not* belong to the stream of ASWJ, among these were "*Islam liberal, [dan] pluralisme agama* (liberal Islam, [and] religious pluralism)". There are no statutory laws on this prohibition, only *fatwa*.

Interestingly enough, the National Fatwa Committee was one of the first to issue a *fatwa* in July 2006, singling out the *Aliran Pemikiran Liberal* (Liberal Thought Stream) for having deviated from the aspects of *akidah* and *syariah* (Jakim 2012, 18–19). This was even before the issuance of the ASWJ *fatwa* in 2012. This 'prohibition of liberalism' *fatwa* was followed, more than a decade later, by the Selangor *fatwa* on *Pemikiran Liberalisme dan Pluralisme Agama* (Thoughts on Liberalism and Religious Pluralism) in 2014. The Selangor *fatwa* specifically lists Sis Forum Sdn Bhd—better known as Sisters in Islam, a Muslim women's organisation—in this category as a group that had allegedly gone astray and deviated from the teachings of Islam. The narrative and professing of correct *akidah* has thus been elevated as the absolute way of determining one's commitment and subject identity to Islam, as embodying firmness and absolutism to the faith (*kemuktamadan, keyakinan, pegangan, keutuhan dan kepercayaan*) (Mohd Aizam 2015, 22).

A bureaucratic scientific-rational measurement for Islamic permissibility is one of the latest in the succession of narratives and method for 'authentic' Islam. The benchmark of *syariah* compliance is an instrument of Islamic capitalism. Although not tantamount to the definitive validation of *halal* (permissible) versus *haram* (prohibited), the *syariah*-compliant narrative has also added to the germaneness of a bureaucracy in its charge, and in its growth within the corporate realms. The collusion of *syariah* and civil judicial institutions, the augmentation of *syariah* by legitimising it as a constitutional provision, and its syncretic absorption of various traditions of law, including secular laws and customary practices, are some of the developments that have paradoxically contributed to deepening what is purportedly the 'pure', 'authentic' and 'immutable' Islam of today. The state and its Divine Bureaucracy perform this role by extending and deepening the uses of Islamic elements, from ethics to *syariah* to *akidah*, and, in so doing, project the agenda of an Islamising state seemingly countering the dangers of secularism.

On the part of the everyday life of Muslims, their time-honoured obligations of daily prayers, annual fasting, paying *zakat* (religious tithe/tax), performing the *hajj* and assuming a new Muslim 'lifestyle' through dressing and *halal* consumption are now being performed more extensively due to state resources for *dakwah* (propagation) being available on a larger and more organised scale. The coordination of these activities was made possible by an extensive bureaucracy leading to the minimisation of social interactions with non-Muslims, reproduction of social distancing and the proliferation of more community enclaves (Kamaludeen et al. 2010). All these have rendered the Muslim social life more exclusivist than ever before.

Looking deeper, there are ensuing conflicts. The state pushes for more laws, regulations and stipulations on homogeneity to govern the Muslim subject more definitively, less ambivalently. However, citizens are also going the opposite direction, pushing for more freedom of expression, pluralism and heterogeneity within Islam. Besides the urban-based so-called liberal Muslim civil society that is targeted by the Divine Bureaucracy, the mushrooming of *tarekat* (Sufi) groups and forms of 'deviant' religious followings is also a manifestation of an unstoppable Islamic plurality. Islamisation through bureaucratic rationality also appears to have failed to exclude Malay spirit cults, shamanism and mysticism in the social life of Muslims, one reason being, "Malays continue to be extremely fearful and anxious about being poisoned and sorcerized" (Peletz 1993, 102).

The rationalisation process merely gave rise to another class of Malays who have been able to use their bureaucratic position and authority to 'de-magicalise' Malay religious life with rules, procedures, policies and laws (Mohd Aizam 2015, 395–444) but whose success is still questionable. Despite its overpowering regulations, methods and enforcement procedures, the Divine Bureaucracy has continued to see threats to itself—as the bearer of absolute Islam—in the form of magic and mysticism, of syncretic devotional practices and of the 'contaminating' ideologies of liberalism, pluralism, feminism and all forms of human rights discourse. The relevance of the Divine Bureaucracy, and to a lesser extent its corporate domain, appears almost hinged on the assertion and invention of enemies and adversaries. This has provided the Divine Bureaucracy with an excuse to exercise its superordinate authority to standardise and ring-fence Muslims. Of particular note is how the corporate Islamic bureaucracy has been shown to be different in sense that its 'antagonists' can emerge from the traditional *negeri* or federal Islamic bureaucracies and also from ordinary Muslims who have yet to benefit from a monetised Islam.

Divine Bureaucracy and Political Transition

The discussion of the Divine Bureaucracy would be incomplete if its existence and manifestations are not examined within the context of a politically transitioning Malaysia. About a month after the victory of the Pakatan Harapan (PH) coalition in the country's 14th general election in May 2018, the Group of 25 (G25) called on the new government to conduct a review of Jakim and abolish several government institutions (The Star Online 2018a). Zan Azlee, a columnist in the online news portal *Malaysiakini*, targeted Jakim as the main focus in his laundry list of possible reforms in the area of Islamic affairs, questioning its stance on matters such as the LGBT community and the exclusive use of the word 'Allah' by Muslims. Citing PM Mahathir Mohamad, he argued that Jakim should ensure that Islam was not portrayed as a cruel and inconsiderate religion (Zan 2018). Not long after, however, the new de facto Minister-in-Charge of Islamic Affairs, Mujahid Yusof Rawa, sparked controversy when he introduced a dress code for Muslim women in the private sector, supposedly to prevent discrimination against them (Shakira 2018). A local women's NGO, Women's Aid Organisation (2018), argued that "the minister ha[d] missed the point completely. Restricting what women wear is, in and of itself, discriminatory, and this policy would end up discriminating women who do not conform to the code".

One of the more 'radical' ideas of the new Minister was to stop religious enforcers from carrying out midnight raids on couples found in close proximity (*khalwat*) (Zakiah 2018). He distinguished between committing wrongs in private versus in public spaces, noting that what transpired in private was not the concern of enforcement officers. PM Mahathir supported this view saying that, "If you have to climb inside a person's house and all that (to find wrongdoings), that is not Islam" (Alyaa 2018). All this was not well received by the traditional bureaucracy, especially the *mufti* from various *negeri*. Those from Pahang, Perak and Negeri Sembilan, in particular, flexed their muscles and asserted that it was within their assigned powers to prevent vice wherever it happened (Malaysiakini 2018a). A day later, the Minister distanced himself from his own earlier statement and claimed the news report had misrepresented his views (Malaysiakini 2018b). The backtracking was confirmed after the Pahang regent, who also headed the Pahang Religious and Malay Custom Council, stressed that the anti-vice raid operations would continue as long as these were done in accordance to the law and regulations of the *negeri* (Bernama 2018c). Subsequently, the Minister sought an apology from the newspaper (Malaysiakini 2018c), which then declared that it regretted the misrepresentation (The Star Online 2018b).

Long before being re-elected as the country's seventh Prime Minister, Mahathir had already expressed his disagreement with Jakim's excessive moral policing tendencies (Dina 2014). He also disagreed with the FT Zakat Council, which said that *zakat* should not be paid directly to the poor but had to be channelled through the government collection centre. He was reiterating the position that believed there was no compulsion in Islam (Izra 2015). A month after taking office as Malaysia's newest Prime Minister, Mahathir announced that a group of former civil servants, intellectuals and scholars, with and without Islamic backgrounds, would review and assess Jakim (Malaysiakini 2018d). Anwar Ibrahim also agreed that Jakim's role in certain areas such as *halal* certification was excessive and that its RM1 billion annual budget was very large (Malaysiakini 2018e). The PM's proposal was not well received by some quarters, particularly a Malay-rights group called Pemantau Malaysia Baru, which threatened to hold a rally if Jakim's role was reviewed, at the same time to protest against the alleged withholding of mosque upgrading funds and salaries of teachers of *quranic* classes (Faisal 2018).

Nevertheless, the Mahathir government went ahead to establish the Jawatankuasa Tertinggi Institusi Hal Ehwal Islam Peringkat Persekutuan (High-Level Committee on Federal Islamic Affairs Institutions) in July 2018, with the approval of the Council of Rulers. Accordingly, several Islamic institutions were asked for feedback on the management of Islamic affairs, including the restructuring of Jakim. The Committee was headed by Ahmad Sarji Abdul Hamid, former Chief Secretary to the federal government; Afifi Al-Akiti, a fellow at the Oxford Centre for Islamic Studies, was named his deputy. There were also five other members in this body (Anne 2018; Ismail 2018). It welcomed the public and NGOs to send feedback pertaining to any aspect of Islamic administration by 1 October 2018 (Rizanizam 2018), and proposed dividing its study of 102 institutions into five clusters: finance and economy, education, *syariah* and law, political organisations and NGOs (Mohd Iskandar 2018). The Committee was to meet for three days each week for a period of five months at the old Istana Negara (National Palace) in Kuala Lumpur (Bernama 2018d).

After the May 2018 electoral turnaround, there seemed to be two opposing trends where Islamic administration and authority was concerned. On the one hand, the old agenda and orientations of the Divine Bureaucracy seemed to be too resilient to undo. On the other, the newly elected government appeared to be responding positively to criticisms of the excesses of the previous Islamic governance. Below is a further discussion of the two oppositional tendencies.

New Government, Old Orientations

Thus far, Mujahid Yusof Rawa, the de facto Islamic affairs Minister, has frequently fallen back on the narratives and policies already set in motion by his predecessor in the Najib government, Jamil Khir Baharom. This pertains particularly to stances on ring-fencing 'unacceptable' groups, such as the LGBT community, liberals, pluralists and feminists. LGBTs remain the most persistent target of vilification as well as enforced rehabilitation. A few months after Mujahid's appointment, he attempted to show a conciliatory face by meeting with a well-known transgender activist Nisha Ayub, though maintaining that this did not mean that he agreed with LGBT struggles (Bernama 2018a). Subsequently, he launched an e-book entitled *Panduan Hijrah Diri* (Guide for Rehabilitation), a project started by his predecessor (Bernama 2018b). In late 2018, the new government also backed down from its intention to ratify the United

Nations International Convention on the Elimination of All Forms of Racial Discrimination (Icerd). This was after Malay and Muslim parties and NGOs held a rally to protest against the treaty, claiming that it would abolish the rights of Malays, privileges of Malay rulers and religious strictures of Islam (Malaysiakini 2018e; Hariz and Fakhrull 2018).

Following an International Women's Day rally in the capital city in March 2018, Mujahid again came under the spotlight when he chastised its organisers for allegedly promoting LGBT rights, which he insisted was an abuse of democracy (Malaysiakini 2019a). This invited counter-reactions from civil society, including the Centre for Independent Journalism. It said his misogynistic insinuations were uncalled for and were tantamount to the government trivialising women's issues (Malaysiakini 2019b). The following month, social activist Maryam Lee launched her book, *Unveiling Choice*, at a forum titled 'Malay Women and De-Hijabbing' with two other women speakers, Dian Sofia and Mohani Niza. Complaints through social media prompted the same Minister to ask Jais, the Selangor religious department, to probe the event (Anne and Lee 2019). The three women responded that they would not cooperate with the probe as they had not broken any laws by having a rational and intellectual dialogue on the issue (Malaysiakini 2019c). A Pas woman senator, Nuridah Mohd Salleh, subsequently called for the book to be banned under the Printing and Printing Presses Act 1984, as the action was considered "disconcerting and shook the minds of many people" (*perbuatan yang tidak disenangi dan menggemparkan fikiran orang ramai*) (Nuridah 2019). This news was carried by the international press, including *The Guardian*, *The Straits Times*, *The Jakarta Post* and the *South China Morning Post*.

Compassionate Islam: New Vision or Platitude?

One of the new government's first targets for closure was Institut Kajian Strategik Islam Malaysia (Iksim, Institute of Islamic Strategic Research Malaysia). This outfit was created in 2012, ostensibly to redress the LGBT issue that was portrayed as threatening the Muslim *akidah*. Formed with the approval of MKI, Jakim and the SIRCs, Iksim was registered as a company, not a government agency. It was headed by the then de facto Minister of Islamic Affairs, Jamil Khir Baharom (Khairil 2017). Iksim also claimed that it was part of the strategy to fight the influence of the Islamic State (IS). It recommended that a compulsory "anti-IS" module be offered to students pursuing their studies overseas, presumably to prevent them from being 'brainwashed' when they are abroad (The Star Online 2015). Funded by Maiwp's *zakat* funds under the *fisabilillah* recipient category—those who serve in the path of Allah to defend and uphold Islam—Iksim claimed to have reached 300,000 participants within three years to influence them on the dangers of liberalism, secularism and extreme evangelism (Mahamad Naser 2018). It was later disclosed that the amount of *zakat* funds transferred from Maiwp to the institute was RM10 million in 2018 (Malaysiakini 2019). A prominent academic and legal expert, Shad Faruqi wrote about how Iksim had produced a booklet to declare that secularism, liberalism and cultural diversity could undermine the Islamic agenda, while asserting that the country should not be obliged to protect other religions (Faruqi 2017). The group subsequently lodged a police report against Faruqi (The Star Online 2017b). In October 2017, the then opposition Member of Parliament Khalid Abdul Samad threatened to sue the Iksim CEO for defamation if he did not publicly apologise in mainstream newspapers and pay a compensation of RM1 million. This was after the Iksim CEO had accused him of opposing the aforementioned RU355 to increase the limits of punishments by *syariah* courts and pave the way for *hudud* law in the country (Anne 2017). Early in 2018, one of its research fellows even urged that a *fatwa* be issued to make it *haram* for Muslims to vote for the Democratic Action Party (DAP) in the forthcoming general election allegedly because it was anti-Islam (Roketkini.com 2018). Iksim had also labelled Mujahid Rawa and other Muslim opposition politicians as supporters of liberalism, pluralism and LGBTs (Danial 2018). These actions represented the different ways in which Jakim employed the *akidah* narrative to defend its regulation and demonisation of competing groups of non-compliant, Muslim civil society.

After the victory of the PH coalition, Noor Farida Ariffin, founding head of G25, called for the dismantling of Iksim, stating that they "were not sure what they [Iksim] are doing… maligning other Muslims as apostates and liberals" (Carvalho 2018). In July 2018, the government froze public funding to Iksim pending investigation into its status (The Star Online 2018c). The organisation was also alleged to have mismanaged its funds, of which some RM7 million from the government had been unaccounted (Utusan Online 2018). When Iksim's funding was withdrawn, it attacked the PH government claiming that it had been voted in by non-Muslims and upholders of the liberal-secular agenda, hence supporting those who threatened the supremacy of Islam in the country (Mahamad

Naser 2018). It is difficult not to associate the formation of Iksim with the political agenda of Umno, which may have utilised the anti-liberalism and anti-secularism narrative (as protection of *akidah*) to dissuade Muslims from voting for the then opposition.

Was there then a move to 'cleanse' Jakim of its increasingly partisan and religious and ethnically divisive role under the new PH government? The G25 also called on the Council of Rulers to review Jakim's functions, with one member pressing for its immediate dissolution since it was not established according to constitutional provisions that place Islam under the purview of *negeri* rather than federal authority (Carvalho 2018). In terms of funding, the federal budget allocation for Islamic development in 2019 was around RM1 billion, up by RM13 million from the previous year. An additional RM50 million was allocated to religious schools not under the administration of either *negeri* or federal governments, namely *tahfiz* (*quranic* memorisation) schools, and RM25 million for registered *pondok* (traditional religious) schools. Another RM150 million was set aside for mosque and *surau* (community prayer hall) repairs (Mujahid 2019, 34). Islamic development administration under the PM's Department was also reorganised into seven clusters—(1) law and the judiciary, (2) education and human development, (3) *dakwah* and media, (4) socio-economy, (5) *hajj* management and *halal* certification, (6) mosque management and (7) research and *maqasid* culture—with *maqasid syariah* and *rahmatan lil 'alamin* as the foundational guide (Mujahid 2019, 36–37).

In fact, *rahmatan lil 'alamin* and *maqasid syariah* are two of the three pillars under the PH government's new thrust for Islamic development in the country, the third is the Malaysian Model. The concept *rahmatan lil 'alamin* denotes the universal good, that God's blessing is for the whole universe regardless of ethnicity and culture, with love, unity and tolerance as the key underpinnings (Mujahid 2019, 30). *Maqasid syariah* stresses that every decision and action must take into consideration the interests of a multiracial society to avoid hate and religious and racial misunderstanding (Mujahid 2019, 31). The Malaysian Model or the *manhaj Malizi* requires that the approach to all of this be appropriately local, taking into account Malaysia's ethnic, religious and cultural diversity (Mujahid 2019, 32). Diversity and plurality must be suited to Malaysia's own method (*manhaj*) of addressing Islam and other religions that is particular and unique to its setting. In short under the new government there is now an aspiration to instil a more compassionate form of Islam.

Aside from harmony and avoidance of hatred and enmity among religions appropriate to the Malaysian Model of ethnic pluralism, the terms blessings (*rahmah*), peace (*aman*), harmony (*harmoni*), friendly (*mesra*) and respect (*hormat*) are to be emphasised as well (Mujahid 2019, 29). This approach is derived from the Quran, *Surah al-Anbiya:21*, verse 107 that states, “We have sent you forth as nothing but mercy to people of the whole world[2] (*Kami tidak mengutuskan engku, wahai Muhammad, melainkan sebagai rahmat bagi seluruh manusia*)”. It gives the sense that Islam is a religion of blessing or love (*rahmat*) for all, and hence the possibility of interfaith dialogue and understanding (Nidhal 2019).

This approach to cultivating harmony has not been taken too kindly by detractors on social media who insisted that this would place Islam on par as other religions, while others claimed that this was the usual platitudes of new governments, as in *Penerapan Nilai-Nilai Islam* under Mahathir, *Islam Hadhari* (Civilisational Islam) under Abdullah Badawi and *wasatiyyah* (‘moderation’ or ‘moderate’ Islam) under Najib.[3] The Minister himself was accused of being a liberal in implementing the *rahmatan lil alamin* (Zanariah 2018). According to one Muslim scholar, even though the notion of universal tolerance and acceptance is derived from a *quranic* verse, it must still be accepted with caution and not mean being ‘apologetic’ to the extent of compromising on Islamic principles against LGBT for example (Abdul Ghafar 2018).

As expected, Umno and Pas also criticised this approach. Now in opposition, Umno claimed that it would be abused for vote-baiting and promoting the freedom of ‘deviant’ groups such as Syiahs, Qadiani and LGBTs (Mohd Anwar 2018). Pas maintained that the PH government appeared to be trying to protect the rights of non-Muslims over Muslims. It also reminded the Minister to ensure the Muslim faith was still strongly based on *akidah* rather than anything else (Aslani 2019). This resort to *akidah* replays the strategy of Jakim under the old administration to draw a line between compliant Muslims and those outside the ambit of the Divine Bureaucracy. To be sure, *rahmatan lil alamin* has spurred some intellectual debates over the appropriateness of its usage by the present government, although for now it is still ambiguously accepted by sceptical Islamic factions (Ahmad Sanusi and Mohd Yusuf 2018).

Minister Muhajid’s bowing to pressure from the Divine Bureaucracy and its allies shows how this entity can draw power beyond that of the elected authority. The bureaucracy is a “permanent machine” for the use of different rulers (Allen 2004, 113). At least for the few months after the installation of the new government, the Divine Bureaucracy prevailed over most questions related to Islam, as it was not answerable to any constituency or vote bank and continued to operate as per usual despite the change in political leadership. Its roles in the overarching project and resurgence of Islamisation span at least three domains of Islamic bureaucratisation—*negeri*, federal and corporate—attesting to the vast and interlocking extent of its governance, authority and control over the social life of Muslims.

Bureaucratisation, Rationalisation and Disenchantment Restated

This book has affirmed that when religious-based values are inscribed into a formal bureaucratic legal system, *syariah* as a legal and philosophical body of ideas takes on a Weberian paradigm with its concomitant execution of rational means and ends. Bureaucracies can mutate from serving as the means to a larger goal, eventually becoming an end in themselves (Constas 1958, 400–401). This study of Malaysia's Divine Bureaucracy has shown that at times it can veer towards an authoritarian bureaucracy, though not one that fully challenges democratic procedures since both can almost coexist in parallel as in *syariah* court jurisdiction alongside civil court jurisdiction. An exception to this synchrony was litigation involving Muslim-non-Muslim family units, discussed in Chap. 6. The Malaysian case also demonstrates that formerly traditional *ulama* have been absorbed into the bureaucracy and occupy sinecure positions. The extraordinary quality of old *ulama*-saints or their charisma, which draws people into their circle of beliefs and devotion, would have been routinised through the bureaucratisation process.

Yet, being a bureaucracy in the service of religion has imparted a Divine quality to bureaucrats, even if in a routinised form. The Divine Bureaucracy thrives on both modernity and antiquity. As revealed, postcolonial Islamisation has been strongly driven by temporal devices for its vitalisation, for instance, the systematic technologies of governance, rational legal structures and the free market. The utilisation of the knowledge base and epistemological foundations of the sacred realm and collection of texts of an imagined authentic past, while at the same time constituting the bureaucratic structures as a storehouse of religious resources, often impregnable to the ordinary Muslim, seals the divinity of this bureaucracy. In effect, Islamisation in Malaysia has become naturalised, normalised and engrained into the wide swathe of Muslim social life as religious orderliness and a regular code of conduct. This is an outcome that would be unattainable by political movements or disparate charismatic saints competing for followers and devotees.

Conclusion

This study has shown that Islamic development has taken a hold over the state itself, precisely because of its Divine Bureaucracy. The latter has been exceptionally privileged in realising its goals and agenda through the disbursement of generous state funding. Nevertheless, in doing so, the advancement of religion and religiosity has taken on the form of the secular, becoming more rationalised, differentiated, measurable, accountable, worldly and disenchanted. Here it is in theology's precise "possession of sacred values" that religion is being rationalised (Weber 1991, 153). It is a rationalisation that has led to the transformation, rather than the rejection of religion. In its distinctiveness, the Divine Bureaucracy is the formidable this-worldly power—*standardising* Islamic beliefs and practices, *ring-fencing* the Muslim subject, *perfecting* the Islamic family and *purifying* money in the emergent Islamic economy. Unavoidably, social life has become disenchanted, even though disenchantment itself may be embraced and even celebrated by those under its spell.

Notes

1. Primarily in his work, *Discipline and Punish*, and also in *History of Madness*, Foucault expounds the notion of how power is linked to norms and normalisation. His "technologies of disciplinary power" is appropriate in the understanding of how coercion works through a normalised process, involving "hierarchical observation, normalizing judgement, and examination" resulting in positive and unquestionable compliance (Lawlor and Nale 2014, 113).
2. From Islamicstudies.info, http://islamicstudies.info/reference.php?sura=21&verse=107, accessed 19 April 2019.
3. See some 40 comments to Nidhal's article (2019), the majority of which are not supportive of the interpretation, claiming that it had a liberal slant.

References

Abdul Ghafar, Don (2018) "'Rahmatan lil alamin' perlu ditafsir secara hikmah, cermat', *Berita Harian Online*, 28 September.

Ahmad Fauzi, Abdul Hamid (2007) "Patterns of State Interaction with Islamic Movement in Malaysia during the Formative Years of Islamic Resurgence", *Southeast Asian Studies*, Vol. 44, No. 4, 444–465.

Ahmad, Ibrahim and Mahmud Saedon Awang Othman (1988) *Ke Arah Islamisasi Undang-Undang Islam di Malaysia (Towards the Islamization of Law in Malaysia)*, Kuala Lumpur: Yayasan Dakwah Islamiyah Malaysia.

Ahmad Sanusi, Azmi and Mohd Yusuf Ismail (2018) "Konsep *Rahmatan lil alamin* dalam Hadith: Penerokaan Makna Serta Aplikasi di Malaysia", *Journal of Hadith Studies*, Vol. 3, No. 1, 1–13.

Allen, Kieran (2004) *Max Weber: A critical introduction*, London, Ann Arbor, MI: Pluto Press.

Alyaa, Alhadjri (2018) "Dr M: Islam doesn't teach us to pry into others' lives to find sin", *Malaysiakini*, 6 October.

Anne, Muhammad (2017) "Khalid tuntut bos Iksim mohon maaf, bayar RM1 juta", *Malaysiakini*, 17 October.

——— (2018) "Memperkasa Islam: Jawatankuasa Tertinggi akan panggil lebih 100 institusi", *Malaysiakini*, 9 August.

Anne, Muhammad and Annabelle Lee (2019) "Jais confirms probe into 'de-hijabbing' forum", *Malaysiakini*, 16 April.

Aslani, M (2019) "'Rahmatan Lil Alamin' tanpa ikatan Akidah", *Harakah Daily*, 1 February.

Benjamin, Geoffrey (2014) *Temiar Religion 1964–2012: Enchantment, disenchantment and re-enchantment in Malaysia's uplands*, Singapore: NUS Press.

Bernama (2018a) "Meeting Nisha Ayub doesn't mean agreeing to LGBT struggle – Mujahid", *Malaysiakini*, 11 August.

——— (2018b) "Gov't launches e-book on LGBT rehabilitation", *Malaysiakini*, 23 October.

——— (2018c) "Pahang will continue with vice raids, says regent", *Malaysiakini*, 7 October.

——— (2018d) "Anggota Jawatankuasa Tertinggi Institusi Hal Ehwal Islam terima watikah pelantikan", 9 August.

Carvalho, Martin (2018) "G25 wants sweeping reforms to key public institutions", *The Star Online*, 31 May.

Constas, Helen (1958) "Max Weber's Two Conceptions of Bureaucracy", *The American Journal of Sociology*, Vol. 63, No. 4, 400–409.

Danial, Dzulkifly (2018) "Suspended by Putrajaya, Iksim blames audit for untraceable RM7.4m allocation", *Malay Mail*, 7 August.

Daniels, Timothy P (2017) *Living Sharia: Law and practice in Malaysia*, Seattle: University of Washington Press.

Dina, Murad (2014) "No to Syariah police, says Dr Mahathir", *The Star Online*, 28 January.

Faisal, Asyraf (2018) "New group to rally against gov't to 'save' Islamic institutions", *Malaysiakini*, 19 June.

Faruqi, Shad Saleem (2017) "Religious radicalism on the rise", *The Star Online*, 23 November.

Frisk, Sylva (2009) *Submitting to God: Women and Islam in urban Malaysia*, Copenhagen: NIAS Press.

Hariz, Mohd and Fakhrull Halim (2018) "Harapan gov't does not need Icerd unlike others, says Dzulkefly", *Malaysiakini*, 16 December.

Hoffstaedter, Gerhard (2014) "Islamic Praxis and Theory: Negotiating orthodoxy in contemporary Malaysia" in Bernard Platzdasch and Johan Saravanamuttu (eds) *Religious Diversity in Muslim-majority States in Southeast Asia*, Singapore: ISEAS Publishing, 253–267.

Ismail, Mat (2018) "Raja-raja Melayu tubuhkan Jawatankuasa Tertinggi Hal Ehwal Islam", *Berita Harian Online*, 30 July.

Izra, Abdul Rahman (2015) "Dr Mahathir: Jakim imposing 'its version of Islam'", *The Star Online*, 20 November.

Jakim (2012) *Keputusan Muzakarah Jawatankuasa Fatwa Majlis Kebangsaan Bagi Hal Ehwal Ugama Islam Malaysia*, Putrajaya: Jabatan Kemajuan Islam Malaysia.

Kamaludeen, Mohamed Nasir, Alexius A Pereira and Bryan S Turner (2010) *Muslims in Singapore: Piety, politics and policies*, London, New York: Routledge.

Khairil, Ashraf (2017) "Mujahid persoal pembentangan Iksim label golongan liberal berbahaya", *Free Malaysia Today*, 28 November.

Lawlor, Leonard and John Nale (2014) "Discipline" in Leonard Lawlor and John Nale (eds), *The Cambridge Foucault Lexicon*, Cambridge: Cambridge University Press, 110–119.

Liow, Joseph Chinyong (2009) *Piety and Politics: Islamism in contemporary Malaysia*, Oxford: Oxford University Press.

Mahamad Naser, Disa (2018) "Iksim bukan 'ghanimah' untuk direbut politikus", *Harakah Daily*, 22 July.

Mahmood, Saba (2005) *Politics of Piety: The Islamic revival and the feminist subject*, Princeton: Princeton University Press.

Mahmood Zuhdi, Hj. Ab. Majid (2001) (ed). *Bidang Kuasa Jenayah Mahkamah Syariah di Malaysia* (Jurisdiction of Syariah Criminal Court), Kuala Lumpur: Dewan Bahasa dan Pustaka.

Malaysiakini (2018a) "Muftis split on Mujahid's call to end vice raids", 6 October.

——— (2018b) "'No khalwat raid' headline didn't come from my mouth – Mujahid", 7 October.

——— (2018c) "Mujahid's aide issue ultimatum to the Star over 'khalwat' article", 7 October.
——— (2018d) "PM: Kerajaan mahu Islam bukan berimej zalim, keras", 30 May.
——— (2018e) "Mujahid meets with Islamic NGOs, lawyers, academicians to discuss Icerd", 8 November.
——— (2019) "BN-era Iksim protests audit over alleged zakat fund mismanagement", 6 May.
——— (2019a) "Defending LGBTs at Women's March an abuse of democracy", 9 March.
——— (2019b) "Marina accuses Mujahid, Wan Saiful of 'misogyny' over Women's March remarks', 10 March.
——— (2019c) "Why fear intellectual discourse on de-hijabbing, ask forum panelists", 17 April.
Mohd Aizam, bin Mas'od (2015) *Diskusi Isu Akidah dan Pemikiran Semasa Di Malaysia*, Putrajaya: Jabatan Kemajuan Islam Malaysia.
Mohd Anwar, Patho Rohman (2018) "Jangan guna konsep 'Rahmatan lil'alamin' untul raih undi", *Berita Harian Online*, 29 September.
Mohd Iskandar, Ibrahim (2018) "102 institusi akan dipanggil – Ahmad Sarji", *Berita Harian Online*, 9 August.
Mohd Izani, Mohd Zain (2005) *Islam dan Demokrasi: Cabaran politik Muslim kontemporari di Malaysia* (*Islam and Democracy: Contemporary challenges to Muslim politics in Malaysia*), Kuala Lumpur: Penerbit Universiti Malaya.
Moustafa, Tamir (2018) "The Judicialization of Religion", *Law and Society Review*, Vol. 52, No. 3, 685–708.
Mujahid, bin Yusof (2019) "Gagasan Pentadbiran Islam di Era Malaysia Baharu", speech given at Sempena Perhimpunan Agensi-Agensi di Bawah YB Menteri di Jabatan Perdana Menteri (Hal Ehwal Agama), Jabatan Kemajuan Islam Malaysia, Putrajaya, 7 January.
Nasr, Seyyed Vali Reza (2001) *Islamic Leviathan: Islam and the making of state power*, Oxford, New York: Oxford University Press.
Nidhal, Rawa (2019) "Ada apa dengan Islam Rahmatan lil alamin?", *Malaysiakini*, 25 February.
Norhashimah, Mohd Yasin (1996) *Islamisation/Malayanisation: A study on the role of Islamic law in the economic development of Malaysia, 1969–1993*, Kuala Lumpur: AS Noordeen.
Norshahril, Saat (2018) *The State, Ulama and Islam in Malaysia and Indonesia*, Singapore: ISEAS Publishing.
Nuridah, Mohd Salleh (2019) "Provokasi Syariah: Apa tindakan selepas Jais siasat?", *Harakah Daily*, 19 April.
Peletz, Michael G (1993) "Sacred Texts and Dangerous Words: The Politics of Law and Cultural Rationalization in Malaysia", *Comparative Studies in Society and History*, Vol. 35, No. 1, 66–109.

Rizanizam, Abdul Hamid (2018) "Serah memorandum sebelum 1 Oktober", *Berita Harian Online*, 20 August.

Robinson, Francis (2004) "Other-Worldly and This-Worldly Islam and the Islamic Revival. A Memorial Lecture for Wilfred Cantwell Smith", *Journal of the Royal Asiatic Society*, Third Series, Vol. 14, No. 1, 47–58.

Roketkini.com (2018) "Jangan guna pendekatan Isis dalam politik Malaysia, pendakwah terkenal tegur Iksim", 26 January.

Shakira, Buang (2018) "Gov't working on syariah-compliant dress code for private sector", *Malaysiakini*, 6 August.

Sloane-White, Patricia (2017) *Corporate Islam: Sharia and the modern workplace,* Cambridge: Cambridge University Press.

The Star Online (2015) "Iksim: Students should take anti-IS module", 31 December.

The Star Online (2017a) "Say no to RUU355 for Malaysia's sake", 7 May.

——— (2017b) "G25 voices concern over police investigation into Prof Shad's article", 23 December.

——— (2018a) "Jakim, Iksim appear on the radar", 1 June.

——— (2018b) "The Star clarifies Mujahid interview on khalwat raids", 9 October.

——— (2018c) "Iksim's allocation frozen, Parliament told", 19 July.

Utusan Online (2018) "Ada bukti kukuh mengenai perbelanjaan Iksim – Mujahid", 8 August.

Weber (1991) "Science as a Vocation", in HH Gerth and C Wright Mills (trans and eds), *From Max Weber: Essays in sociology*, London: Routledge, 129–156.

Women's Aid Organisation (2018) "Stop Policing Women's clothing", *Malaysiakini*, 7 August.

Zakiah, Koya (2018) "No more night khalwat raids or intrusion into Muslims' private lives says Mujahid", *The Star Online*, 6 October.

Zan, Azlee (2018) "Will our handling of Islamic affairs really be reformed?", *Malaysiakini*, 20 July.

Zanariah, Abd Mutalib (2018) "'Rahmatan lil alamin' bukan berlembut dengan perbuatan mungkar", *Berita Harian Online*, 7 September.

Zulkifli, Sulong, Sheridan Mahavera and Diyana Ibrahim (2017) "So why is Umno helping Pas with RUU355 again?", *The Malaysian Insight*, 11 October.

Correction to: The Divine Bureaucracy and Disenchantment of Social Life

Correction to:

M. Mohamad, *The Divine Bureaucracy and Disenchantment of Social Life*,
https://doi.org/10.1007/978-981-15-2093-8

The chapters were inadvertently published with incorrect texts which have affected the meaning of the content. These texts have been corrected as below:

Chapter 5, page 179: "It is not true because the contents are full of loving elements, teaching prayers and to get to know Allah **pbh** (*Ia tidak benar kerana pengisiannya penuh dengan elemen kasihsayang, mengajar solat dan mengenal Allah SWT*)"

Chapter 5, page 180: Within these two categories, there are also various subcategories of people "**hackled** and bonded" in accordance to their identity (as "transsexual", "tomboy", "pengkid") or their activities (as in "prostitutes" or "gigolo"), all specified in the fatwa. Zakat allocations are not

The updated versions of these chapters can be found at
https://doi.org/10.1007/978-981-15-2093-8_5
https://doi.org/10.1007/978-981-15-2093-8_7
https://doi.org/10.1007/978-981-15-2093-8_8

M. Mohamad, *The Divine Bureaucracy and Disenchantment of Social Life*, Contestations in Contemporary Southeast Asia,
https://doi.org/10.1007/978-981-15-2093-8_9

given directly to these groups and individuals but are instead channelled to those (institutions or individuals) who are involved in work and programmes to rehabilitate them.

Chapter 7, page 259: The **Penang** government had apparently paid RM1.48 million to Maik for the *wakaf* land and planned to build a new *surau* (community prayer hall) in the mall to replace the old Madrasah Salihiah that was demolished (Star Online 2011).

Chapter 8, page 282: The **Malaysian** also demonstrates that formerly traditional *ulama* have been absorbed into the bureaucracy and occupy sinecure positions.

Changed to:

Chapter 5, page 179: "It is not true because the contents are full of loving elements, teaching prayers and to get to know Allah The **Almighty** (*Ia tidak benar kerana pengisiannya penuh dengan elemen kasih sayang, mengajar solat dan mengenal Allah SWT*)"

Chapter 5, page 180: Within these two categories, there are also various subcategories of people "**shackled** and bonded" in accordance to their identity (as "transsexual", "tomboy", "pengkid") or their activities (as in "prostitutes"or "gigolo"), all specified in the *fatwa*. Zakat allocations are not given directly to these groups and individuals but are instead channelled

to those (institutions or individuals) who are involved in work and programmes to rehabilitate them.

Chapter 7, page 259: The **Kedah** government had apparently paid RM1.48 million to Maik for the *wakaf* land and planned to build a new *surau* (community prayer hall) in the mall to replace the old Madrasah Salihiah that was demolished (Star Online 2011).

Chapter 8, page 282: The **Malaysian case** also demonstrates that formerly traditional *ulama* have been absorbed into the bureaucracy and occupy sinecure positions.

Appendixes

Table A.1 Timeline on the formation of religion-related social movements and incidences of political conflict and violence in Malaysia

Year	*Incident/controversy*	*Description*	*Related incidents*
1968	Darul Arqam founded by Ashaari Muhammad. First base was in the Kuala Lumpur suburb of Dato' Keramat		
1969	May 13 'racial riots' in Kuala Lumpur		
1971	Establishment of Abim		
1973	Darul Arqam moves to its own Sungai Penchala commune in the outskirts of Kuala Lumpur		
1977	Emergency rule and curfew in Kelantan	Breakdown of Umno-Pas coalition in the Kelantan State government leading to street demonstrations	
1978	Incident in Kerling	Four Muslims killed and one injured by temple caretakers. They were caught desecrating idols in a Hindu temple in Kerling, north of Kuala Lumpur	Start of the Iranian Revolution

(*continued*)

M. Mohamad, *The Divine Bureaucracy and Disenchantment of Social Life*, Contestations in Contemporary Southeast Asia,
https://doi.org/10.1007/978-981-15-2093-8

Table A.1 (continued)

Year	*Incident/controversy*	*Description*	*Related incidents*
1979			Islamic Republic of Iran formed
1980	Batu Pahat police station violence	23 people slashed, 6 attackers (in white and armed with swords) shot to death.	
1981	Speech known as the *Amanat Haji Hadi* delivered	Outlined the following: (1) Umno was a continuation of foreign colonialism; (2) all who struggled and contributed towards the cause of Pas would be performing the *jihad*, and if they died in the process they would become martyrs; and (3) one who separated religion from politics was a *kafir*. Led to polarisation of Muslims at the everyday level	
Mid-1980s	*Fatwa* on *kafir* (infidels)	Pas Ulama Council issues a *fatwa* pronouncing Umno as *kafir* for cooperating with non-Muslim political parties in the general election	
1984	Ban on Pas gatherings in Kelantan, Terengganu, Kedah and Perlis		
1984		Pas members incriminated as extremists and being involved in subversive activities	Tabling of White Paper 'The Threat to Muslim Unity and National Security'
1985	Pas supporter killed by Umno-paid thugs at a pre-by-election gathering in Lubok Merbau, Kedah	Pas legal advisor detained under the ISA	
1985	Memali incident	18 people and 4 policemen killed in armed clashes in the village of Memali, Kedah. Those killed included leader Ibrahim Mahmood, a Pas member accused of leading a *jihad* (holy war) against the *kafir* (infidel) government	

(*continued*)

Table A.1 (continued)

Year	*Incident/controversy*	*Description*	*Related incidents*
1988	Sandakan attacks on policemen	Eight men with machetes in white and red robes shot to death after going on a rampage	
1988	Malaysian Home Ministry bans the book by Ashaari Muhammad, leader of Darul Arqam, titled *Aurad Muhammadiah Pegangan Darul Arqam*		
1994	Banning of Darul Arqam, the detention of Ashaari Muhammad under the Internal Security Act (ISA)	Prevent the spread of Ashaari Muhammad's Sufi teachings known as the *Aurad Muhammadiah*	
1998	Sacking of Anwar Ibrahim as Deputy Prime Minister		
1999	Detention of Anwar Ibrahim under the ISA		
1999		Malaysia's 10th general election	Pas captures two *negeri* (State), Kelantan and Terengganu in the 1999 general election. In partnership with DAP and PKR, they won the most number of seats in their history of contesting national elections
2000	Al-Ma'unah arms heist	Four-day standoff between a group of 26 men who stole weapons from a military camp, with the deployment of 2000 government troops in the jungles of Perak. One policeman and a soldier held hostage were killed. Leader Mohamed Amin Mohamed Razali and 2 followers sentenced to death, 16 given life sentences, 10 others jailed for 7–10 years	

(*continued*)

Table A.1 (continued)

Year	*Incident/controversy*	*Description*	*Related incidents*
2001	Activists of *Mujahidin* Group of Malaysia (KMM—Kumpulan al-Ma'unah Malaysia) arrested	Alleged to have attacked a police station, non-religious sites and assassinated a politician, Joe Fernandez, for his evangelical activities among Malay youths. Also for allegedly raiding the Guar Chempedak police station, and setting-off a bomb near a temple in Kuala Lumpur	
2016	Abduction and disappearance of Amri Che Mat, founder of NGO Perlis Hope	Abducted by men in five vehicles while driving near his home in Perlis, and not seen since. Before this, Amri had been monitored for his alleged links to Syiah teachings	
2016	Bomb blast in a nightclub in Puchong, Selangor	Carried out by local supporters of Isis in Syria and Iraq	8 people injured
2016	Disappearance of Pastor Joshua Hilmi and his wife Ruth Sitepu	Joshua was formerly Jamaluddin Othman, a Muslim who converted to Christianity, and was previously arrested and tortured in detention under the ISA in 1987	
2017	Abduction and disappearance of Pastor Raymond Koh, founder of Harapan Komuniti	Abducted by a group of men in Petaling Jaya while driving, and not seen since. Previously, Jais (Jabatan Agama Islam Selangor), acting on complaints that there were 12 Muslims in attendance, raided a thanksgiving and charity dinner organised by Pastor Koh's group	

Table A.2 Timeline of the establishment of federal-level Islamic agencies

Year	*Events*	*Institutions formed*	*Functions*
1962–1995		Perbadanan Wang Simpanan Bakal-Bakal Haji (Pilgrims' Savings and Deposits Bank) established in 1962, converted to Lembaga Tabung Haji (Pilgrims Fund Board) in 1995	Pilgrims' Savings and Deposits Bank, to date 9 million depositors and 125 branches nationwide
1965		National Mosque	
1966–1998	First state-sponsored school for *quranic* study under the National Mosque. Upgraded as division in Jakim and moved to own campus in 1998	Ma'ahad Tahfiz established in 1966. Rebranded as Darul Quran (Quran Study Institute) in 1997	
1968	First national-level body on Islamic affairs formed by the Conference of Rulers, chaired by Prime Minister (PM) with the religious unit (Unit Agama) as secretariat	Majlis Kebangsaan Bagi Hal Ehwal Agama Islam, MKI (National Council for Islamic Affairs)	Highest forum to discuss and advise Council of Rulers on Islamic matters of *negeri*. Coordinates Islamic affairs under the Prime Minister's Department (PM's Department)
1971	Resolution from 1969 Islamic Conference of Malaysia	Pusat Penyelidikan Islam, PPI (Islamic Research Centre) housed within the National Mosque	Research themes: *akidah*, *Syariah*, *akhlak*. First research officer was from Al-Azhar University, Egypt. Upgraded and placed under Jakim in 1997
1972	Committee to study status of *Syariah* and *Kadi* courts set up by MKI		Concerns over marginal status of *syariah* courts and terms of service of judges under this system
1973	Launch of Islamic Missionary Fund by PM Abdul Razak; approved by MKI		

(*continued*)

Table A.2 (continued)

Year	*Events*	*Institutions formed*	*Functions*
1974		Institut Dakwah dan Latihan Islam, Indah (Islamic Dakwah and Training Institute)	
		Kuala Lumpur becomes a Federal Territory, i.e. autonomous from Selangor	
	Unit Agama upgraded, with new portfolios added on	Bahagian Agama (Religious Section), PM's Department	
	Formation of Wilayah Persekutuan (WP) of Kuala Lumpur (Federal Territory (FT) of Kuala Lumpur)	Majlis Agama Islam Wilayah Persekutuan, Maiwp (Federal Territories Islamic Religious Council)	Runs religious schools, training institutions, religious welfare and charity, ***dakwah***, develops ***wakaf***, increases ***zakat*** collections, strengthens Islamic law and upgrades economic activities and investments. Provides welfare assistance from ***zakat*** payments
		Jabatan Agama Islam Wilayah Persekutuan (Jawi)	Strengthens faith, ***syariah*** and conduct of Muslims, manages Muslim family affairs, education for ***ummah*** based on the Quran and ***Sunnah***, builds mosques and ***surau***
		Jawatankuasa Undang-Undang Islam, WP (Committee on Islamic Law FT)	Conducts research and formulates laws on administration of Islam. First to produce draft Islamic Family Law (Federal Territory). Subsequently prepared draft of model Islamic family to be adopted uniformly by all ***negeri*** in the early 1980s

(*continued*)

Table A.2 (continued)

Year	*Events*	*Institutions formed*	*Functions*
	Launched by PM Abdul Razak	Yayasan Dakwah Islamiah (Yadim)	Missionary activities, training of missionaries, organisation of international seminars, Ibu Mithali programmes, *dakwah* month, national *dakwah* programmes. Nurtures young *dakwah* leaders, sponsors *dakwah* champion awards (categories include national, women, NGO, new converts, entertainers). Has its own trained *muballigh* (missionaries) to achieve "Government's goal of channelling Islamic evangelism to promote national development, and guarantee national security"
1976–1984	Formation of body for Islamic economic development in 1976; relaunched by PM Mahathir Mohamad in 1984	Yayasan Pembangunan Ekonomi Islam Malaysia, Yapeim (Islamic Economic Development Foundation)	
1978	Launched by PM Hussein Onn	*Dakwah* month	Theme: 'Islam Guarantees the Nation's Security'
1979		Special religious division within the Ministry of Education formed to "keep tabs on the *dakwah* movement and ensure that religious teachings conform to the right interpretation"	

(*continued*)

Table A.2 (continued)

Year	*Events*	*Institutions formed*	*Functions*
1981	Report by Committee to Study Status of Syariah and Kadi Courts (established by MKI) submitted to government		Proposed differentiation and separation of powers of Islamic authority: *syariah* courts to be separate from SIRC, status of *syariah* court to be upgraded and scope of jurisdiction enlarged, status of *syariah* judges upgraded and civil service scheme applied to *syariah* officers
1983		Bank Islam (Islamic Bank)	First bank to offer Islamic banking products
1984		Maiwp Labuan Jawi Labuan	
	Bahagian Agama enlarged, to implement programmes under the PM's Department and continue to function as MKI Secretariat	Bahagian Hal Ehwal Islam, Baheis (Division of Islamic Affairs)	
1985	Government policy on "Inculcation of Islamic Values in Administration" implemented		
1988	Constitutional amendment to Article 121(1)(A) passed in Parliament	Civil courts to have no jurisdiction on all matters within the jurisdiction of *syariah* courts	
	Launched by Minister-in-Charge of Islamic affairs, PM's Department	Technical Committee on Syariah and Civil Laws	Drafts statutes on various categories of Islamic law; members comprise judges, academics, lawyers; secretariat is the legal unit of Jakim

(*continued*)

Table A.2 (continued)

Year	*Events*	*Institutions formed*	*Functions*
1991	First corporation set up to privatise *zakat* collection. Launched by PM Mahathir	Pusat Pungutan Zakat – Majlis Agama Islam Wilayah Persekutuan, PPZ-Maiwp (Zakat Collection Centre – Federal Territories Islamic Religious Council)	
1992	Islamic think-tank launched by PM Mahathir	Institut Kefahaman Islam Malaysia, Ikim (Institute of Islamic Understanding)	Research, publications, seminars
1996		Syariah Advisory Council of the Securities Commission of Malaysia	
1997	Baheis upgraded to a department within the PM's Department. Scope of functions enlarged	Jabatan Kemajuan Islam Malaysia, Jakim (Islamic Development Department of Malaysia)	Formulates and standardises Islamic laws, coordinates Islamic administration, coordinates and develops Islamic education
		Syariah Advisory Council (SAC) of Bank Negara Malaysia (BNM, Central Bank Malaysia)	Ascertains laws for Islamic-related businesses (banking, *takaful*, finance or any other business) based on *syariah* principles, supervised and regulated by BNM
1996	Cabinet decision in July 1986 to restructure the national *syariah* courts system	Jabatan Kehakiman Syariah Malaysia, JKSM (Department of Syariah Judiciary Malaysia)	Introduces *Syariah* Appeal Courts. Engages in policy-making research to improve *syariah* justice system, monitors maintenance orders, distributes 'advance' maintenance payments, provides transit facilities for needy families using FT Kuala Lumpur and Putrajaya *syariah* courts

(*continued*)

Table A.2 (continued)

Year	*Events*	*Institutions formed*	*Functions*
	Mufti's Office (Istinbat Section) separated from Jawi; restructuring exercise by the Public Services Department	Pejabat Mufti WP (FT Mufti's Office)	Issues *fatwa* to foster understanding of *Ahli Sunnah wal Jamaah* (followers of Sunni Islam) beliefs and rehabilitates 'deviationists'
2000	FT Mufti's Office, fully autonomous and directly under the PM's Department		
2001		Maiwp Putrajaya	
2001		Jawi Putrajaya	
2004		Pejabat Mufti Labuan (Labuan Mufti's Office)	
	Launched by PM Abdullah Ahmad Badawi	Jabatan Wakaf, Zakat dan Haji, Jawhar (Wakaf, Zakat and Hajj Department)	Plans, monitors and coordinates development of *wakaf*, *zakat* and pilgrimage institutions. Develops *wakaf* with Government-Link Corporations (GLCs) and "High Networth Individual Muslim (HNIM)". Conducts research; has publications. Owns several hotels
2008		Yayasan Waqaf Malaysia (YWM—Waqaf Foundation of Malaysia)	Develops *wakaf* land, *wakaf* foundation, conducts investment and welfare programmes
2010	Free-to-air television network, owned by the PM's Department	Al-Hijrah media	Produces Islamic-oriented and religious programmes

Glossary

adat customs/traditions
agong king
ahl/ahli family/followers/group/members
Ahli Sunnah Wal Jamaah Sunni Islam
ajaran sesat deviant teachings
akad nikah marriage solemnisation
akal reasoning
akhlak morals/moral conduct
akidah (Ar. 'aqa'id) faith/creed
al-gharimin those in debt
al-ijarah thumma al-bai use of two contracts, one for lease, the other for sale and purchase
Al-Riqab those in slavery/bondage
Allah God
aman peace
amanat mandate
amil designated *zakat* collector
asnaf *zakat* recipients
aurat hair, other bodily parts
Bahagian Ugama Religious Section
bai' bi thaman ajil contract

M. Mohamad, *The Divine Bureaucracy and Disenchantment of Social Life*, Contestations in Contemporary Southeast Asia,
https://doi.org/10.1007/978-981-15-2093-8

baitulmal Islamic treasury whose revenues come from religious taxation and penalties
Bank Islam Islamic Bank
berbogel beramai-ramai group nudity
berpesta partying
berzina having sex outside of marriage
bid'ah heresy/deviation/innovation
bilal caller to prayer
budaya songsang perverted culture
bumiputera sons of the soil (*lit.*)
cerai taklik divorce by stipulation
corporate Islamic bureaucracy the religious bureaucracy emerging out of the development of an Islamic banking and financial services industry, and the commercialisation and corporatisation of activities like *zakat* collection
cuka wain wine vinegar
daerah district
dakwah Islamic propagation
Darul Arqam House of Arqam
Darul Quran Quran Study Institute
Divine Bureaucracy the religious bureaucracy comprising State, Federal and Corporate domains
do'a prayers and supplications
ekonomi economy
Entzauberung demagification/disenchantment
faraid Muslim inheritance
fasakh judicial divorce
fatwa legal opinion
fatwa munakahat fatwa on marriage
Federal Islamic bureaucracy the central/federalised religious bureaucracy which became prominent from the 1980s onwards
fiqh Islamic philosophy and method of law, Islamic jurisprudence
fisabilillah those who serve in the path of Allah to defend and uphold Islam
fitrah dues/payment
fuqaha jurists
fuqara, wal masakin poor and needy
gejala LGBT ills of LGBT
gejala sosial social ills

Gerbang Perkahwinan Gateway of Marriage
gharar chance/risky and speculative behaviour
guru agama religious teacher
habitus taste
hadhanah childcare rights
hadith word of the Prophet
haiwan animals
hajj religious pilgrimage
hakim judge
halal permissible
haram prohibited
harmoni harmony
harta sepencarian matrimonial property
harus obligatory though not mandatory
hijab/tudung veil/headscarf
hormat respect
hudud law Islamic criminal law with harsh and capital punishment
hukum syarak syariah law
hukum muamalat laws regulating economic exchange, transactions, contracts
ibadah worship
ibnu sabil stranded travellers
ibrar an instrument to retrieve default payments
ibu buapak lesser chief in the State of Negeri Sembilan
iddah period of waiting before a divorce is finalised
iftar breaking of fast
ijarah leasing contract
ijtihad rational reasoning
imam head of prayer
Islam madani Islamic civil society
Istana Negara National Palace
istilah terminology
jampi spell
jihad call to holy war
ka'abah sacred structure at the centre of mosque complex in Mecca
kadi/kathi judge/registrar of an Islamic court
kafir infidel
Kaum Muda Young Turks
Kaum Tua Old Guards

kebulatan process of unanimity practised in the State of Negeri Sembilan
Ketuanan Melayu Malay supremacy
khalwat to be in close proximity that may lead to illicit sexual relations
khatib quranic reciter/orator
kiamat doomsday
kitab books
kuasa authority
lembaga clan chiefs in the State of Negeri Sembilan
luak district in the State of Negeri Sembilan
madrassah community prayer centre
mahar dowry
Mahkamah Adat Customary Court
Mahkamah Negeri Territorial Court
mahmudah good values and virtues
makanan dan minuman food and drinks
makruf do good
maksiat sinful acts
manhaj method
manhaj Malizi Malaysian model/method
maqasid al-Shari'ah for the greater well-being
masalah problems
mas kahwin dowry
maslahah ummah greater good of the community
mati syahid martyr
mazhab school of thought or Islamic jurisprudence
mazmunah loathsome akhlak
mengadakan majlis tari menari having dance functions
menutup aurat cover forbidden bodily parts
menyantuni engage
mesra friendly
minum arak drinking alcohol
Mohammedan laws laws for Muslims
muallaf convert to Islam
muamalat transaction and commercial exchange between humans
mudarabah trading contract
mufti jurisconsult
mukim subdistrict
Muktazilah/Mu'tazilah group of Muslims who primarily advocate use of reason and rationality in theological questions
munafik traitors

munakahat marriage and family
mungkar avoid evil
murtad apostates
musahamah joint contributors in a takaful insurance contract
mutaah post-divorce gift
mutawwali wakaf management trustee
myasir gaming and gambling
nafkah maintenance
naib kathi deputy kathi
negeri State(s), subnational units of governance
nikah, cerai dan rujuk marriage, divorce and reconciliation
nikah daaim permanent marriage
nikah mutaah temporary marriage
nilai values
nusyuz act of disobedience
Orang Asli indigenous people of Peninsular Malaysia
Orang Kaya Imam Tuan community religious leader
pakaian clothing
panduan guidelines
para sahabat disciples
pawang healer
Pejabat Mufti Mufti's Office
Penerapan Nilai-Nilai Islam dalam Pentadbiran The Integration of Islamic Values in Administration
penghulu village head
pengkid masculine looking woman, usually young and Malay
Perbadanan Wang Simpanan Bakal-Bakal Haji Pilgrims' Savings and Deposits Banking Corporation
perkhidmatan rundingcara arbitration services
perubatan medicine
perut sub-clan in the State of Negeri Sembilan
pondok school traditional religious schools
Puteri Umno Umno young women's wing
qawwamun guardians/guardianship
rahmah blessings
rahmatan lil 'alamin mercy and blessings to all creations
rahn collateral-based contract
raja ruler
rakyat subjects

riba interest/usury
Salafism an Islamic religious orientation towards purity and ways of the Prophet
Seksualiti Merdeka Independent Sexualities
Shaikh-al-Islam Learned authority of Islam
Shi'ism (adj.) Islamic sect tracing the line of leadership directly to the Prophet
silat Malay art of self-defence
siput babi garden snails
Sky Kingdom religious sect which had its site in Terengganu
sosial social
State Islamic bureaucracy religious bureaucracy originally formed in the Malay States during British rule
Sufi Islamic mysticism
suku clan in the State of Negeri Sembilan
sukuk Islamic bonds
sultan ruler of a State
sunna/sunnah/suna ways of the Prophet
surau community prayer hall
syahadah pronouncement of faith
syariah (also shari'a, shariah, syarak) path to the water (lit); Islamic law
Syeikh Mursyid spiritual director of a Sufist tarekat
Syiah Islamic sect tracing the line of leadership (*n*)
syiar Islam the calling of Islam
tahfiz quranic memorisation
takaful Islamic insurance
talak divorce by the repudiation of marriage
tarekat/tariqah Sufi sect
tasawwuf Sufi belief and practice
tauhid oneness of God
tauliah authorisation
Temiar group of indigenous people in Peninsular Malaysia
to' kweng community heads in the State of Kelantan
tudung/hijab headscarf/veil
ulama Islamic scholar
ulama muktabar legitimate ulama
umrah small religious pilgrimage
undang district chief in the State of Negeri Sembilan
Unit Agama Religious Unit

usul fiqh the origin of Islamic law
wakaf trusts/endowments
wakaf am general endowment with no specific purpose
wakaf khas special endowment for specific purpose
wakaf korporat corporate *wakaf*
wakalah bi al-istithmar given proxy to act on someone else's behalf
Wahhabism Religious orientation with strict application of *quranic* doctrines to life, originates from the ruling Wahhabi clan of Saudi Arabia
wali lawful guardian giving away the bride to marriage
wali hakim proxy appointed by the court to represent the bride
Wilayatul Faqih leadership by the clerics
Yayasan Taqwa Wilayah Persekutuan Federal Territory Taqwa Foundation
zakat religious tithe/tax
zakat al-mal religious tax on income and business earnings
zakat mal religious tax on one's wealth
zakat fitrah individual gifts extended to the poor
zakat padi religious tax on paddy harvest
zikir (dhikr) incantations
zina illicit sex/fornication between unmarried persons

Index[1]

[1] Note: Page numbers followed by 'n' refer to notes.

M. Mohamad, *The Divine Bureaucracy and Disenchantment of Social Life*, Contestations in Contemporary Southeast Asia, https://doi.org/10.1007/978-981-15-2093-8

The manufacturer's authorised representative in the EU is Springer Nature Customer Service Centre GmbH, Europaplatz 3, 69115 Heidelberg, Germany. If you have any concerns regarding our products, please contact ProductSafety@springernature.com

Printed and bound by CPI Group (UK) Ltd, Croydon, CR0 4YY
25/09/2026
02222902-0010